THE SOCIAL PSYCHOLOGY OF LIVING WELL

How to live well and the search for meaning have long been of intense concern to humans, perhaps because Homo sapiens is the only species aware of its own mortality. In the last few decades, empirical psychology made a major contribution to this quest. This book surveys groundbreaking work by leading international researchers, demonstrating that social psychology is the core discipline for understanding well-being and the search for meaning. Basic conceptual and theoretical principles are discussed, drawing on philosophy, evolutionary theory and psychology, followed by a review of the role of purposeful, motivated activity and self-control in achieving life satisfaction. The role of emotional and cognitive processes and the influence of social, interpersonal and cultural factors in promoting a happy and meaningful life are discussed. The book will be of interest to students, practitioners and researchers in the behavioral and social sciences, as well as to laypersons for whom improving the quality of human life and understanding the principles of well-being are of interest.

Joseph P. Forgas is Scientia Professor at the University of New South Wales, Australia. He has received numerous awards, including the Distinguished Scientific Contribution Award from the Australian Psychological Society.

Roy F. Baumeister is Professor of Social Psychology at the University of Queensland, Australia. In 2013, he received the William James Fellow Award from the Association for Psychological Science in recognition of his lifetime achievements.

The Sydney Symposium of Social Psychology series

This book is Volume 19 in the *Sydney Symposium of Social Psychology* series. The aim of the Sydney Symposia of Social Psychology is to provide new, integrative insights into key areas of contemporary research. Held every year at the University of New South Wales, Sydney, each symposium deals with an important integrative theme in social psychology, and the invited participants are leading researchers in the field from around the world. Each contribution is extensively discussed during the symposium and is subsequently thoroughly revised into book chapters that are published in the volumes in this series. For further details see the website at www.sydneysymposium.unsw.edu.au

Previous Sydney Symposium of Social Psychology volumes:

SSSP 1. FEELING AND THINKING: THE ROLE OF AFFECT IN SOCIAL COGNITION★★ ISBN 0-521-64223-X (Edited by J.P. Forgas). *Contributors*: Robert Zajonc, Jim Blascovich, Wendy Berry Mendes, Craig Smith, Leslie Kirby, Eric Eich, Dawn Macauley, Len Berkowitz, Sara Jaffee, EunKyung Jo, Bartholomeu Troccoli, Leonard Martin, Daniel Gilbert, Timothy Wilson, Herbert Bless, Klaus Fiedler, Joseph Forgas, Carolin Showers, Anthony Greenwald, Mahzarin Banaji, Laurie Rudman, Shelly Farnham, Brian Nosek, Marshall Rosier, Mark Leary, Paula Niedenthal and Jamin Halberstadt.

SSSP 2. THE SOCIAL MIND: COGNITIVE AND MOTIVATIONAL ASPECTS OF INTERPERSONAL BEHAVIOR★★ ISBN 0-521-77092-0 (Edited by J.P. Forgas, K.D. Williams & L. Wheeler). *Contributors*: William & Claire McGuire, Susan Andersen, Roy Baumeister, Joel Cooper, Bill Crano, Garth Fletcher, Joseph Forgas, Pascal Huguet, Mike Hogg, Martin Kaplan, Norb Kerr, John Nezlek, Fred Rhodewalt, Astrid Schuetz, Constantine Sedikides, Jeffry Simpson, Richard Sorrentino, Dianne Tice, Kip Williams and Ladd Wheeler.

SSSP 3. SOCIAL INFLUENCE: DIRECT AND INDIRECT PROCESSES★ ISBN 1-84169-038-4 (Edited by J.P. Forgas & K.D. Williams). *Contributors*: Robert Cialdini, Eric Knowles, Shannon Butler, Jay Linn, Bibb Latane, Martin Bourgeois, Mark Schaller, Ap Dijksterhuis, James Tedeschi, Richard Petty, Joseph Forgas, Herbert Bless, Fritz Strack, Eva Walther, Sik Hung Ng, Thomas Mussweiler, Kipling Williams, Lara Dolnik, Charles

Stangor, Gretchen Sechrist, John Jost, Deborah Terry, Michael Hogg, Stephen Harkins, Barbara David, John Turner, Robin Martin, Miles Hewstone, Russell Spears, Tom Postmes, Martin Lea and Susan Watt.

SSSP 4. THE SOCIAL SELF: COGNITIVE, INTERPERSONAL, AND INTERGROUP PERSPECTIVES★★ ISBN 1-84169-062-7 (Edited by J.P. Forgas & K.D. Williams). *Contributors*: Eliot R. Smith, Thomas Gilovich, Monica Biernat, Joseph P. Forgas, Stephanie J. Moylan, Edward R. Hirt, Sean M. McCrea, Frederick Rhodewalt, Michael Tragakis, Mark Leary, Roy F. Baumeister, Jean M. Twenge, Natalie Ciarocco, Dianne M. Tice, Jean M. Twenge, Brandon J. Schmeichel, Bertram F. Malle, William Ickes, Marianne LaFrance, Yoshihisa Kashima, Emiko Kashima, Anna Clark, Marilynn B. Brewer, Cynthia L. Pickett, Sabine Otten, Christian S. Crandall, Diane M. Mackie, Joel Cooper, Michael Hogg, Stephen C. Wright, Art Aron, Linda R. Tropp and Constantine Sedikides.

SSSP 5. SOCIAL JUDGMENTS: IMPLICIT AND EXPLICIT PRO-CESSES★★ ISBN 0-521-82248-3. (Edited by J.P. Forgas, K.D. Williams & W. von Hippel). *Contributors*: Herbert Bless, Marilynn Brewer, David Buss, Tanya Chartrand, Klaus Fiedler, Joseph Forgas, David Funder, Adam Galinsky, Martie Haselton, Denis Hilton, Lucy Johnston, Arie Kruglanski, Matthew Lieberman, John McClure, Mario Mikulincer, Norbert Schwarz, Philip Shaver, Diederik Stapel, Jerry Suls, William von Hippel, Michaela Waenke, Ladd Wheeler, Kipling Williams and Michael Zarate.

SSSP 6. SOCIAL MOTIVATION: CONSCIOUS AND UNCON-SCIOUS PROCESSES★★ ISBN 0-521-83254-3 (Edited by J.P. Forgas, K.D. Williams & S.M. Laham). *Contributors*: Henk Aarts, Ran Hassin, Trish Devine, Joseph Forgas, Jens Forster, Nira Liberman, Judy Harackiewicz, Leanne Hing, Mark Zanna, Michael Kernis, Paul Lewicki, Steve Neuberg, Doug Kenrick, Mark Schaller, Tom Pyszczynski, Fred Rhodewalt, Jonathan Schooler, Steve Spencer, Fritz Strack, Roland Deutsch, Howard Weiss, Neal Ashkanasy, Kip Williams, Trevor Case, Wayne Warburton, Wendy Wood, Jeffrey Quinn, Rex Wright and Guido Gendolla.

SSSP 7. THE SOCIAL OUTCAST: OSTRACISM, SOCIAL EXCLU-SION, REJECTION, AND BULLYING★ ISBN 1-84169-424-X (Edited by K.D. Williams, J.P. Forgas & W. von Hippel). *Contributors*: Kipling D. Williams, Joseph P. Forgas, William von Hippel, Lisa Zadro, Mark R. Leary, Roy F. Baumeister, C. Nathan DeWall, Geoff MacDonald, Rachell Kingsbury, Stephanie Shaw, John T. Cacioppo, Louise C. Hawkley, Naomi I. Eisenberger, Matthew D. Lieberman, Rainer Romero-Canyas, Geraldine Downey, Jaana Juvonen, Elisheva F. Gross, Kristin L. Sommer, Yonata Rubin, Susan T. Fiske, Mariko Yamamoto, Jean M. Twenge, Cynthia L. Pickett, Wendi L. Gardner, Megan Knowles, Michael A. Hogg, Julie Fitness, Jessica L. Lakin, Tanya L.

Chartrand, Kathleen R. Catanese, Dianne M. Tice, Lowell Gaertner, Jonathan Iuzzini, Jaap W. Ouwerkerk, Norbert L. Kerr, Marcello Gallucci, Paul A. M. Van Lange and Marilynn B. Brewer.

SSSP 8. AFFECT IN SOCIAL THINKING AND BEHAVIOR★ ISBN 1-84169-454-2 (Edited by J.P. Forgas). *Contributors*: Joseph P. Forgas, Carrie Wyland, Simon M. Laham, Martie G. Haselton, Timothy Ketelaar, Piotr Winkielman, John T. Cacioppo, Herbert Bless, Klaus Fiedler, Craig A. Smith, Bieke David, Leslie D. Kirby, Eric Eich, Dawn Macaulay, Gerald L. Clore, Justin Storbeck, Roy F. Baumeister, Kathleen D. Vohs, Dianne M. Tice, Dacher Keltner, E.J. Horberg, Christopher Oveis, Elizabeth W. Dunn, Simon M. Laham, Constantine Sedikides, Tim Wildschut, Jamie Arndt, Clay Routledge, Yaacov Trope, Eric R. Igou, Chris Burke, Felicia A. Huppert, Ralph Erber, Susan Markunas, Joseph P. Forgas, Joseph Ciarrochi, John T. Blackledge, Janice R. Kelly, Jennifer R.Spoor, John G. Holmes and Danu B. Anthony.

SSSP 9. EVOLUTION AND THE SOCIAL MIND★ ISBN 1-84169-458-0 (Edited by J.P. Forgas, M.G. Haselton & W. von Hippel). *Contributors*: William von Hippel, Martie Haselton, Joseph P. Forgas, R.I.M. Dunbar, Steven W. Gangestad, Randy Thornhill, Douglas T. Kenrick, Andrew W. Delton, Theresa E. Robertson, D. Vaughn Becker, Steven L. Neuberg, Phoebe C. Ellsworth, Ross Buck, Paul B.T. Badcock, Nicholas B. Allen, Peter M. Todd, Jeffry A. Simpson, Jonathon LaPaglia, Debra Lieberman, Garth J.O. Fletcher, Nickola C. Overall, Abraham P. Buunk, Karlijn Massar, Pieternel Dijkstra, Mark Van Vugt, Rob Kurzban, Jamin Halberstadt, Oscar Ybarra, Matthew C. Keller, Emily Chan, Andrew S. Baron, Jeffrey Hutsler, Stephen Garcia, Jeffrey Sanchez-Burks, Kimberly Rios Morrison, Jennifer R. Spoor, Kipling D. Williams, Mark Schaller and Lesley A. Duncan.

SSSP 10. SOCIAL RELATIONSHIPS: COGNITIVE, AFFECTIVE, AND MOTIVATIONAL PROCESSES★ ISBN 978-1-84169-715-4 (Edited by J.P. Forgas & J. Fitness). *Contributors*: Joseph P. Forgas, Julie Fitness, Elaine Hatfield, Richard L. Rapson, Gian C. Gonzaga, Martie G. Haselton, Phillip R. Shaver, Mario Mikulincer, David P. Schmitt, Garth J.O. Fletcher, Alice D. Boyes, Linda K. Acitelli, Margaret S. Clark, Steven M. Graham, Erin Williams, Edward P. Lemay, Christopher R. Agnew, Ximena B. Arriaga, Juan E. Wilson, Marilynn B. Brewer, Jeffry A. Simpson, W. Andrew Collins, SiSi Tran, Katherine C. Haydon, Shelly L. Gable, Patricia Noller, Susan Conway, Anita Blakeley-Smith, Julie Peterson, Eli J. Finkel, Sandra L. Murray, Lisa Zadro, Kipling D. Williams and Rowland S. Miller.

SSSP 11. PSYCHOLOGY OF SELF-REGULATION: COGNITIVE, AFFECTIVE, AND MOTIVATIONAL PROCESSES★ ISBN 978-1-84872-842-4 (Edited by J.P. Forgas, R. Baumeister & D.M. Tice). *Contributors*: Joseph P. Forgas, Roy F. Baumeister, Dianne M. Tice, Jessica L. Alquist,

Carol Sansone, Malte Friese, Michaela Wänke, Wilhelm Hofmann, Constantine Sedikides, Christian Unkelbach, Henning Plessner, Daniel Memmert, Charles S. Carver, Michael F. Scheier, Gabriele Oettingen, Peter M. Gollwitzer, Jens Förster, Nira Liberman, Ayelet Fishbach, Gráinne M. Fitzsimons, Justin Friesen, Edward Orehek, Arie W. Kruglanski, Sander L. Koole, Thomas F. Denson, Klaus Fiedler, Matthias Bluemke, Christian Unkelbach, Hart Blanton, Deborah L. Hall, Kathleen D. Vohs, Jannine D. Lasaleta, Bob Fennis, William von Hippel, Richard Ronay, Eli J. Finkel, Daniel C. Molden, Sarah E. Johnson and Paul W. Eastwick.

SSSP 12. PSYCHOLOGY OF ATTITUDES AND ATTITUDE CHANGE★ ISBN 978-1-84872-908-7 (Edited by J.P. Forgas, J. Cooper & W.D. Crano). *Contributors*: William D. Crano, Joel Cooper, Joseph P. Forgas, Blair T. Johnson, Marcella H. Boynton, Alison Ledgerwood, Yaacov Trope, Eva Walther, Tina Langer, Klaus Fiedler, Steven J. Spencer, Jennifer Peach, Emiko Yoshida, Mark P. Zanna, Allyson L. Holbrook, Jon A. Krosnick, Eddie Harmon-Jones, David M. Amodio, Cindy Harmon-Jones, Michaela Wänke, Leonie Reutner, Kipling D. Williams, Zhansheng Chen, Duane Wegener, Radmila Prislin, Brenda Major, Sarah S.M. Townsend, Frederick Rhodewalt, Benjamin Peterson, Jim Blascovich and Cade McCall.

SSSP 13. PSYCHOLOGY OF SOCIAL CONFLICT AND AGGRESSION★ ISBN 978-1-84872-932-2 (Edited by J.P. Forgas, A.W. Kruglanski & K.D. Williams). *Contributors*: Daniel Ames, Craig A. Anderson, Joanna E. Anderson, Paul Boxer, Tanya L. Chartrand, John Christner, Matt DeLisi, Thomas F. Denson, Ed Donnerstein, Eric F. Dubow, Chris Eckhardt, Emma C. Fabiansson, Eli J. Finkel, Gráinne M. Fitzsimons, Joseph P. Forgas, Adam D. Galinsky, Debra Gilin, Georgina S. Hammock, L. Rowell Huesmann, Arie W. Kruglanski, Robert Kurzban, N. Pontus Leander, Laura B. Luchies, William W. Maddux, Mario Mikulincer, Edward Orehek, Deborah South Richardson, Phillip R. Shaver, Hui Bing Tan, Mark Van Vugt, Eric D. Wesselmann, Kipling D. Williams and Lisa Zadro.

SSSP 14. SOCIAL THINKING AND INTERPERSONAL BEHAVIOR★ ISBN 978-1-84872-990-2 (Edited by J.P. Forgas, K. Fiedler & C. Sekidikes). *Contributors*: Andrea E. Abele, Eusebio M. Alvaro, Mauro Bertolotti, Camiel J. Beukeboom, Susanne Bruckmüller, Patrizia Catellani, Cindy K. Chung, Joel Cooper, William D. Crano, István Csertő, John F. Dovidio, Bea Ehmann, Klaus Fiedler, Joseph P. Forgas, Éva Fülöp, Jessica Gasiorek, Howard Giles, Liz Goldenberg, Barbara Ilg, Yoshihisa Kashima, Mikhail Kissine, Olivier Klein, Alex Koch, János László, Anne Maass, Andre Mata, Elisa M. Merkel, Alessio Nencini, Andrew A. Pearson, James W. Pennebaker, Kim Peters, Tibor Pólya, Ben Slugoski, Caterina Suitner, Zsolt Szabó, Matthew D. Trujillo and Orsolya Vincze.

SSSP 15. SOCIAL COGNITION AND COMMUNICATION* ISBN 978-1-84872-663-5 (Edited by J.P. Forgas, O. Vincze & J. László). *Contributors:* Andrea E. Abele, Eusebio M. Alvaro, Maro Bertolotti, Camiel J. Beukeboom, Susanne Bruckmüller, Patrizia Catellani, István Cserto, Cindy K. Chung, Joel Coooper, William D. Crano, John F. Dovidio, Bea Ehmann, Klaus Fiedler, J.P. Forgas, Éva Fülöp, Jessica Gasiorek, Howard Giles, Liz Goldenberg, Barbara Ilg, Yoshihisa Kahima, Mikhail Kissine, Alex S. Koch, János László, Olivier Klein, Anne Maass, André Mata, Elisa M. Merkel, Alessio Nencini, Adam R. Pearson, James W. Pennebaker, Kim Peters, Tibor Pólya, Ben Slugoski, Caterina Suitner, Zsolt Szabó, Matthew D. Trujillo and Orsolya Vincze.

SSSP 16. MOTIVATION AND ITS REGULATION: THE CONTROL WITHIN* ISBN 978-1-84872-562-1 (Edited by J.P. Forgas & E. Harmon-Jones). *Contributors:* Emily Balcetis, John A. Bargh, Jarik Bouw, Charles S. Carver, Brittany M. Christian, Hannah Faye Chua, Shana Cole, Carsten K.W. De Dreu, Thomas F. Denson, Andrew J. Elliot, Joseph P. Forgas, Alexandra Godwin, Karen Gonsalkorale, Jamin Halberstadt, Cindy Harmon-Jones, Eddie Harmon-Jones, E. Tory Higgins, Julie Y. Huang, Michael Inzlicht, Sheri L. Johnson, Jonathan Jong, Jutta Joormann, Nils B. Jostmann, Shinobu Kitayama, Sander L. Koole, Lisa Legault, Jennifer Leo, C. Neil Macrae, Jon K. Maner, Lynden K. Mile, Steven B. Most, Jaime L. Napier, Tom F. Price, Marieke Roskes, Brandon J. Schmeichel, Iris K. Schneider, Abigail A. Scholer, Julia Schüler, Sarah Strübin, David Tang, Steve Tompson, Mattie Tops and Lisa Zadro.

SSSP 17. SOCIAL PSYCHOLOGY AND POLITICS* ISBN 978-1-13882-968-8 (Edited by J.P. Forgas, K. Fiedler & W.D. Crano). *Contributors:* Stephanie M. Anglin, Luisa Batalha, Mauro Bertolotti, Patrizia Catellani, William D. Crano, Jarret T. Crawford, John F. Dovidio, Klaus Fiedler, Joseph P. Forgas, Mark G. Frank, Samuel L. Gaertner, Jeremy Ginges, Joscha Hofferbert, Michael A. Hogg, Hyisung C. Hwang, Yoel Inbar, Lee Jussim, Lucas A. Keefer, Laszlo Kelemen, Alex Koch, Tobias Krüger, Mark J. Landau, Janos Laszlo, Elena Lyrintzis, David Matsumoto, G. Scott Morgan, David A. Pizarro, Felicia Pratto, Katherine J. Reynolds, Tamar Saguy, Daan Scheepers, David O. Sears, Linda J. Skitka, Sean T. Stevens, Emina Subasic, Elze G. Ufkes, Robin R. Vallacher, Paul A.M. Van Lange, Daniel C. Wisneski, Michaela Wänke, Franz Woellert and Fouad Bou Zeineddine.

SSSP 18. THE SOCIAL PSYCHOLOGY OF MORALITY* ISBN 978-1-138-92907-4 (Edited by J.P. Forgas, L. Jussim & P.A.M. Van Lange). *Contributors:* Stephanie M. Anglin, Joel B. Armstrong, Mark J. Brandt, Brock Bastian, Paul Conway, Joel Cooper, Chelsea Corless, Jarret T. Crawford, Daniel Crimston, Molly J. Crockett, Jose L. Duarte, Allison K. Farrell, Klaus Fiedler, Rebecca Friesdorf, Jeremy A. Frimer, Adam D. Galinsky, Bertram Gawronski,

William G. Graziano, Nick Haslam, Mandy Hütter, Lee Jussim, Alice Lee, William W. Maddux, Emma Marshall, Dale T. Miller, Benoît Monin, Tom Pyszczynski, Richard Ronay, David A. Schroeder, Simon M. Laham, Jeffry A. Simpson, Sean T. Stevens, William von Hippel and Geoffrey Wetherell.

SSSP 19. THE SOCIAL PSYCHOLOGY OF LIVING WELL★ ISBN 978-0-8153-6924-0 (Edited by J.P. Forgas & R.F. Baumeister). *Contributors*: Yair Amichai-Hamburger, Peter Arslan, Roy F. Baumeister, William D. Crano, Candice D. Donaldson, Elizabeth W. Dunn, Ryan J. Dwyer, Jami Eller, Shir Etgar, Allison K. Farrell, Klaus Fiedler, Joseph P. Forgas, Barbara L. Fredrickson, Megan M. Fritz, Shelly L. Gable, Karen Gonsalkorale, Alexa Hubbard, Chloe O. Huelsnitz, Felicia A. Huppert, David Kalkstein, Sonja Lyubomirsky, David G. Myers, Constantine Sedikides, James Shah, Kennon M. Sheldon, Jeffry A. Simpson, Elena Stephan, Yaacov Trope, William von Hippel and Tim Wildschut.

★ Published by Routledge
★★ Published by Cambridge University Press

THE SOCIAL PSYCHOLOGY OF LIVING WELL

Edited by Joseph P. Forgas
and Roy F. Baumeister

Routledge
Taylor & Francis Group

NEW YORK AND LONDON

First published 2018
by Routledge
711 Third Avenue, New York, NY 10017

and by Routledge
2 Park Square, Milton Park, Abingdon, Oxon, OX14 4RN

Routledge is an imprint of the Taylor & Francis Group, an informa business

© 2018 Taylor & Francis

The right of Joseph P. Forgas and Roy F. Baumeister to be identified
as the authors of the editorial material, and of the authors for their
individual chapters, has been asserted in accordance with sections 77 and
78 of the Copyright, Designs and Patents Act 1988.

Library of Congress Cataloging-in-Publication Data
Names: Forgas, Joseph P., editor. | Baumeister, Roy F., editor.
Title: The social psychology of living well / edited by Joseph P. Forgas and
  Roy F. Baumeister.
Description: New York, NY : Routledge, 2018. | Series: The Sydney
  Symposium of Social Psychology series | Includes bibliographical
  references and index.
Identifiers: LCCN 2017044354 | ISBN 9780815369233 (hardback : alk.
  paper) | ISBN 9780815369240 (pbk. : alk. paper) | ISBN 9781351189712
  (ebook)
Subjects: LCSH: Happiness. | Well-being. | Quality of life—Psychological
  aspects.
Classification: LCC BF575.H27 S63 2018 | DDC 302—dc23
LC record available at https://lccn.loc.gov/2017044354

ISBN: 978-0-8153-6923-3 (hbk)
ISBN: 978-0-8153-6924-0 (pbk)
ISBN: 978-1-351-18971-2 (ebk)

Typeset in Bembo
by Apex CoVantage, LLC

CONTENTS

List of Contributors   *xiv*

1 The Social Psychology of Living Well: Historical,
   Social and Cultural Perspectives   1
   Joseph P. Forgas and Roy F. Baumeister

PART I
Conceptual Issues   **19**

2 Happiness and Meaningfulness as Two Different and
   Not Entirely Compatible Versions of the Good Life   21
   Roy F. Baumeister

3 Evolutionary Imperatives and the Good Life   34
   William von Hippel and Karen Gonsalkorale

4 On the Adaptive Functions of Good Life: Going
   Beyond Hedonic Experience   48
   Klaus Fiedler and Peter Arslan

5 Living Life Well: The Role of Mindfulness
   and Compassion   65
   Felicia A. Huppert

PART II
The Role of Purposeful Activities in Living Well   83

6   For What It's Worth: The Regulatory Pleasure
and Purpose of a Good Life   85
James Shah

7   Whither Happiness? When, How, and Why Might
Positive Activities Undermine Well-Being   101
Megan M. Fritz and Sonja Lyubomirsky

8   Understanding the Good Life: Eudaimonic Living
Involves Well-Doing, Not Well-Being   116
Kennon M. Sheldon

9   Religious Engagement and Living Well   137
David G. Myers

PART III
Affective and Cognitive Aspects of Living Well   161

10   Biological Underpinnings of Positive Emotions
and Purpose   163
Barbara L. Fredrickson

11   Nostalgia Shapes and Potentiates the Future   181
Constantine Sedikides, Tim Wildschut, and Elena Stephan

12   Negative Affect and the Good Life: On the Cognitive,
Motivational and Interpersonal Benefits
of Negative Mood   200
Joseph P. Forgas

13   Expansive and Contractive Learning Experiences:
Mental Construal and Living Well   223
David Kalkstein, Alexa Hubbard, and Yaacov Trope

PART IV
Social and Cultural Factors in Living Well   237

14   Satisfying and Meaningful Close Relationships   239
Shelly L. Gable

15 Early Social Experiences and Living Well: A Longitudinal
    View of Adult Physical Health   257
    Jeffry A. Simpson, Allison K. Farrell, Chloe O. Huelsnitz,
    and Jami Eller

16 Positive Parenting, Adolescent Substance Use Prevention,
    and the Good Life   277
    William D. Crano and Candice D. Donaldson

17 Internet and Well-Being   298
    Yair Amichai-Hamburger and Shir Etgar

18 Technology and the Future of Happiness   319
    Elizabeth W. Dunn and Ryan J. Dwyer

Index   *336*

CONTRIBUTORS

Amichai-Hamburger, Yair, IDC, Herzliya, Israel.

Arslan, Peter, University of Heidelberg, Germany.

Baumeister, Roy F., University of Queensland, Australia.

Crano, William D., Claremont Graduate University, USA.

Donaldson, Candice D., Claremont Graduate University, USA.

Dunn, Elizabeth W., University of British Columbia, Canada.

Dwyer, Ryan J., University of British Columbia, Canada.

Eller, Jami, University of Minnesota, USA.

Etgar, Shir, IDC, Herzliya, Israel.

Farrell, Allison K., Wayne State University, USA.

Fiedler, Klaus, University of Heidelberg, Germany.

Forgas, Joseph P., University of New South Wales, Sydney, Australia.

Fredrickson, Barbara L., University of North Carolina, USA.

Fritz, Megan M., University of California, Riverside, USA.

Gable, Shelly L., University of California, Santa Barbara, USA.

Gonsalkorale, Karen, University of Sydney, Australia.

Hubbard, Alexa, New York University, USA.

Huelsnitz, Chloe O., University of Minnesota, USA.

Huppert, Felicia A., University of Cambridge, UK.

Kalkstein, David, New York University, USA.

Lyubomirsky, Sonja, University of California, Riverside, USA.

Myers, David G., Hope College, USA.

Sedikides, Constantine, University of Southampton, UK.

Shah, James, Duke University, USA.

Sheldon, Kennon M., University of Missouri, USA.

Simpson, Jeffry A., University of Minnesota, USA.
Stephan, Elena, Bar-Ilan University, Israel.
Trope, Yaacov, New York University, USA
Von Hippel, William, University of Queensland, Australia.
Wildschut, Tim, University of Southampton, UK.

1

THE SOCIAL PSYCHOLOGY OF LIVING WELL

Historical, Social and Cultural Perspectives

Joseph P. Forgas and Roy F. Baumeister

The topic of this book, how to live well, is one of the oldest and most universal questions that has preoccupied human beings since the dawn of history. Philosophers, writers and artists and, more recently, empirical social scientists struggled to understand how life should be lived, and how well-being and life satisfaction could be optimized. The ability to think about and reflect on the nature of our own existence and its possibilities is a uniquely human capability and in a sense is as defining a hallmark of our species as is our intelligence. The way we respond to these questions has a profound metaphysical significance and, at the same time, also has powerful practical implications for the ways that individuals, groups and societies at large should regulate their affairs.

Topics that deal with the question of how to live well were traditionally addressed by scientists working in a number of interlinked disciplines, including psychology, evolutionary theory, economics, sociology, history and political science. In the present book, we would like to argue that social psychology occupies an important and privileged position when it comes to understanding the nature of human well-being. In this introductory chapter in particular, we will start with a brief review of the alternative philosophical orientations that speak to the question of how to live well.

Next, the role of some of the most important social psychological processes in achieving a 'good life' will be discussed, and the functions of specific strategies in promoting well-being will be considered. And finally, the contribution of the different chapters included here to the achievement of life satisfaction will be summarized.

Philosophical Antecedents

How to live well has been a perennial question asked by philosophers since time immemorial. It is perhaps not surprising that it was philosophers who were among the first to seek such answers, possibly because such philosophical reflection might in themselves produce a degree of dysphoria. Many of their insights may still strike us as highly relevant today—indeed, ancient philosophers such as Socrates, Epicurus, Epictetus, Zeno and many others offer us advice that could come straight out of a popular book of positive psychology today. Thus, in introducing this book, it seems appropriate to start where it all began. . . .

Seeking Happiness and Avoiding Pain: Hedonism

The philosophy of hedonism is sometimes considered as the most important simple and sovereign principle that can explain all human behaviour (Allport, 1954/1968). This idea is almost as old as human civilization. Already in the Babylonian *Epic of Gilgamesh*, probably the first ever recorded advocacy of hedonism, Siduri suggested that the main concern of humans should be to fill their bellies, make merry, and let their days be full of joy. Looking at the message conveyed by most contemporary marketing and advertising gurus, one could be forgiven for thinking that secretly they are all disciples of Siduri.

Subsequent antique philosophers such as Democritus and later the Cyrenaics elaborated the doctrine of hedonism further, emphasizing the importance of immediate sensations as the most relevant criteria of knowledge and conduct. According to them, the wise person should be in control of pleasures, and this requires judgment to evaluate the different pleasures. Love, friendship, altruism and justice can all provide pleasure; these are ideas that are frequently echoed in contemporary positive psychology, and in several of the chapters here as well (see also Baumeister; Huppert; Gable; and Fiedler and Arslan, this volume).

Ultimately, it was Epicurus (*c.* 341–*c.* 270 BC), probably the greatest philosophical exponent of hedonism, who believed that the highest good was to seek modest, sustainable 'pleasures' such as a state of tranquility and freedom from fear. These are states that can be obtained by knowledge, reflection, friendship and living a virtuous and temperate life. Epicurus gave much useful advice about how to live well, advice that is reiterated in many contemporary books on well-being, and indeed in this volume. His emphasis on friendship, communality and aesthetic pleasures rather than seeking material possessions is echoed by some of the contributors here (for example, Sedikides, Wildschut & Stephan; Simpson et al.; Amichai-Hamburger & Etgar, this volume).

Utilitarianism

The philosophy of hedonism was neglected in subsequent centuries when the ascetic precepts of dogmatic Christianity focused attention on the promised (and yet to be confirmed . . .!) pleasures of the afterlife, as distinct from the well-deserved suffering in this life derived from the concept of original sin. However, the presumptuous notion that a good life can and perhaps should be lived in this world did not entirely disappear. It was as an indirect consequence of the Renaissance, the Reformation and the Enlightenment that the notion of hedonism in this world re-emerged in a new guise and with renewed force in Europe. It was utilitarian philosophers like Jeremy Bentham and John Stuart Mill who sought to translate Epicurean principles into an ethical theory of appropriate social and collective behaviour that provides the foundations of the contemporary rational, rather than religious, system of morality and well-being.

Utilitarian ethics argues that all action should be directed toward achieving the greatest total amount of happiness for the largest number of people. Utilitarian ethics assumes that all actions can be evaluated in terms of their moral worth, and so the desirability of an action is determined by its resulting hedonistic consequences. This is a consequentialist creed, assuming that the moral value and desirability of an action can be determined from its likely outcomes. Jeremy Bentham suggested that the value of hedonistic outcomes can be quantitatively assessed, so that the value of consequent pleasure can be derived by multiplying its intensity and its duration. In contrast, the other major exponent of utilitarianism, John Stuart Mill, argued for a more qualitative approach, assuming that there can be different subjective levels of pleasure. Higher-quality pleasures are more desirable than lower-quality pleasures. Less sophisticated creatures (like pigs!) have an easier access to the simpler pleasures, but more sophisticated creatures like humans have the capacity to access higher pleasures and should be motivated to seek those.

Hedonism and utilitarianism are rather optimistic creeds, assuming that through rational thought and analysis humans can achieve positive outcomes and live a good life. This rational and hopeful approach to the good life they share with most modern psychological thinking on the topic, and indeed, it is this orientation that motivates this volume. A somewhat more pessimistic approach to the perennial question of how to live well is provided by the philosophical tradition of Stoicism, that emphasizes the acceptance and understanding of inevitable negative outcomes. However, both philosophical schools, hedonism and Stoicism, share a belief in the ultimate power of individuals to live a good life through their own efforts and rational processes.

Accepting Negative Outcomes: Stoicism

Perhaps the earliest philosophical tradition that explicitly teaches the need to accept and manage adversity is Stoicism, a school founded by Zeno in the 3rd century BC. Stoicism emphasizes the development of self-control as a means of managing destructive emotions, through becoming a clear and unbiased thinker. We can readily recognize the recurrence of this idea in several of the contributions to this book, including the chapters by Baumeister; Fiedler and Arslan; Forgas; Sheldon; Fritz & Lyubomirsky, and others. Stoicism is a means for improving a person's ethical and moral well-being, by learning to accept the natural order of things. A Stoic adapts and amends his or her desires to suit the world and so remains contented even in the face of adversity.

The Stoics taught that destructive emotions always resulted from errors in judgment, a conflict between the will and the natural order. To live a good life, we need to understand and accept the rules of the natural order; thus, the sage person becomes immune to misfortune. There is more than a passing resemblance here to some of the basic tenets of Buddhism. It is rather remarkable that whereas Eastern ideologies such as Buddhism have become highly influential and had a huge influence on popular culture as an attractive means to improve well-being, essentially similar messages coming to us from antiquity from the Stoics remain largely unheeded (see also Kalkstein, Hubbard & Trope, this volume).

The solution to evil and unhappiness, according to Stoic philosophy, is to examine one's own judgments and behavior and determine where they diverge from the universal reason of nature. Stoics also accepted that suicide is permissible for a wise person in circumstances that prevent them from living a virtuous life. Suicide could also be justifiable if one fell victim to severe pain or disease. Stoicism is not just a philosophy but a way of life requiring constant practice, including focusing on the present and daily reflection—these are ideas that indeed share a great deal of similarity with Eastern practices of meditation and mindfulness.

Stoics were also the first tolerant cosmopolitans. They held that every individual is part of the universal spirit, and differences in birth, rank and status should be of no importance in social relationships. They advocated the universal brotherhood of humanity and the natural equality of all human beings. Stoic writers such as Epictetus, Seneca, Cicero and Marcus Aurelius anticipated a kind of thought system based on individualism, tolerance, self-knowledge, acceptance and self-control that had a major influence on Western civilizations ever since. Just like Stoicism, Christianity also asserts an inner freedom in the face of the external world, and the futility and ephemeral nature of worldly possessions and attachments. The *Meditations* of Marcus Aurelius in particular have been highly regarded by many Christians throughout the ages, and would not be out of place in any contemporary book of advice on how to live a good life.

Evolutionary Considerations

In contemporary Western societies, at least since the Enlightenment and the industrial revolution, living well in many people's minds is inextricably linked to material wealth. Even at the political level, it is typically assumed that well-being is somehow directly linked to measures of economic performance such as annual growth or gross domestic product (GDP) per capita. In fact, there is now very strong evidence that this relationship between wealth and well-being only holds up to a certain standard of living. Once societies reach that level, further increases in wealth do not produce an appreciable increase in well-being and happiness. So, something quite fundamental is wrong with the overwhelming emphasis on economic progress as the sole means of improving well-being, at least once a reasonable standard of living has been reached.

Why should this be so? Modern humans in fundamental ways are no different from our evolutionary hunter-gatherer ancestors, who eked out a precarious existence living in small, intimate social groups. We all evolved as thoroughly social creatures, surrounded by the same small group of people from birth to death, and humans derived and maintained a sense of identity and status from the daily face-to-face interactions within that group. This pattern of living changed fundamentally about three hundred years ago, when the philosophy of Enlightenment, the French Revolution and the industrial revolution ushered in a fundamentally different epoch in human affairs, the age of the individual. Radical social changes, including dramatic increases in social and geographical mobility, also created new opportunities for living well while at the same time disrupting the traditional social bases of identity and interpersonal connection.

Liberating individuals from the social constraints of small group life had a revolutionary effect. It enabled us to become much freer, much richer and much healthier, live much longer and, up to a point, become much happier. But we also lost something: we lost the natural sense of belonging, identity and community that comes from the intense social life of the small group. Most of us probably only experience this kind of belonging for a short time, perhaps in our high school years. So a sense of connectedness—perhaps a kind of brotherhood or 'fraternite' in the sense that the French Revolution emphasized—is also essential to human well-being, as several of the chapters here also suggest (see, for example, Gable; Simpson et al.; Sheldon; Kalkstein, Hubbard & Trope, this volume). By way of contrast, the medieval European peasant may have seen barely a couple hundred other human beings in his or her entire lifetime, but such a person was firmly entrenched in social bonds that remained stable until death. In contrast, the modern European urban dweller often sees more people than that in a single day, has social interactions and contacts with countless others—but relationship partners come and go, and apart from the strongest family bonds, almost no social connections endure for decades. Quantity has replaced intensity (quality) in human interaction.

While freedom and individualism are certainly liberating, the loss of social connection and identity will become more problematic and more debilitating as our material well-being progresses. In a way, what limits further increases in well-being in modern societies is the problematic nature of our social contacts. For human beings, naturally selected by evolution to be intensely sociable and to rely on others for their daily survival, living as an isolated individual is not without its problems. Yet social trends also show that more and more people do live alone, often by choice.

We see plenty of evidence for this 'attachment gap' all around us. Survey evidence for loneliness, isolation and social shyness is all around us (Zimbardo, 1990). Of course, people are not lonely because they are forced to be—they are lonely as a consequence of their freely made individual choices. People prefer independence, privacy, autonomy and freedom. These are all desirable objectives, but they can only be effectively achieved if we chose to liberate ourselves from the social constraints that enduring close relationships demand. Even though these are freely made choices, the unforeseen consequence of remaining isolated from our fellow human beings can be a great source of discomfort and unhappiness.

Consumption and Well-Being

There is another intriguing and less obvious line of evidence demonstrating the unsatisfied need for identity and connectedness, coming from the fields of *marketing and advertising*. Increasingly, the goods we work for, desire and purchase are not bought because of their actual usefulness, but because they promise to tell others (and ourselves) something about the kind of people we are (or would like to be). Often, the things we buy are not bought for their actual utility, but are *identity products* that promise to satisfy the deep-seated desire for social status and connectedness.

Advertised brand names are increasingly not about guarantees of quality and reliability, but are indications of status. What is the possible point of branding an expensive watch or a perfume with brand names such as 'Burberry' (a rain coat maker), 'Gucci' (a fashion house), 'Porsche' (a car maker) or 'Mont Blanc' (a pen maker)? These brands never made a watch and never will—attaching their name to an overpriced but otherwise undistinguished luxury product has nothing to do with utility or quality, it is purely and simply a badge of desired social status and identity. Or take the example of running shoes; these used to be humble items of great utility, mass produced and sold cheaply everywhere. A few decades ago, manipulative advertisers managed to convince customers that running shoes are more than just shoes—they can be important sources of status and identity. The illusion of rugged individualism ('Just do it') can now be bought, communicated and displayed by paying exorbitant prices for a particular brand of shoes by masses of misguided consumers.

Even more bizarre is the huge international business that developed around selling branded water in bottles—a colourless, tasteless, transparent liquid that flows freely from every tap (and actually, about a quarter of bottled water sold is actually tap water; e.g. Torres, 2016). Who would have thought that people can be persuaded to pay outrageous prices, often in excess of what a bottle of reasonable wine might cost, for water, just because it is labelled 'Evian' or 'San Pellegrino'? This is truly a triumph of advertising over common sense. Clearly, what is being sold and bought here is not water, but an image, a badge of identity and social status, all supported by a huge advertising budget that the consumers actually pay for.

The point is, if people are willing to pay their hard-earned money to buy such otherwise useless identity products, there must be a huge unsatisfied need out there for a *real* sense of status and identity, something that normally could not be purchased but must be achieved within an organic and meaningful social environment such as a group. The lack of increase in well-being and life satisfaction for some decades now in rich Western countries despite our increasing affluence suggests that we might have reached the limits of improving well-being through material progress alone. Clearly the key issue has something to do with the way ever-increasing material wealth is now spent on increasingly useless products. Identity products sell because they promise social status and position, but they actually fail to deliver, since no amount of such symbolic identity consumption can actually make us *feel* more important, more connected, more popular, more liked and of higher status.

Technology and the Good Life

A special case of the growing disconnect between material progress and well-being is also illustrated by the influence of new technology on the way people interact with each other. Technological progress has given us new devices that may fundamentally change the way we spend our time, and the way we relate to each other (see also Dunn & Dwyer; and Amichai-Hamburger & Etgar, this volume). These developments emerged unannounced and were driven by the possibilities of technological progress, not by any kind of thoughtful or rational consideration of what human beings really need to improve our quality of life. Yet they have the potential to fundamentally change the way human beings relate to each other. As argued above, we cannot forget that modern humans were essentially shaped by the demands of survival in a Stone Age environment, and our needs for belonging and connectedness were determined by the demands of intimate, face-to-face small group life. To what extent can such needs be satisfied by the fundamentally different communication features that prevail on the Internet and in the virtual world? There is growing evidence that cyber-connectedness and cyber-communication are characterized by psychological features such as, for example, anonymity, superficiality, and widespread deception (including self-deception) that make their usefulness for improving human connectedness highly questionable.

Psychology's Well-Being Agenda

Psychology's contribution to understanding and promoting the good life has expanded in multiple directions in recent decades. For much of psychology's history, a primary focus was on reducing mental illness. Freud's theories about human nature, including his views on happiness (e.g. in his *The Future of an Illusion*; Freud 1927/1990), were based largely on his work with patients suffering from various forms of mental illness.

It was not surprising that helping people resolve their pain and suffering came first. The basic principle that bad is stronger than good (Baumeister, Bratslavsky,

Finkenauer & Vohs, 2001) dictates that most people will give priority to getting out of a bad state and into a neutral one, rather than moving from a neutral state to a positive one. The primacy of pain in mental content (Scarry, 1985) suggests that the very evolution of consciousness was partly driven by the importance of recognizing and stopping harm to the body.

The focus on alleviating mental illness in early psychology was thus not really about the good life—merely how to avoid a bad one. This was conceded in Freud's famous quip that with successful psychotherapy the patient could escape from neurotic misery into ordinary unhappiness.

It was not until the humanistic psychology movement (e.g., Maslow, 1968) that researchers began to assert that psychology could and should move beyond the narrow focus on curing illness. Health is not simply the absence of disease, as such writers asserted.

More recently, the positive psychology movement took up the banner of promoting positive good states rather than just alleviating bad ones. The movement has been spearheaded by Martin Seligman, a clinical psychologist who became famous by doing research on learned helplessness—itself one of the most dismally negative states in the history of psychological theory. Having spent so much of his career focusing on the negative, Seligman was able to inspire many others to recognize the importance of the good life and to explore ways of celebrating and cultivating it. The positive psychology movement learned from the mistakes of the humanistic psychology movement, which lost some scientific credibility by its uncritical embrace of touchy-feely subjectivism.

The Self-Esteem Movement

The interim between the decline of humanistic psychology in the early 1980s and the rise of positive psychology in the 1990s was marked by the self-esteem movement, based on the assumption that lives could be improved in widely assorted and substantial ways by getting people to love themselves more. Its intellectual roots extended back at least to Carl Rogers's notion of unconditional positive regard, but it was firmly based in research findings showing correlations between self-esteem and a broad assortment of positive and negative outcomes (Mecca, Smelser & Vasconcellos, 1989; see also California Task Force, 1990). At the zenith of the movement, its adherents confidently predicted that boosting self-esteem could alleviate all manner of problems, including teen pregnancy, unemployment, school failure, drug abuse, domestic violence, divorce, and crime (see also Crano & Donaldson, this volume).

In retrospect, the self-esteem movement was unfortunately based on mistaking correlation for causation. Yes, high self-esteem was correlated with higher grades among schoolchildren (e.g., Wylie, 1979)—but longitudinal studies gradually revealed that high self-esteem resulted from getting good grades, rather than leading to them later (Bachman & O'Malley, 1977, 1986; Maruyama, Rubin & Kingsbury, 1981).

Yet not all was lost. A review of the benefits of high self-esteem concluded that thinking well of oneself does in fact increase happiness (Baumeister, Campbell, Krueger & Vohs, 2003). Subsequent work has sought to show further benefits, but these again tend to be in the domain of subjective rather than objective indicators of success and well-being. In particular, an impressive investigation by Orth et al. (2012) showed that high self-esteem led to having more positive views of one's life and circumstances but did not actually lead to objectively better circumstances. Thus, people with high self-esteem enjoyed their jobs more than other people, but they did not attain higher levels of occupational success or promotion.

The self-esteem findings highlight an important gap between subjective and objective outcomes, which is a central substantive as well as methodological issue in any attempt to understand and promote the good life (see also Baumeister; and Fiedler & Arslan, this volume). Must psychology strive to make life objectively better—or is it enough to help people adopt a happier, more positive attitude toward life, without necessarily improving it in any objectively discernible way? Despite the overreach and resulting loss of credibility of the self-esteem movement, it may still claim to offer much if all it does is make people subjectively enjoy their lives more. After all, insofar as the good life is something that resides in how the individual feels about his or her circumstances, then enhancing feelings may be enough.

To be sure, some may think that simply changing attitudes without improving circumstances is a feeble effort, unlikely to endure. Yet much of psychotherapy continues to be focused on teaching clients to learn to accept the inevitability of circumstances they may not be able to change. This philosophical approach has its roots in the ancient philosophy of the Stoics. Perhaps approaches to well-being should also embrace the principle that positive change may often come from internal changes in how we see and interpret the world, rather than any unfettered ability to change our prevailing circumstances.

Another intriguing line of objections to the view that it is enough to change subjective factors comes from ideological perspectives suggesting that such approaches can smack of oppression. Ruling elites want their oppressed classes to be content with the status quo and not make trouble. They would eagerly embrace solutions that make the downtrodden content with being trodden upon. Marx's (1977) concept of 'false consciousness' is one such well-known attempt to discredit the validity of an individual's internal representations when they contradict what he took to be 'objective' reality. His characterization of religion as the opiate of the masses was perhaps the most famous version of this critique. The ruling elites foist religion on working people to reduce social protest and revolution, so that the rulers can continue exploiting the working classes while the latter look to an afterlife in heaven for happiness. Jost's work on system justification

(Jost & van Toorn, 2012) is another example of a recent reincarnation of Marx's ideas on false consciousness. These criticisms focusing on criteria for, and the validity of, subjective versus objective well-being beg the question of who is actually qualified to decide whether an individual is or is not allowed to be satisfied with his or her circumstances. Arguably a radical liberal approach can only be based on unconditionally accepting that each person must be the ultimate arbiter of his or her own well-being.

Self-Control

For those who think psychology should strive to improve objective outcomes as well as subjective ones, the personality emphasis has shifted from self-esteem to self-control (see also Shah, this volume). Like self-esteem, trait self-control is associated with many positive outcomes (e.g., de Ridder et al., 2012). But unlike self-esteem, self-control appears to actually predict desirable future outcomes and indeed cause them. The sorts of longitudinal data that gradually demolished the myth that self-esteem led to objective benefits have upheld the value and power of self-control. Multiple studies have found that self-control assessed in childhood predicts positive outcomes in adulthood, including better performance in work and school, better relationships and popularity, better interpersonal trust, less aggression and crime including less likelihood of being arrested, reduced risk of unemployment, less cigarette smoking, fewer mental and physical health problems, and ultimately improvements in longevity (Moffitt et al., 2011; Mischel, Shoda & Peake, 1988; Daly et al., 2015; Tangney et al., 2004; Righetti & Finkenauer, 2011; Ainsworth et al., 2014).

All of this brings up the question as to whether subjective happiness is the essence of the good life. Indeed, rather paradoxically, emphasis on self-control could be seen as potentially detrimental to happiness, insofar as its exercise often consists in denying oneself pleasures. Fortunately, the evidence has now become fairly solid that high self-control does ultimately lead to happiness as well as improved objective indicators of success and well-being (see Hofmann, Luhmann, Fisher, Vohs & Baumeister, 2013). Self-control thus has a well-supported claim to be an essential component of the good life, both in its subjective and its objective aspects.

Still, there is more to the good life than happiness. The lives of others that we admire most are not necessarily the happiest. In the USA, Abraham Lincoln is probably the single most admired president, but his life was not a happy one, and indeed it is generally accepted that he suffered from severe depression at times. He is admired for holding the nation together, but one wonders how much joy that brought him, as it was a nightmarish struggle marked by hundreds of thousands of deaths—and just when the war was ending, he was shot to death.

The Lincoln example suggests that perceived virtue and achievement are major components in how people evaluate others' lives. Other people's happiness may be something to envy or emulate but not necessarily to admire. Positive psychology has itself continued to struggle with overarching tendencies to put happiness first, despite periodic reminders that meaningfulness, achievement and other emotions including temporary periods of nostalgia, melancholia and even dysphoria are also valuable parts of the human emotional repertoire that are well worth cultivating (see also Baumeister; Fiedler & Arslan; Sedikides, Wildschut & Stephan, this volume). Indeed, there is now growing experimental evidence suggesting that temporary episodes of dysphoria are actually necessary and adaptive contributors to better managing life's challenges (see also Forgas, this volume).

Health is also a component of the good life (see also Simpson et al., this volume). Most lives contain stretches of good health punctuated by illnesses. Health is appreciated more during its absence than presence, given the tendency to take it for granted. A remark attributed to Benjamin Franklin asserted that if mankind could ever find a way to cure or avoid toothaches, everyone would live happily ever after. That remark reminds us of the intense, inescapable suffering that many of our forebears endured on a regular basis in the era preceding modern dentistry. It also shows how easily we come to take for granted things such as the absence of pain that earlier generations yearned to have. Obviously, Franklin's prediction was dead wrong: toothaches have mostly vanished from daily life in the modern world, but somehow mutual ongoing bliss for all mankind remains elusive.

The role of health in the good life brings up another aspect of the psychological agenda: measurement. Health can be measured objectively, unlike happiness, for which subjective self-reports seem difficult to avoid. Indeed, subjectivity is essential to happiness in a way that it is not for health. One can be mistaken about one's good health or one's illness, as the familiar cases of hypochondriacs and sickness deniers illustrate. But it makes little sense to say that someone is mistaken about how happy he or she is. No objective data can be cited to prove that your honest sense of your own happiness is mistaken, unlike with health. The very question of how well-being should be defined and measured remains a perennial challenge for psychologists, as the contributions by Fiedler and Arslan, and Sheldon et al. (this volume) illustrate.

The volume is the result of leading researchers with an interest in the nature, measurement and promotion of well-being attempting to summarize what social psychology can contribute to living life well. In the next, final section of this introductory chapter, a brief summary and overview of their contributions is provided.

Overview of the Volume

The book is organized into four parts. The first part, after this introductory chapter, is devoted to discussing **basic conceptual issues** concerning the social psychology of well-being.

Chapter 2 by **Roy Baumeister** explores one of the most the fundamental questions about how to live a good life: the link between happiness and meaning.

Living well has both a hedonic and a moral connotation, denoting either pleasure or virtue. Baumeister argues that pleasure is a more evolutionary, natural category, while virtue and meaning are profoundly social constructions, where it is shared social values that allow the experiences of kindness, gratitude and connectedness to exert a positive influence on well-being. Empirical evidence suggests that the two criteria tend to overlap, although pleasure and meaning are linked to different psychological processes, and pleasure is mainly experienced in the present, while meaning involves a more inclusive past and future perspective. Happiness appears the simpler and in an evolutionary sense older of the two, while meaningful lives are linked to giving to others and being highly involved in complex social undertakings.

In Chapter 3, **von Hippel and Gonsalkorale** develop an evolutionary approach to understanding what it takes to live a good life. They point out that the very contemplation of this issue by masses of people is probably a modern luxury, as our Stone Age ancestors had little choice in how they made a living. Although living the good life may well be a matter of meeting our evolutionary imperatives, these imperatives are often at cross-purposes with each other, as is often the case with the goals of reproduction and survival, manifest in frequent tension between many of our short-term and long-term goals. Such an evolutionary perspective can help us to make sense of many of the pitfalls of the modern world, such as our weaknesses in the face of what Trivers called 'phenotypical indulgences', such as drugs, computer games, television, or potato chips.

In chapter 4, **Fiedler and Arslan** discuss the common fallacy that maximizing positive hedonic experiences is the best strategy for a happy and fulfilling life. As they point out, the dialectics of adaptive behavior implies that happy outcomes are necessarily rare, and depend on effortful past learning. Happiness is relative to modest aspirations, and paradoxically, deprivation often enhances subsequent enjoyment. Thus, as a matter of principle, optimal learning and personal growth necessarily depend on the contrasting experiences of hedonically positive and negative outcomes.

Chapter 5 by **Felicia Huppert** explores the dual roles of mindfulness and compassion in living a good life. She proposes that these two mental practices are foundational to life going well. Mindfulness trains the skills of awareness, attention and self-regulation, while compassion trains the skills of empathy and kindness and motivation to help. The chapter reviews evidence from behavioural science and neuroscience demonstrating the individual and interpersonal benefits of these practices.

The second part of the book looks at the role of **purposeful, motivated activities in living well**. In Chapter 6, **James Shah** outlines a regulatory focus approach (emphasis on promotion, or prevention objectives) to consider the purpose of a good life and the basic self-regulatory functions it may serve. In support of this approach, research is presented suggesting that regulatory focus may impact not only whether individuals come to define the good life in terms of what is desired or required in such a life, but also how they work in pursuit of such a life and how they experience living it. The research suggests that regulatory focus may impact not only how one defines, pursues and experiences a good life but how one considers it ending.

Chapter 7 by **Fritz and Lyubomirsky** discusses the implications for well-being of the 'positive activity model' that suggests that people can increase their own happiness by intentionally engaging in positive activities. The chapter considers the importance of mediators and moderators that determine the relationship between positive activities and increased well-being. However, positive activities may also have paradoxical effects when they can actively backfire. The chapter posits several key moderators and mechanisms by which performing presumably happiness-increasing activities may give rise to iatrogenic effects, producing *un*happiness.

Ken Sheldon in Chapter 8 offers a thoughtful examination of the increasingly popular concept of 'eudaimonic well-being', and proposes an 'Eudaimonic Activity Model' which reserves the term eudaimonia to refer to specified characteristics of people's conative activity, not to a positive psychological state or emotional condition. The model asks researchers to test purportedly eudaimonic activities as causes of subjective well-being. Such an approach can help to discriminate between eudaimonic-type activities (which typically produce subjective well-being) and merely hedonic-type activities (which typically do not).

In Chapter 9, **David Myers** explores the role of religion in well-being. Is religiosity indeed "one of the world's great evils" (Dawkins, 2006), or does religion serve an adaptive evolutionary purpose, fostering morality, cohesion and group survival? On balance, is religious engagement today associated more with the good life or with misery? Does religion promote human virtues such as humility, forgiveness, health, happiness and longevity, or does it produce arrogance, pride, hypocrisy and, ultimately, stress, depression and illness? Myers presents intriguing results from big data sources showing a curious *religious engagement paradox*. Religious engagement correlates *negatively* with well-being across aggregate, societal levels (for example, when comparing more vs. less religious countries or American states), yet religiosity correlates *positively* with well-being when measured across individuals. Intriguingly, actively religious individuals *and* irreligious places are generally more flourishing. Some possible explanations for this paradox are considered.

The third part of the book deals with the **affective and cognitive variables** that have an influence on living well. In Chapter 10, **Barbara Fredrickson** explores the plausible biological pathways by which positive mind states, such as positive emotions and purpose, are linked to physical health. Positive emotions can prospectively predict increases in purpose and meaning, and purpose-laden activities, such spirituality and meditation, predict positive emotions. The capacities to experience positive emotions and purpose are human universals shaped over millennia by natural selection. Based on findings from Fredrickson she offers a provisional model specifying how various biological attributes—ranging from leukocyte gene expression profiles to cardiac vagal tone and oxytocin—can function as mechanisms (mediators and moderators) that undergird both positive emotions and purpose.

Chapter 11 by **Sedikides, Wildschut and Stephan** discusses the important role that such puzzling emotions as nostalgia can play in human well-being. They argue that nostalgia, although oriented towards the past, has implications for one's future, and for living 'the good life' in general. The chapter suggests that nostalgia shapes the future by sparking an approach orientation, increasing optimism, and evoking inspiration. Further, nostalgia potentiates the future by strengthening motivation for goal pursuit, boosting creativity, and guiding behavior.

Chapter 12 by **Joseph Forgas** makes the counterintuitive point that accepting and even embracing negative affective states can serve useful and adaptive functions and, paradoxically, may actually contribute to well-being and life satisfaction. He argues that the representation, cultivation and understanding of negative affective states has long been a hallmark of Western culture and civilization, and most great works of art. The chapter reviews extensive laboratory evidence documenting the psychological benefits of mild negative affect, consistent with evolutionary theories suggesting an adaptive function for *all* affective states. The studies show that mild negative affect can improve memory, reduce judgmental errors, improve motivation and result in more effective interpersonal strategies. The practical implications of recognizing the adaptive benefits of negative affect for well-being are also considered.

Chapter 13 by **Kalkstein, Hubbard and Trope** turns to the cognitive domain, discussing the role of more or less abstract—expansive versus contractive—mental construals in promoting well-being. The chapter explores construal level (abstractness of thought) as a psychological process that allows people to adaptively learn from others in a social landscape that is evolving to include a more diverse array of near and distant others than ever before. Whereas low-level construals serve to contract people's mental horizons by immersing them in the finer details of the shared content, higher-level construals serve to expand people's mental horizons by focusing on shared and stable content. Through the strategic employment of varying construal levels, people are able to improve their well-being and take full advantage of the richness of today's social learning environment.

Part four of the book turns to discussing the **social and cultural factors involved in well-being**. Chapter 14 by **Shelly Gable** explores the role that meaningful personal relationships play in well-being. Current scientific thinking acknowledges that forming bonds with people is a fundamental and evolutionarily determined need. The chapter reviews extensive evidence demonstrating that when people have abundant and satisfying social ties they also report higher well-being, and most theories of well-being contain social relationships as a necessary ingredient. The benefits of social relationships for well-being are manifold—

having meaningful relationships can help regulate stress, and relationships are also a primary vehicle for the experience of positive emotions. Social relationships are also essential for having a sense of meaning and purpose. In sum, one cannot live the good life without good relationships.

Simpson, Farrell, Huelsnitz and Eller in Chapter 15 take this connection one step further, by exploring the role of early attachment patterns in subsequent physical health. In this chapter, they describe a series of studies based on a 40-year longitudinal project—the Minnesota Longitudinal Study of Risk and Adaptation (MLSRA)—demonstrating how early life events can prospectively predict physical health outcomes in middle adulthood. They also discuss how one important interpersonal experience early in life—the quality of care received from one's mother—appears to protect individuals who experienced early life stress from having health problems later in life. The empirical demonstration of such a link between early interpersonal experiences and subsequent health outcomes has important implications for optimizing well-being throughout the life cycle.

In Chapter 16, **Crano and Donaldson** also turn to the importance of family relationships and parenting in preventing seriously detrimental events in adolescents' lives, such as drug abuse. They show that positive parenting can make a critical contribution to family well-being, by preventing adolescent substance abuse. The family is a major determinant of life satisfaction, and there are few things that are more destructive of family life than an addicted child. Social psychology can make a substantial positive contribution to life satisfaction by bringing an evidence-based focus to substance use prevention in youth. For this reason, the authors argue that campaigns that affect parents' communicative behaviors about substance use might prove effective in affecting adolescents' substance-related behaviors. Such a campaign should involve instructing parents about the importance of positive parent-child communication, warmth, and setting democratic and fair guidelines and boundaries.

Amichai-Hamburger and Etgar in Chapter 17 discuss one of the most important contemporary issues relevant to living well: How does the Internet influence our well-being? The Internet has created a unique psychological space, characterized by features such as anonymity, control over physical exposure and communications, accessibility and feelings of equality. In such an environment the online user feels protected and empowered. While this can promote empathy and altruism, the same empowerment can also facilitate hostility, aggression and anti-social behaviors. Altogether the Internet creates startling interpersonal complexity, with varied and as yet poorly understood consequences for the individual, the group and the community. The chapter discusses the impact of this complexity for four specific areas: personality, relationships, e-therapy and online intergroup contacts.

In the final chapter, Chapter 18, **Dunn and Dwyer** discuss a closely related topic: how future well-being is intricately tied to technological developments that will determine how we communicate with and relate to each other. Smartphones in particular have altered the way we work, play, travel and communicate. This technological revolution holds the potential to increase human well-being—but may also carry less obvious costs. The chapter describes the authors' recent research showing that mobile technology can both enhance and undermine happiness. The chapter also considers how, in the more distant future, interconnected machines may largely replace the need for human labour. Anticipating these changes, the chapter discusses how happiness research can be used to plan for and navigate the more technologically advanced future.

Overall, then, this book seeks to contribute to social psychology and human well-being by surveying the most recent developments in research in this intriguing area. As editors, we are deeply grateful to our contributors for accepting our invitation to attend the Sydney Symposium of Social Psychology and sharing their valuable ideas with our readers. We sincerely hope that the insights contained in these chapters will contribute not only to the emerging science of how to live well but will also hold some value for readers as they contemplate their own lives and challenges.

Bibliography

Ainsworth, S. E., Baumeister, R. F., Vohs, K. D., & Ariely, D. (2014). Ego depletion decreases trust in economic decision making. *Journal of Experimental Social Psychology*, *54*, 40–49. doi:10.1016/j.jesp.2014.04.004

Allport, G. W. (1954/1968). The historical background of modern social psychology. In G. Lindzey (Ed.), *The handbook of social psychology* (Vol. 1, pp. 3–56). Cambridge, MA: Addison-Wesley.

Bachman, J. G., & O'Malley, P. M. (1977). Self-esteem in young men: A longitudinal analysis of the impact of educational and occupational attainment. *Journal of Personality & Social Psychology*, *35*, 365–380.

Bachman, J. G., & O'Malley, P. M. (1986). Self-concepts, self-esteem, and educational experiences: The frog pond revisited (again). *Journal of Personality & Social Psychology*, *50*, 35–46.

Baumeister, R. F., Bratslavsky, E., Finkenauer, C., & Vohs, K. D. (2001). Bad is stronger than good. *Review of General Psychology*, *5*, 323–370. doi:10.1037/1089–2680.5.4.323

Baumeister, R. F., Campbell, J. D., Krueger, J. I., & Vohs, K. D. (2003). Does high self-esteem cause better performance interpersonal success, happiness, or healthier lifestyles? *Psychological Science in the Public Interest*, *4*, 1–44. doi:10.1111/1529–1006.01431

California Task Force to Promote Self-Esteem and Personal and Social Responsibility. (1990). *Toward a state of self-esteem*. Sacramento: California State Department of Education.

Daly, M., Delaney, L., Egan, M., & Baumeister, R. F. (2015). Childhood self-control and unemployment throughout the lifespan: Evidence from two British cohort studies. *Psychological Science*, *26*, 709–723. doi:10.1177/0956797615569001

Dawkins, R. (2006). *The God delusion*. New York, NY: Bantam Books.

de Ridder, D., Lensvelt-Mulders, G., Finkenauer, C., Stok, F. M., & Baumeister, R. F. (2012). A meta-analysis of how trait self-control relates to a wide range of behaviors. *Personality and Social Psychology Review*, *16*, 76–99. doi:10.1177/1088868311418749

Freud, S. (1990). *The future of an illusion*. New York, NY: Norton. (Original work published 1927)

Hofmann, W., Luhmann, M., Fisher, R. R., Vohs, K. D., & Baumeister, R. F. (2013). Yes, but are they happy? Effects of trait self-control on affective well-being and life satisfaction. *Journal of Personality*, *82*, 265–277. doi:10.1111/jopy.12050

Jost, J. T., & van der Toorn, J. (2012). System justification theory. In P.A.M. van Lange, A. W. Kruglanski, & E. T. Higgins (Eds.), *Handbook of theories of social psychology* (Vol. 2, pp. 313–343). London: Sage.

Maruyama, G., Rubin, R. A., & Kingsbury, G. G. (1981). Self-esteem and educational achievement: Independent constructs with a common cause? *Journal of Personality and Social Psychology*, *40*, 962–975.

Marx, K. (1977). *Capital* (Vol. 1). New York, NY: Vintage.

Maslow, A. H. (1968). *Toward a psychology of being*. New York, NY: Van Nostrand.

Mecca, A. M., Smelser, N. J., & Vasconcellos, J. (Eds.). (1989). *The social importance of self-esteem*. Berkeley, CA: University of California Press.

Mischel, W., Shoda, Y., & Peake, P. (1988). The nature of adolescent competencies predicted by preschool delay of gratification. *Journal of Personality and Social Psychology*, *54*, 687–696.

Moffitt, T. E., Arseneault, L., Belsky, D., Dickson, N., Hancox, R. J., Harrington, H., . . . Caspi, A. (2011). A gradient of childhood self-control predicts health, wealth, and public safety. *Proceedings of the National Academy of Sciences*, *108*, 2693–2698. doi:10.1073/pnas.1010076108Orth, 20xx

Orth, U., Robins, R. W., & Widaman, K. F. (2012). Life-span development of self-esteem and its effects on important life outcomes. *Journal of Personality and Social Psychology*, *102*, 1271–1288.

Righetti, F., & Finkenauer, C. (2011). If you are able to control yourself, I will trust you: The role of perceived self-control in interpersonal trust. *Journal of Personality and Social Psychology*, *100*, 874–886. doi:10.1037/a0021827

Scarry, E. (1985). *The body in pain: The making and unmaking of the world*. New York, NY: Oxford University Press.

Tangney, J. P., Baumeister, R. F., & Boone, A. L. (2004). High self-control predicts good adjustment, less pathology, better grades, and interpersonal success. *Journal of Personality*, *72*, 271–324. doi:10.1111/j.0022-3506.2004.00263.x

Torres, P. (2016). Bottled water vs. tap water: Rethink what you drink. *Reader's Digest*. Retrieved from www.rd.com/health/diet-weight-loss/rethink-what-you-drink/

Wylie, R. C. (1979). *The self-concept: Theory and research on selected topics* (Vol. 2). Lincoln, NE: University of Nebraska Press.

Zimbardo, P. (1990). *Shyness: What it is and what to do about it*. Cambridge, MA: Perseus Books.

PART I
Conceptual Issues

2

HAPPINESS AND MEANINGFULNESS AS TWO DIFFERENT AND NOT ENTIRELY COMPATIBLE VERSIONS OF THE GOOD LIFE

Roy F. Baumeister

What makes life good? Happiness is certainly one answer. Someone who has lived happily for decades is much more likely to view life as good than someone whom happiness has eluded. Hence studying happiness is one prominent pathway for learning about the good life.

Yet happiness does not exhaust the concept of the good life. In ordinary discourse, the word "good" is used in both hedonic and moral senses, denoting either pleasure or virtue (see also Fiedler & Arslan, this volume). People seek not just pleasure but meaningfulness, some of which is tied up with earning the respect of one's peers, or perhaps imagining respect from posterity. Some of that is moral. There is also "good" in the sense of competence, which like morality is a dimension of cultural respect.

Meaning and happiness overlap but are far from the same. This chapter will focus on how these two competing versions of the good life differ.

As point of departure, we suggest that nature and culture are differently relevant. Happiness presumably began in evolution when organisms felt pleasure in connection with having their needs satisfied (see also von Hippel & Gonsalkorale, this volume). Happiness may therefore be relatively natural. In contrast, meaning may be generally cultural. A solitary animal's ability to process meaning may be limited to simple associations. Language exists only in human cultures, and without language, the ability to process meaning is severely limited. What makes a life meaningful may be tied up not only with having social interactions but indeed participating in a cultural system with shared values and understandings that allows the experiences of kindness, gratitude, and connectedness to exert a positive influence on experiences of well-being (see also Sheldon; Huppert; Gable; and Fritz & Lyubomirsky, this volume).

Meaning Versus Happiness

One recent effort to disentangle meaning from happiness was a series of studies by Baumeister, Vohs, Aaker, and Garbinsky (2013). Unlike most of my research, it went beyond college student samples, and the main study was a series of large national surveys of 397 adults, ranging in age from 18 to 78. The average age was 35, and half of the respondents were parents. (Men were underrepresented, as is the norm in social psychology.) Thus, many different walks of life were represented. The data had been collected by Aaker and Garbinsky, who invited Vohs and then me to delve into them. Thus, the conclusions were all post hoc, at least in the sense that they had not been formulated prior to data collection.

Empirical Approach

Six items formed the core of our effort to learn about meaning and happiness. The three happiness items were "In general, I consider myself happy," "Taking all things together, I feel I am happy," and "Compared to most of my peers, I consider myself happy." The meaning items were roughly parallel: "In general I consider my life to be meaningful," "Compared to most of my peers, my life is meaningful," and "Taking all things together, I feel my life is meaningful." The two sets of three items were summed to create an index of how much each person rated his or her life as meaningful and happy.

The survey had collected a wealth of data about how people rated various aspects of their lives, feelings, attitudes, and experiences. Our goal was to exploit the data set to learn about differences between meaning and happiness. We got stuck at first on one troublesome fact, which was that meaning and happiness were significantly correlated with each other, indeed in the .6–.7 range. Thus, the two measures shared nearly half their variance.

The overlap between meaning and happiness self-reports might hold a profound insight. It is plausible that many things that make life meaningful would also increase happiness, and vice versa (see also Sheldon, this volume). An early survey of research on life's meaning by Baumeister (1991) concluded tentatively that meaning was often a prerequisite for happiness, but not vice versa. Lack of meaning would reduce happiness, but lack of happiness would not preclude meaningfulness.

Then again, the overlap might not hold a profound insight. It is plausible, even likely, that when people respond to surveys, they have a global attitude that informs all their responses—especially when talking about themselves. This problem has been recognized in the self-esteem literature. Much spurious evidence of the ostensible benefits of self-esteem has consisted of showing correlations between self-report questionnaires. People score high in self-esteem by rating themselves favorably, and those same people may also rate their relationship skills, intelligence, and sex appeal favorably, thereby tempting researchers to conclude that high self-esteem is closely linked to having those qualities. Objective evidence often contradicts them, however (for review, see Baumeister, Campbell, Krueger, & Vohs, 2003). For example, Gabriele, Critelli, and Ee (1994) found that self-esteem had a significant positive correlation with self-reported intelligence—but had a nonsignificant negative correlation with scores on an actual IQ test.

Thus, some of the overlap between meaningfulness and happiness may reflect genuine kinship between those two dimensions of the good life, and some of it may boil down to simple tendencies for some people to furnish more globally optimistic and positive self-reports than others. Our solution was to discard the shared variance and focus on the differences. Hence our main analyses involved finding what correlated with happiness after controlling for meaningfulness, and vice versa.

All of this made our study explicitly exploratory, and the conclusions should not be taken as definitive. Statistically, discarding half the variance on the main measures (and conceding some of the rest to error variance) raises the possibility that the controls distorted the findings. Conceptually, it is possible that the correlates of the variance that is shared between happiness and meaning are different from the correlates that attend the non-shared parts. (Indeed, I assume that both the shared variance and the unshared parts are of theoretical interest, so our focus on what makes meaning and happiness different is only part of the story.) Put another way, the things that make life both happy and meaningful may differ from the things that give meaning without happiness, and from those that give happiness without meaning.

A useful analogy was offered by Fredrickson (this volume), who used a similar analysis strategy. She said it is like the notion of "empty calories," that is, getting food energy that lacks nutritional value. Some happiness comes in connection with high meaningfulness. Our analysis focuses on the rest, the happiness that comes without meaningfulness. It is real, and important, but it is not the only kind.

Getting What You Want

A first pattern of findings was that people who were able to satisfy their basic needs and wants were happier than other people. Satisfying needs and wants was largely irrelevant to meaning. Items such as whether one generally finds life easy, has to struggle, or finds life difficult correlated with happiness but were mostly irrelevant to meaning. Health was linked to happiness but completely irrelevant to meaning. A sickly person can have as meaningful a life as a robustly healthy one, but the latter is likely to be happier (not surprisingly).

Having enough money to buy the things one wants and needs correlated substantially with happiness but again seemed completely irrelevant to meaning. A scarcity of money reduced happiness but hardly made a dent in meaningfulness.

Emotions and feelings are often tied up with getting what one wants. As one would expect almost by definition, frequent good feelings were linked to high happiness, and frequent bad feelings correlated with low happiness. Again, they had no relation to meaningfulness. The only exception was boredom: Frequent feelings of boredom were linked to low scores on both meaning and happiness. Boredom is the opposite of the good life: boring lives lack both happiness and meaning.

All of this suggests that happiness is in many ways simpler, and presumably linked to earlier steps in evolution, than meaningfulness. Creatures feel good when they satisfy their needs and feel bad when denied satisfaction. Among human beings, getting the things one wants and needs boosts happiness but is surprisingly irrelevant to whether they find life meaningful. Money is a product of culture, not nature, yet its power to get people what they want links it to happiness more than meaning (see also von Hippel & Gonsalkorale; and Kalkstein, Hubbard, & Trope, this volume).

Past, Present, Future, and Combinations

One distinctive, remarkable, and profoundly important aspect of the human psyche is the ability to think about past and future events (Suddendorf, 2013). Most animals live in the present, "stuck in time" (Roberts, 2002), whereas humans adjust their behavior based on events that are hours, years, or even centuries removed from the here and now. These connections by which the distant past or future influences the present are mediated by meanings (for example, the symbolism of anniversaries or holidays, or the simulation of relevance to long-term values and goals; for review and extended discussion, see Baumeister, Vohs, & Oettingen, 2016). Based on this analysis, we began to test the idea that time span would be linked to meaningfulness. Happiness, in contrast, seemed much more present-focused, as the preceding section already indicated: People are happy in the present when an urge finds satisfaction.

The surveys asked simply how much time people spent thinking about the past, the present, and the future. This is obviously a crude and simplistic measure. Yet the results were striking.

Happiness is apparently in the present. The more people thought about the present, the happier they were. The more they thought about the past and/or the future, the less happy they were (but see also Sedikides, Wildschut, & Stephan, this volume). Even an additional item asking how often people imagine the future yielded a negative correlation with happiness. Apparently, if you want to be happy, live in the present and don't think about past or future. This approach resonates with research on mindfulness: Training in mindfulness emphasizes focusing on the here and now (Huppert, this volume).

For meaning, the pattern was markedly different, though the correlations were weaker. Thinking about the past was marginally correlated with higher meaningfulness, as was thinking about the future. Combining those items into an index of mental time travel (that is, simply adding together the self-reported amounts of thinking about past and thinking about future) did yield a significant difference.

Thinking about the present was irrelevant, and imagining the future more frequently was linked to higher meaningfulness.

A follow-up study confirmed the differential effect of future and present. Students rated happiness as fleeting but meaningfulness as lasting over time. This may be more perception than reality. In our main study, self-rated happiness was quite stable, as indicated by a correlation of .82 between reports of happiness across different waves separated by three weeks. Prior work has found happiness to be remarkably stable even across a decade (e.g., Costa, McCrae, & Zonderman, 1987). Phrases referring to the present were rated as relevant to happiness, whereas those referring to the future were rated as more meaningful.

These findings on time perspective were provocative, and fortunately some of us soon embarked on a large experience sampling study of people's thoughts, with emphasis on time perspective (Baumeister, Hofmann, & Vohs, 2015, unpublished; see Baumeister, Vohs, & Oettingen, 2016). A large community sample (N = 497) was contacted at random points during their daily activities and reported on their most recent thought. Each thought was rated separately as to whether it referred to past, present, and/or future, so that it was possible to indicate none or any combination of them.

The experience sampling study yielded strong confirmation of the view that happiness is present-focused whereas meaningfulness involves linking across time. Happiness was highest when people focused on the present and declined as thoughts roamed farther into future or past. The past was unhappier than the future. Thus, again, to maximize happiness, the advice would seem to be to remain focused on the here and now.

Meaning, meanwhile, showed a dramatically different pattern. Focus on the present was low in meaningfulness, whereas thoughts that invoked past or future were more meaningful—with thoughts about the future being far more meaningful than thoughts about the past. As further evidence of the link between meaning and time, the fairly large (25%) category of thoughts for which people reported no time aspect—that is, not past nor present nor future—were generally low in meaningfulness. Conversely, thoughts that invoked combinations of different times (e.g., both present and future) were highly meaningful. The highest average meaningfulness ratings attended thoughts that invoked all three of past, present, and future. This pattern may bear some resemblance to the proposed distinction of different levels of cognitive construals discussed by Kalkstein, Hubbard, and Trope (this volume).

To be sure, these patterns of findings generalize across all thoughts that invoke the past. There may be special cases. Sedikides et al. (this volume) have made a persuasive case that nostalgic thoughts bring happiness and meaning. Nostalgia is, however, not just thinking about the past, in their view, and indeed it connects the past to present and future.

Thus, time may be antithetical to happiness but is vital for meaning. At best, happiness is focused on the present. But to render life meaningful, it is apparently most effective to maintain some focus on the future, including integrating the future with the present (and occasionally the past). Planning links the present to the future, and in fact the activity of planning was relatively pleasant (especially as compared to other thoughts about the future, such as worries). Planning is obviously a highly pragmatic, active way of thinking about aspects of one's life in time, especially in that it lays out the requisite steps to reach desired goals.

Social Relations and Engagement

Earlier I suggested that happiness may have its roots in early evolution, such that solitary beings felt pleasure upon satisfying their needs (see also von Hippel & Gonsalkorale, this volume). Almost certainly, however, social animals gain happiness by social contact and connection (see Gable, this volume; Simpson et al., this volume). Meaningfulness, meanwhile, seems heavily intertwined with social connection, to the point that most people would be hard put to imagine how a solitary life could be highly meaningful.

Thus, social relationships may be positively linked to both happiness and meaning. This was certainly evident in the Baumeister et al. (2013) data. There were multiple positive correlations with measures of feeling socially connected, spending time with friends, spending time with loved ones, and thinking that others regard oneself as connected to them. Conversely, there were negative correlations with recalling hours spent alone, anticipating being alone in the future, and the like. Both happiness and meaning showed these positive links.

Thus, both happiness and meaning gain from involvement in social relationships. On closer inspection, however, some important differences can be found. These were perhaps epitomized in two simple items that asked whether the person agreed with the statements "I am a giver" and "I am a taker." Being a giver was positively associated with rating one's life as meaningful and negatively associated with happiness. Being a taker showed the opposite pattern, though the effects were weaker and fell short of significance, though they differed significantly from each other (see also Fritz & Lyubomirsky; and Huppert, this volume).

The broader implication is that meaning comes from doing things for others, whereas happiness arises when others do things for oneself. Takers may be happier than givers, whereas givers have more meaningful lives than takers.

The giver-taker difference may be one area in which the analytical strategy concealed some important effects of overlap between meaning and happiness. With simple, uncorrected analyses, people who (claim to) do things for others are relatively happy. Correcting for meaning reverses the sign, from positive to negative. The implication is that doing things for other people does increase happiness—but mainly by increasing meaningfulness. If the connection via meaning is taken out, doing things for others detracts from happiness. (In contrast, meaning is positively linked to doing things for others, and controlling for happiness does not change that.)

Two other interpersonal measures are revealing. One had to do with taking care of children. Recalling time spent caring for children had a negligible effect on happiness and a trend toward increasing meaning among people who were not parents. They were presumably recalling taking care of someone else's children. Among parents, who presumably were thinking about taking care of their own children, there was a significant increase in meaning but a trend toward less happiness. These findings speak to the so-called parenthood paradox, which is that most people want to become parents and want to be happy—but most evidence indicates that being a parent reduces happiness, so those two goals conflict. Baumeister (1991) provided one review of that evidence and speculated that people want both meaning and happiness, and parenthood may be a powerful source of meaning even if it does reduce happiness somewhat. That fits the findings indicating that parents gain in meaning as they recall taking care of children but, if anything, lose happiness. (Anecdotally, the optimal strategy for happiness would be to have grandchildren rather than children!)

The other interpersonal measure involved asking whether arguing was an activity that expressed and reflected the self. Arguing involves interpersonal conflict, almost by definition. This item yielded significant correlations with both meaning and happiness—but in opposite directions. Rating oneself as an argumentative person was associated with less happiness but greater meaning.

That arguing reduces happiness is hardly surprising. Arguing involves conflict and negative emotion. Happy people may avoid arguments. The positive link to meaning is, however, more complex and even puzzling. I hesitate to recommend that people pick fights and arguments with other people as a way of pursuing the good life via increased meaningfulness. It is hard to see how life could be enriched by arguing about, say, who ate the last doughnut or who should empty the trash.

Most likely, arguing is a side effect of factors that increase meaning. People who are seriously involved in complex cultural undertakings and care passionately about them may find themselves needing to argue when they encounter someone who has a different view. It is thus not the interpersonal activity of arguing per se, but the passionate involvement, that enhances meaning. The next section will pursue this.

Involved in Society

Multiple findings suggested that being seriously involved in the affairs and events that go beyond one's own life has effects on both meaning and happiness. In general, such involvements increase meaning, but some of them detract from happiness. We have already indicated some of these, namely helping others and seeing arguing as central to one's identity.

Having major good and/or bad events occur in one's life seems like it should have a potentially major impact on happiness and meaning, and indeed it did. Not surprisingly, people who reported plenty of good events rated their lives as both happier and more meaningful than other people. Having had plenty of bad events in one's life was linked to lower happiness—but was correlated with higher meaning. To be sure, these results are correlational. I am inclined to think that suffering bad events is a cause of unhappiness, but there may well be some reverse causation too: Unhappy people probably remember more bad events than happy people! Still, what matters is that perceiving one's life as having had an ample share of misfortune is linked to lower happiness but higher meaningfulness.

The occurrence of bad events is thus important for understanding the good life. A first point is that the impact of bad events on happiness far outweighed the impact of good events, indeed with about four times the impact in terms of percent of variance. This is consistent with a vast literature indicating that bad events have much stronger psychological impact than good events (Baumeister, Bratslavsky, Finkenauer, & Vohs, 2001). The Chinese proverb "May you never live in interesting times" expresses the sentiment that happiness is more easily found in quietude, because the intrusion of major historical and societal events (the hallmark of what people regard as interesting times, for society as a whole) into one's life has more power to reduce than to increase happiness.

The increase in meaningfulness linked to high rates of negative events is perhaps most puzzling. Again, I hesitate to recommend that people seek out personal and historical disasters as a pathway to finding a good, meaningful life. A more plausible interpretation of this finding is that meaningful lives are deeply enmeshed in important activities that go beyond the self and are thus partly beyond the self's control. That fact brings the possibility that things will not turn out as one wishes and that one's efforts and strivings will be in vain.

Thus, it is more likely that having a very meaningful life leads to more negative experiences than the reverse. A meaningful life means getting involved in things beyond oneself, which often means exposing oneself to risks and to forces that are beyond one's control—so, almost inevitably, sometimes things will turn out for the worse. The prescription for the good life is to pursue meaningful involvement in culture and society, not to seek out bad experiences.

Multiple other findings fit the conclusion that meaningful involvement brings risks and outcomes that can reduce happiness. Self-reported stress was linked to lower happiness and higher meaningfulness. Even worrying showed the same pattern: People who reported more worrying had less happy but more meaningful lives.

Both stress and worry are future-oriented. Stress is not so much the occurrence of bad events as living with the ongoing, threatening possibility that bad events will occur (e.g., Brady, 1958). Worry is by definition thinking about possible bad future events; no one worries about the outcome of the Thirty Years War any more, even though plenty of people in the early 1600s worried about it. Thus, the stress and the worry findings are consistent with the pattern that thinking about the future increases meaningfulness but may sacrifice happiness.

Expressing Oneself

It is possible to live and create behavior without caring a fig for finding oneself, expressing oneself, discovering one's true or hidden self, and the like. Presumably that is what most nonhuman animals do, almost exclusively. However, some peculiarities in human evolution have created a psyche that is capable of self-reflection and the attendant cultivation of concerns with self-discovery and self-expression. Hence some people are highly concerned with those matters, while others are less perturbed by them (see also Kalkstein, Hubbard & Trope, this volume).

The surveys reported by Baumeister et al. (2013) asked people whether issues of personal identity were important to them. The higher importance people assigned to identity issues, the more meaningful their lives were. Importance of identity was unrelated to happiness, and in fact the trend was in the opposite direction (i.e., more identity importance went with less happiness). Caring about how one defines, understands, expresses, and fulfills the self is apparently an important component of a meaningful life.

Survey respondents were given a list of 37 different activities, and for each one they rated whether they thought engaging in that activity "reflects me," a colloquial term for self-engagement and self-expression. The activities were widely assorted, ranging from working to sex to watching television to shopping. Of the 37 activities, 25 were significantly correlated with meaningfulness—and all those correlations were positive. In contrast, whether people thought these activities reflected their self-concepts was mostly irrelevant to happiness. Only two items (socializing, and partying without alcohol) correlated positively with happiness, whereas five correlated negatively, and the vast majority showed no significant link (see also Fritz & Lyubomirsky, this volume).

Thus, doing things that express or engage the self is important for meaning but appears to have little to do with happiness. The implication is that people make life meaningful by doing things that express themselves.

The five items that correlated negatively with happiness all correlated positively with meaningfulness. These were worrying, arguing, taking care of children, buying gifts for others, and watching television. Admittedly, that is an odd set, but they do bring up themes to which I have already alluded. Meaningful involvement in challenging, contentious social affairs can require worrying and arguing, neither of which is pleasant. Social involvement is apparent in buying things for others and taking care of children, which again reflect the theme that happiness comes when social interactions benefit the self but making sacrifices for others reduces happiness while bolstering meaning.

The fifth item, watching television, may seem an outlier, especially as a source of meaning. The meaning aspect may come from the pseudo-intimate relationships that people form, mostly in their imagination, with fictional characters in television series. Gabriel, Valenti, and Young (2015) have elaborated how such characters function as "social surrogates," thereby counteracting loneliness and making people feel connected to other social worlds. Thus, perhaps becoming involved via television in a fictitious social world can furnish a sense of meaning, similarly perhaps to how involvement in real social worlds can furnish meaning. Another factor to consider is that not all television watching involves fiction. After all, people may watch news shows and political talk shows to increase their sense of involvement in world affairs. Others watch sports events, which are technically reality shows depicting genuine competition, although typically these have no material consequences for the fans and casual viewers. (Watching a sports contest on which one has wagered may also provide a sense of meaning.) Further work may examine whether fictional shows or nonfiction ones—or both—increase meaningfulness, and by what pathway.

Self-Reward and Self-Control

One survey item asked simply whether people ever reward themselves. People who reward themselves rated their lives as more meaningful than people who do not reward themselves. Perhaps surprisingly, self-reward was irrelevant to happiness, indeed trending in the opposite direction (happy people do not reward themselves).

Rewarding oneself is different from simply giving oneself pleasures. As one sign, giving oneself pleasures was (as already mentioned) positively linked to happiness but irrelevant to meaning. The difference lies presumably in that self-reward is part of a self-regulation process: One earns rewards by good behavior. The difference is perhaps something like just having a doughnut because you like doughnuts and having a doughnut to reward yourself after completing a tough assignment. If the person had decided, "I can have a doughnut if and when I complete this task," it can form part of a self-regulatory loop.

It is risky to place much emphasis on a single item, especially when the item addresses only part of the broader phenomenon (i.e., rewarding oneself is only part of self-control). Still, the correlation of self-reward with meaning and not happiness could suggest that self-control is possibly orthogonal or even detrimental to happiness. Hofmann, Luhmann, Fisher, Vohs, and Baumeister (2014) derived what they called the "Puritan hypothesis," which asserted that high levels of self-control may foster disciplined pursuit of goals and success at various endeavors but at the cost of pervasive self-denial, so that life becomes a joyless performance of duties. Their studies found, however, that higher trait self-control was positively linked to happiness. In fact, this held up across a broad variety of measures of happiness, including balance between momentary positive and negative affect, as well as life satisfaction and global happiness ratings that integrate across time.

The findings linking high self-control to happiness (from Hofmann et al., 2014) did not control for meaningfulness, as in the Baumeister et al. (2013) surveys, so it is possible that the contribution of self-control to increasing happiness occurs by way of bolstering meaningfulness and even that controlling for meaning would eliminate or reverse the pattern. This remains for future research.

Nonetheless, the positive link is itself relevant to the broader question of the good life. It is possible to look at social life in zero-sum fashion, such that the individual has to make sacrifices to comply with the rules and demands of society. Self-control in that context would seemingly reduce happiness, because it overrides one's own inclinations so as to enable one to conform to rules and other standards.

Instead, however, it appears that self-control is beneficial to the self. Ample prior work had provided evidence of benefits of self-control, such as increased success in work and school, increased popularity, fewer mental and physical health problems, and fewer behavioral problems (see Tangney, Baumeister, & Boone, 2004; Moffitt et al., 2011; for reviews, see de Ridder et al., 2012; Baumeister & Tierney, 2011). These all suggest indirect pathways by which self-control could bolster longer-term happiness, by way of improving the quality of life. Direct enhancement is also quite plausible, insofar as good self-control includes control over one's emotions: People with good affect regulation skills may be able to manage negative emotions and sustain positive ones better than other people.

The positive impact of self-control on happiness is good news for people with good self-control (and perhaps bad news for people who lack it). It is also good in a broader sense, however. The extensive capacity for self-regulation is part of the distinctively human psychology, and it reflects the ability to alter oneself based on rules, norms, and other standards. Often this means sacrificing one's own wishes for the sake of doing what specific others, or society in general, would prefer. Some theorists have thus seen self-control as essentially self-harming. Freud (1930), for example, proposed that the super-ego (his term for the self-regulatory moral part of the psyche) was constructed by redirecting one's aggressive instinct back toward the self, and he saw the operation of the super-ego as essentially denying oneself pleasures and satisfactions, with the added cost of guilt. The Hofmann et al. (2014) findings paint self-control in a much more positive light. Even if it does bring some guilt and self-denial, its long-term rewards apparently far outweigh its costs. Self-control enables people to live and work together effectively.

Conclusions

A good life would ideally be both happy and meaningful. A pretty good life would presumably at least be one or the other. The two criteria tend to overlap in people's self-ratings, some of which may be affected by general halo effects and other tendencies to rate oneself positively or negatively. Nonetheless, they are different in important ways.

This chapter surveyed some of the key differences between the correlates of happiness and meaningfulness. Happiness appears to be the simpler and in evolutionary sense older of the two, and it remains closely tied to natural inclinations.

People feel happy when they get what they want and feel unhappy when they do not. Happiness is increased by interpersonal interactions and relationships that provide benefits to the self. It is diminished by struggle, stress, argument, worry, and anxiety, and it appears to thrive with a narrow focus on the present.

In contrast, meaningful lives are linked to giving to others and to being highly involved in complex social undertakings (even if these bring struggle, stress, argument, worry, and anxiety). Concern with building one's personal identity and with expressing the self through diverse activities also goes with a highly meaningful life. A mental time span that encompasses past and future, indeed integrating past and present and future, is linked to finding life meaningful.

The enemies of both happiness and meaning include boredom and social exclusion. Being socially connected to other human beings is central to the human condition, and people who lack such connections tend to have trouble finding either happiness or meaning. Boredom appears to combine features of both unhappiness and meaninglessness, including being rooted in an unpleasant present moment that lacks redeeming connections to past or future.

Thus, our work suggests two different versions of the good life, with different pathways. The happy life is one of ease and enjoyment, focused on taking pleasures in the present. The meaningful life is oriented toward the future, concerned with constructing and expressing the self, and heavily involved in complex sociocultural activities. Inevitably, involvement in such activities will bring some stress and struggle, and most likely some failures and disappointments, and these may be very unhappy phases. But very likely they are part and parcel of a highly meaningful life.

Bibliography

Baumeister, R. F. (1991). *Meanings of life*. New York, NY: Guilford Press.

Baumeister, R. F., Bratslavsky, E., Finkenauer, C., & Vohs, K. D. (2001). Bad is stronger than good. *Review of General Psychology, 5*, 323–370. doi:10.1037/1089–2680.5.4.323

Baumeister, R. F., Campbell, J. D., Krueger, J. I., & Vohs, K. D. (2003). Does high self-esteem cause better performance interpersonal success, happiness, or healthier lifestyles? *Psychological Science in the Public Interest, 4*, 1–44. doi:10.1111/1529–1006.01431

Baumeister, R. F., Hofmann, W., & Vohs, K. D. (2015). Everyday thoughts about the past, present, and future: An experience sampling study of mental time travel. Manuscript under review, Florida State University.

Baumeister, R. F., & Tierney, J. (2011). *Willpower: Rediscovering the greatest human strength*. New York, NY: Penguin Press.

Baumeister, R. F., Vohs, K. D., Aaker, J. L., & Garbinsky, E. N. (2013). Some key differences between a happy life and a meaningful life. *Journal of Positive Psychology, 8*, 505–516. doi:10.1080/17439760.2013.830764

Baumeister, R. F., Vohs, K. D., & Oettingen, G. (2016). Pragmatic prospection: How and why people think about the future. *Review of General Psychology, 20*, 3–16. doi:10.1037/gpr0000060

Brady, J. V. (1958). Ulcers in "executive" monkeys. *Scientific American, 199*, 95–100.

Costa, P. T., McCrae, R. R., & Zonderman, A. B. (1987). Environmental and dispositional influences on well-being: Longitudinal follow-up of an American national sample. *British Journal of Psychology*, *78*, 299–306.

De Ridder, D., Lensvelt-Mulders, G., Finkenauer, C., Stok, F. M., & Baumeister, R. F. (2012). Taking stock of self-control: A meta-analysis of how trait self-control relates to a wide range of behaviors. *Personality and Social Psychology Review*, *16*, 76–99. doi:10.1177/1088868311418749

Freud, S. (1930) *Civilization and its discontents*. (J. Riviere, trans.). London: Hogarth Press.

Gabriel, M. T., Critelli, J. W., & Ee, J. S. (1994). Narcissistic illusions in self-evaluations of intelligence and attractiveness. *Journal of Personality*, *62*, 143–155.

Gabriel, S., Valenti, J., & Young, A. F. (2015). Social surrogates, social motivations, and everyday activities: The case for a strong, subtle, and sneaky social self. In J. Olson & M. Zanna (Eds.), *Advances in experimental social psychology* (Vol. 53, pp. 189–243). Amsterdam: Elsevier.

Hofmann, W., Luhmann, M., Fisher, R. R., Vohs, K. D., & Baumeister, R. F. (2014). Yes, but are they happy? Effects of trait self-control on affective well-being and life satisfaction. *Journal of Personality*, *82*, 265–277. doi:10.1111/jopy.12050

Moffitt, T. E., Arseneault, L., Belsky, D., Dickson, N., Hancox, R. J., Harrington, H., . . . Caspi, A. (2011). A gradient of childhood self-control predicts health, wealth, and public safety. *Proceedings of the National Academy of Sciences*, *108*, 2693–2698. doi:10.1073/pnas.1010076108

Roberts, W. A. (2002). Are animals stuck in time? *Psychological Bulletin*, *128*, 473–489.

Suddendorf, T. (2013). *The gap: The science of what separates us from other animals*. New York, NY: Basic Books.

Tangney, J. P., Baumeister, R. F., & Boone, A. L. (2004). High self-control predicts good adjustment, less pathology, better grades, and interpersonal success. *Journal of Personality*, *72*, 271–322. doi:10.1111/j.0022-3506.2004.00263.x

3

EVOLUTIONARY IMPERATIVES AND THE GOOD LIFE

William von Hippel and Karen Gonsalkorale

Pondering the good life and how to lead it is probably a modern luxury (or perhaps a curse; people seem to differ on this issue). Our hunter-gatherer ancestors appear to have had plenty of spare time for reflection (Winterhalder, 1993), but because they had so little choice in how they made a living, it seems unlikely that this topic was a source of concern or contemplation for them. Nevertheless, even if the question is a uniquely modern one, there is reason to believe that a substantial part of the answer can be found in our distant past. Evolutionary pressures shaped our motivational system to guide us toward reproductive success, and thus consideration of our evolutionary imperatives might help us gain some traction on what it means to lead a good life.

On first reflection, an evolutionary guide to happiness would seem to be a pretty short pamphlet, or even just the simple advice to eat more and have more sex, and perhaps there is some truth to this. But the story is also much more complex. First, living the good life may well be a matter of meeting our evolutionary imperatives, but these imperatives are often at cross-purposes with each other, and thus it requires a good deal of wisdom and self-knowledge to navigate between them. The clearest example of these cross-purposes can be seen in our paramount goals of reproduction and survival. Despite their joint centrality, reproduction is actually the currency of evolution and survival is only of significance to the degree that it serves that goal. The resultant tension between reproduction and survival is evident throughout our motivational system,[1] most notably in the competition between many of our short-term and long-term goals.

These challenges in meeting our competing evolutionary imperatives are then magnified by numerous other complexities, some ancient and some modern. On the ancient side, although our imperatives are universal, our strategies to achieve them are not. For many species there is only one way to get dinner or a mate, but for us the number of strategies we can adopt is limited only by our imagination. Thus, to understand how to achieve happiness it is also necessary to understand individual differences. This is not to say that all roads can lead to happiness, as they assuredly cannot, but it is to say that people need to find a solution of best fit.

On the modern side, our highly technological world continues to develop new tricks to short-circuit our pursuit of happiness via what Robert Trivers calls *phenotypic indulgences*. Alcohol and other drugs, television, and even potato chips are all phenotypic indulgences, as they are designed to mimic ancient pleasures without actually delivering the outcomes that made those ancient activities adaptive (television may provide some of the benefits it is designed to mimic, but more on this issue later). Baumeister's research (this volume) on happiness in the absence of meaning is conceptually similar to the notion of phenotypic indulgences.

Lastly, and perhaps most importantly, lest all this discussion of meeting our evolutionary imperatives seem overly deterministic, it is important to keep in mind that humans evolved to be the most cognitively flexible species on the planet (see also Kalkstein, Hubbard, & Trope, this volume). Indeed, we evolved to fill the cognitive niche that we created; *we actively learn most of what we need to know to survive and thereby create our own life course.* For this reason, our genes are only one of many influences on the way our lives unfold. Again, that doesn't mean that we can find happiness just about anywhere, but it does mean that we decide the importance of happiness in our life as well as the most fruitful way to pursue it. Understanding our evolved nature and the pressures exerted by our deep past can help guide us in this pursuit.

In the remainder of this chapter we consider our most important evolutionary imperatives, from reproduction and survival to learning, cooperation, and competition. We consider how to avoid being derailed by phenotypic indulgences, and conclude with a discussion of strategies of best fit. These strategies not only differ as a function of personality and abilities, but they also change in important ways across the life course.

Reproduction

Reproduction is the currency of evolution, but as Hamilton (1964) pointed out, our own reproduction is not necessary so long as we enhance the reproductive success of our relatives. The central importance of reproduction does not mean that humans or any other animals have a desire to reproduce (e.g., Confer et al., 2010; Tooby & Cosmides, 1990). Indeed, it would have been a strange outcome if we had evolved a desire to have children, given that until very recently in our evolutionary history we would have had no idea how to achieve that desire. Thus, it should come as no surprise that evolution gave us a desire to have sex rather than a desire to reproduce, and then a tendency to feel nurturant to those children who came along as a consequence. One might argue that such a desire for sex in the absence of a desire for children is inefficient, and indeed it is. Humans have all sorts of sex that cannot lead to reproduction, but so long as they mix in enough of the reproductive sort of sexual activity, the biological costs of masturbation, oral and anal sex, and even sex with other species is likely to be low.

For this reason, sexual desire is a fundamental human motive and hence *frequent sexual activity likely to be a key to living the good life*. But frequent sexual activity alone is insufficient to successfully reproduce. The long period of dependency in human children dictates that parenthood is also critically important for reproduction, and indeed grandparenthood is important as well. For this reason, nurturance is also a fundamental human motive and hence *raising and teaching our children and grandchildren are likely to be important to living the good life*. Although this may sound sexist, given the much greater obligatory investment required by women than men in creating offspring, it seems likely that raising children (and probably also grandchildren) plays a larger role in female than male life satisfaction. Nevertheless, it is in both men's and women's interest to facilitate the survival of their offspring and those of their close family, and thus providing for the next generation of our kin is likely to be an important source of happiness for everyone (see also Crano & Donaldson; Simpson et al., this volume).

This recipe for happiness—have more sex and do a good job raising your children—probably seems inherently obvious to the most casual observer. But reproduction is more complicated than that, and so are its implications for life satisfaction. Probably the most complicated aspect of reproduction is finding the right partner in the first place. Choosing a partner involves a fair degree of predicting the future, which is always a gamble. The difficulty of this problem is further exacerbated in pair-bonding species like our own, as partnership is a mutual decision, so it is not possible for all males to mate with the most desirable female and vice versa. Due to the compromises necessitated by limited availability and mutual choice, it also follows that different people are likely to make different trade-offs when making these choices (given the importance of individual differences discussed above).

In response to these rather complex and fluid demands, the human motivational system appears to have evolved to maximize effectiveness in intra-sexual competition for the best and most individually suitable partner. In this manner, reproductive pressures ensure that happiness is driven by more than just sex and parenting, as it is also a product of those variables that increase our chances of pair bonding with the person with whom we most want to have sex and children. In other words, our motivational system is shaped by sexual selection; we want to be what the other sex is looking for.

What the other sex is looking for often feels like one of life's great mysteries, but the broad brushstrokes are not so mysterious at all. Men and women want many of the same things—for example, kindness and generosity are near the top of everyone's list—and differences in their desires have been also well documented (Buss, 1989; see also Gable, this volume). Setting aside the details, sexual selection pushes both men and women to strive for greater status than the people around them—not necessarily in all domains, but certainly in those domains in which people have the best prospects. This drive need not emerge in a conscious desire to put ourselves above others, but it should emerge in a desire for mastery and an aversion to inequality when others are above us. Mastery is important because our unique skill set differentiates us from others and make us desirable as a mate. Inequality aversion is also fundamental, largely because it is difficult to attract a mate from the bottom of the heap, and hence we prefer egalitarianism unless our social status is high.

In our modern world, both of these preferences can easily put us on a hedonic treadmill, whereby we endlessly pursue wealth and status, forever hoping that a little more will make us happier than we are today. Unfortunately, the data suggest that wealth does little for us unless we have more than those around us do, suggesting that in fact it is status that we are really after (see also Fiedler & Arslan, this volume). Two sets of findings illustrate this point nicely. With regard to status, research in macaques demonstrates that when monkeys rise to the top of the status hierarchy they increase the availability of dopamine receptors in their brain. As a result of this increase, they no longer experience benefits from cocaine (a drug designed to hijack the dopamine system), showing no preference to self-administer cocaine over salt water (Morgan et al., 2002). Monkeys at the bottom of the status hierarchy, in contrast, become avid cocaine users.

Second, with regard to wealth, the data show that although it makes people happier when they become richer, once they get out of poverty the effects are not as strong as people think. And more importantly, if all of society rises in wealth at the same time, increased wealth provides no increase in happiness at all (Easterlin, 1994). This effect can be seen by plotting life satisfaction against purchasing power over fifty-five years in the United States (Figure 3.1a) and thirty years in the European Union (Figure 3.1b). These data suggest that my flat screen TV, granite countertops, and convertible don't actually make me any happier unless I have them and you don't. This impact of relative wealth clearly implicates status, and with it, the role of sexual selection in life satisfaction.

Unfortunately, getting off this hedonic treadmill is no easy matter. Millions of years of sexual selection have ingrained status concerns into the deepest levels of our psyche, so turning them off or even ignoring them is impossible for most of us. But awareness of the issue probably helps, particularly as it can allow us to focus our attention on other aspects of our lives that have the potential to provide more lasting happiness (see Gable; Huppert, this volume). One partial solution is to spend money on activities rather than material goods—buy things to do rather than to have (see Fritz & Lyubomirsky; Sheldon, this volume). Particularly when people move into the middle class and go from buying necessities to luxuries, their experiential purchases make them a lot happier than their material ones (van Boven & Gilovich, 2003). The things we own lose their allure as soon as we reset our status goals, but the things we do become a part of us. Experiences give

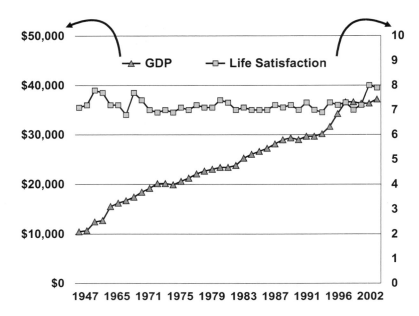

FIGURE 3.1A Income and Life Satisfaction in the United States

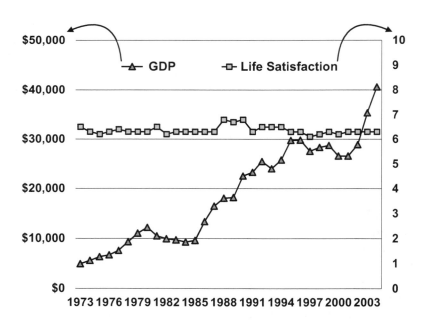

FIGURE 3.1B Income and Life Satisfaction in the European Union

us the stories that we tell friends and family, our most important memories, and continue to provide satisfaction long after the physical experience has ended.

Survival

Survival goals are fundamental, and a great deal of our positive and negative emotions are tuned to our survival. We love fat, sugar, and salt because they were rare in our ancestral environment, but critical for survival. We feel anxious and afraid when we walk through the woods at night, because we are far more likely to be prey than predator once darkness falls. We are highly attuned to the possibility that our friends or group members might reject us, and devastated when it happens, because expulsion from our group was a major life threat for our ancestors (Gruter & Masters, 1986). And we feel comfort and security from home and hearth, as these were sources of protection from the elements and predators.

Nevertheless, despite their importance, survival goals are often trumped by reproduction goals, and we see this in numerous trade-offs. Perhaps the most notable example is senescence itself. We age and die in part because we evolved to spend precious resources in our efforts to reproduce rather than in tissue maintenance and repair (Hunt et al., 2004). In a world full of predators and parasites, such a trade-off made good sense because we had little chance of living forever anyway. Furthermore, a trait that helps us reproduce when we're young will typically have a selective advantage, even if it kills us when we're old. Perhaps the most famous example of such an effect can be found in the ε4 allele of the ApoE gene, which is associated with an increased likelihood of developing Alzheimer's disease late in life (Corder et al., 1993). Somewhat ironically, this allele is also associated with better attention and memory early in life (Han et al., 2007). As a consequence of the benefits it brings when we are young, the ε4 allele is widespread in our population. Because evolution often favors our tendency to sacrifice long-term survival in service of short-term reproduction goals, our motivational system shows substantial support for such trade-offs.

The clearest illustrations of such effects can be seen in dating and mating strategies themselves. Men take greater physical risks when in the presence of attractive women, and this rise in risk taking is mediated by increases in testosterone (Ronay & von Hippel, 2010). Similar effects can be seen in many other animals. Because men are much more likely than women to leave behind no offspring at all, selection favors men who will risk their survival in service of the goal to reproduce. Physical risk taking also communicates reliable information about how robust and skilled a person is, which means that women use male risk taking as a sign of genetic quality. As a consequence, men are more likely than women to enjoy thrill seeking, which is why being a young male is one of the highest causes of mortality in industrialized countries (Owens, 2002). Of course, women compete for men too, and the widespread use of dieting pills, tanning salons, and various other unhealthy mating strategies show clear evidence of female willing-ness to sacrifice long-term health for short-term gains in attraction.

Cooperation and Competition

Our capacity for cooperation and social coordination was probably a key element that allowed our ancestors to survive their move from the trees. In the savannah our ancestors were much more susceptible to predation, as lions, saber-toothed tigers, and even hyenas are much faster and more powerful than bipedal hominins (Hart & Sussman, 2005). Although chimpanzees are probably best characterized as occasional cooperators (Boesch, 1994; Gilby, 2006; Hare & Tomasello, 2004), reliable cooperation would have been essential for our ancestors to protect them-selves from these predators, perhaps by collectively throwing stones (Bingham, 2000; Calvin, 1982; Isaac, 1987). Evidence for this possibility can be seen as far back as *Australopithecus*, in changes to the bone structure of our hands that enable better throwing than the hands of chimpanzees (Marzke, 1983; Napier, 1993; Young, 2003). Evidence for our fundamentally cooperative nature can also be seen in the whites of our eyes, which, in contrast to the brown eyes of other apes, display our gaze direction. The fact that we advertise the direction of our attention suggests that it is to our advantage to broadcast our intentions to other members of our group (Tomasello et al., 2007).

These anatomical data suggest that we evolved to cooperate with each other, and there are numerous changes in our minds and brains that support this conclu-sion. Our capacity to understand the different contents of the minds of others is much better developed than our chimpanzee cousins (Call & Tomasello, 2008), and just as importantly humans seem to be unique in the desire to share the contents of our minds (Suddendorf, 2013). Thus, it comes as no surprise that our motivational system is also tightly tuned to cooperation and group living.

Economists often seem surprised when people share resources with stran-gers that they could readily keep for themselves (Thaler, 1988), but this surprise only emerges from a misunderstanding of our evolutionary history. Because we evolved to cooperate with each other, we also evolved the capacity to readily detect free riders, who reap the benefits of cooperation but do not themselves contribute (Cosmides, Barrett, & Tooby, 2010). Along with our cheater-detection system, we evolved a strong emotional response to free riders, feeling anger and righteous indignation when others take advantage of us (Fehr & Gächter, 2002). These abilities and emotional responses ensure that others in our group cooperate with us, but they have also shaped the underlying cooperative motive itself. We don't like people who cooperate with us only to reciprocate, or to gain future cooperation in return. Rather, we like people who are friendly, kind, trusting, and generous without regard to consequences. In other words, we like people who enjoy cooperating for its own sake. And that, of course, means that other people like us for the same reasons, which would have given a substantial evolutionary advantage to our ancestors who genuinely enjoyed cooperating.

This is why we often share resources with strangers who will never be able to help us in return. Even though generous people occasionally get exploited, in the long run they win far more than they lose. Generous people are more popular than stingy or calculating people all over the world. When Hadza hunter-gatherers in Tanzania break camp and go off in different directions, the generous ones have lots of people who want to be with them while the stingy ones are at constant risk of being left alone (Apicella, Marlowe, Fowler, & Christakis, 2012). Similarly, when the Martu people of Western Australia head off on their morning hunts, the generous people are always chosen as partners even if they're not the best hunters, while the stingy ones are often forgotten (Bird & Power, 2015).

The result of these evolutionary pressures is a motivational system that is highly attuned to cooperation. We enjoy spending time with our friends and kin, and we also get satisfaction from helping them. In the most recent World Values Survey of nearly one hundred countries (www.worldvaluessurvey.org), people around the world rated family as the single most important thing in their lives. But our sources of satisfaction extend beyond close friends and kin to our entire community. Our communities may be much larger now than the ones in which we originally evolved, but the psychological principles that link us to our community have the same effects that they have always had. As a consequence, *integration with our community is one of the keys to living the good life*. Accumulation without sharing may be important at some stages in life as people attempt to ascend the hierarchy, but to retain high status in a group it is necessary to form long-term and mutually beneficial relationships with others; that is, it is necessary to be regarded as a good and reliable friend. For this reason, life satisfaction is achieved by being a long-term resident in a stable set of social networks, and by supporting community members who are in need (see also Huppert, this volume).

Supporting community members in need is often accomplished through charity, but making a contribution to the community itself is probably the more important manifestation of this effect. We need to be of value to our community—our ancestors who were not judged to be of value were at risk of ostracism and hence death—and the most notable way to be of value is to produce more than you cost. This calculus probably lies in the backs of all of our minds, and drives us to be contributing members of society. When someone asks how you would like to be remembered (and hopefully eulogized) at your funeral, essentially they are asking what is the nature of your contribution to your community.

Learning

As we mentioned at the outset of this chapter, humans actively learn most of what we need to know to survive. We are born knowing very little and with a brain that is really only half-baked, but that would be too large to birth once fully cooked. As a consequence, we have an inordinately long period of development before we can become a viable and contributing member of our community. This period of development is consumed almost entirely by learning the means of survival used by our group. The importance of learning ensures that evolution linked learning tightly to our motivational system, and consistent with this possibility, humans all over the globe love to learn. Curiosity is one of our fundamental drives (Kidd & Hayden, 2015), and the satisfaction associated with learning and mastery is universal (Deci & Ryan, 2000).

Despite widespread awareness of these principles, there are two important aspects of learning—and hence two important sources of life satisfaction—that are given relatively short shrift in the psychological literature: play and storytelling. Play is universal among mammals, most notably before they reach maturity, as it is a form of learning the rules and strategies of an adult life. Because humans are unique in how much they need to learn to survive and thrive, and how long that learning takes, the importance of play has extended beyond our childhood into our adult lives. As adults, play enhances the quality of close relationships by fostering intimacy and improving conflict resolution skills (van Vleet & Feeney, 2015). For these reasons, play has a fundamental role in life satisfaction. This effect can be seen in the enjoyment of sport (and sport spectating) across the lifespan, and also in the importance of various games into late adulthood. In the absence of play, life is not nearly as worth living.

The importance of play is shared with all mammals, but storytelling appears to be unique to humans. Human learning has an enormous advantage over the learning of other animals, as our incredible communicative abilities allow us to incorporate the learning and accomplishments of others into our own understanding of the world (see Kalkstein et al., this volume). The oldest and most important form of this learning process is probably storytelling (McBride, 2014). Storytelling is ubiquitous in all human cultures, and assuredly began as our hunter-gatherer ancestors sat around in small groups at the end of the day and regaled each other with their experiences. Those who enjoyed telling stories and were talented at it would have gained stature in the group. Furthermore, everyone would have evolved a tendency to enjoy listening to stories, as that would provide a cost-free manner in which difficult and sometimes expensive lessons could be learned. Finally, storytelling would have connected community members to each other through shared emotional experiences, a sense of shared reality, and a common knowledge of how to approach the world.

For these reasons, telling and listening to stories are two of the great sources of human happiness and life satisfaction. When we feel that our stories are valued by others and they share our understanding of the world, we feel validated and that our importance to our group is assured. When our stories are dismissed or misunderstood, we feel marginalized and unhappy. Perhaps this is one of the reasons for the proliferation of urban legends, as research suggests that people exaggerate and invent components of the stories they tell to ensure that others share their emotional reactions (Heath, Bell, & Sternberg, 2001). If I tell a tale of woe that fails to sadden the listener, then my story has failed its purpose, and the next time I tell it the details will become more outrageous to ensure my audience feels as I did.

Personality and Development

As we suggested at the outset of this chapter, there is more than one way to be a success as a human and hence more than one route to happiness. If I'm big and strong I might attract a mate through sport or other physical competition, but if I'm small and weak I might be better off using humor or kindness. As a consequence, people naturally tend to choose a strategy of best fit by maximizing their advantages. That is, people pursue activities that rely on their strengths and that minimize the impact of their weaknesses. Because our motivational system is attuned to the potential for success and the degree to which our group values us, this means that different activities will make different people happy, largely depending on how their abilities compare to others. If I am a better artist than most people but a worse athlete, I will probably find greater satisfaction from art than from sport.

These individual differences, in turn, also change over the course of our lifespan. As a child it is very difficult to contribute to one's group, and hence children gain most of their sense of happiness and satisfaction from their activities with one another and from acceptance and support by their parents. Because their unique features are more likely to be noticed by others than their common ones (McGuire & Padawer-Singer, 1976), children's sense of self nevertheless becomes most tightly tied to the ways that they can differentiate themselves positively from their group. That is, children start to develop their unique set of talents that will make them most productive when they reach adulthood.

Once we attain adulthood, our contribution to the community becomes important, and we start to rely on those skills that we learned in an effort to rise up in the status hierarchy and be valued by other members of our group. These skills and activities are relatively stable in most people throughout their young and middle adulthood but begin to show reliable changes in late life. At that point, physical skills often deteriorate. Older adults tend to have a larger body of knowledge, which made them valuable in our ancestral past and offset their deteriorating physical skills. Unfortunately, in our modern and rapidly changing world that knowledge can become obsolete as well. But the evolutionary pressures that push us to contribute to our group don't change just because we have gotten older, and thus many older adults strive to find ways to continue to make a positive impact on their community. This is one of the reasons why approximately one third of people who are recently retired have a great deal of difficulty adjusting to their new life, even if they were looking forward to it previously.

As a consequence of these processes, the sources of our life satisfaction also change as we enter late adulthood. Because we evolved to feel happy when we contribute to our community, we also evolved to seek different sources of life satisfaction as the nature of those contributions changes over the lifespan. Issues of legacy and care for others become increasingly important among older adults, as these are often their greatest opportunities to remain connected and helpful to others.

Pitfalls of the Modern World

Pondering the good life may be a uniquely modern pastime, but the ways that we achieve the good life are by following the ancient strategies that made our ancestors successful. Sex and eating, parenthood and play, mastery and storytelling, friendship and kin, hearth and home, community and contribution—these were the keys to success in our past, and they remain the keys to our happiness today. Nonetheless, our modern world provides many new opportunities for happiness, and it is not at all clear when the modern version is just as good as the original.

For example, movies and television have replaced some aspects of storytelling, and they remain some of the most fun things that we do (Kahneman et al., 2004). But storytelling is much more than just relating a series of events, and movies and television don't connect people to each other in the same way that conversations do (until we talk about them later). To some degree, movies and television are thus a phenotypic indulgence (like potato chips), and so it is no surprise that people rarely cite television programs as an important source of life satisfaction. Anecdotal experience suggests that books are more likely to have an important and lasting effect on us than TV, which (if true) raises the possibility that a critical part of storytelling is the imaginative and generative processes taking place in our minds when someone tells a tale that we cannot physically experience. But even books are typically less memorable and important than the stories we tell and are told, because reading is typically done alone.

Other aspects of our modern world that are designed to mimic important ancestral experiences provide much thinner gruel and leave us a lot less satisfied. Drugs and alcohol are probably the most notable example of such phenotypic indulgences, as they go straight to the brain regions responsible for pleasure without providing the physical or experiential basis from which that pleasure was meant to emanate. After drugs and alcohol, junk food comes a close second, as the sugar, fat, and salt that our ancestors desperately sought in the past are overabundant today. One need only look at the dentition of Neanderthals—who never owned a toothbrush but never got a cavity—to see the health consequences of our modern agricultural diet. Sadly, our struggle is now against what was once a healthy goal to eat as much sugar, fat, and salt as possible.

The costs that we pay when we have too much of a good thing bring us to the final lesson that our evolutionary history can teach us about how to live a happy and meaningful life. Long-term relationships were our ancestors' best recipe for raising successful offspring, and as a result we find long-term relationships particularly rewarding (see Gable; Simpson et al., this volume). When people part-ner with the right person, they have their best shot at a lasting increase in happi-ness. But evolution also gave us a preference for novel partners, as both men and women gain reproductive benefits when they put their genetic eggs in more than one basket. The problem is that novel partners were relatively rare in our ancestral environment, as we spent our entire lives in the same small group of people. But just like fat, salt, and sugar, we now live in a world in which there is an unend-ing supply of novel potential partners, who serve as a constant temptation for us to abandon our current relationship to try out a new and more exciting one. Of course, the new relationship will soon become old, and hence the allure of novelty is fleeting by definition, and eventually unsatisfying. Nevertheless, that fact doesn't prevent many of us from being serial monogamists now, and it didn't prevent our ancestors from adopting a similar mating strategy back then.

Most people are better at avoiding temptation than resisting it, and sure enough, people who escape the lure of novelty usually achieve this goal by not exposing themselves to it. Marriages last longer in rural areas than in cities, and much longer still if you're a nobody than if you're a famous actor or rock star. This fact brings us to the German folk saying, "Vorfreude ist die schönste Freude" (*anticipated joy is the greatest joy*), which describes the inevitable disappointment we experience when we achieve our goals. Universal adoration and fame are some of the most common dreams of people all over the world, but you need only reflect on the turbulent lives and repeated divorces of celebrities to realize how much happier you are being unknown.

Note

1 For example, the possibility of sharing bodily fluids typically evokes disgust in service of our survival goals, but when sexual goals are activated these disgust responses are inhibited.

Bibliography

Apicella, C. L., Marlowe, F. W., Fowler, J. H., & Christakis, N. A. (2012). Social networks and cooperation in hunter-gatherers. *Nature, 481*, 497–501.

Bingham, P. M. (2000). Human evolution and human history: A complete theory. *Evolutionary Anthropology, 9*, 248–257.

Bird, R. B., & Power, E. A. (2015). Prosocial signaling and cooperation among Martu hunt-ers. *Evolution and Human Behavior, 36*, 389–397.

Boesch, C. (1994). Cooperative hunting in wild chimpanzees. *Animal Behaviour, 48*, 653–667.

Buss, D. (1989). Sex differences in human mate preferences: Evolutionary hypotheses tested in 37 cultures. *Behavioral and Brain Sciences, 12*, 1–49.

Call, J., & Tomasello, M. (2008). Does the chimpanzee have a theory of mind? 30 years later. *Trends in cognitive sciences, 12*, 187–192.

Calvin, W. H. (1982). Did throwing stones shape hominid brain evolution? *Ethology and Sociobiology, 3*, 115–124.

Confer, J. C., Easton, J. A., Fleischman, D. S., Goetz, C. D., Lewis, D. M., Perilloux, C., & Buss, D. M. (2010). Evolutionary psychology: Controversies, questions, prospects, and limitations. *American Psychologist, 65*, 110–126.

Corder, E. H., Saunders, A. M., Strittmatter, W. J., Schmechel, D. E., Gaskell, P. C., Small, G. W., Roses, A. D., Haines, J. L., & Pericak-Vance, M. A. (1993). Gene dose of apolipo-protein E type 4 allele and the risk of Alzheimer's disease in late onset families. *Science, 261*, 921–923.

Cosmides, L., Barrett, H. C., & Tooby, J. (2010). Adaptive specializations, social exchange, and the evolution of human intelligence. *Proceedings of the National Academy of Sciences, 107*, 9007–9014.

Deci, E. L., & Ryan, R. M. (2000). The "what" and "why" of goal pursuits: Human needs and self-determination of behavior. *Psychological Inquiry, 11*, 227–268.

Easterlin, R. (1994). Will raising the incomes of all increase the happiness of all? *Journal of Economic Behaviour and Organization, 27*, 35–47.

Fehr, E., & Gächter, S. (2002). Altruistic punishment in humans. *Nature, 415*, 137–140.

Gilby, I. C. (2006). Meat sharing among the Gombe chimpanzees: Harassment and recipro-cal exchange. *Animal Behaviour, 71*, 953–963.

Gruter, M., & Masters, R. D. (1986). Ostracism as a social and biological phenomenon: An introduction. *Ethology and Sociobiology, 7*, 149–158.

Hamilton, W. D. (1964). The genetical evolution of social behaviour. II. *Journal of Theoreti-cal Biology, 7*, 17–52.

Han, S. D., Drake, A. I., Cessante, L. M., Jak, A. J., Houston, W. S., Delis, D. C., . . . Bondi, M. W. (2007). Apolipoprotein E and traumatic brain injury in a military population: Evidence of a neuropsychological compensatory mechanism? *Journal of Neurology, Neu-rosurgery, and Psychiatry, 78*, 1103–1108.

Hare, B., & Tomasello, M. (2004). Chimpanzees are more skilful in competitive than in cooperative cognitive tasks. *Animal Behaviour, 68*, 571–581.

Hart, D., & Sussman, R. W. (2005). *Man the hunted: Primates, predators, and human evolution.* Boulder, CO: Westview Press.

Heath, C., Bell, C., & Sternberg, E. (2001). Emotional selection in memes: The case of urban legends. *Journal of Personality and Social Psychology, 81*, 1028–1041.

Hunt, J., Brooks, R., Jennions, M. D., Smith, M. J., Bentsen, C. L., & Bussiere, L. F. (2004). High-quality male field crickets invest heavily in sexual display but die young. *Nature, 432*, 1024–1027.

Isaac, B. (1987). Throwing and human evolution. *African Archaeological Review, 5*, 3–17.

Kahneman, D., Krueger, A. B., Schkade, D. A., Schwarz, N., & Stone, A. A. (2004). A survey method for characterizing daily life experience: The day reconstruction method. *Sci-ence, 306*, 1776–1780.

Kidd, C., & Hayden, B. Y. (2015.) The psychology and neuroscience of curiosity. *Neuron, 88*, 449–460.

Marzke, M. W. (1983). Joint functions and grips of the Australopithecus afarensis hand, with special reference to the region of the capitate. *Journal of Human Evolution, 12*, 197–211.

McBride, G. (2014). Storytelling, behavior planning, and language evolution in context. *Frontiers in Psychology, 5*, 1131.

McGuire, W. J., & Padawer-Singer, A. (1976). Trait salience in the spontaneous self-concept. *Journal of personality and social psychology, 33*, 743–754.

Morgan, D., Grant, K. A., Gage, H. D., Mach, R. H., Kaplan, J. R., Prioleau, O., . . . Nader, M. A. (2002). Social dominance in monkeys: Dopamine D2 receptors and cocaine self-administration. *Nature Neuroscience, 5*, 169–174.

Napier, J. R. (1993). *Hands*. Princeton, NJ: Princeton University Press.

Owens, I. P. (2002). Sex differences in mortality rate. *Science, 297*, 2008–2009.

Ronay, R., & von Hippel, W. (2010). The presence of an attractive woman elevates testosterone and physical risk-taking in young men. *Social Psychological and Personality Science, 1*, 57–64.

Suddendorf, T. (2013). *The Gap: The science of what separates us from other animals*. New York, NY: Basic Books.

Thaler, R. H. (1988). Anomalies: The ultimatum game. *The Journal of Economic Perspectives, 2*, 195–206.

Tomasello, M., Hare, B., Lehmann, H., & Call, J. (2007). Reliance on head versus eyes in the gaze following of great apes and human infants: The cooperative eye hypothesis. *Journal of Human Evolution, 52*, 314–320.

Tooby, J., & Cosmides, L. (1990). The past explains the present: Emotional adaptations and the structure of ancestral environments. *Ethology and Sociobiology, 11*, 375–424.

van Boven, L., & Gilovich, T. (2003). To do or to have? That is the question. *Journal of Personality and Social Psychology, 85*, 1193–1302.

Van Vleet, M., & Feeney, B. C. (2015). Young at heart: A perspective for advancing research on play in adulthood. *Perspectives on Psychological Science, 10*, 639–645.

Winterhalder, B. (1993). Work, resources and population in foraging societies. *Man*, 321–340.

Young, R. W. (2003). Evolution of the human hand: The role of throwing and clubbing. *Journal of Anatomy, 202*, 165–174.

4

ON THE ADAPTIVE FUNCTIONS OF GOOD LIFE

Going Beyond Hedonic Experience

Klaus Fiedler and Peter Arslan

Introduction

The topic of this volume—good life—is as old and prominent as Stoic and Aristotelian ethics. The purpose of the present chapter is to discuss some necessary theoretical and conceptual prerequisites for the scientific study of what makes for a good life. It is also meant to illustrate the often neglected role of theorizing in the current debate about the quality of science. While the literature on appropriate significance testing, statistical power, good practices, and transparency of research data is growing rapidly, stringent theorizing and logic of science continue to be neglected (cf. Earp & Trafimow, 2015; Fiedler, 2017; Meehl, 1990; Platt, 1964).

With regard to research on the notion of good life, we believe that three symptoms of this neglected-theory syndrome must be dealt with. They might be named the symptoms of (a) unwarranted reification, (b) aggregation error, and (c) reverse inference of the *modus tollens*. The literature on behavioral science in general, and on the good-life issue in particular, is replete with all three symptoms, which can be explained as follows: (a) The reification symptom consists in the presupposition that if there is a common verbal label, it must have a truly existing reference object (see also Sheldon, this volume). This presupposition is deeply entrenched in laypeople's as well as scientists' thinking. The mere existence of a term such as "short-term memory" seems to imply the existence of a real corresponding memory system. By analogy, a real reference object of "good life" must exist when scientists and readers of the feuilleton part of a newspaper all refer to the sonorous word.

As to the second symptom, (b) *aggregation errors* are evident in the assumption that empirical laws (correlations, established experimental effects) hold at all levels of aggregation. It is commonly assumed for example that the same causal factors that link religion and life satisfaction at the individual level must also exist at the aggregate level of states (see also Myers, this volume). By analogy, any answer about the good life of humanity at large is assumed to apply to the good life of individuals.

And thirdly, although scientists should know that logical implications of the form *If p, then q* do not imply *If q, then p*, in reality they often accept such reverse inferences (from q to p), for example, when it is easier to manipulate the consequent (q) than the antecedent condition (p). Thus, when studying causes (p) of accidents, diseases, professional success or life satisfaction (q), it is hardly possible to manipulate hundreds of causal factors (p) to demonstrate outcomes (q). In these cases, researchers sometimes engage in a reverse strategy, basing causal analyses on reverse inferences from samples of accidents, diseases, or life satisfaction. In other words, while it is virtually impossible to investigate the conditions of good life experimentally, researchers often resort to reverse inferences from success versus failure on good-life tasks to antecedent causal conditions (traits, lifestyles, ethical rule).

We do need to focus on the almost insurmountable limitations imposed by all three symptoms on the psychological study of good life. Specifically, (a) it is very difficult to assign an invariant meaning or real reference object to the term 'good life'; and (b) even if a meaning is defined, measures of good life at different aggregation levels (past vs. present vs. future, within individuals vs. groups or nations) can diverge dramatically (Diener, Diener & Diener, 1995; see also Sheldon; and Myers, this volume). Moreover, (c) reversed inferences about the social conditions that seem to correlate with personal or historical cases of good life are as weak as many other instances of reverse inferences (Fiedler, 2008; Wason, 1960).

The Relativity of Positive and Negative Valence

Let us start by examining the evidence whether there is a construct called good life that can be defined clearly enough to warrant its scientific study. All humans evaluate persons and outcomes as good or bad, approaching the former and avoiding the latter (Denrell, 2005; Thorndike, 1927). It seems obvious that the hedonic distinction between good and bad is real. Despite the existence of ambivalence in some cases, the distinction between pleasant and unpleasant experience appears to be easy to manipulate experimentally or to measure reliably.

However, the hedonic reaction to momentary positive or negative experiences such as food, pain, love and hate does not easily map onto enduring hedonic states. What is pleasant and comfortable in the short run is often unhealthy and demotivating in the long run (see also Forgas, this volume). Using one's own car or a public bus to commute is much more pleasant than having to walk three miles to work, but the latter experience may be far better for one's physical and mental health. Receiving extra reward for learning and performance may be greatly enjoyed but may undermine subsequent intrinsic motivation (Gallus & Frey, 2016; Lepper, Greene & Nisbett, 1973; see also Forgas, this volume). Being always protected is nice but prevents the immune system from producing antibodies. Rich people have trouble enjoying small monetary gains; very attractive people cannot appreciate social approval; and being satiated with delicious food precludes the possibility of further culinary enjoyment.

Thus, the simple distinction of hedonically pleasant or unpleasant experiences becomes much more complicated. And the underlying dialectical principle of valence regulation—good and bad experiences are mutually supportive—is not the exception but rather the rule. That bad things are inherently linked to good things can be the result of several regulatory mechanisms. Three of these may be termed (1) relativity, (2) deprivation, and (3) self-generated reinforcement.

The Relativity of Pleasant Experiences and Well-Being

The principle of relativity is ubiquitous in the psychology of affective experiences and life satisfaction (Heck, 2016; Lyubomirsky, 2013; Fritz & Lyubomirsky, this volume; Parducci, 1968). The effective reward value of any experience is not fully inherent in the obtained outcome. Rather, it strongly depends on the aspiration level or comparison standard—that is, on the value of the outcomes forgone. A ten-dollar tip seems generous, but it is frustrating if it is only 3% of the overall bill. A silver medal in an Olympic competition is a big success, but not if an athlete was strongly expected to receive the gold medal (Medvec, Madey & Gilovich, 1995). Even animals who like cucumbers as a reward may refuse them if neighboring animals get more delicious grapes (as illustrated in a YouTube film clip: www.youtube.com/watch?v=HL45pVdsRvE).

Thus, the relativity of well-being is a natural consequence of the Weber-Fechner law applied to evaluative judgment. Just as a discrimination threshold, or just-noticeable difference, in weight, loudness, brightness or any other sensory dimensions increase with the absolute level of the magnitude in question, the threshold for a pleasant increment (or unpleasant decrement) in well-being is relative to the current status quo, or comparison standard. As a consequence, the reward value of an experience is not inherent in the stimulus; it rather lies in the eye of the beholder. To take an obvious example, a hundred dollars has far greater hedonic value to a homeless person than to a millionaire.

As impressively explained in Parducci's (1965, 1968) seminal work on the range-frequency principle, the relativity principle extends to even extreme intensities of experience. Accordingly, even the poorest people imprisoned in a concentration camp can feel happiness and joy, relative to their extremely modest comparison level. Conversely, the most blessed people may be dissatisfied when experiences fail to match their extremely high comparison levels. Parducci's

(1968) psychological explanation of relativity is built on the range-frequency principle, which quantifies psychophysical judgments relative to the distribution of all stimuli in a reference set. For example, in a right-skewed distribution of mostly negative experiences, the same experience gets a higher relative position than in a left-skewed distribution of mostly positive experiences.

Such an outcome is an almost necessary consequence of natural regulation processes. Rich people live in more exclusive and privileged neighbourhoods, successful sports teams rise into a higher league, and so their comparison standards and expectations rise accordingly. The natural consequence of such regulation is the big-fish-little-pond effect (Marsh, 1987). The same achievement is worth much less in an elite environment than in an average environment, and this may affect not only the person's self-concept (Marsh, 2016) but also the evaluations of others (Moore, Swift, Sharek & Gino, 2010). Thus, the relativity of good and bad experience is real and consequential; this is the rule rather than the exception.

The relativity principle even applies to such a fundamental paradigm as conditioning, which has been traditionally treated like an epitome of automatic, stable and invariable, biologically determined behavior. In classical conditioning, the crucial determinant of learning is not the positive (appetitive) or negative (aversive) value of unconditioned stimuli (US) per se. What counts is rather the surprise value of the US, that is, whether it is more positive or negative than could be expected in the present stage of the learning process (cf. Rescorla & Wagner, 1972).

A similar principle underlies Mellers, Schwartz and Ritov's (1999) decision affect theory, which says: $R_{obtained} = u_{obtained} + d(u_{obtained} - u_{forgone})(1 - s_{obtained})$. Accordingly, the reward value $R_{obtained}$ of an obtained decision outcome is not solely a function of the utility $u_{obtained}$ of the obtained outcome but also of the regret or disappointment function $d(u_{obtained} - u_{forgone})$, which specifies the relative utility difference between obtained and forgone options. To the extent that the utility of the forgone option exceeds the utility of the chosen and obtained option, the resulting reward value will be reduced. A closer look at the formula above reveals that it not only predicts that the effective reward value will shrink when disappointment d increases, it also predicts that disappointment is strongest when the weighting factor $1 - s_{obtained}$ is high—that is, when the subjective probability $s_{obtained}$ of the obtained option is low. In other words, people are most disappointed and their satisfaction with the chosen option is lowest when the forgone option gained by most others is common and the inferior chosen option is rare.

Relativity in Evaluative Conditioning

It is important to understand the psychological mechanisms that underlie the relativity of well-being. Recent evidence on evaluative conditioning from our own lab (Unkelbach & Fiedler, 2017) confirms the relative nature of positive and negative stimulation. We used neutral faces as conditioned stimuli (CSs) and clearly unlikeable or likeable faces as unconditioned stimuli (USs). Contrary to the common assumption that CSs take on the valence of the USs with which they are paired repeatedly, we aimed to demonstrate that the simple association of CS and US does not determine the outcome of evaluative learning. Rather, taking a propositional learning perspective (Mitchell, de Houwer & Lovibond, 2009), we hypothesized that the impact of US valence on the learned CS evaluation is moderated by the type of predicate (Pred) linking CS and US in the conditioning task: CS—Pred—US. For example, when the task asks participants in a forced-choice task to decide whether either the CS face or the US face is more likeable, the predicate (Pred) implies an opposition between CS and US. As a consequence of such a predicate, the final evaluation of CS should be contrasted away from the valence of US. In other words, after a forced choice contrasting a neutral CS face against a positive (negative) US face, the CS face should take on the valence opposite to the US face against which it is pitted.

The empirical results support this expectation. When participants were asked to make forced choices between all pairs of six neutral CS faces and six clearly negative US faces, the neutral CS faces "won the comparisons" and were subsequently evaluated positively, despite the fact that they had been consistently paired with negative US faces. Conversely, when in another condition participants had to make forced choices between all pairs of six neutral CS faces and six positive US faces, the CSs lost the comparisons and were devalued afterwards, despite the repeated association with positive USs. In other words, the relative value of CS and US overrode the valence of the US as a determinant of conditioning.

Apparently, then, the allegedly automatic and biologically anchored process of conditioning is not determined by the intrinsically pleasant or unpleasant US experience per se. It is rather subject to strong (disordinal) interactions regulated by the relational predicate (Pred) between CS and US. If Pred implies mutual exclusion and opposition between CS and US, as in a forced-choice task, the evaluative learning effect of pleasant versus unpleasant US is reversed.

To cross-validate this interpretation, Unkelbach and Fiedler (2017) also tested the inverse implication that it is possible to obtain a "normal" (i.e., congruent) conditioning effect when the same CSs are paired with the same USs and only the Pred is replaced. Indeed, when participants in different experimental conditions were either asked to make comparative (competitive) evaluations of CS versus US or joint evaluations of CS and US together, the evaluative learning influence on CS was incongruent (opposite to the US valence) in the former condition but congruent (same as US valence) in the latter condition.

Deprivation Creates the Potential for Satisfaction

A special case of the relativity principle that is highly relevant to our understanding of well-being as well is the concept of deprivation. It deserves to be emphasized because it has a long tradition in animal learning and in existentialist philosophy. Whenever behavioral goals depend on drives, such as hunger, curiosity or sexuality, the strength of the drive increases with increasing deprivation. In other words, the deprivation experience creates the potential for positive motivation and satisfying goal attainment. Conversely, saturation after excessive goal consumption (e.g., overeating, excessive exploration, frequent sexual activities) reduces motivation and the pleasure resulting from goal attainment.

This dialectic regulation of deprivation and fulfillment, frustration and satisfaction, blocking and empowerment of drives, is not peculiar to artificial experimental paradigms nor is it confined to the realm of animal behavior (see also von Hippel & Gonsalkorale, this volume). It is rather ubiquitous in daily life, it lies at the heart of many existential conflicts, and it is of course crucial for the regulation of subjective well-being and life satisfaction. This wisdom is illustrated in social psychology's most prominent theoretical framework, that is, in Festinger's (1957) theory of cognitive dissonance. Accordingly, strong intrinsic motivation and positive attitudes toward an activity often originate in a lack of external reinforcement, creating a state of under-justification. In contrast, abundant reinforcement and frequent prior satisfaction cause over-justification and thereby undermine the resulting intrinsic motivation and attitude towards the action goal. Thus, providing strong rewards to perform activities we already enjoy may undermine motivation, due to over-justification (Deci, 1971; Gallus & Frey, 2016; Lepper et al., 1973). In contrast, people will be strongly motivated and develop the most positive attitude toward those goals and activities that they had to wait and struggle for over a long time, that is, after under-justified effort expenditure.

The internal and external validity (Campbell, 1957) of this important regulation principle was demonstrated in a monograph by Lawrence and Festinger (1962), who basically applied dissonance theory to animal learning. They explained a number of well-established laws of animal learning and performance as analogous to the phenomena of under-justification and over-justification in human behavior. For instance, the well-known learning advantage associated with partial reinforcement schedules can also be interpreted in terms of under-justification. If animals have to overcome many obstacles, to struggle a lot, and to expend much effort until they are finally rewarded on only a small part of the trials, their motivation is maximal and the learning effects are most endurable. If the animals receive full and abundant reinforcement on every trial, in contrast, their performance and the persistence of their learning will be lower due to over-justification. The same basic principles should also apply to the way humans value different activities and are motivated to engage in them—clearly an important insight into understanding the psychology of well-being. Thus, animal research highlights the same insight as dissonance research with human participants, namely, that good life is not self-perpetuating. What creates success and satisfaction in the long run is not any constant lifestyle or steady state called good life. It is rather the repeated deviation from, and deprivation of, that alleged ideal of good life.

This ironic state of affairs is indicative of the more general principle of home-ostatic system regulation. In economics, high prices of precious goods reflect their scarcity, whereas low prices reflect over-production and abundant supply. As explained in a remarkable article by Pleskac and Hertwig (2014), the same principle seems to hold for the relationship between the value of an object and its frequency (probability) of occurrence in the environment in general. Rare objects tend to be highly valued relative to frequent and abundant objects, which are worth little or even experienced as a plague. There are many historical examples: pineapples were luxury goods as long as they were scarce; aluminium cutlery was considered precious, until it became common.

Notwithstanding the existence of cross-sectional statistics documenting that people's happiness increases on average with economic wealth or with social sup-port, a plethora of empirical and historical evidence (e.g., Lavin, Joesting, Chiu, Moon, Meng, Dilger & Freund, 2011; Sonnentag, Venz & Casper, 2017) testifies that optimal motivation, ultimate satisfaction, strongest immune system and lowest depression rates are mostly experienced after marked periods of deprivation (such as wars, threatening disease, natural disaster). There is no logical contradiction at all between cross-sectional evidence for happiness under fortunate conditions and longitudinal evidence for increased happiness after unfortunate conditions. The coexistence of both phenomena is actually quite essential from a behavior-regulation perspective. It is however hard to reconcile this evidence with any simplistic psychological attempt to specify a recipe for good life. The ultimate purpose of studying behavior regulation is to understand the acquisition of wis-dom and personal growth and the attainment of equilibrium states emerging as (not plannable) consequences of contrast experience, conflict resolution and the ups and downs in the social and physical environment. From this perspective, it is unnecessary, and actually unlikely and unwarranted, to assume that an equilibrium of good life can be specified positively or prescribed in terms of injunctive norms.

Well-Being and Constructing Self-Generated Reinforcement

The relativity and malleability of good and bad experiences is even more impres-sive. The reward value and the behavioral consequences of positive and negative experiences depend not only on the relative frequency of obtained and forgone outcomes, on expectations and comparison standards, and on relational predi-cates between environmental stimuli (such as CS–US pairs). Rather, the effective reward value of real-life experience is additionally subject to internally generated inferences and subjective interpretations that go way beyond externally provided outcomes. Thus, it is well known that psychosomatic diseases are not so much determined by the objective degree of stressors but by the subjective attribution of stress as avoidable or unavoidable, personal or impersonal, intentional and predict-able or incidental and unwanted. Depressives' online diary entries are less negative than their biased retrospective memory reports. Or, impressions and evaluation of the same target persons or groups can vary dramatically as a function of the manner in which social hypotheses are tested during interaction (Fiedler & Walther, 2004; Snyder, 1984).

Let us go beyond such commonplace arguments and try to understand the full power of constructive memory and judgment. To get a glimpse of the general importance of self-generated information, let us consider another piece of evidence from evaluative conditioning (Fiedler & Unkelbach, 2011). All participants repeatedly observed several neutral CS faces, subsets of which were paired with positive, negative or neutral US faces. In different experimental conditions, participants were either asked to estimate the likelihood that the two persons are friends or the likelihood that they are enemies. The idea was that the effective stimulus is always a joint function of a passively received stimulus and what the learner actively does with the offered stimulus. Just as the notion of preparedness (Seligman, 1970) emphasizes the fact that organisms are internally prepared to link particular CSs to types or modalities of USs (Davey, 1992), we expected that, in principle, the same pairing of CS and US can be construed in essentially different ways and that this active construal process can even override the valence of the US.

To understand the basic psychological idea, assume that you are presented with a series of faces paired with wicked terrorists like Bin Laden. By default, you may encode stimulus pairs as faces belonging to closely related individuals, and this default predicate will probably produce a standard conditioning effect: originally neutral CS faces will take on the same negative valence as aversive US faces. This seemingly normal conditioning effect may be strengthened when the encoding task refers to pairs of faces introduced as friends. Clearly, persons paired with Bin Laden as a friend are particularly likely to be charged with negative valence. However, now assume that the same experiment refers to CSs as victims of Bin Laden's inhuman torture regime, thus imposing an inverse relational predicate on the construal of stimulus pairs. Would it not be possible, and even plausible and psychologically predictable, that victims of Bin Laden will be construed in a benevolent manner, charged with empathy, compassion, and maybe with respect and admiration for somebody who dared to be Bin Laden's antagonist?

The empirical findings supported this possibility. Whether observers expected the faces to be friends or enemies made a significant difference to the kinds of associations they formed. When the encoding task during learning asked participants to estimate the probability that the persons represented by CS and US might be friends, CS faces that had been paired with positive US faces were liked more in the posttest. In contrast, when participants estimated the probability that the same CS faces and the same US faces were enemies, then CS faces took on negative valence (provided the estimated probability was not too low). An analogous reversal was obtained for CS faces paired with negative US faces. More precisely, the impact of the relational predicate (is friend of vs. is enemy of) was restricted to subjective likelihood estimates of no less than about 20%. That is, when participants believed it was highly unlikely (i.e., < 20%) that CS and US can be friends, then the evaluative learning effect did not conform to the predicate. However, over a wide range of probability estimates, CS valence was assimilated to the US valence in the friendship condition but contrasted away from the US valence in the enemy condition.

Moreover, to rule out any problems of demand effects and self-selected likelihood estimates (which are not under experimental control), convergent evidence was obtained in an additional experiment in which the encoding task asked participants to indicate reasons why CS and US are either friends or enemies. Thus, in this experiment, friendship versus enmity was presupposed as a given property to be explained in the encoding task. Still, the presupposed friendship relation led to an evaluative shift of the formerly neutral faces toward the US valence, whereas the presupposed enmity relation produced a contrast effect, away from the US valence.

The plasticity of hedonic experience that can be framed and construed in different and even opposite ways was already demonstrated in an earlier study by Strack, Schwarz and Gscheidinger (1985) on the impact of prior life experiences on current life satisfaction. Prior to evaluating satisfaction with their life as a whole, participants were asked to think of something in their biography that was either very pleasant and positive or very unpleasant and negative. In different experimental conditions, they were instructed either to remember *how* that earlier life experience felt or to provide an explanation of *why* that experience occurred. How questions elicited an assimilation effect—positive memories produced higher life satisfaction than negative memories. In contrast, why questions led participants to construe life experiences in a way that elicited contrast effects—explaining prior positive episodes made one's current life appear more negative than explaining negative episodes. This study further illustrates that subjective well-being and life satisfaction judgments are fundamentally influenced by the subjective comparison and constructive interpretations and mindset of the individual.

The opposite effects of how and why questions are presumably related to the fact that, as a principle, every affective experience exerts a twofold influence: (a) Affective experiences may be included in the valenced construal of the current judgment object (i.e., one's life satisfaction). At the same time, (b) they influence the construal of the comparison standard or aspiration level (cf. Bless & Schwarz, 2010). Apparently, *how* questions induce an affective mindset that strongly influences the valenced construal of one's life satisfaction, whereas *why* questions induce an analytic mindset that has a relatively stronger influence on the reliance of a comparison standard, or reference scale. In any case, this evidence nicely demonstrates that subtle manipulations of the mindset or of the framing used for a judgment task can strongly moderate the manner in which autobiographical memories shape one's current satisfaction.

Elated and Depressed Mood States, Promotion and Prevention Focus

The same relativity that characterizes the hedonic value of positive versus negative life experiences holds for the functional value of positive versus negative affective states (Fiedler, 1988). The impact of different mood states on behavior can be explained as a self-corrective regulatory cycle. The behavioral style triggered by euphoric mood states entails the potential for outcomes inducing negative mood, whereas the style triggered by dysphoric mood carries the potential for mood repair (see also Forgas, this volume). Positive mood supports adaptive strategies of the assimilation type, encouraging intuitive decisions based on small samples of information, self-confident risk taking, curiosity, creativity, nonconformity, and constructive inferences beyond the information given (Fiedler & Hütter, 2013). While this style serves important adaptive functions—such as exploring novel behaviors and testing the limits—it is only a matter of time until the increased probability of social conflicts, transgressions, and accidents will cause a shift from positive to negative mood. Conversely, the adaptive style triggered by negative mood states supports adaptive functions of the accommodation type. Depressed or dysphoric people resort to cautious and very careful behavior, conservative strategies, sticking to the facts and to their well-learned repertoire, conforming to norms of politeness and compliance, and refraining from creative inferences beyond the information given. Inherent in this adaptive style is the potential for mood repair; it is only a matter of time until such accommodative strategies will reduce the rate of mischief and transgressions and more benevolent social feedback will re-establish better mood states.

Because of this dialectic homeostatic circle, there is no unequivocal answer to the often asked question of whether good or bad mood induces higher performance or success (Fiedler & Beier, 2014; Fiedler & Hütter, 2013). Again, the regulatory cycle produces strong and disordinal interactions, with negative mood leading to better performance on accommodative tasks (Forgas, this volume) but positive mood facilitating performance on other tasks of the assimilative type (Fiedler & Hütter, 2013; see also Fredrickson, this volume). For example, depressed mood reduces the prevalence of false memories (Storbeck & Clore, 2005), erroneous eyewitness reports (Forgas, Laham & Vargas, 2005) or impoliteness in social communication (Forgas, 1999). Elated mood states, in contrast, facilitate creativity (Rowe et al., 2007), flexible decision making (Fiedler, Renn & Kareev, 2010) and self-efficacy (Kavanagh & Bower, 1985).

In a similar way, one cannot expect to find an overall main effect of good or bad mood (or good or bad life) on success, health or personal well-being. Mood states are not only self-correcting (i.e., entailing the potential to induce opponent states) but are also differentially suited for different types of tasks. The coexistence of costs and benefits associated with either mood state is even visible simultaneously within the same task. Let us illustrate this memorable insight with reference to a sequential decision-making task developed by Fiedler et al. (2010).

On every trial, participants were asked to make a choice between a pair of job candidates, each one described by a binary sample of juror opinions represented on the screen by smileys (☺) or frowneys (☹). If candidates did not differ sufficiently, participants could also decide not to choose and pass on to the next pair. Participants were told that these opinions were randomly sampled from the universe of all evaluations obtained during an assessment session. Instructions reminded participants of a speed-accuracy trade-off: gathering as many observations as necessary to identify the better candidate (according to the records in the assessment center) but also making as many personnel selection choices as possible in the given time. Decision accuracy was analyzed as a function of task difficulty (i.e., similarity of positivity proportions of the two candidates in a pair) and thoroughness of decision strategies (i.e., self-determined sample size), which were in turn expected to depend on the participants' positive versus negative mood (induced by film clips at the beginning of the experimental session).

How would decision accuracy depend on thoroughness, that is, on self-determined sample size? On one hand, of course, expending more effort in collecting larger samples should reduce sampling error and lead to better decisions. On the other hand, in a self-truncated information search, a characteristic primacy effect will produce a small-sample advantage. Thus, when the first few observations in a choice task happen to show a clear-cut difference between candidates, information search will be truncated early and small samples will lead to quick and confident decisions, which will be accurate most of the time. In contrast, when early observations happen to produce a mixed and equivocal picture on other trials, then larger samples will lead to less confident choices that are not always correct. Thus, low effort expenditure or laziness (i.e., the tendency to make do with small samples) might either reduce or improve decision accuracy. There is a clear conceptual parallel between this experimental task and the way people make similar decisions in everyday life that come to determine their life satisfaction and well-being.

Indeed, an expected finding was that participants in a positive mood were inclined to make more quick and intuitive decisions; they relied on smaller samples, expending lesser effort than participants in negative mood. However, the primacy effect prevented such risky strategies from reducing decision accuracy. Apparently, making quick and effortless decisions on easy trials, when the first few observations happened to reveal a clear-cut difference between candidates, was adaptive. Exploiting the primacy advantage for quick and effortless decision—a strategy supported by positive mood—and exploiting the thoroughness of large and laborious samples—a strategy induced by negative mood—are just different ways of improving decision performance.

Both strategies were actually shown in the same study to foster decision performance, though at different aggregation levels. Within most individual participants, the correlation across all decision trials between sample size and the size of the observed sample difference was negative; smaller samples made the actually existing difference between options more apparent (due to the primacy advantage). However, at the same time, the correlation across participants between their average sample size (i.e., thoroughness) and their decision accuracy (averaged across trials) was positive. Thus, sufficient thoroughness was a precondition for an individual participant's effective exploitation of the small sample advantage across trials (resulting from the primacy effect). These findings highlight, once more, that advantages and disadvantages of positive and negative mood, or lazy or laborious strategies, are likely to co-occur in the same problem context. This is a common insight from the analysis of behavior regulation in a world that is often characterized by trade-offs rather than by simple main effects.

Recent research by Arslan and Fiedler (2017) illustrates still another aspect of the dialectic relation between opposite affective or motivational states in achieving and maintaining well-being and life satisfaction. To investigate the relationship between regulatory focus and creativity, participants were asked to think and write either about their hopes and desires or about their duties and obligations. Note that such a manipulation of promotion focus versus prevention focus refers to motives and imaginations rather than emotions and mood states, but it clearly taps into another central aspect of good versus bad life (see also Shah, this volume). Orthogonal to this regulatory-focus state manipulation, we also manipulated the presence versus absence of a shift in regulatory focus. That is, a promotion or a prevention focus was either induced after a neutral task or after an opposite regulatory focus had been induced in participants (i.e., writing about hopes after writing about obligations or vice versa). Consistent with the postulated dynamic, dialectic mechanism, we expected the contrasting experience to intensify the regulatory focus manipulation. The dependent measure consisted of a battery of four different tests of creativity.

As expected, creativity was enhanced in a promotion focus state relative to a prevention focus state induced immediately before the creativity tests. However, this difference was amplified after a shift in regulatory focus. That is, participants were most creative when a current promotion focus followed a preceding prevention focus, and creativity was lowest after a shift from promotion to prevention focus. Indeed, a separate manipulation check (i.e., an accessibility measure for promotion- versus prevention-related word meanings) showed that the current regulatory-focus state was strongest after a shift from an opposite state. Apparently, a negative motive at t_1 energizes a positive motive at t_2, and vice versa. It thus seems justifiable to conclude that, indirectly, a prevention focus is also helpful for the mobilization of creative performance, in addition to the direct impact of a promotion focus.

Thus, upon closer inspection, the simplifying idea of a main effect of positive affective or motivational states on creativity is subject to strong regulatory interactions. The same relativity that characterizes the hedonic experience of happiness and sadness also holds for the functional consequences of positive or negative states. Creativity is not just a reflection of pleasant states; it is rather influenced by a regulatory cycle of creativity that entails both loosening and tightening (Kelly, 1955), relaxation and persistence (see also Fredrickson, this volume). This dualism is evident in the coexistence of the two Latin verbs *crear* (expressing innovation) and *crescere* (expressing effortful growth; personal communication by Rainer Holm-Hadulla).

Similarly, the tendency of positive affective states to release people from conformity and social norms can have different consequences for moral and ethical behavior. Using a commons-dilemma game, Hertel and Fiedler (1994) have shown that good mood enhances cooperative behavior, freeing people from egoistic profit maximization. At the same time, however, good mood also enhances the rate of playful transgressions and teasing provocations, much in line with the finding that good mood makes people impolite and more forward (Forgas, 1999).

One-sided main effects of negative affective states, such as ego depletion (Ainsworth, Baumeister, Ariely & Vohs, 2014; Baumeister, Vohs & Tice, 2007) or the hot-stove effect (Denrell & March, 2001) are subject to similar interactions. Thus, it has been argued that a hot-stove effect after aversive experience (e.g., sickness after eating in a restaurant) causes a negativity bias, as the subsequent avoidance of the negative stimulus prevents one from revising transitory negative evaluations (Denrell, 2005; Denrell & Le Mens, 2012; Fazio, Eiser & Shook, 2004). However, such a hot-stove effect only works when negative stimuli are avoided radically. When avoidance is not absolute, the tendency to sample more from pleasant than from unpleasant sources will produce a polarization of positive evaluations (i.e., more extreme evaluations of positive than negative stimuli), as demonstrated by Forgas (1990) or by Fiedler et al. (2013).

In the same vein, although self-control tasks have been shown to cause ego depletion (Baumeister et al., 2007), we have recently found that ego depletion will not result from effortful cognitive processing that is self-determined and assimilative, rather than other-determined and accommodative (Arslan & Fiedler, 2017).

Concluding Remarks

Thus, the relativity effects and the regulatory interactions we have discussed throughout this chapter have obvious implications for the psychology of the good life. Although this is certainly a fascinating topic for those who would provide simplified self-help advice, the conceptual and empirical issues we have reviewed here suggest that it is a far more complex process than commonly assumed. Thus, with regard to the first symptom of insufficient theorizing that we had identified at the outset, the reification symptom, we have seen (a) that it is virtually impossible to define good life, due to the relativity of good and bad evaluations. With regard to the second symptom, related to the problem of aggregation levels, we have discussed (b) the divergence of hedonic and even moral values in the short run and in the long run, and the disjunction between well-being at the individual and at the national level (see also Myers, this volume). And, last but not least, with regard to the logical fallacy of reverse inferences, even when there is some family resemblance (Wittgenstein, 1958) between good-life phenomena, (c) these phenomena may represent the consequence rather than the antecedent (causal) conditions of psychological mechanisms leading to well-being. Because it is ethically, legally and pragmatically impossible to randomize and manipulate the causal antecedent conditions under experimental control, there is no logically sound rationale for backward inferences from the observed consequences to antecedent conditions and processes leading to good life.

Being dissatisfied with such a disclaimer, one might conclude that the ultimate purpose of "positive psychology" or the "psychology of good life" is to highlight the relativity of good and bad, the prevalence of trade-offs rather than optimal solutions, and the importance of dynamic regulation as distinguished from static equilibrium. While this might well be in the spirit of the findings reviewed in this chapter, it does not amount to a satisfactory solution of the ultimate problem of every scientific endeavor, the search for invariant laws or valid insights that inform social, political and therapeutic interventions, conflict resolutions, and rational action. Simply pointing out that well-being is relative, that contrast experience is the key to happiness, that delay-of-gratification problems call for wise regulation, or that aggregation levels exist is just the beginning of a truly scientific approach that may go beyond the popular approach to the meaning of good life. A truly compelling theoretical approach leading to useful practical advice would have to offer functional recipes for optimal solutions (if only heuristic ones) for delay-of-gratification problems, foraging conflicts, and aggregation gaps. We believe that a precondition for such ultimate progress is to develop robust theoretical frameworks that take the social and physical environment into account and that allow us to understand the adaptive interplay of the individual and the environment.

Author Note

The work underlying this chapter was supported by a grant provided by the Deutsche Forschungsgemeinschaft to the first author (FI 294/26–1).

Bibliography

Ainsworth, S. E., Baumeister, R. F., Ariely, D., & Vohs, K. D. (2014). Ego depletion decreases trust in economic decision making. *Journal of Experimental Social Psychology*, *54*, 40–49. doi:10.1016/j.jesp.2014.04.004

Arslan, P., & Fiedler, K. (2017). *Creativity depends on regulatory focus and, more strongly, on regulatory-focus shift*. Manuscript submitted for publication.

Baumeister, R. F., Vohs, K. D., & Tice, D. M. (2007). The strength model of self-control. *Current Directions in Psychological Science*, *16*(6), 351–355.

Bless, H., & Schwarz, N. (2010). Mental construal and the emergence of assimilation and contrast effects: The inclusion/exclusion model. In M. P. Zanna, M. P. Zanna (Eds.), *Advances in experimental social psychology, Vol 42* (pp. 319–373). San Diego, CA, US: Academic Press.

Campbell, D. T. (1957). Factors relevant to the validity of experiments in social settings. *Psychological Bulletin, 54*(4), 297–312.

Davey, G. L. (1992). An expectancy model of laboratory preparedness effects. *Journal of Experimental Psychology: General, 121*(1), 24–40.

Deci, E. L. (1971). Effects of externally mediated rewards on intrinsic motivation. *Journal of Personality and Social Psychology, 18*, 105–115.

DeciBless, H., & Schwarz, N. (2010). Mental construal and the emergence of assimilation and contrast effects: The inclusion/exclusion model. In M. P. Zanna (Eds.), *Advances in experimental social psychology* (Vol. 42, pp. 319–373). San Diego, CA: Academic Press.

Denrell, J. (2005). Why most people disapprove of me: Experience sampling in impression formation. *Psychological Review, 112*(4), 951–978.

Denrell, J., & Le Mens, G. (2012). Social judgments from adaptive samples. In J. I. Krueger (Ed.), *Social judgment and decision making* (pp. 151–169). New York, NY: Psychology Press.

Denrell, J., & March, J. G. (2001). Adaptation as information restriction: The hot stove effect. *Organization Science, 12*(5), 523–538.

Diener, E., Diener, M., & Diener, C. (1995). Factors predicting the subjective well-being of nations. *Journal of Personality and Social Psychology, 69*(5), 851.

Earp, B. D., & Trafimow, D. (2015). Replication, falsification, and the crisis of confidence in social psychology. *Frontiers in Psychology, 6*.

Fazio, R., Eiser, J., & Shook, N. (2004). Attitude formation through exploration: Valence asymmetries. *Journal of Personality and Social Psychology, 87*(3), 293–311.

Festinger, L. (1957). *A theory of cognitive dissonance.* Stanford, CA: Stanford University Press.

Fiedler, K. (1988). Emotional mood, cognitive style, and behavior regulation. In K. Fiedler & J. P. Forgas (Eds.), *Affect, cognition, and social behavior* (pp. 100–119). Toronto: Hogrefe.

Fiedler, K. (2008). The ultimate sampling dilemma in experience-based decision making. *Journal of Experimental Psychology: Learning, Memory & Cognition, 34*, 186–203.

Fiedler, K. (2011). Voodoo correlations are everywhere—not only in neuroscience. *Perspectives on Psychological Science, 6*, 163–171.

Fiedler, K. (2017). What constitutes strong psychological science? The (neglected) role of diagnosticity and a priori theorizing. *Perspectives on Psychological Science, 12*(1), 46–61.

Fiedler, K., & Beier, S. (2014). Affect and cognitive processes in educational contexts. In R. Pekrun, L. Linnenbrink-Garcia, R. Pekrun, & L. Linnenbrink-Garcia (Eds.), *International handbook of emotions in education* (pp. 36–55). New York, NY: Routledge/Taylor & Francis Group.

Fiedler, K., & Hütter, M. (2013). Memory and emotion. In T. Perfect & S. Lindsay (Eds.), *Sage handbook of applied memory* (pp. 145–161). London: Sage Publications.

Fiedler, K., Renn, S., & Kareev, Y. (2010). Mood and judgments based on sequential sampling. *Journal of Behavioral Decision Making, 23*(5), 483–495.

Fiedler, K., & Unkelbach, C. (2011). Evaluative conditioning depends on higher order encoding processes. *Cognition & Emotion, 25*, 639–656.

Fiedler, K., & Walther, E. (2004). *Stereotyping as inductive hypothesis testing.* New York, NY: Psychology Press.

Fiedler, K., Wöllert, F., Tauber, B., & Hess, P. (2013). Applying sampling theories to attitude learning in a virtual school class environment. *Organizational Behavior and Human Decision Processes, 122*, 222–231.

Forgas, J. P. (1990). Affective influences on individual and group judgments. *European Journal of Social Psychology, 20*(5), 441–453.

Forgas, J. P. (1999). On feeling good and being rude: Affective influences on language use and request formulations. *Journal of Personality and Social Psychology, 76*(6), 928–939.

Forgas, J. P. (2013). Don't worry, be sad! On the cognitive, motivational, and interpersonal benefits of negative mood. *Current Directions in Psychological Science, 22*(3), 225–232.

Forgas, J. P., Laham, S. M., & Vargas, P. T. (2005). Mood effects on eyewitness memory: Affective influences on susceptibility to misinformation. *Journal of Experimental Social Psychology, 41*(6), 574–588.

Gallus, J., & Frey, B. S. (2016). Awards: A strategic management perspective. *Strategic Management Journal, 37*(8), 1699–1714.

Heck, P. R. (2016). Happiness: A theory of relativity. *The American Journal of Psychology, 129*(2), 197–200.

Hertel, G., & Fiedler, K. (1994). Affective and cognitive influences in a social dilemma game. *European Journal of Social Psychology, 24*(1), 131–145.

Hofmann, W., De Houwer, J., Perugini, M., Baeyens, F., & Crombez, G. (2010). Evaluative conditioning in humans: A meta-analysis. *Psychological Bulletin, 136*, 390–421.

Kavanagh, D. J., & Bower, G. H. (1985). Mood and self-efficacy: Impact of joy and sadness on perceived capabilities. *Cognitive Therapy and Research, 9*(5), 507–525.

Kelly, G. A. (1955). *The psychology of personal constructs. Vol. 1. A theory of personality. Vol. 2. Clinical diagnosis and psychotherapy*. Oxford, UK: W. W. Norton.

Klayman, J., & Ha, Y. (1987). Confirmation, disconfirmation, and information in hypothesis testing. *Psychological Review, 94*(2), 211–228.

Kuppens, T., & Pollet, T. V. (2014). Mind the level: Problems with two recent nation-level analyses in psychology. *Frontiers in Psychology, 5*.

Lavin, D. N., Joesting, J. J., Chiu, G. S., Moon, M. L., Meng, J., Dilger, R. N., & Freund, G. G. (2011). Fasting induces an anti-inflammatory effect on the neuroimmune system which a high-fat diet prevents. *Obesity, 19*(8), 1586–1594.

Lawrence, D. H., & Festinger, L. (1962). *Deterrents and reinforcement: The psychology of insufficient reward*. Palo Alto, CA: Stanford University Press.

Lepper, M. R., Greene, D., & Nisbett, R. E. (1973). Undermining children's intrinsic interest with extrinsic reward: A test of the "overjustification" hypothesis. *Journal of Personality and Social Psychology, 28*, 129–137.

Lyubomirsky, S. (2013). *The myths of happiness: What should make you happy, but doesn't, what shouldn't make you happy, but does*. New York: Penguin.

Marsh, H. W. (1987). The big-fish-little-pond effect on academic self-concept. *Journal of Educational Psychology, 79*(3), 280–295.

Marsh, H. W. (2016). Cross-cultural generalizability of year in school effects: Negative effects of acceleration and positive effects of retention on academic self-concept. *Journal of Educational Psychology, 108*(2), 256–273.

Medvec, V. H., Madey, S. F., & Gilovich, T. (1995). When less is more: Counterfactual thinking and satisfaction among Olympic medalists. *Journal of Personality and Social Psychology, 69*(4), 603–610.

Meehl, P. E. (1990). Appraising and amending theories: The strategy of Lakatosian defense and two principles that warrant it. *Psychological Inquiry, 1*(2), 108–141.

Mellers, B., Schwartz, A., & Ritov, I. (1999). Emotion-based choice. *Journal of Experimental Psychology: General, 128*(3), 332–345.

Mitchell, C. J., de Houwer, J., & Lovibond, P. F. (2009). The propositional nature of human associative learning. *Behavioral and Brain Sciences, 32*, 183–198.

Moore, D. A., Swift, S. A., Sharek, Z. S., & Gino, F. (2010). Correspondence bias in performance evaluation: Why grade inflation works. *Personality and Social Psychology Bulletin, 36*(6), 843–852.

Myers, D. G., & Diener, E. (1995). Who is happy? *Psychological Science, 6,* 10–19.

Oishi, S. (2012). *The psychological wealth of nations: Do happy people make a happy society?* New York, NY: Wiley-Blackwell.

Parducci, A. (1965). Category judgment: A range-frequency model. *Psychological Review, 72*(6), 407.

Parducci, A. (1968). The relativism of absolute judgments. *Scientific American, 219,* 84–90.

Platt, J. R. (1964). Strong inference. *Science, 146,* 347–353.

Pleskac, T. J., & Hertwig, R. (2014). Ecologically rational choice and the structure of the environment. *Journal of Experimental Psychology: General, 143*(5), 2000–2019.

Popper, K. R. (1959). *The logic of scientific discovery.* New York, NY: Basic books.

Rescorla, R. A., & Wagner, A. R. (1972). A theory of Pavlovian conditioning: Variations in the effectiveness of reinforcement and nonreinforcement. In A. H. Black & W. F. Prokasy (Eds.), *Classical conditioning II.* New York: Appleton-Century-Crofts, 1972.

Rowe, G., Hirsh, J. B., Anderson, A. K., & Smith, E. E. (2007). Positive affect increases the breadth of attentional selection. *PNAS Proceedings of The National Academy of Sciences of The United States of America, 104*(1), 383–388.

Seligman, M. E. (1970). On the generality of the laws of learning. *Psychological Review, 77*(5), 406–418.

Snyder, M. (1984). When belief creates reality. *Advances in Experimental Social Psychology, 18,* 247–305.

Sonnentag, S., Venz, L., & Casper, A. (2017). Advances in recovery research: What have we learned? What should be done next? *Journal of Occupational Health Psychology, 22*(3), 365–380.

Stewart, N., Chater, N., & Brown, G. A. (2006). Decision by sampling. *Cognitive Psychology, 53*(1), 1–26.

Storbeck, J., & Clore, G. L. (2005). With sadness conies accuracy; with happiness, false memory: Mood and the false memory effect. *Psychological Science, 16*(10), 785–791.

Strack, F., Schwarz, N., & Gschneidinger, E. (1985). Happiness and reminiscing: The role of time perspective, affect, and mode of thinking. *Journal of Personality and Social Psychology, 49*(6), 1460–1469.

Thorndike, E. L. (1927). The law of effect. *The American Journal of Psychology, 39*(1/4), 212–222.

Unkelbach, C., & Fiedler, K. (2017). Contrastive CS-US relations reverse evaluative conditioning effects. *Social Cognition, 34.*

Wason, P. C. (1960). On the failure to eliminate hypotheses in a conceptual task. *The Quarterly Journal of Experimental Psychology, 12,* 129–140.

Wittgenstein, L. (1958). *The Blue and Brown books: Preliminary studies for the "Philosophical Investigations".* Oxford: Basil Blackwood.

5

LIVING LIFE WELL

The Role of Mindfulness and Compassion

Felicia A. Huppert

Introduction

Most of us lead extraordinarily busy lives. We immerse ourselves in our work or studies, in family and social activities, we go to the gym or engage in other forms of physical activity, we may participate in community events or volunteer our time for good causes. It is common to feel we are hurtling through our lives as we strive relentlessly towards our goals, driven by expectations and social pressures. We are spurred on by our 24/7 culture and the ubiquity of mobile technology, including the social media with its addictive quality (Amichai-Hamburger & Etgar, this volume; Dunn & Dwyer, this volume). It has been said that we have become human doings not human beings. The question we need to ask is whether our obsession with doing, striving, and constant busyness is conducive to living well.

The rising rates of stress and distress, and of mental health problems such as anxiety, depression, self-harm, and substance misuse, suggest that for a large part of the population, life is not going well (see also Crano & Donaldson, this volume). Alarmingly, the highest prevalence of these disorders is occurring at an increasingly young age, presumably reflecting the increasing academic and social pressures experienced by young people, along with their high expectations of success, appearance, and material goods (Zisook et al., 2007). Fifty per cent of young adults with psychiatric disorders already have clinically significant psychopathology by 15 years, 75% by age 24 (Kessler et al., 2005). These problems, while manifesting in individual children or adults, have serious repercussions on those around them. Through emotional contagion, our negative affect can spread to family members, friends, workmates, or fellow commuters. High levels of stress or distress make us turn inwards, focusing on ourselves and reducing our ability to care about others. They are also associated with poor physical health and burnout, whose prevalence appears to be increasing among teachers and health care workers, as well as other high-stress occupational groups such as lawyers, social workers, and police officers (Finney et al., 2013; Khamisa, Peltzer, & Oldenburg, 2013; Khan, Yusoff, & Khan, 2014).

So what can we do to bring more balance and tranquillity into our lives? The simple answer is to slow down, reflect, take stock, and make more conscious choices. This view is congruent with ideas passed down from the ancient Greek philosophers, to whom we frequently turn for an authoritative account of the good life. Socrates is reported by Plato to have believed that to "know thyself" is the beginning of all wisdom, and to have said "the unexamined life is not worth living" (Plato, *Apology* 38a). A few decades later, Aristotle said "contemplation is . . . the highest form of activity" (Aristotle, *Ethics*, 10.7). For these Greek philosophers, the good life was not about individual pleasure and the fulfilment of desires, but about using our uniquely human capacity for rationality to make conscious ethical choices which would benefit the whole community (see also Fiedler & Arslan, this volume).

Centuries earlier, Buddhist philosophy had not only identified awareness and contemplation as necessary for living well, but also developed techniques of mental training to support these processes. One of the attractions of Buddhism for many people today is its empirical approach to the good life. In place of dogma, Buddhism invites people to explore for themselves what makes them feel good and act wisely. While a number of Buddhist scholars and teachers have introduced these ideas into the West, Jon Kabat-Zinn is often credited with the widespread adoption of mindfulness as a secular program of mental training. Kabat-Zinn, a biomedical scientist from the University of Massachusetts Medical Center, founded the Mindfulness-Based Stress Reduction Clinic in 1979. The resulting eight-week program, known as Mindfulness-Based Stress Reduction (MBSR), was initially developed for the alleviation of pain and other medical conditions but, over the decades, is being used increasingly to enhance the quality of people's lives in general population settings. The success of the MBSR program, and the closely related Mindfulness-Based Cognitive Therapy (MBCT) program, may be attributable in part to the well-designed curriculum and associated manuals, which have facilitated program fidelity across mindfulness teachers, along with an emphasis from their inception on the importance of scientific research to establish evidence of their benefits. While clinical applications of mindfulness training continue to be prominent (e.g. the NHS National Institute for Health and Clinical Excellence recommends mindfulness training for the treatment of depression), non-clinical applications include its widespread use in education, organisations, sport, and relationship building.

What Is Mindfulness and How Does It Promote Living Well?

Mindfulness is a way of paying attention to our ongoing experience as it unfolds in the moment. We become aware of bodily sensations, of thoughts and emotions in our mind, and of the people, objects, and events in our immediate environment. Being mindful is the antithesis of the state in which most people find themselves—immersed in their memories, thoughts, or plans, swept away by their emotions, barely noticing what is going on around them or inside them, and functioning on automatic pilot. In this state, we tend to react in habitual or impulsive ways rather than pausing and reflecting on the best way to respond. As a result, we may say and do things we later regret, that we would have done differently if we had stepped back and observed our experience rather than being embroiled in the drama of our lives.

Being mindful is a capability, and as with any capability there are wide individual differences in dispositional mindfulness. It has been shown that a high level of dispositional mindfulness is associated with greater well-being (e.g. Brown & Ryan, 2003). However, mindfulness can be learned and strengthened. Mindfulness training usually takes the form of longer or shorter periods of meditation, where participants are invited to adopt a comfortable and upright posture and to focus on one type of experience, such as bodily sensations or the flow of the breath. They are invited to observe their experiences with interest and curiosity, noticing large sensations as well as smaller, more subtle ones, and noticing how the sensations are constantly changing. While trying to focus, they inevitably notice that their mind has wandered, and they are encouraged to notice where it has wandered to, gently bringing their attention back to whatever they were focusing on. The repeated practice of focusing, becoming distracted, noticing the distraction, and returning to their focus is the most basic form of attention training. Mindfulness training may also encompass focusing attention on experiences such as sounds, thoughts, or movement, and in each case, the practice is to really notice the quality and changing nature of whatever one is experiencing, and to keep returning to it despite repeated distraction. An important part of the training is to treat all experiences with equal interest and curiosity, neither clinging to pleasant experiences nor pushing away unpleasant ones (Sahdra, Ciarrochi, & Parker, 2016).

Learning to intentionally control attention can also have more indirect long-term effects, such as an increase in the sense of agency and self-efficacy in relation to unpleasant thoughts and emotions (Allen et al., 2009). These more persisting effects can lead to long-term reductions in suffering.

From the earliest sessions of mindfulness training, a number of important processes are already being developed: awareness, attentional control, and self-regulation. The most fundamental of these is awareness—bodily awareness and self-awareness. This involves a perceptual shift, the ability to stand back from our experience, and this shift promotes emotion regulation and helps us to differentiate between our thoughts and reality (Shonin et al., 2015). Attention training is another fundamental process intrinsic to mindfulness. The attentional processes of focusing, maintaining, and shifting attention can also be viewed as examples of self-regulation training.

Embedding the basic skills of noticing whatever we are experiencing, focusing on these experiences whenever we choose to, and regulating our attention is likely to make us more successful in carrying out the tasks of our daily lives. For example, it has been suggested that situational awareness can increase our ability to understand the physical and social environment, which is likely to lead to better relationships, decision-making, and job performance (Shonin & Van Gordon, 2016). Awareness of our feelings is an important step towards emotion regulation and resulting resilience and mental health outcomes, while awareness of our thoughts is an important step towards clarifying our motivations and values (Nila et al., 2016; Shonin & Van Gordon, 2016). Support for this is provided in a series of experiments by Papies et al. (2015), who found that following mindful attention training participants became more conscious of their motivations and subsequently altered their preferences and made healthier choices. It has further been proposed that mindfulness training can ultimately lead to a deepened capacity for meaning-making and greater engagement in life (Garland et al., 2015).

The What and How of Mindfulness

The above description focuses on what we do when practising mindfulness. This practice leads to the development or strengthening of a number of basic cognitive, metacognitive, and affective skills. These are:

- Awareness of ongoing experience
- Attention to the experience we choose to focus on
- Perceptual shift—"stepping back" from our experience
- Non-reactivity to our experiences ("responding rather than reacting")
- Emotion regulation—managing strong emotions through the application of the above skills

But just as important as *what* we do is *how* we do it. We enact these skills not in a cold, harsh, disinterested manner, but with friendly curiosity and openness, accepting whatever we are experiencing in the moment, without judging it. As we will see later when we discuss the research evidence, it is in large part the curious, kind, and gentle manner in which we observe and relate to our experience that leads to the mental health and well-being benefits of mindfulness training. Avoiding, suppressing, or denying difficult or painful experiences is a common symptom in mental health problems. With mindfulness training, we learn to be as curious about our unpleasant or painful emotions and experiences as about our positive ones, and the kindly attitude we take towards all experiences helps us to work with them rather than push them away (see also Forgas, this volume, on accepting negative emotions). Germer has a sequence of stages in managing difficult emotions: turning towards, noticing, allowing, tolerating, and finally befriending (Germer, 2009).

What Is the Relationship Between Mindfulness and Meditation?

As indicated above, the mental training we call mindfulness involves periods of regular, formal practice, known as meditation. These practices are akin to the regular periods of practice required when training the body. MBSR or MBCT courses typically recommend 20 to 45 minutes of daily formal practice, but as little as 10 minutes a day has been shown to provide benefits (Creswell, 2017; Mrazek et al., 2013; Reitz & Chaskalson, 2016). There are also very short, "on the go" practices that can be used anytime and anywhere, such as the "three-minute briefing space". This is a useful calming, grounding practice, and it can be used before, during, or after any challenging situation or simply as a way of savouring an experience or moving consciously from one task to another, such as from commuting to work, or from work to family. Throughout the day, there are also unlimited opportunities for informal mindfulness practice. We can brush our teeth mindfully, walk mindfully from the parking lot to the office, or mindfully observe the voices and body language of our colleagues in a meeting. In short, we can be mindful without meditating, although the formal and regular practice of meditation is important for achieving mental training.

It is also possible to meditate without being mindful. In contrast to mindfulness meditation, which brings awareness to the full range of our experiences and mental contents, some meditation practices try to block out mental activity (e.g. concentrated focus on a candle flame), while others try to empty the mind. So it is possible to be mindful without meditating, and to meditate without being mindful.

Is Mindfulness Incompatible With Imagination and Future Orientation?

On the surface it may appear that imagination, which involves mentally departing from the present stimulus environment, is incompatible with mindfulness, which involves attending to present moment experience. Yet a deeper understanding of these two concepts makes it clear that they are not mutually exclusive and can work in harmony. The concern seems to be that if we are focusing on experiences in the present moment, we miss out on the important functions served by certain forms of mind wandering, as well as the uniquely human ability to envisage and plan for possible futures. The idea that some forms of mind wandering are beneficial is captured by the term "positive constructive daydreaming", which promotes creativity and allows us to plan for and rehearse possible future scenarios (McMillan et al., 2013).

An important distinction is that between stimulus-dependant experience and self-generated thought. In contrast to what some have assumed, mindfulness is not restricted to mental events triggered by momentary experiences but can also encompass the present experience of various temporal orientations such as past memories and future projections. Remembering, imagining, and future planning can only be done in the present moment. Being mindful of such stimulus-independent thoughts or experiences is a choice we can make (e.g. MacLeod, 2017).

It is helpful to make a distinction between the mind unintentionally drifting off when we are trying to focus on something else (which in excess has been linked to negative affect and lower psychological well-being; Mrazek et al., 2012; Stawarczyk et al., 2012) versus *choosing* to follow a train of thought. Perhaps the misunderstanding about the relationship between mindfulness and the temporal orientation of thoughts has come about through the emphasis on the formal practice that takes place in the early stages of mindfulness training. There is an obvious need to practice grounding our attention and coming back to the breath or bodily sensations (or to some other anchor) in order to learn the attentional skills needed for awareness to emerge. During this early stage of practice, novices are advised to just treat thoughts as thoughts and let them dissipate. As mindfulness practice develops, additional skills are introduced, including open monitoring and reflective thinking. In an investigation comparing the effects of two different styles of attentional monitoring on creative thinking, it was found that in contrast to focused attention, open monitoring induces a control state that promotes divergent thinking, a style of thinking that allows many different ideas to be generated (Colzato, Szapora, & Hommel, 2012). In relation to reflective thinking, there are times when focused attention may be the preferred process and other times where open monitoring, with its wide and spacious focus, may be more helpful. The overall effect of this is to liberate us from habitual or automatic ways of thinking and responding, leaving us free to see more clearly the thoughts that are occurring and then to choose how best to respond to them.

Evidence for the Well-Being Benefits of Mindfulness

Research and application of mindfulness training have grown exponentially over the past decade. Mindfulness programs have become particularly widespread in clinical settings for both physical and mental health problems, in schools for teachers and students, and in business organisations where the focus is often on mindful leadership. For instance, Google has been offering a mindfulness course, "Search Inside Yourself", since 2007, believing that it will enhance personal well-being, effectiveness, and leadership capacity through better judgment and emotional balance, increased emotional and cognitive resilience, and renewed vision to achieve goals and improve creativity and productivity (Tan, 2012). Other applications include its use in sport to enhance performance of both individuals and teams, in relationship building (e.g. couples counselling, mindful parenting), as well as its adoption in high-stress environments such as prisons or the military. Indeed, as with many new ideas, mindfulness has become something of a fad, and many people are jumping on the bandwagon as mindfulness teachers who may be ill equipped to teach it, lacking adequate training or their own personal practice of mindfulness. Being a good mindfulness trainer is not simply about imparting skills and information but also requires a deep understanding of how mental processes are experienced. Without having this deep understanding and a personal practice, it would be difficult or impossible to impart to others an authentic understanding of the principles and practice of present moment awareness (see Crane et al., 2012). Mindfulness is probably at or near the peak of inflated expectations in the "hype cycle", and as always happens, is beginning to come under attack from detractors, who point out that it may not be beneficial for everyone. The key to the sustainability of mindfulness training is the conduct of high-quality research, together with quality control guidelines or accreditation for mindfulness teachers.

The quality of the research has been improving steadily over recent years, with an increasing number of studies using randomised controlled trial (RCT) methodology, often with an active control group. The vast majority of research has been undertaken either in a clinical or an educational context (e.g. Baer, 2015; Weare, 2016), and there is a real need for more research on other applications of mindfulness training, particularly in businesses where this training has become so widely adopted. A recent review of research which focused only on high-quality studies, mainly methodologically rigorous RCTs, has provided some very encouraging results across a variety of outcome measures, including clinical outcomes, cognitive and affective processes, and interpersonal relationships (Creswell, 2017). Key findings can be summarised as follows.

There are clear and large benefits for patients with mental health problems, specifically depression, anxiety, and substance abuse. For example, a recent review finds that following MBCT, patients with a history of recurrent depression were 31% less likely to have a relapse over a 60-week period compared to usual treatment, and 21% less likely compared to an active treatment group (anti-depressant medication or psycho-education; Kuyken et al., 2016). An additional benefit of mindfulness training over anti-depressant medication is that unlike medication, which can only facilitate changes in neural firing but not alter the structure of neural pathways, mindfulness training can create or strengthen neural pathways that are conducive to healthy behaviour (Rossouw, 2013). Mindfulness training also produces large benefits in relation to physical health problems, including chronic pain and high stress, significantly reducing both the subjective experience of pain and stress, and the physiological responses associated with them (Chiesa & Serretti, 2011; Zeidan et al., 2012).

Mindfulness training (MT) has also been shown to increase many of the specific cognitive and affective processes which are the focus of the training, and hypothesised mechanisms through which it exerts its effects. For example, there are improvements on behavioural measures of sustained attention and working memory (Hölzel et al., 2011b; Mrazek et al., 2013), although the evidence does not at present support improvements in other aspects of attention such as set-shifting (Jensen et al., 2012). There is evidence for improved problem-solving following MT (e.g. Ostafin & Kassman, 2012). Numerous studies have shown increases in positive affect and emotion regulation following MT (e.g. Jain et al., 2007; Lindsay & Creswell, 2015).

Although MT focuses primarily on within-person processes, there is evidence of benefit across a range of interpersonal processes. For example, following participation in a mindfulness training program both members of a couple showed significant improvement on survey and daily diary measures of levels of relationship satisfaction, autonomy, relatedness, closeness, and acceptance of one another (Carson et al., 2004). Other studies have shown that MT increased the ability to see things from another person's perspective (Karremans et al., 2016), and the likelihood of undertaking pro-social actions such as giving up a seat in a waiting room to a person on crutches (e.g. Lim et al., 2015).

Less encouraging findings have been reported by Goyal et al. (2014), whose systematic review and meta-analysis was restricted to 47 studies which had an active control group. Although moderate benefits of mindfulness training were found for a range of clinical outcomes (depression, anxiety, and pain), there was no significant effect in relation to positive well-being outcomes. However, of the eight studies which examined positive well-being outcomes, the majority were conducted on small clinical samples, including patients with cancer, organ transplants, depression, and anxiety. Only three studies used non-clinical samples; two showed a significant difference between the mindfulness group and the active control group (Moritz et al., 2006; Delgado et al., 2010), while only one failed to show a difference (Barrett et al., 2012). Further work is needed to establish the reliability of this finding in general population samples, as opposed to clinical samples.

In the Goyal study there was a wide variety of active control conditions, including cognitive behaviour therapy (CBT), anti-depressant medication, psychoeducation, exercise, and various relaxation programs. Overall, mindfulness produced clinical outcomes that were either greater than or equivalent to the effects of these active control conditions. However, in the case of complex interventions such as mindfulness training, great care needs to be taken in selecting active control conditions, since some of the mechanisms through which mindfulness has its effects may be incorporated, inadvertently or otherwise, in the active control condition. A case in point is the work of MacCoon et al. (2012, 2014), who have taken care to design the Health Enhancement Program (HEP), which is structurally very similar to a standard MBSR. Components of HEP include physical activity, music therapy, and nutrition education, but a detailed reading of the program reveals that mindfulness practice is introduced in the music therapy component (mindfulness of sounds), thereby overlapping with a key process in MBSR training (MacCoon et al., 2011).

Neuroscience also supports the conclusion that mindfulness training does indeed have its desired effects. In studies of functional neuroimaging, participants experience short mindfulness-induction procedures (e.g. focusing on the breath) while undergoing magnetic resonance imaging. High levels of activation are seen in specific brain regions and networks which have previously been shown to be involved in the processes of attention control, emotion regulation, and self-awareness (Tang et al., 2015), processes which are hypothesised to change following mindfulness practice. Research has also been undertaken on how long it takes for structural changes in relevant brain regions to be observed. The surprising finding is that by the end of a standard eight-week MBSR course, there are significant increases in the density of grey matter (i.e. strengthened neuronal pathways) in virtually all of the expected regions, including networks associated with cognitive processes (attention, learning, memory), emotion regulation, self-awareness, interoception (bodily awareness), and compassion (Hölzel et al., 2011a).

Overall, the behavioural and neuroscience evidence converges to support the idea that dispositional mindfulness and mindfulness training enhance well-being through the promotion of skills and processes that enable us to live well. These include the basic skills of awareness, attention, and self-regulation, which help us both to savour positive experiences and tolerate unpleasant experiences. It has been suggested that there are "downstream effects of mindfulness on other regulatory processes integral to successful adaptation and flourishing in the world", including meaning-making and engagement with life (Garland et al., 2015, p. 385; see also Baumeister, this volume), which are often regarded as integral to living well. Interpersonal relationships, including perspective taking and compassion, are also enhanced through mindfulness practice, thereby contributing to the well-being of the wider community.

What Is Compassion and How Does It Promote Living Well?

As we have seen, mindfulness alone has been found to produce many well-being benefits, but according to ancient Buddhist teaching, true well-being requires both mindfulness and compassion, and these have been the concerns of many wisdom traditions. The role of compassion is beautifully captured in the quote: "If you want others to be happy, practice compassion. If you want to be happy, practice compassion" (Dalai Lama, 2010).

Modern science supports the view that humans are fundamentally social, and the quality of our relationships has a profound effect on our well-being and the well-being of those around us (see also Simpson et al., and Gable, this volume), with empathy and compassion playing an important role. For example, neuroimaging research has shown that the emotional pain that results from being ostracised produces activation in the same brain regions as physical pain (Eisenberger & Lieberman, 2004). There is also recent evidence that ostracising others causes emotional pain for the ostraciser as well as the ostracised (Legate, DeHaan, Weinstein, & Ryan, 2013; Legate, DeHaan, & Ryan, 2015), and it has been suggested that a possible mechanism of this effect is the empathetic understanding that their act inflicts pain on others and damages relationships (Chen et al., 2014). Feelings of warmth and concern for others produce activation in the reward centres of the brain, as well as regions associated with affiliation and positive affect (Singer & Klimecki, 2014). We later show increased activation in these regions following compassion training.

Self-Compassion

Compassion encompasses not only caring attitudes and behaviours towards others but also a caring and kindly attitude towards ourselves. Many of us take a very harsh, self-critical attitude towards ourselves when we suffer, fail, or feel inadequate. Self-compassion is the ability to treat yourself in the same kind and caring way you would treat a dear friend who is suffering, along with the recognition that suffering and personal inadequacy is part of the shared human experience (Neff, 2003). The most widely used self-compassion program, Mindful Self-Compassion (MSC), recognises that mindfulness is crucial to the ability to give oneself compassion. It is based on the eight-week structure of the standard MBSR program and includes both formal (sitting meditation) and informal (during daily life) self-compassion practices. According to the authors, "the program makes it clear how judging oneself when things go wrong tends to exacerbate emotional pain, while self-compassion helps to alleviate that pain" (Neff & Germer, 2013, p. 31).

Compassion Towards Others

Compassion towards others is characterised by feelings of warmth and concern for the other, as well as a strong motivation to help. This contrasts with empathy, which is *sharing* the feelings of another. Empathic responses can be seen in very young children and appear to be hard-wired, having probably evolved to enable us to understand what is going on in someone else's mind (e.g. de Waal, 2010). Empathy may be a prerequisite for compassion, but sharing someone's pain can be distressing, so if a person stays in empathy this can lead to withdrawal, avoidance, and burnout (Singer & Klimecki, 2014). Further, there is evidence that there are entirely different patterns of brain activation following empathy training compared to compassion training (Singer & Klimecki, 2014).

The most widely used program to enhance compassion towards others is probably loving-kindness meditation (LKM), which derives from an ancient Buddhist practice that involves goodwill or well-wishing (Salzberg, 2011). The LKM training usually begins with wishing oneself well, then extending the practice to a loved one, to a neutral person, and finally to someone with whom one has a difficult relationship. Many people find the practice very challenging, and experience a sense of failure (Galante et al., 2014), possibly because they are unable to *feel* loving towards all these people. However, although unconditional love might be seen as the long-term goal of this meditation practice, teachers often find it helpful to emphasise that loving kindness is an intention of well-wishing rather than a feeling of love.

It is interesting to consider how this view compares with Greek philosophy. In the following quote Aristotle differentiates between goodwill on the one hand, and friendship and love/affection on the other:

> Goodwill appears to be an element of friendly feeling, but it is not the same thing as friendship; for it can be felt towards strangers, and it can be unknown to its object, whereas friendship cannot . . . Neither is goodwill the same as affection. For it has no intensity, nor does it include desire, but these things are necessarily involved in affection.
>
> *(Aristotle, Nicomanchean Ethics, 9.5)*

Evidence for the Well-Being Benefits of Compassion

Practising self-compassion is integral to mindfulness training, and this is evident in the kindly, gentle attitude taken towards difficult experiences. Research demonstrates that an increase in self-compassion is the principal mediator of the effect of mindfulness training on relapse prevention in depressed patients (Kuyken et al., 2010). Self-compassion also produces benefits on positive well-being. A study examining mindfulness training in a non-clinical adolescent sample showed that change in self-compassion was found to be a stronger predictor of well-being outcomes than change in mindfulness (Galla, 2016). A recent systematic review and meta-analysis concluded that self-compassion training produced significant increases in optimism, self-efficacy, life satisfaction, and happiness (Zessin et al., 2015). There is also evidence that short self-compassion exercises can produce beneficial effects on well-being. For example, a lab-based self-compassion induction increased motivation to change behaviour for the better (Breines & Chen, 2012), and a one-week self-compassion program increased happiness for up to six months compared to an active control group (Shapira & Mongrain, 2010).

Turning to compassion towards others, there is evidence that compassionate feelings and helping behaviour increase well-being. In a randomised controlled trial conducted with employees in an information technology company, Fredrickson and colleagues (2008) found that training in loving-kindness meditation produced increases in positive emotions and life satisfaction, as well as purpose in life and social support, and decreased symptoms of depression and physical illness (see also Fredrickson, this volume). A systematic review of the effects of compassion meditations found significant improvements across five psychological outcomes: positive and negative affect, psychological distress, positive thinking, interpersonal relations, and a performance measure of empathic accuracy (Shonin et al., 2015). In addition, compassion meditations have been shown to increase pro-social behaviour (Jazaieri et al., 2013; Leiberg et al., 2011), and pro-social behaviour is known to improve interpersonal and social well-being. There is also evidence for a direct benefit of pro-social behaviour on the helper (Weinstein & Ryan, 2010). In other words, doing good makes us feel good.

Compassion interventions are being embraced in the contexts of education and business organisations. In schools, this may be in part a response to ineffective anti-bullying programs, which have tended to focus on the reduction of harm, rather than taking a more positive approach and promoting kindness. The new programs usually combine mindfulness and compassion. A 12-week randomised controlled trial of a Kindness Curriculum on a small sample of pre-school children found significant benefits to pro-social behaviour and relationships, as well as to cognitive flexibility and delayed gratification, a self-regulation capability (Flook et al., 2015). Among primary school students, a randomised trial of the Call to Care program showed significant decreases in symptoms of stress and anxiety, along with large reductions in prejudice and stereotyping, and an increased willingness to help the "out-group" (Berger & Tarrach, 2017; Berger et al., 2017). Similar effects in both adults and children have been reported in an earlier generation of studies, which used the term "empathy training" (e.g. Stephan & Finlay, 1999), although the earlier studies did not differentiate between empathy and compassion.

The interpersonal process of compassion has recently received substantial attention from organisational researchers and practitioners (Dutton et al., 2014). The research at present appears to be limited to anecdotal reports, or qualitative surveys of pre-existing institutional approaches towards handling employee suffering. To date, there are no published reports of the organisational benefits of compassion training offered to employees. A study by Fredrickson et al. (2008) did offer loving-kindness meditation to employees in an IT organisation, but the study outcomes were focused on individual benefits rather than organisational benefits. A recently published volume, *Awakening Compassion at Work: The Quiet Power That Elevates People and Organizations* (Worline & Dutton, 2017), makes a compelling case for why compassion training should be encouraged in the organisational context, and the authors highlight the need for high-quality research in this field.

Conclusion: The Interconnectedness of Mindfulness, Compassion, and Living Well

Mindfulness and compassion should be viewed as complementary practices. As we have seen, self-compassion is an integral part of mindfulness training, and now an increasing number of mindfulness programs are incorporating explicit training in compassion towards others. This combined approach acknowledges that well-being arises in part from the relationship we have with our ongoing experience, and in part from the way we respond to and act towards others. One hypothesis is that compassion meditation interventions affect outcomes primarily via positive affect mechanisms, whereas mindfulness interventions affect outcomes primarily through metacognitive awareness and decentring mechanisms (Feldman et al., 2010; Creswell, 2017).

In this chapter, I have briefly explored two ancient well-being practices, mindfulness and compassion. I have shown that the skills people learn are so fundamental, and their impacts on daily life so wide-ranging, that these practices could be regarded as foundational for living life well. After all, what could be more foundational mental skills than awareness, attention, and self-regulation? And what could be more foundational to relationships than empathy and acting with kindness?

Mindfulness and compassion science are relatively new endeavours, and there is much further work to be done at all levels of potential impact—individual, interpersonal, organisational, and societal. Funding for larger, long-term studies should be regarded as a priority, to establish the most effective training methods and the breadth and sustainability of their effects. Nevertheless, the existing evidence of foundational benefits from mindfulness and compassion training suggests that if we genuinely desire to improve individual well-being and reduce social ills such as hatred, intolerance, violence, and greed, we would do well to consider embracing and extending these programs, while maintaining the quality and integrity of the training.

This chapter has emphasised the contribution of psychological processes to how well our lives are going, but of course, external circumstances also play a role. None has received more attention than economic factors, and innumerable national and international studies have shown that measures of wealth, such as income and income inequality, are related to measures of well-being and life satisfaction (Huppert, 2014; Oishi & Kesebir, 2015). It is worth asking what economic policy would look like if it prioritised well-being. Singer (2015) has recently set out a vision of what life could be like if we had a caring economy, based on the principles of mindfulness and compassion. There is a real chance that the widespread adoption of the foundational skills described in this chapter could support this vision, increasing the numbers of happy, fulfilled, socially responsible individuals and thriving, productive, inclusive organisations and communities.

Bibliography

Allen, M., Bromley, A., Kuyken, W., & Sonnenberg, S. J. (2009). Participants' experiences of mindfulness-based cognitive therapy: It changed me in just about every way possible. *Behavioural and Cognitive Psychotherapy*, *37*, 413–430.

Aristotle (1934). *Aristotle in 23 Volumes* (Vol. 19, H. Rackham, Trans.). Cambridge, MA: Harvard University Press; London: William Heinemann Ltd.

Baer, R. A. (Ed.). (2015). *Mindfulness-based treatment approaches: Clinician's guide to evidence base and applications*. San Diego, CA: Academic Press.

Barrett, B., Hayney, M. S., Muller, D., Rakel, D., Ward, A., Obasi, C. N., . . . Coe, C. L. (2012). Meditation or exercise for preventing acute respiratory infection: A randomized controlled trial. *Annals of Family Medicine*, *10*(4), 337–346.

Berger, R., & Tarrach, R. (2017). *Enhancing resiliency, well being and pro-social behavior among Israeli elementary school children by using a mindfulness and compassion-based program: Call to Care—Israel.*

Berger, R., Brenick, A., & Tarrach, R. (2017). *Reducing stereotyping and prejudice among Israeli-Jewish elementary school children via a mindfulness and compassion-based program.*

Breines, J. G., & Chen, S. (2012). Self-compassion increases self-improvement motivation. *Personality and Social Psychology Bulletin, 38*(9), 1133–1143.

Brown, K. W., & Ryan, R. M., 2003. The benefits of being present: Mindfulness and its role in psychological well-being. *Journal of personality and social psychology, 84*(4), 822.

Carson, J. W., Carson, K. M., Gil, K. M., & Baucom, D. H. (2004). Mindfulness-based relationship enhancement. *Behavior Therapy, 35*(3), 471–494.

Chen, Z., Poon, K. T., Bernstein, M. J., & Teng, F. (2014). Rejecting another pains the self: The impact of perceived future rejection. *Journal of Experimental Social Psychology, 50,* 225–233.

Chiesa, A., & Serretti, A. (2011). Mindfulness-based interventions for chronic pain: A systematic review of the evidence. *The Journal of Alternative and Complementary Medicine, 17*(1), 83–93.

Colzato, L. S., Szapora, A., & Hommel, B. (2012). Meditate to create: The impact of focused-attention and open-monitoring training on convergent and divergent thinking. *Frontiers in Psychology, 3,* 116.

Crane, R. S., Kuyken, W., Williams, J. M. G., Hastings, R. P., Cooper, L., & Fennell, M. J. (2012). Competence in teaching mindfulness-based courses: Concepts, development and assessment. *Mindfulness, 3*(1), 76–84.

Creswell, J. D. (2017). Mindfulness interventions. *Annual Review of Psychology, 68,* 491–516.

Dalai Lama. (2010). Retrieved from https://twitter.com/dalailama/status/193352334972 10880

Delgado, L. C., Guerra, P., Perakakis, P., Vera, M. N., Reyes del Paso, G., & Vila, J. (2010). Treating chronic worry: Psychological and physiological effects of a training programme based on mindfulness. *Behaviour Research and Therapy, 48*(9), 873–882.

De Waal, F. (2010). *The age of empathy: Nature's lessons for a kinder society.* New York, NY: Broadway Books.

Dutton, J. E., Workman, K. M., & Hardin, A. E. (2014). Compassion at work. *Annual Review of Organizational Psychology and Organizational Behavior, 1*(1), 277–304.

Eisenberger, N. I., & Lieberman, M. D. (2004). Why rejection hurts: A common neural alarm system for physical and social pain. *Trends in Cognitive Sciences, 8*(7), 294–300.

Feldman, G., Greeson, J., & Senville, J. (2010). Differential effects of mindful breathing, progressive muscle relaxation, and loving-kindness meditation on decentering and negative reactions to repetitive thoughts. *Behaviour Research and Therapy, 48*(10), 1002–1011.

Finney, C., Stergiopoulos, E., Hensel, J., Bonato, S., & Dewa, C. S. (2013). Organizational stressors associated with job stress and burnout in correctional officers: A systematic review. *BMC Public Health, 13*(1), 82.

Flook, L., Goldberg, S. B., Pinger, L., & Davidson, R. J. (2015). Promoting prosocial behavior and self-regulatory skills in preschool children through a mindfulness-based kindness curriculum. *Developmental Psychology, 51*(1), 44.

Fredrickson, B. L., Cohn, M. A., Coffey, K. A., Pek, J., & Finkel, S. M. (2008). Open hearts build lives: Positive emotions, induced through loving-kindness meditation, build consequential personal resources. *Journal of Personality and Social Psychology, 95*(5), 1045.

Galante, J., Galante, I., Bekkers, M. J., & Gallacher, J. (2014). Effect of kindness-based meditation on health and well-being: A systematic review and meta-analysis. *Journal of consulting and clinical psychology, 82*(6), 1101.

Galla, B. M., 2016. Within-person changes in mindfulness and self-compassion predict enhanced emotional well-being in healthy, but stressed adolescents. *Journal of Adolescence*, *49*, 204–217.

Garland, E. L., Farb, N. A., Goldin, P. R., & Fredrickson, B. L. (2015). The mindfulness-to-meaning theory: Extensions, applications, and challenges at the attention—appraisal—emotion interface. *Psychological Inquiry*, *26*(4), 377–387.

Germer, C. K. (2009). *The mindful path to self-compassion: Freeing yourself from destructive thoughts and emotions.* New York, NY: Guilford Press.

Gilbert, P. (2014). The origins and nature of compassion focused therapy. *British Journal of Clinical Psychology*, *53*(1), 6–41.

Goyal, M., Singh, S., Sibinga, E. M., Gould, N. F., Rowland-Seymour, A., Sharma, R., . . . Ranasinghe, P. D. (2014). Meditation programs for psychological stress and well-being: A systematic review and meta-analysis. *JAMA Internal Medicine*, *174*(3), 357–368.

Hölzel, B. K., Carmody, J., Vangel, M., Congleton, C., Yerramsetti, S. M., Gard, T., & Lazar, S. W. (2011a). Mindfulness practice leads to increases in regional brain gray matter density. *Psychiatry Research: Neuroimaging*, *191*(1), 36–43.

Hölzel, B. K., Lazar, S. W., Gard, T., Schuman-Olivier, Z., Vago, D. R., & Ott, U. (2011b). How does mindfulness meditation work? Proposing mechanisms of action from a conceptual and neural perspective. *Perspectives on Psychological Science*, *6*(6), 537–559.

Huppert, F. A. (2014). The state of wellbeing science: Concepts, measures, interventions, and policies. *Interventions and Policies to Enhance Well-Being*, *6*, 1–49.

Jain, S., Shapiro, S. L., Swanick, S., Roesch, S. C., Mills, P. J., & Schwartz, G. E. (2007). A randomized controlled trial of mindfulness meditation versus relaxation training: Effects on distress, positive states of mind, rumination, and distraction. *Annals of Behavioral Medicine*, *33*(1), 11–21.

Jazaieri, H., Jinpa, G. T., McGonigal, K., Rosenberg, E. L., Finkelstein, J., Simon-Thomas, E., . . . Goldin, P. R. (2013). Enhancing compassion: A randomized controlled trial of a compassion cultivation training program. *Journal of Happiness Studies*, *14*(4), 1113–1126.

Jensen, C. G., Vangkilde, S., Frokjaer, V., & Hasselbalch, S. G. (2012). Mindfulness training affects attention—or is it attentional effort? *Journal of Experimental Psychology: General*, *141*(1), 106–123.

Karremans, J. C., Schellekens, M. P. J., & Kappen, G. (2016). Bridging the sciences of mindfulness and romantic relationships: A theoretical model and research agenda. *Personality and Social Psychology Review* doi:10.1177/1088868315615450

Kessler, R. C., Berglund, P., Demler, O., Jin, R., Merikangas, K. R., & Walters, E. E. (2005). Lifetime prevalence and age-of-onset distributions of DSM-IV disorders in the National Co-morbidity Survey replication. *Archives of General Psychiatry*, *62*, 593–602.

Khamisa, N., Peltzer, K., & Oldenburg, B. (2013). Burnout in relation to specific contributing factors and health outcomes among nurses: A systematic review. *International Journal of Environmental Research and Public Health*, *10*(6), 2214–2240.

Khan, F., Yusoff, R. M., & Khan, A. (2014). Job demands, burnout and resources in teaching a conceptual review. *World Applied Sciences Journal*, *30*(1), 20–28.

Kuyken, W., Warren, F. C., Taylor, R. S., Whalley, B., Crane, C., Bondolfi, G., . . . Segal, Z. (2016). Efficacy of mindfulness-based cognitive therapy in prevention of depressive relapse: An individual patient data meta-analysis from randomized trials. *JAMA Psychiatry*, *73*(6), 565–574.

Kuyken, W., Watkins, E., Holden, E., White, K., Taylor, R. S., Byford, S., . . . & Dalgleish, T. (2010). How does mindfulness-based cognitive therapy work? *Behaviour Research and Therapy*, *48*(11), 1105–1112.

Legate, N., DeHaan, C., & Ryan, R. (2015). Righting the wrong: Reparative coping after going along with ostracism. *The Journal of Social Psychology, 155*(5), 471–482.

Legate, N., DeHaan, C. R., Weinstein, N., & Ryan, R. M. (2013). Hurting you hurts me too: The psychological costs of complying with ostracism. *Psychological Science, 24*(4), 583–588.

Leiberg, S., Klimecki, O., & Singer, T. (2011). Short-term compassion training increases prosocial behavior in a newly developed prosocial game. *PloS One, 6*(3), e17798.

Lim, D., Condon, P., & DeSteno, D. (2015). Mindfulness and compassion: An examination of mechanism and scalability. *PloS One, 10*(2), e0118221.

Lindsay, E. K., & Creswell, J. D. (2015). Back to the basics: How attention monitoring and acceptance stimulate positive growth. *Psychological Inquiry, 26*(4), 343–348.

MacCoon, D., Sullivan, J., Lutz, A., Stoney, C. M., Johnson, L. L., Christmas, P., Thurlow, J., & Davidson, R. (2011). *Health-enhancement program (HEP) guidelines.* Madison: University of Wisconsin.

MacCoon, D. G., Imel, Z. E., Rosenkranz, M. A., Sheftel, J. G., Weng, H. Y., Sullivan, J. C., . . . Lutz, A. (2012). The validation of an active control intervention for Mindfulness Based Stress Reduction (MBSR). *Behaviour Research and Therapy, 50*(1), 3–12.

MacCoon, D. G., MacLean, K. A., Davidson, R. J., Saron, C. D., & Lutz, A. (2014). No sustained attention differences in a longitudinal randomized trial comparing mindfulness based stress reduction versus active control. *PloS One, 9*(6), e97551.

MacLeod, A. (2017). *Prospection, well-being, and mental health.* Oxford, UK: Oxford University Press.

McMillan, R., Kaufman, S. B., & Singer, J. L. (2013). Ode to positive constructive daydreaming. *Frontiers in Psychology, 4*, 626.

Mooneyham, B. W., & Schooler, J. W. (2013). The costs and benefits of mind-wandering: A review. *Canadian Journal of Experimental Psychology / Revue canadienne de psychologie expérimentale, 67*(1), 11.

Moritz, S., Quan, H., Rickhi, B., Liu, M., Angen, M., Vintila, R., . . . Toews, J. (2006). A home study-based spirituality education program decreases emotional distress and increases quality of life: A randomized, controlled trial. *Altern Therapies in Health and Medicine 12*(6), 26–35.

Mrazek, M. D., Franklin, M. S., Phillips, D. T., Baird, B., & Schooler, J. W. (2013). Mindfulness training improves working memory capacity and GRE performance while reducing mind wandering. *Psychological Science, 24*(5), 776–781.

Mrazek, M. D., Smallwood, J., & Schooler, J. W. (2012). Mindfulness and mind-wandering: Finding convergence through opposing constructs. *Emotion, 12*(3), 442.

Neff, K. D. (2003). Self-compassion: An alternative conceptualization of a healthy attitude toward oneself. *Self and Identity, 2*(2), 85–101.

Neff, K. D., & Germer, C. K. (2013). A pilot study and randomized controlled trial of the mindful self-compassion program. *Journal of Clinical Psychology, 69*(1), 28–44.

Nila, K., Holt, D. V., Ditzen, B., & Aguilar-Raab, C. (2016). Mindfulness-Based Stress Reduction (MBSR) enhances distress tolerance and resilience through changes in mindfulness. *Mental Health & Prevention, 4*(1), 36–41.

Oishi, S., & Kesebir, S. (2015). Income inequality explains why economic growth does not always translate to an increase in happiness. *Psychological Science,* 0956797615596713.

Ostafin, B. D., & Kassman, K. T. (2012). Stepping out of history: Mindfulness improves insight problem solving. *Consciousness and Cognition, 21*(2), 1031–1036.

Papies, E. K., Pronk, T. M., Keesman, M., & Barsalou, L. W. (2015). The benefits of simply observing: Mindful attention modulates the link between motivation and behavior. *Journal of Personality and Social Psychology, 108*(1), 148.

Plato. (1966). *Plato in twelve volumes* (Vol. 1, Harold North Fowler, Trans.). Introduction by W. R. M. Lamb. Cambridge, MA: Harvard University Press; London: William Heinemann Ltd.

Reitz, M., & Chaskalson, M. (2016). How to bring mindfulness to your company's leadership. *Harvard Business Review.* Retrieved from https://hbr.org/2016/12/how-to-bring-mindfulness-to-your-companys-leadership

Rossouw, P. J. (2013). The end of the medical model? Recent findings in neuroscience regarding antidepressant medication: Implications for Neuropsychotherapy. *Neuropsychotherapy in Australia,* (19), 3–10.

Sahdra, B., Ciarrochi, J., & Parker, P. (2016). Nonattachment and mindfulness: Related but distinct constructs. *Psychological Assessment, 28*(7), 819.

Salzberg, S. (2011). Mindfulness and loving-kindness. *Contemporary Buddhism, 12*(01), 177–182.

Seligman, M. E., Railton, P., Baumeister, R. F., & Sripada, C. (2013). Navigating into the future or driven by the past. *Perspectives on Psychological Science, 8*(2), 119–141.

Shapira, L. B., & Mongrain, M. (2010). The benefits of self-compassion and optimism exercises for individuals vulnerable to depression. *The Journal of Positive Psychology, 5*(5), 377–389.

Shonin, E., & Van Gordon, W. (2016). The mechanisms of mindfulness in the treatment of mental illness and addiction. *International Journal of Mental Health and Addiction,* 1–6.

Shonin, E., Van Gordon, W., Compare, A., Zangeneh, M., & Griffiths, M. D. (2015). Buddhist-derived loving-kindness and compassion meditation for the treatment of psychopathology: A systematic review. *Mindfulness, 6*(5), 1161–1180.

Singer, P. (2015). How to build a caring economy. *World Economic Forum.* Retrieved from www.weforum.org/agenda/2015/01/how-to-build-a-caring-economy/

Singer, T., & Klimecki, O. M. (2014). Empathy and compassion. *Current Biology, 24*(18), R875–R878.

Smallwood, J., & Andrews-Hanna, J. (2013). Not all minds that wander are lost: The importance of a balanced perspective on the mind-wandering state. *Frontiers in Psychology, 4,* 441.

Stawarczyk, D., Majerus, S., Van der Linden, M., & D'Argembeau, A. (2012). Using the daydreaming frequency scale to investigate the relationships between mind-wandering, psychological well-being, and present-moment awareness. *Frontiers in Psychology, 3,* 363.

Stephan, W. G., & Finlay, K. (1999). The role of empathy in improving intergroup relations. *Journal of Social issues, 55*(4), 729–743.

Tan, C. M. (2012). *Search inside yourself.* New York, NY: Harper Collins.

Tang, Y. Y., Hölzel, B. K., & Posner, M. I. (2015). The neuroscience of mindfulness meditation. *Nature Reviews Neuroscience, 16*(4), 213–225.

Weare, K. (2016). Mindfulness in education. In M. A. West (Ed.), *The psychology of meditation: Research and practice* (pp. 259–281). Oxford: Oxford University Press.

Weinstein, N., & Ryan, R. M. (2010). When helping helps: Autonomous motivation for prosocial behavior and its influence on well-being for the helper and recipient. *Journal of Personality and Social Psychology, 98*(2), 222.

Worline, M., & Dutton, J. E. (2017). *Awakening compassion at work: The quiet power that elevates people and organizations.* Oakland, CA: Berrett-Koehler Publishers.

Zeidan, F., Grant, J. A., Brown, C. A., McHaffie, J. G., & Coghill, R. C. (2012). Mindfulness meditation-related pain relief: Evidence for unique brain mechanisms in the regulation of pain. *Neuroscience Letters, 520*(2), 165–173.

Zessin, U., Dickhäuser, O., & Garbade, S. (2015). The relationship between self-compassion a nd well-being: A meta-analysis. *Applied Psychology: Health and Well-Being, 7*(3), 340–364.

Zisook, S., Lesser, I., Stewart, J. W., Wisniewski, S. R., Balasubramani, G. K., Fava, M., . . . Trivedi, M. H. (2007). Effect of age at onset on the course of major depressive disorder. *American Journal of Psychiatry, 164*(10), 1539–1546.

PART II
The Role of Purposeful Activities in Living Well

6

FOR WHAT IT'S WORTH

The Regulatory Pleasure and Purpose of a Good Life

James Shah

> When one does not know what harbor one is making for, no wind is the right wind.
>
> —Seneca

Why is living a good life often so challenging? Why might it be difficult, at times, even to define? Research and theorizing in social psychology on the nature of well-being have long understood that pursing a good life involves more than simply the continued pursuit of good times (see Baumeister; Forgas & Arslan; and Forgas, this volume). Indeed, much of this work has distinguished a hedonic sense of well-being, which emphasizes the actual experience of positivity in a good life (for instance, Diener, Suh, Lucas & Smith, 1999; Kahneman, Diener & Schwarz, 1999), from a eudaemonic sense, which focuses on the process, and purpose, of living such a life (see Baumeister, Vohs, Aaker & Garbinsky, 2013; Cheung, 2010; Deci & Ryan, 2008; Gallagher, Lopez & Preacher, 2009; Keyes, Shmotkin & Ryff, 2002; Ryan, Huta & Deci, 2006; Ryff, 1989; but also Sheldon, this volume). The approach outlined here elaborates on this distinction by considering recent work on the nature and process of self-regulation in order to better understand not only how individuals may come to define the good life, but how they pursue and experience it and why they may be challenged by it.

The Pleasure and Purpose of a Good Life

The current approach starts by assuming that individuals have a varied sense of the good life that nevertheless is ultimately defined in terms of what makes them happy and what gives them purpose and meaning. Clearly a good life is one that involves positivity and personal happiness, and models of well-being have traditionally acknowledged the significance of hedonic experience (see Diener, 1984, 2000). The recent rise in interest for positive psychological processes has renewed focus in social psychology on the benefits of happiness and positive affective experiences for general well-being (Lyubomirsky, King & Diener, 2005; Fredrickson, this volume). In a review of the literature, for instance, Lyubomirsky et al. (2005) found happiness to be associated with a wide variety of successful work, health and social outcomes. Similarly, Fredrickson's (2001, 2004) broaden-and-build theory proposes that the positive emotions commonly associated with the good life, such as enjoyment and happiness, generally encourage novel and exploratory thought and behavior that may promote skill development and mastery over time. Pleasant social interactions, for example, may encourage future interactions and ultimately help to refine the social skills required to navigate these interactions smoothly. Research has also suggested, however, that the pursuit of happiness and positivity can prove surprisingly challenging (see Fiedler & Arslan, this volume; Gilbert, 2006). Work by Gilbert, Wilson and their colleagues, for instance, has found that individuals often fail to understand exactly what will make them happy (Wilson & Gilbert 2003) and overestimate how long and how consistently happiness may last (see Quoidbach, Gilbert & Wilson 2013). We may also hold mistaken beliefs about how choice impacts our well-being and the ultimate control we have over our own happiness (see Schwartz, Ward, Monterosso, Lyubomirsky, White & Lehman, 2002). A good life defined solely in terms of levels of happiness and positivity, then, may be one that individuals often have difficulty realizing and maintaining. Moreover, such a life may also prove to be costly, as the motivation literature has long recognized that negativity and negative emotions can often serve productive self-regulatory ends (see, for instance, Oettingen, 2015; Forgas, this volume).

Like other recent eudaimonic approaches to well-being, then, the current approach assumes that the good life is one that not only provides positivity but also purpose in fulfilling fundamental regulatory needs (see also Emmons, 1986; McGregor, McAdams & Little, 2006; Romero, Villar, Luengo & Gómez-Fraguela, 2009; Steger, Kashdan & Oishi, 2008). Indeed, the self-regulatory purpose of a good life may determine how such a life is ultimately lived, how it impacts daily behavior and experience, and the role it plays in general well-being. In this assumption, the current approach is similar to other recent perspectives on the good life that have focused on the purpose of pursuing it and the process through which it is best realized. Research on self-determination and self-concordance, for instance, has assumed that well-being is linked to the pursuit and fulfillment of intrinsic needs for autonomy, connectedness and growth (see Deci & Ryan, 2000; Sheldon & Houser-Marko, 2001). From this perspective, a good life is one that addresses individuals' intrinsic needs. Perceiving how one's life should be shaped to address such needs may pose an ongoing challenge, especially given the pervasiveness of extrinsic pressures and rewards. Indeed, studies spanning elementary through medical school, a variety of workplace settings and a diversity of cultures have consistently demonstrated that goals motivated for autonomous reasons (vs. controlled reasons) may be pursued differently than when pursued for extrinsic reasons. Intrinsic goals may be pursued more creatively (Amabile, 1983), for instance, with more cognitive flexibility and depth (Grolnick & Ryan, 1987; McGraw & McCullers, 1979; Williams & Deci, 1996), and with more perseverance (Vallerand & Bissonnette, 1992). Grolnick and Ryan (1987) found that students who were more autonomous in reading text material showed greater conceptual understanding of the material than those who were more externally motivated (see also Black & Deci, 2000; Grolnick, Ryan & Deci, 1991). Similarly, Ryan and Connell (1989) found that although both internally and externally motivated children adopted achievement goals in the classroom, children's external motivation for pursuing classroom goals was positively correlated with anxiety in school and maladaptive coping with failures, whereas their internal motivation was positively correlated with enjoyment of school and proactive coping with failures.

Perhaps it is not surprising, then, that the pursuit of intrinsically motivated goals is ultimately linked to more satisfaction (Deci, Connell & Ryan, 1989) as well as greater well-being and self-esteem (Deci, Nezlek & Sheinman, 1981; Langer & Rodin, 1976). Sheldon and Elliot (1999) reported that more intrinsic (autonomous) reasons for pursing achievement goals among college students (rather than external reasons) were associated with more goal commitment and goal attainment. Moreover, Sheldon and Kasser (1998) found that when students were more intrinsically motivated in their goal pursuits they made more goal-related progress and this progress had more positive effects on well-being (relative to those motivated for external reasons). Such findings inspired the self-concordance model (see Sheldon & Elliot, 1999; Sheldon & Houser-Marko, 2001), which asserts that when individuals pursue self-concordant goals (i.e., goals consistent with their intrinsic motivations) they do so with more effort and with greater likelihood of attainment. Moreover, such attainment is more likely to benefit well-being. In this model, then, well-being depends not only on realizing one's goals but realizing the "right" goals, those that satisfy intrinsic needs for autonomy, competence, relatedness and meaning (see also Baumeister, this volume). Supporting their model, Sheldon and Houser-Marko (2001) found evidence for an "upward spiral" in students' pursuit of self-concordant goals. Incoming freshmen with self-concordant goals for their first semester were more likely to attain them, which in turn predicted increased psychological adjustment as well as even greater self-concordance for the next semester's goals. This increase in self-concordance was linked to even greater goal attainment during students' second semester, which led to further increases in psychological adjustment by the end of the year. The benefits of self-concordance, then, are not only immediate but may build over time. Ryan, Huta and Deci (2006) have suggested that a good life should be defined by how it satisfies basic needs for competence, relatedness and autonomy, how it encourages the pursuit of intrinsic goals for personal growth, relationships, community and health (rather than extrinsic goals, such as wealth, fame, image and power), and how it supports autonomous, volitional, consensual behavior as well as a general sense of awareness. Yet these need-based life assessments may themselves prove challenging. Work on self-infiltration, for instance, has suggested that individuals can often be mistaken in the inferences they make about their own needs, confusing them with the desires and needs others may have for them (Baumann & Kuhl, 2003).

The Focus of a Good Life

The approach taken here is inspired by research and theorizing on regulatory focus theory (see Higgins, 1997), which also encourages a definition of the good life that emphasizes its underlying regulatory purpose (see Higgins, Cornwell & Franks, 2014). Regulatory focus theory proposes that individuals develop distinct regulatory systems in pursuit of basic needs for achievement and gain (promotion), and for safety and security (prevention). Individuals' promotion focus on achievement and gain is, in turn, represented by their hopes, wishes and aspirations (labeled their "ideals"). Alternatively, individuals' prevention focus on safety and security is defined by their duties, responsibilities and obligations (collectively labeled individuals' "oughts"). The theory suggests that individuals may differ in their focus on promotion and prevention either because the situation calls for it (as when they are in immediate danger or sense a golden opportunity) or because of chronic differences that arise from distinct histories of punishment and reward (as may arise, for instance, because of differences in parental discipline and affection). Differences in individuals' focus on promotion and prevention in turn may affect how they respond to everyday events. Outcomes may be experienced quite differently when seen in terms of one's promotion needs for advancement and gain or in terms of one's prevention needs for safety and security. Indeed, considerable research over the last two decades has examined how differences in regulatory focus may influence the process of self-regulation from beginning to end: from goal adoption to ongoing pursuit to the emotional consequences of successful and unsuccessful outcomes (see Higgins, 2014).

Perceiving the good life in terms of how it addresses fundamental needs for promotion and prevention may not only shape what one looks for in such a life, it may ultimately impact the strategies and behaviors one employs in pursuing it and the experiences one has in living it. Indeed, past research has suggested that whereas a promotion focus is associated with eagerness-related strategies for goal attainment, a prevention focus is associated with strategic vigilance (see Higgins, 1997). Freitas, Liberman, Salovey and Higgins (2002), for instance, found that participants with a prevention focus prefer to initiate goal pursuit more quickly than individuals with a promotion focus, presumably because duties and obligations often demand immediate fulfillment. Consistent with a tendency towards eagerness, Förster, Higgins and Bianco (2003) have found that a promotion focus is associated with a preference for speed in completing task goals. Consistent with a tendency for vigilance, however, a prevention focus was associated with a preference for accuracy.

Taken together, then, past research has suggested that duties and obligations demand immediate, careful attention, whereas ideals and aspirations may often be more flexibly pursued (see also Shah & Kruglanski, 2000a). Of course, living the good life involves more than the use of general strategies. Like other pursuits, they must also invoke specific behavior and action. Here, too, regulatory focus may play an important role. Shah, Higgins and Friedman (1998) examined how regulatory focus affected the specific ways in which goals were pursued behaviorally. In particular, they found that whereas promotion-focused individuals eagerly employed approach-related means in pursuing their ideals, prevention-focused individuals more vigilantly pursued duties and obligations via avoidance-related means. Thus, if academic success is seen as an ideal, promotion-focused individuals might utilize approach-related behaviors designed for the success of "straight A's" and the raising of their GPA, such as studying extra hours and seeking out teachers. Alternatively, if academic success is viewed as an obligation, prevention-focused individuals might instead focus on avoidance-related strategies designed to prevent harm to their GPA, such as forgoing parties and social activities on the weekend (see also Higgins, Roney, Crowe & Hymes, 1994). Moreover, these distinct behavioral tendencies may only grow stronger over the course of a pursuit. By measuring approach and avoidance intensity through arm flexion and extension, for instance, Förster, Higgins and Idson (1998) found that approach and avoidance inclinations increased as progress was made towards goal attainment and the goals themselves "loomed larger". Subsequent research on regulatory fit has found that individuals are generally more successful, committed and engaged when the specific demands and opportunities of a goal pursuit "fit" the strategic preferences of one's current regulatory focus (see Higgins, 2000; Higgins, Cornwell & Franks, 2014). Frietas, Liberman and Higgins (2002), for example, found that prevention-focused individuals were more engaged and effective with goal pursuits that required them to resist temptations or distractions, as the avoidance involved fit their prevention focus (see also Spiegel, Grant-Pillow & Higgins, 2004). As is soon discussed, the same behavioral and strategic preferences may be evident in our pursuit of the good life generally.

Finally, a consideration of regulatory focus may also be useful for understanding the various ways living a good life may be felt, both positively and negatively, as differences in regulatory focus have long been linked to qualitative differences in positive and negative emotional experiences. Realizing one's ideals have consistently been found to be experienced in happy terms, whereas failing to do so is experienced as dejection and loss. Not living up to one's obligations, alternatively, invokes anxiety and agitation, whereas fulfilling one's obligations brings relief and calm (see Higgins, 1987, 1997). Moreover, one's engagement and immersion in pursuits, regardless of their ultimate outcome, may depend on the fit between one's regulatory focus and how these pursuits unfold behaviorally (see Higgins, Cornwell & Franks, 2014).

What's Desired in a Good Life and What's Required

Similarly, how individuals come to perceive a good life may reflect their general orientations toward promotion through the realization of their personal aspirations or toward prevention through fulfillment of their duties and obligations.

A promotion focus, then, may lead one to define the good life in terms of what one truly wants and desires in such a life (the ideals involved). A prevention focus, alternatively, may lead one to define the good life in terms of what is necessary or required for such a life (the obligations involved). Moreover, construing the good life in terms of what we require versus what we desire in such a life may also come to determine how we ultimately pursue and experience such a life (see Fritz & Lyubomirsky, this volume). Shah (2017) recently asked online participants to complete a composite measure of regulatory focus (Haws et al., 2010) and then assess the extent to which they personally desired and the extent to which they felt they needed more states and traits commonly associated with the good life. Specifically, participants were asked to rate their current need and desire for "growth", "spirituality", "wisdom", "joy", "social connection", "health", "security", "success", "wealth" and "status" (see, for instance, Baumeister et al., 2013; Gallagher et al., 2009, Morris & Small, 1971).

After separately calculating totals for participants' focus on promotion and prevention and their overall desire and necessity ratings, participants' promotion focus was found to be positively correlated with their desire ratings total, representing the degree to which they ideally desired more of the traits and states that defined the good life. Alternatively, participants' prevention focus was found to be positively correlated with their necessity ratings total, representing the degree to which they felt it necessary to have more of these same traits and states. Perhaps more importantly, this study also found that participants' regulatory focus moderated the importance of their desire and necessity rating totals for their well-being overall. Indeed, participants' promotion focus was found to significantly increase the impact of their desire rating total on their overall satisfaction with life, as measured by the Satisfaction with Life Scale (SWLS; see Diener et al., 1985; Pavot & Diener, 1993). Alternatively, participants' prevention focus was found to significantly increase the impact of their necessity rating total on their overall satisfaction with life.

And as discussed, focusing on what's desired and what's required in a good life may also lead to differences in how such a life is pursued. With this in mind, Shah (2017) asked the same online participants about potential origins of the good life. Specifically, the extent to which the good life originated with them and with others, as well as the extent to which it was the result of various behavioral strategies, such as enthusiasm, vigilance, assertion and restraint. As is illustrated in Table 6.2, participants' promotion focus was associated with an orientation toward assertion and enthusiasm in pursuing the good life whereas their prevention focus was associated with restraint and self-control.

A follow-up study gave participants an online version of Morris's 13-item Ways of Living scale (Morris & Stone, 1971) after again completing the composite measure of regulatory focus (Haws et al., 2010). As illustrated in Table 6.3, participants' promotion focus score was found to be associated with the items from the Ways of Living scale that reflected challenge and risk whereas participants' prevention focus was found to be associated with those items that reflected obedient and vigilant ways of living.

TABLE 6.1 Partial Correlations of Regulatory Focus With What Is Desired and Required for a Good Life

N = 606	Desires for Good Life	Requirements for Good Life
Promotion Focus	.14***	0.06
Prevention Focus	−.11**	.09*

*p < .05, **p < .01, ***p < .001

TABLE 6.2 Partial Correlations of Regulatory Focus With Perceived Determinants of the Good Life

The Good Life Comes From

N = 606	Enthusiasm	Vigilance	Assertion	Restraint	Self	Others
Promotion Focus	.13*	−0.05	.15***	0.07	0.24***	−0.03
Prevention Focus	0.05	.17**	0.07	.12*	.081*	.14***

*p < .05, **p < .01, ***p < .001

In a third study, Shah (2017) had online participants again complete the composite regulatory focus strength measure (Haws et al., 2010) and then asked them to imagine an individual they knew well who had a resolution to exercise at least 15 days a month on average in the upcoming year. Ultimately, this person does exercise, on average, 15 days a month over the course of the year, and the participants were randomly shown one of two charts indicating how the individual's days of exercise each month varied over the course of the year. Although the charts showed an identical number of exercise days across the entire year, one chart indicated a rather consistent monthly performance while the other chart showed a monthly performance that increased over the course of the year, as illustrated in Figure 6.1.

After viewing the charts participants were asked to indicate how positive and satisfied they predicted the individuals would be with their performance overall and how satisfied they would be with this performance. As illustrated in Table 6.4, participants' promotion focus strength was associated with greater positivity predictions and self-reports for the performance that increased over time. Participants' prevention focus strength, alternatively, was associated with greater positivity predictions and self-reports for performance that was consistent over the course of the year.

Participants' regulatory focus, then, may impact how individuals ultimately experience positivity in their own lives. For promotion-focused individuals, the good life may be experienced most positively to the extent to which their lives allow them to fulfill their ideals and personal desires in a manner that fits with a focus on achievement and gain. Alternatively, for prevention-focused individuals the good life may be experienced most positively to the extent to which their lives

TABLE 6.3 Partial correlations of regulatory focus with ratings of ways of living

Proactive and Reactive Ways of Living

$N = 348$	Constantly Master Changing Conditions	Wait in Quiet Receptivity	Chance Adventuresome Deeds	Obey the Cosmic Purpose
Promotion Focus	.21***	−0.05	.21***	0.07
Prevention Focus	0.04	.11*	−0.07	.12*

*p < .05, ***p < .001

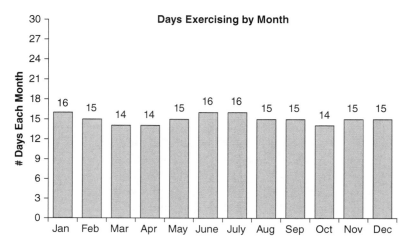

FIGURE 6.1 Hypothetical Resolution Performance Over the Course of a Year

TABLE 6.4 Partial correlations of regulatory focus with predicted and own satisfaction from growth and stability in fulfilling a new year's resolution

N = 307	Predicted Positivity from Growth	Own Positivity from Growth	Predicted Positivity from Stability	Own Positivity from Stability
Promotion Focus	.14*	.11*	−0.04	−0.05
Prevention Focus	0.05	0.02	.15**	.14**

*p < .05, **p < .01

allow them to address their basic needs and requirements in a manner best fitting with a focus on security and safety (see also Higgins, Cornwell & Franks, 2014).

Pursuing a Good End: Regulatory Focus and End-of-Life Planning

Finally, recent work by Tyszkowski and Shah (2016) has examined whether regulatory focus may come to impact not only how we pursue, maintain and experience good lives but also the significance and manner in which we plan for their ending (see also Shah, 2017). Indeed, despite significant benefit for themselves and their loved ones, individuals are often reluctant to consider and plan for their death and end-of-life care (see Vail, Juhl, Arndt, Vess, Routledge & Rutjens, 2012). As a result, end-of-life decisions are often left to loved ones, which often results in care that is inconsistent with individuals' wishes or intentions (Brinkman-Stoppelenburg, Rietjens & van der Heide, 2014). Tyszkowski and Shah (2016) examined whether end-of-life and advanced-care discussions could be encouraged through different social and behavioral pathways, as determined by individuals' regulatory focus on promotion or prevention. Through their differing tendencies towards eagerness and approach versus vigilance and avoidance, it was predicted that regulatory focus may influence not only the likelihood of considering end-of-life care, but the manner in which this consideration would best unfold through medical intervention. To examine these possibilities, 311 participants were recruited for an online survey that included a measure of participants' regulatory focus towards promotion and prevention (the RFQ-SR; see Summerville & Roese, 2008), as well as assessments of the frequency of their medical care over the last 12 months and the ease with which they felt they could discuss medical issues with their doctor or doctors. Finally, this survey included a four-item assessment of participants' consideration of their end-of-life medical care as well as assessments of their overall health, age and income. Consistent with past work, Tyszkowski and Shah (2016) found that the extent to which participants had thought about, discussed and planned end-of-life medical treatment was positively related to both the frequency of their medical care visits and the ease with which they could talk with their doctor. Moreover, the strength of participants' prevention focus was found to encourage consideration of end-of-life care both directly and indirectly (by increasing the frequency of medical care). Although the strength of participants' promotion focus was not found to directly encourage consideration of end-of-life care, it was found to relate indirectly by increasing the ease with which participants proactively initiated discussions with their doctors about end-of-life care, as illustrated in Figure 6.2.

Additionally, Shah (2017) examined whether differences in regulatory focus may influence not just how one goes about planning for the end-of-life but the impact such plans may have on current subjective well-being. To examine this influence, 327 participants were recruited for an online survey that included a composite measure of participants' regulatory focus towards promotion and prevention (the RFQ-CP; see Haws et al., 2010), as well as a seven-item assessment of the degree to which they had thought about, discussed and made plans for their will and their end-of-life care. Finally, participants completed the Satisfaction With Life Scale (SWLS), a five-item measure meant to assess one's general satisfaction with life (see Diener et al., 1999).

Overall, end-of-life planning was found to be significantly positively related to participants' satisfaction with life scores, though the relationship varied significantly as a function of participants' promotion and prevention focus. As illustrated

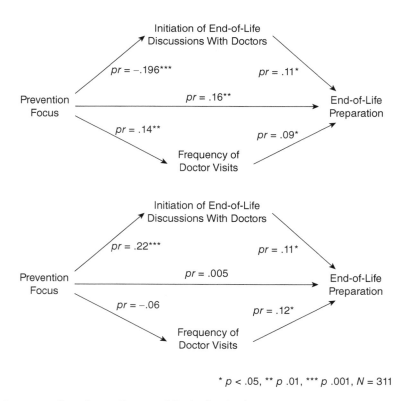

$* p < .05, ** p .01, *** p .001, N = 311$

FIGURE 6.2 Regulatory Focus and End-of-Life Planning

in Figure 6.3, participants' promotion focus strength, although significantly positively related to their satisfaction with life scores overall, was found to negatively moderate the impact of planning for end-of-life on their satisfaction with
life scores. Alternatively, participants' prevention focus strength did not predict
their satisfaction with life scores overall but was found to positively moderate the
impact of planning for end-of-life on their satisfaction with life scores, as also
illustrated in Figure 6.3.

Taken together, the results of these initial studies have implications for understanding not only the psychological importance of end-of-life planning for
subjective well-being, but how such plans likely come about. Indeed, identification of individuals as either prevention or promotion focused may ultimately
allow for the tailoring of clinical interventions meant to highlight the regulatory

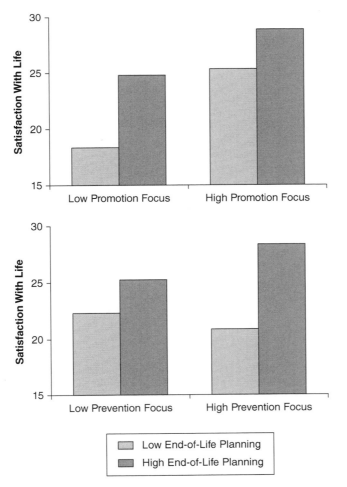

FIGURE 6.3 Planning for the End-of-Life, Regulatory Focus, and Satisfaction with Life

significance of information on end-of-life planning as well as the way it may be most effectively conveyed by medical and legal professionals to those who may have come to define their life primarily in terms of promotion and prevention.

A Good Life With Purpose

In detailing the implications of considering the basic regulatory purposes of leading a good life, the present analysis has sought to highlight the utility of a self-regulatory approach to understanding the challenges involved in defining and leading a good life. In doing so, it has considered why individuals might come to define such a life differently and why they might ultimately pursue and experience it in very different ways. Though this analysis is hardly complete, it perhaps provides a framework for understanding other self-regulatory challenges that may arise as individuals define, pursue, experience and maintain their good life, as well as the benefits and challenges they may face in planning for its inevitable end.

Bibliography

Amabile, T. M. (1983). The social psychology of creativity: A componential conceptualization. *Journal of Personality and Social Psychology, 45*(2), 357.

Baumann, N., Kaschel, R., & Kuhl, J. (2005). Striving for unwanted goals: Stress-dependent discrepancies between explicit and implicit achievement motives reduce subjective well-being and increase psychosomatic symptoms. *Journal of Personality and Social Psychology, 89*, 781–799.

Baumann, N., & Kuhl, J. (2003). Self-infiltration: Confusing assigned tasks as self-selected in memory. *Personality and Social Psychology Bulletin, 29*(4), 487–497.

Baumeister, R. F. (2017). Happiness and meaningfulness as two different and not entirely compatible versions of the good life. Chapter to appear in J. Forgas & R. Baumeister (Eds.), *The social psychology of the good life.* New York, NY: Psychology Press.

Baumeister, R. F., Vohs, K. D., Aaker, J. L., & Garbinsky, E. N. (2013). Some key differences between a happy life and a meaningful life. *Journal of Positive Psychology, 8*(6), 505–516.

Black, A. E., & Deci, E. L. (2000). The effects of instructors' autonomy support and students' autonomous motivation on learning organic chemistry: A self-determination theory perspective. *Science education, 84*(6), 740–756.

Brinkman-Stoppelenburg, A., Rietjens, J. A. C., & van der Heide, A. (2014). The effects of advance care planning on end-of-life care: A systematic review. *Palliative Medicine, 28*(8), 1000–1025.

Brunstein, J. C., Schultheiss, O. C., & Grässmann, R. (1998). Personal goals and emotional well-being: The moderating role of motive dispositions* 1. *Journal of Personality and Social Psychology, 75*(2), 494–508.

Caprara, G. V., & Steca, P. (2005). Affective and social self-regulatory efficacy beliefs as online determinants of positive thinking and happiness. *European Psychologist, 10*, 275–286.

Cheung, C. K. (2010). Toward a theoretically based measurement model of the good life. *The Journal of Genetic Psychology, 158*(2), 200–215.

Deci, E. L., Connell, J. P., & Ryan, R. M. (1989). Self-determination in a work organization. *Journal of Applied Psychology, 74*(4), 580.

Deci, E. L., Nezlek, J., & Sheinman, L. (1981). Characteristics of the rewarder and intrinsic motivation of the rewardee. *Journal of Personality and Social Psychology*, *40*(1), 1.

Deci, E. L., & Ryan, R. M. (2008). Hedonia, eudaimonia, and well-being: An introduction. *Journal of Happiness Studies*, *9*, 1–11.

Diener, E. (1984). Subjective well-being. *Psychological Bulletin*, 95, 542–575.

Diener, E. (2000). Subjective well-being. The science of happiness and a proposal for a national index. *American Psychologist*, *55*(1), 34–43.

Diener, E., Emmons, R. A., Larsen, R. J., & Griffin, S. (1985). The satisfaction with life scale. *Journal of Personality Assessment*, *49*, 71–75.

Diener, E., & Fujita, F. (1995). Resources, personal strivings, and subjective well-being: A nomothetic and idiographic approach. *Journal of Personality and Social Psychology*, *68*(5), 926–935.

Diener, E., Suh, E. M., Lucas, R. E., & Smith, H. E. (1999). Subjective well-being: Three decades of progress. *Psychological Bulletin*, *125*, 276–302.

Dunn, E. W., Gilbert, D. T., & Wilson, T. D. (2011). If money doesn't make you happy, then you probably aren't spending it right. *Journal of Consumer Psychology*, *21*(2), 115–125.

Emmons, R. A. (1986). Personal strivings: An approach to personality and subjective well-being. *Journal of Personality and Social Psychology*, *51*(5), 1058.

Fiedler, K., & Arslan, P. (2017). From a hedonic perspective on good life to an analysis of underlying adaptive principles. Chapter to appear in J. Forgas & R. Baumeister (Eds.), *The social psychology of the good life*. New York, NY: Psychology Press.

Forgas, J. P. (2017). Negative affect and the good life: On the cognitive, motivational and interpersonal benefits of negative mood. Chapter to appear in J. Forgas & R. Baumeister (Eds.), *The social psychology of the good life*. New York, NY: Psychology Press.

Förster, J., Higgins, E. T., & Bianco, A. T. (2003). Speed/accuracy decisions in task performance: Built-in trade-off or separate strategic concerns? *Organizational Behavior and Human Decision Processes*, *90*(1), 148–164.

Förster, J., Higgins, E. T., & Idson, L. C. (1998). Approach and avoidance strength during goal attainment: Regulatory focus and the "goal looms larger" effect. *Journal of Personality and Social Psychology*, *75*(5), 1115.

Fredrickson, B. L. (2001). The role of positive emotions in positive psychology. *American Psychologist*, *56*(3), 218–226.

Fredrickson, B. L. (2004). The broaden-and-build theory of positive emotions. *Philosophical Transactions of the Royal Society B: Biological Sciences*, *359*(1449), 1367–1377.

Freitas, A. L., Liberman, N., & Higgins, E. T. (2002). Regulatory fit and resisting temptation during goal pursuit. *Journal of Experimental Social Psychology*, *38*(3), 291–298.

Freitas, A. L., Liberman, N., Salovey, P., & Higgins, E. T. (2002). When to begin? Regulatory focus and initiating goal pursuit. *Personality and Social Psychology Bulletin*, *28*(1), 121–130.

Gallagher, M., Lopez, S. J., & Preacher, K. J. (2009). The hierarchical structure of well-being. *Journal of Personality*, 77, 1025–1049.

Gilbert, D. (2006). *Stumbling on happiness*. New York, NY: Vintage.

Gilbert, D. T., & Ebert, J. E. J. (2002). Decisions and revisions: The affective forecasting of changeable outcomes. *Journal of Personality and Social Psychology*, *82*(4), 503–514.

Gilbert, D. T., Pinel, E. C., Wilson, T. D., Blumberg, S. J., & Wheatley, T. P. (1998). Immune neglect: A source of durability bias in affective forecasting. *Journal of Personality and Social Psychology*, *75*(3), 617.

George, L. S., & Park, C. L. (2016). The multidimensional existential meaning scale: A tripartite approach to measuring meaning in life. *The Journal of Positive Psychology*, 1–15.

Grant, H., & Higgins, E. (2003). Optimism, promotion pride, and prevention pride as predictors of quality of life. *Personality and Social Psychological Bulletin, 29*(12), 1521–1532.

Grolnick, W. S., & Ryan, R. M. (1987). Autonomy in children's learning: An experimental and individual difference investigation. *Journal of Personality and Social Psychology, 52*(5), 890.

Grolnick, W. S., Ryan, R. M., & Deci, E. L. (1991). Inner resources for school achievement: Motivational mediators of children's perceptions of their parents. *Journal of Educational Psychology, 83*(4), 508.

Haws, K., Dholakia, U., & Bearden, W. (2010). An assessment of chronic regulatory focus measures. *Journal of Marketing, 47*, 967–982.

Heller, D., Komar, J., & Lee, W. B. (2007). The dynamics of personality states, goals, and well-being. *Personality and Social Psychological Bulletin, 33*(6), 898–910.

Herrmann, M., & Brandstätter, V. (2013). Overcoming action crises in personal goals—longitudinal evidence on a mediating mechanism between action orientation and well-being. *Journal of Research in Personality, 47*(6), 881–893.

Heyl, V., Wahl, H.-W., & Mollenkopf, H. (2007). Affective well-being in old age: The role of tenacious goal pursuit and flexible goal adjustment. *European Psychologist, 12*(2), 119–129.

Higgins, E. T. (1997). Beyond pleasure and pain. *American Psychologist, 52*(12), 1280.

Higgins, E. T. (2000). Making a good decision: value from fit. *American Psychologist, 55*(11), 1217.

Higgins, E. T. (2012). *Beyond pleasure and pain: How motivation works.* New York, NY: Oxford University Press.

Higgins, E. T., Cornwell, J. F., & Franks, B. (2014). "Happiness" and "the good life" as motives working together effectively. *Advances in Motivation Science, 1*, 135–179.

Kahneman, D., Diener, E., & Schwarz, N. (1999). *Well-being: The foundation of hedonic psychology.* New York, NY: Russell Sage Foundation.

Kashdan, T. B., Biswas-Diener, R., & King, L. A. (2008). Reconsidering happiness: The costs of distinguishing between hedonics and eudaimonia. *Journal of Positive Psychology, 3*, 219–233.

Keyes, C. L. M. (2007). Promoting and protecting mental health as flourishing: A complementary strategy for improving national mental health. *American Psychologist, 62*, 95–108.

Keyes, C. L. M., Shmotkin, D., & Ryff, C. D. (2002). Optimizing well-being: The empirical encounter of two traditions. *Journal of Personality and Social Psychology, 82*, 1007–1022.

King, L. A. (2001). The hard road to the good life: The happy, mature person. *Journal of Humanistic Psychology, 41*(1), 51–72.

King, L. A., & Napa, C. K. (1998). What makes a life good? *Journal of Personality and Social Psychology, 75*(1), 156–165.

Langer, E. J., & Rodin, J. (1976). The effects of choice and enhanced personal responsibility for the aged: A field experiment in an institutional setting. *Journal of Personality and Social Psychology, 34*(2), 191.

Linley, P. A., Maltby, J., Wood, A. M., Osborne, G., & Hurling, R. (2009). Measuring happiness: The higher order factor structure of subjective and psychological well-being measures. *Personality and Individual Differences, 47*, 878–884.

Little, B. R., & Chambers, N. C. (2004). Personal project pursuit: On human doings and well-beings. In *Handbook of Motivational Counseling* (p. 65). Chichester, UK: Wiley.

Lyubomirsky, S., & Fritz, M. M. (2017). Wither happiness? When, how, and why might positive activities undermine well-being. Chapter to appear in J. Forgas & R. Baumeister (Eds.), *The social psychology of the good life.* New York, NY: Psychology Press.

Lyubomirsky, S., King, L., & Diener, E. (2005). The benefits of frequent positive affect: Does happiness lead to success? *Psychological Bulletin, 131*(6), 803–855.

Lyubomirsky, S., Sheldon, K. M., & Schkade, D. (2005). Pursuing happiness: The architecture of sustainable change. *Review of General Psychology, 9*(2), 111–131.

McConnell, A., Renaud, J., Dean, K., Green, S., Lamoreaux, M., Hall, C., & Rydell, R. (2005). Whose self is it anyway? Self-aspect control moderates the relation between self-complexity and well-being. *Journal of Experimental Social Psychology, 41*, 1–18.

McGraw, K. O., & McCullers, J. C. (1979). Evidence of a detrimental effect of extrinsic incentives on breaking a mental set. *Journal of Experimental Social Psychology, 15*(3), 285–294.

McGregor, I., McAdams, D. P., & Little, B. R. (2006). Personal projects, life stories, and happiness: On being true to traits. *Journal of Research in Personality, 40*(5), 551–572.

Morris, C., & Small, L. (1971). Changes in conceptions of the good life by American college students from 1950 to 1970. *20*(2), 254–260.

Myers, D. G., & Diener, E. (1995). Who is happy? *Psychological Science, 6*, 10–19.

Oettingen, G. (2015). *Rethinking positive thinking: Inside the new science of motivation*. New York, NY: Current.

Oishi, S., & Diener, E. (2001). Goals, culture, and subjective well-being. *Personality and Social Psychological Bulletin, 27*(12), 1674–1682.

Pavot, W., & Diener, E. (1993). Review of the satisfaction with life scale. *Psychological Assessment, 5*, 164–172.

Platt, J. R. (1964). Strong inference. *Science, 146*, 347–353.

Quoidbach, J., Gilbert, D. T., & Wilson, T. D. (2013). The end of history illusion. *Science, 339*(6115), 96–98.

Romero, E., Villar, P., Luengo, M. Á., & Gómez-Fraguela, J. A. (2009). Traits, personal strivings and well-being. *Journal of Research in Personality, 43*(4), 535–546.

Ryan, R. M., & Connell, J. P. (1989). Perceived locus of causality and internalization: examining reasons for acting in two domains. *Journal of Personality and Social Psychology, 57*(5), 749.

Ryan, R., & Deci, E. (2000). Self-determination theory and the facilitation of intrinsic motivation, social development, and well-being. *American Psychologist, 55*(1), 68–78.

Ryan, R. M., & Deci, E. L. (2001). On happiness and human potentials: A review of research on hedonic and eudaimonic well-being. *Annual Review of Psychology, 52*, 141–166.

Ryan, R. M., Huta, V., & Deci, E. L. (2006). Living well: A self-determination theory perspective on eudaimonia. *Journal of Happiness Studies, 9*(1), 139–170.

Ryff, C. D. (1989). Happiness is everything, or is it? Explorations on the meaning of psychological well-being. *Journal of Personality and Social Psychology, 57*(6), 1069.

Ryff, C. D., & Keyes, C. L. M. (1995). The structure of eudaimonic well-being revisited. *Journal of Personality and Social Psychology, 69*, 719–727.

Ryff, C. D., & Singer, B. H. (2008). Know thyself and become what you are: A eudaimonic approach to psychological well-being. *Journal of Happiness Studies, 9*, 13–39.

Schwartz, B., Ward, A., Monterosso, J., Lyubomirsky, S., White, K., & Lehman, D. (2002). Maximizing versus satisficing: Happiness is a matter of choice. *Journal of Personality and Social Psychology, 83*, 1178–1197.

Sedikides, C. (2017). Nostalgia potentiates a positive and attainable future. Chapter to appear in J. Forgas & R. Baumeister (Eds.), *The social psychology of the good life*. New York, NY: Psychology Press.

Shah, J. Y. (2017). *The importance of ending well. Regulatory focus moderates the impact of end-of-life planning on subjective well-being*. Manuscript in preparation.

Shah, J. Y., & Kruglanski, A. W. (2000). The Structure and Substance of Intrinsic Motivation. In Sansone, C., & Harackiewicz, J. M. (Eds.). *Intrinsic and extrinsic motivation: The search for optimal motivation and performance* (pp. 105–127). San Diego, CA: Academic Press.

Sheldon, K. M. (2017). Understanding the good life: Eudaimonic living involves well-doing, not well-being. Chapter to appear in J. Forgas & R. Baumeister (Eds.), *The social psychology of the good life*. New York, NY: Psychology Press.

Sheldon, K. M., & Elliot, A. J. (1999). Goal striving, need satisfaction, and longitudinal well-being: The self-concordance model. *Journal of Personality and Social Psychology, 76,* 482–497.

Sheldon, K. M., & Houser-Marko, L. (2001). Self-concordance, goal attainment, and the pursuit of happiness: Can there be an upward spiral? *Journal of Personality and Social Psychology, 80*(1), 152–165.

Sheldon, K. M., & Kasser, T. (1998). Pursuing personal goals: Skills enable progress, but not all progress is beneficial. *Personality and Social Psychology Bulletin, 24*(12), 1319–1331.

Sheldon, K. M., Ryan, R. M., Deci, E. L., & Kasser, T. (2004). The independent effects of goal contents and motives on well-being: It's both what you pursue and why you pursue it. *Journal of Occupational and Organizational Psychology, 30*(4), 475–486.

Spiegel, S., Grant-Pillow, H., & Higgins, E. T. (2004). How regulatory fit enhances motivational strength during goal pursuit. *European Journal of Social Psychology, 34*(1), 39–54.

Steger, M. F., Kashdan, T. B., & Oishi, S. (2008). Being good by doing good: Daily eudaimonic activity and well-being. *Journal of Research in Personality, 42,* 22–42.

Summerville, A., & Roese (2008). Self-report measures of individual differences in regulatory focus: A cautionary note. *Journal of Research in Personality, 42,* 247–254.

Thrash, T. M., Elliot, A. J., Maruskin, L. A., & Cassidy, S. E. (2010). Inspiration and the promotion of well-being: Tests of causality and mediation. *Journal of Personality and Social Psychology, 98*(3), 488–506.

Tyszkowski, K. A., & Shah, J. (2016). *Motivational orientations toward end-of-life planning.* Paper presented at the 37th meeting of the Society of Behavioral Medicine, Washington, DC.

Vail, K. E., III, Juhl, J., Arndt, J., Vess, M., Routledge, C., & Rutjens, B. T. (2012). When death is good for life. *Personality and Social Psychology Review, 16*(4), 303–329.

Vallerand, R. J., & Blssonnette, R. (1992). Intrinsic, extrinsic, and amotivational styles as predictors of behavior: A prospective study. *Journal of Personality, 60*(3), 599–620.

Vallerand, R. J., Pelletier, L. G., Blais, M. R., Briere, N. M., Senecal, C., & Vallieres, E. F. (1992). The Academic Motivation Scale: A measure of intrinsic, extrinsic, and amotivation in education. *Educational and Psychological Measurement, 52*(4), 1003–1017.

Vittersø, J., Oelmann, H. I., & Wang, A. L. (2007). Life satisfaction is not a balanced estimator of the good life: Evidence from reaction time measures and self-reported emotions. *Journal of Happiness Studies, 10*(1), 1–17.

Waterman, A. S. (1993). Two conceptions of happiness: Contrasts of personal expressiveness (eudaimonia) and hedonic enjoyment. *Journal of Personality and Social Psychology, 64,* 678–691.

Williams, G. C., & Deci, E. L. (1996). Internalization of biopsychosocial values by medical students: A test of self-determination theory. *Journal of Personality and Social Psychology, 70*(4), 767.

Wilson, T. D., & Gilbert, D. T. (2003). Affective forecasting. *Advances in Experimental Social Psychology, 35,* 345–411.

Wilson, T. D., Reinhard, D. A., Westgate, E. C., Gilbert, D. T., Ellerbeck, N., Hahn, C., . . . Shaked, A. (2014). Just think: The challenges of the disengaged mind. *Science, 345*(6192), 75–77.

7

WHITHER HAPPINESS?

When, How, and Why Might Positive Activities Undermine Well-Being

Megan M. Fritz and Sonja Lyubomirsky

Across the globe, most people desire happiness (Diener, 2000; Diener, Suh, Smith, & Shao, 1995), and this desire transcends differences in age, culture, geographical location, political beliefs, religion, and life experiences. The quest for the secret of how to increase and sustain happiness has preoccupied men and women for millennia, from the philosophers of ancient Athens to present-day scientists and scholars (Kesebir & Diener, 2008; McMahon, 2008). Although conceptualizations of happiness may shift across generations and cultures, the goal of attaining it remains ubiquitous (McMahon, 2008; Oishi, Graham, Kesebir, & Galinha, 2013).

Notably, happiness is desirable not just because it is pleasurable, but because it grants numerous benefits to both the individual and those around him or her (see also Fredrickson, this volume). Happiness (or well-being)—which researchers define as the experience of frequent positive emotions relative to negative emotions, coupled with high life satisfaction—predicts, correlates, and begets success across multiple life domains, including work, relationships, and physical health (Lyubomirsky, King, & Diener, 2005; see also von Hippel & Gonsalkorale; and Sheldon, this volume). Relative to their less happy counterparts, happy people have stronger interpersonal relationships, higher incomes, and superior physical and mental health; they receive more favorable job performance reviews, are more likely to get married, and live longer on average (e.g., Boehm & Kubzansky, 2012; Chida & Steptoe, 2008; Lyubomirsky, King, et al., 2005; Simpson, Farrell, Huelsnitz, & Eller, this volume). Positive emotions have also been shown to prompt greater creativity and prosocial behavior (see Lyubomirsky, King, et al., 2005, for a review). Happiness, therefore, does not only feel good—it *is* good. It pays to be happy not just for the individual, but for the individual's social network and his or her community at large. In this chapter, we will use the terms happiness and well-being interchangeably.

Almost two decades of research suggest that individuals can increase their well-being by engaging in so-called positive activities. Longitudinal randomized controlled trials have shown that purposeful and effortful performance of positive activities can markedly impact happiness, with average effect sizes of $r = .29$ for increasing well-being and $r = .31$ for decreasing depressive symptoms (Sin & Lyubomirsky, 2009). These simple, self-administered positive activities are designed to increase well-being by mirroring the behaviors (or habits) that happy people naturally do. They include expressing gratitude or appreciation (Boehm, Lyubomirsky, & Sheldon, 2011; Emmons & McCullough, 2003; Froh, Sefick, & Emmons, 2008; Layous, Lee, Choi, & Lyubomirsky, 2013; Lyubomirsky, Dickerhoof, Boehm, & Sheldon, 2011), doing kind acts for others (Chancellor, Margolis, Bao, & Lyubomirsky, 2017; Dunn, Aknin, & Norton, 2008; Layous, Lee, et al., 2013; Layous, Nelson, Oberle, Schonert-Reichl, & Lyubomirsky, 2012; Nelson, Layous, Cole, & Lyubomirsky, 2016; Pressman, Kraft, & Cross, 2014; see also Huppert, this volume), cultivating optimism (Boehm et al., 2011; Layous, Nelson, & Lyubomirsky, 2013; Lyubomirsky et al., 2011; Peters, Flink, Boersma, & Linton, 2010; Sheldon & Lyubomirsky, 2006), meditating on positive feelings toward the self (Neff & Germer, 2013) and others (Fredrickson, Cohn, Coffey, Pek, & Finkel, 2008), and affirming one's most important values (Nelson, Fuller, Choi, & Lyubomirsky, 2014).

The Positive Activity Model: Summary and Evidence

Recent empirical investigation has shifted from simply focusing on *whether* activities like expressing gratitude or practicing kindness can increase happiness to asking *how*, *when*, *why*, and *for whom* they can do so. Our positive activity model (Figure 7.1, Layous & Lyubomirsky, 2014; Lyubomirsky & Layous, 2013) offers predictions for the conditions under which various positive activities may be more (or less) effective at boosting well-being. This theoretical model identifies specific moderators and mediators underlying the relationship between positive activity engagement and increases in well-being. Key moderators pertain to the activity itself (e.g., how often is the behavior practiced and how novel is it), to the person performing it (e.g., how motivated the person is to become happier and if the person believes the activity will work), or to the congruence between the two (e.g., person-activity fit). Hypothesized mediators, such as the satisfaction of psychological needs, suggest mechanisms by which positive activities operate to increase happiness.

Features of the Activity

Positive activity interventions—that is, randomized controlled experiments aimed to test the success of positive activities—are maximally beneficial under certain strategic conditions. First, like any behavioral or medical intervention, considerations about dosage (e.g., frequency and timing of administration) are critical. For

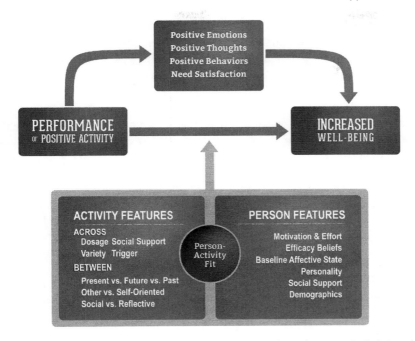

FIGURE 7.1   Model of the Psychological Mediators and Moderators Underlying the Efficacy of Practicing Positive Activities

Source: Adapted with permission from "How Do Simple Positive Activities Increase Well-Being" by S. Lyubomirsky & K. Layous, 2013, *Current Directions in Psychological Science.*

example, one longitudinal study showed that participants who performed five kind acts per week for six weeks showed greater increases in well-being when all five acts were committed on a single day each week, rather than spread across the week (Lyubomirsky, Sheldon, & Schkade, 2005). Thus, kindness interventions may be most effective when packaged in relatively strong and relatively infrequent doses. Furthermore, research on hedonic adaptation suggests that well-being benefits are stronger and more durable when positive activities are novel and varied, rather than repetitive and boring (Lyubomirsky, 2011). In support of this notion, participants in a ten-week kindness intervention reported stronger gains in well-being when they were instructed to vary their kind acts rather than perform the same kind act week after week (Sheldon, Boehm, & Lyubomirsky, 2012, Study 2).

Features of the Person

Person-level features may also impact the efficacy of positive activity interventions. Happiness seekers will likely obtain maximal benefit from engagement in a positive activity when they feel motivated to become happier (Deci & Ryan, 2000; Lyubomirsky et al., 2011), exert effort toward engaging in the activity (Layous,

Lee, et al., 2013; Lyubomirsky et al., 2011), and believe that the activity will be successful (Ajzen, 1991; Bandura, 1986; Dweck & Leggett, 1988; Layous, Nelson, et al., 2013). For example, in a quasi-experimental study, participants who deliberately chose to perform "happiness-increasing" exercises (versus doing "cognitive" exercises) and who mustered more effort (as assessed by observers) into the exercises showed bigger gains in well-being (Lyubomirsky et al., 2011). Theory and research also suggest that baseline attitudes about happiness-increasing strategies (e.g., whether happiness is difficult to change and whether increasing happiness is an appropriate goal; Dweck & Leggett, 1988), as well as baseline affective state (e.g., whether one begins a happiness intervention in a healthy versus vulnerable position), moderate well-being outcomes (Cohn & Fredrickson, 2010; Nelson et al., 2014; see also Fiedler & Arslan, this volume). Cross-cultural work also suggests that intervention effects may differ based on the participant's culture. For example, optimism and gratitude interventions have been shown to increase well-being more strongly in European American participants relative to Asian American participants (Boehm et al., 2011); gratitude activities have stronger effects for participants in the United States than in South Korea (Layous, Lee, et al., 2013); and kindness activities have stronger effects in Hong Kong Chinese (relative to Americans) when directed toward friends and family (versus strangers) (Shin & Lyubomirsky, 2017).

The Role of Person-Activity Fit

An additional factor to consider when designing the optimal happiness practice is the level of "fit" between the activity and the individual. In other words, certain activities appear to work best for certain individuals (Layous & Lyubomirsky, 2014). For example, highly extraverted happiness seekers may reap more benefits from positive activities that require interacting with others, and interventions delivered online or via mobile app may be ideal for tech-savvy users (see also Amichai-Hamburger & Etgar; and Dunn & Dwyer, this volume). One study found that individuals' enjoyment of a positive activity was linked with both greater intervention adherence and increases in well-being (Schueller, 2010). Thus, features of the person may interact with features of the activity to promote or hinder well-being boosts.

Evidence for Mediators

The positive activity model also identifies potential mechanisms by which engagement in a particular positive activity will promote well-being. Positive activities generate well-being via increases in positive emotions, thoughts, and behaviors, as well as by satisfying psychological needs (i.e., autonomy, competence, and social connectedness; Deci & Ryan, 2000). For example, Fredrickson and colleagues (2008) found that participants who engaged in loving-kindness meditation experienced increases in personal resources (e.g., social relationships, physical health) and, in turn, reported greater life satisfaction, and this effect was mediated by increases in positive emotions (see also Fredrickson, this volume). Gratitude and optimism interventions have been shown to increase well-being by promoting positive construals of events—for example, people who practiced gratitude and optimism subsequently perceived their daily experiences as more satisfying (Dickerhoof, 2007; see also Huppert, this volume). Additionally, students assigned to pursue goals related to autonomy and connectedness showed increased well-being over a six-month period, relative to students assigned to pursue goals related to their life circumstances (Sheldon et al., 2010).

Summary and New Questions

Taken together, the empirical and theoretical work we have described so far focuses on the fundamental question of when positive activities are successful at increasing well-being, and when they may have little to no effect. We propose here that the positive activity model can also be applied to suggest the circumstances in which positive activities might actively backfire. In other words, under what conditions might positive activities actually engender *un*happiness? Little is known about when, why, and how happiness-increasing strategies can produce adverse effects (cf. McNulty & Fincham, 2012; see also Fiedler & Arslan, this volume). For example, in what situations and for what types of individuals might gratitude lead people to feel resentful, guilty, indebted, morally inferior, conflicted, and/or uncomfortable? When might kindness lead people to feel taken advantage of, resentful, and overburdened? Accordingly, we discuss here the potential contraindications and iatrogenic effects of the pursuit of happiness.

When Might Positive Activities Backfire?

Activity Overdose

Just as particular activity-level characteristics may promote gains in well-being, such characteristics may also lead to unhappiness. For example, inappropriate, incorrect, or suboptimal dosage and timing of a positive activity may inadvertently undermine well-being.

Gratitude interventions may be particularly susceptible to the perils of "overdose." In the oft-used counting blessings activity (Emmons & McCullough, 2003), individuals are asked to list things in their lives for which they are grateful. However, when people are obligated to think harder to come up with a list of items, they tend to use an effort-as-information heuristic, thereby judging harder-to-generate items to be less common (see Schwarz, Bless, Wanke, & Winkielman, 2003, for a review). For example, people asked to recall 12 examples of their own assertive behaviors subsequently rate themselves as less assertive than those asked to recall only six examples of their own assertive behaviors (Schwarz et al., 1991). This finding holds implications for list-based positive activity interventions, such as the counting blessings activity. If a happiness seeker is compelled to list too many blessings, she may find the exercise challenging and thus conclude that her life must not have many blessings, thus experiencing increased dismay, more sadness, and tempered well-being.

Additionally, gratitude interventions may be detrimental when administered too frequently. In a six-week intervention, students were randomly assigned to count their blessings once per week or three times per week, or to a wait-list control (Lyubomirsky, Sheldon, et al., 2005). While students who counted their blessings once per week showed significant improvements in well-being, those who counted their blessings three times per week slightly decreased in well-being from baseline.

Kindness interventions may also backfire when administered in too high doses. For example, in Sheldon and colleagues' (2012, Study 2) examination of high- versus low-variety kindness interventions, participants instructed to repeat the same act of kindness (i.e., low-variety condition) for ten consecutive weeks reported lower happiness on average at the end of the study, relative to baseline. In other words, this dosage of the kindness intervention did not merely fail to increase well-being, it appeared to have contributed to *reductions* in well-being. It is likely that performing the same kind act (e.g., doing a particular household chore) repeatedly for ten weeks causes the act to feel stale, monotonous, and burdensome, producing negative emotions (e.g., resentment, tedium) and, hence, poor well-being outcomes.

Extremes of Motivation

The positive activity model indicates that the success of any given positive activity is moderated—that is, augmented—by the person's motivation to become happier (for empirical evidence, see Lyubomirsky et al., 2011). However, recent work suggests that *over*valuing happiness (i.e., strongly agreeing with statements like "How happy I am at any given moment says a lot about how worthwhile my life is"; Mauss, Tamir, Anderson, & Savino, 2011) may be linked with lower well-being. In clinical populations, overvaluing happiness is associated with both self-reported and clinician-rated depressive symptoms (Ford, Shallcross, Mauss, Floerke, & Gruber, 2014). Experimental work also suggests that overvaluing happiness can paradoxically reduce it. In one study, participants who were randomly assigned to a happiness-valuation condition reported lower positive affect and more negative affect during a positive experience (i.e., watching a "happy" film clip) than participants not so induced; however, this effect was not present during a negative experience (i.e., watching a "sad" film clip; Mauss et al., 2011). This finding suggests that individuals who are too highly motivated to become happier—those who are preoccupied with being happy and who seek happiness too often and too directly—may find themselves counterintuitively thwarting their own happiness (see also Forgas, this volume).

Overly motivated happiness-seekers may spend too much time monitoring their own well-being and emotions. Consequently, when a particular positive activity (say, expressing gratitude) does not elicit the expected degree of happiness, these individuals attribute the discrepancy to personal failings (e.g., "I'm doing something that is supposed to make me happy—why am I not happier?"; Gruber, Mauss, & Tamir, 2011), engendering negative emotions, dissatisfaction, and reduced happiness. Ultimately, the pursuit of happiness, regardless of one's approach, may produce iatrogenic effects when one's motivation and standards for reaching the goal of happiness are too high, when engagement in positive activities prompts high self-focus and a sense of entitlement to happiness, and when one's explicit aim is the achievement of the goal (i.e., increased happiness) rather than enjoyment of the journey (Ford & Mauss, 2014; Layous & Lyubomirsky, 2014; see also Fiedler & Arslan; and Forgas, this volume).

Person-Activity Misfit

When considering a positive activity intervention, happiness seekers are encouraged to maximize their benefits and adherence by choosing an activity that feels natural, meaningful, and enjoyable (Layous & Lyubomirsky, 2014). However, it is likely that particular interactions between aspects of the individual and the activity may not merely fail to produce well-being benefits but, instead, may markedly diminish happiness.

The positive activity model suggests that baseline affective state may impact the efficacy of a positive activity intervention. After all, if a person is already relatively high in well-being, there may not be much room for improvement; conversely, if the person is experiencing too much acute distress or anxiety, he or she may experience limited improvement in well-being. However, it is also possible that baseline affective state may actively contribute to contraindications of positive activities. For example, consider an individual who is moderately depressed and is attempting to engage in a gratitude letter exercise. She may feel intensely lonely if she cannot think of anyone to whom she can express gratitude. Or, if she does identify an individual to whom she feels grateful, she may feel like a failure for having needed help in the first place, guilty for not having expressed gratitude sooner, or worthless for not having repaid the kind act. Experimental evidence supports the notion that gratitude activities can have detrimental effects for depressed or dysphoric individuals. Dysphoric students prompted to write a gratitude letter actually showed declines in well-being from before to after the intervention (Sin, Della Porta, & Lyubomirsky, 2011). Thus, it seems that a person's baseline affective state can interact with the activity itself (in this case, expressing gratitude) and lead to person-activity misfit.

Another potential person-activity misfit could result from an incongruence between an individual's personality and his or her selected activity. In one study, students were assigned to participate in a campus-based kindness intervention that required them to perform kind acts for passersby (Pressman et al., 2014). Although kindness-givers reported boosts in well-being on average, a small percentage of participants reported *poorer* well-being after the study. For these participants, engagement in a kindness activity reduced life satisfaction, diminished positive affect, and heightened negative affect. Furthermore, discussions with study partici- pants revealed that introverted and shy participants felt negative emotions such as discomfort and anxiety when approaching strangers to perform kind acts. These results suggest that aspects of personality may not simply impact who benefits more or less from engaging in kindness interventions: These interventions may actually undermine happiness among highly introverted individuals.

Finally, a mismatch between an individual's culture and the positive activity he or she chooses to engage in could also result in person-activity misfit and lead to an erosion in well-being. For example, a woman from Japan who attempts to build happiness by striving toward autonomy-related goals (e.g., making her own decisions independently; Sheldon et al., 2010) may find that the collectivist, inter- dependent perspectives inherent in her culture clash with the individualist nature of this activity. Although pursuing autonomy goals may fulfill her desire for more independence, self-sufficiency, and self-esteem, it may also be in conflict with the cultural expectation of social cohesion and obligation to the group, leading her to feel selfish or overly self-focused and thus diminishing well-being. Similarly, an individualist may experience dissonance or discomfort when expressing gratitude if he is socialized to be independent and not rely on others for help.

Mediators Gone Sour

In addition to the role of personality, Pressman and colleagues (2014) posit another reason that their kindness activity had iatrogenic effects for a subgroup of participants. When the kindness-recipients did not respond to the kindness- givers as expected (e.g., did not thank them properly), the givers likely experi- enced increased negative emotions (e.g., frustration, disappointment, resentment) and/or negative thoughts (e.g., questioning whether the kind act was appropriate or appreciated). These negative emotions and thoughts may subsequently have dampened well-being. This account highlights one way that the mediating path- ways proposed in the positive activity model not only suggest mechanisms by which positive activities work (or do not work), but the pathways by which posi- tive activities engender unhappiness.

Individuals are likely to experience poorer well-being outcomes when posi- tive activities produce negative (rather than positive) emotions, thoughts, and behaviors, or when they produce decrements (rather than boosts) in psychologi- cal need satisfaction (i.e., less connectedness, autonomy, and competence) (see

Figure 7.1). For example, a gratitude exercise could make a person feel guilty, embarrassed, and/or indebted for not having thanked the benefactor sooner and bearing the burden of needing to reciprocate. Supporting these ideas, three experiments conducted in the United States and South Korea found that gratitude exercises were more likely to generate mixed emotions than other positive exercises (such as experiencing relief and recalling kind acts). In other words, practicing gratitude made people feel not only connected and uplifted but also guilty and indebted (Layous et al., 2017). Expressing gratitude may also lead individuals to feel ashamed for needing help in the first place, uncomfortable or awkward while trying to share their gratitude, conflicted about having needed help, or subordinate or socially inferior for having been in a position that required assistance. Thus, happiness seekers may feel *less* autonomous and competent, as they needed someone else's assistance to achieve a goal they could not achieve on their own. They may also feel more resentful, and consequently *less* socially connected toward their benefactor. This combination of increased negative emotions and low psychological need satisfaction may bear the potential to reduce happiness in people trying to practice gratitude.

One perhaps surprising example of a positive activity that can trigger negative emotions, thoughts, and behaviors is doing acts of kindness. Kindnesses that are too lavish (like giving away one's personal laptop or cell phone to a stranger) or too burdensome (like spending days helping a neighbor move) may promote feelings of resentment, frustration, or anger. The kindness-giver may perceive him or herself as being taken advantage of or feel exploited or distressed. As mentioned above, the response of the kindness-recipient may also promote negative thoughts or behaviors that contribute to unhappiness. The kindness-giver may feel low autonomy if the recipient expects or demands the kind act, or he or she may feel incompetent if the kind act did not help the recipient as much as he or she had hoped. As a result, she may decide to stop engaging in such prosocial acts in the future or may even start acting more selfishly. Taken together, such factors clearly can contribute to poorer well-being outcomes in both the short term and the long term.

When positive activities result in reduced autonomy (one component of psychological need satisfaction), unhappiness is also likely to result. For example, in a study involving monetary donations, participants randomly assigned to donate freely showed increases in positive affect, while those forced to donate money showed marginally significant decreases in positive affect (Weinstein & Ryan, 2010). Inagaki and Orehek (in press) theorize that the requirement of positive activities to be autonomous in order to boost well-being also applies to another form of prosocial behavior—namely, providing support. For example, the association between chronic caregiving and reduced well-being may be partially explained by the caregivers' sense of necessity or obligation to help (Inagaki & Orehek, in press). Taken together, this work suggests that when positive activities are performed under conditions of low or no autonomy—that is, when positive activities are extrinsically motivated—they may reduce well-being. This phenomenon is consistent with classic work on cognitive dissonance, which has revealed that the perception of autonomy is critical to attitudinal shifts following a dissonance-inducing activity (e.g., writing counterattitudinal essays; Baumeister & Tice, 1984; Linder, Cooper, & Jones, 1967).

The Social Costs of Positive Activities

Very little research has examined the potential costs of the types of positive activities we have been discussing on individuals other than the happiness seeker. Notably, targets of gratitude letters, recipients of kind acts, or partners of individuals trying to practice optimism or savoring may all be impacted.

Kindness interventions, for example, are inherently social or other-oriented—that is, they do not merely affect the person performing the kind act; typically, another individual is involved to receive the generosity. Intuitively, of course, receiving a kind act should always be a positive experience, yet the literature on social support shows that receiving aid can threaten self-efficacy, curb autonomy, and invoke feelings of indebtedness among recipients (Fisher, Nadler, & Whitcher-Alagna, 1982). Researchers suggest that social support may confer deleterious effects on intimate relationships, particularly when efforts to help misfire, undermine the recipient's sense of self-sufficiency, or draw attention to the challenge or stressor the helper was trying to ameliorate (Rafaeli & Gleeson, 2009). Happiness seekers engaging in prosocial behavior should ensure that they are responsive to the recipient's needs (Maisel & Gable, 2009) and ideally demonstrate their generosity face-to-face (see Dunn & Dwyer, 2017). They should also strive to avoid inducing guilt or indebtedness in the recipient, making the recipient feel weak, vulnerable, or like a burden, or blaming the recipient for his or her misfortunes or setbacks (cf. Bolger, Zuckerman, & Kessler, 2000; McClure et al., 2014).

Regarding targets of gratitude, cross-cultural research suggests that receiving an expression of gratitude may not be a purely positive experience in all contexts. In Western cultures, for example, gratitude letters are frequently addressed to parents, but East Asian parents might feel insulted for being thanked for doing something they consider their parental duty. They may even feel disrespected by the implication that helping their child was optional. Such negative emotions may interfere with well-being, and, instead, foster dissatisfaction and unhappiness. Even in Western contexts, recipients of gratitude may feel awkward, uncomfortable, or indebted, thus impairing connectedness and relationship satisfaction.

Even individuals only proximally connected to the happiness seeker might suffer adverse effects on their well-being. In one study, company employees who witnessed acts of kindness in the workplace (i.e., participants who interacted with kindness-recipients) appeared to experience unfavorable social comparisons (Chancellor et al., 2017). It seems that merely viewing others receiving assistance may invoke negative thoughts and emotions for observers, who may wonder,

"Why is everyone suddenly so nice to my colleagues and not to me?" While this effect requires far more empirical investigation and replication, it is possible that *not* being selected as a target of a kind act may functionally diminish happiness.

Implications and Conclusions

In this chapter, we have put forward a number of pathways by which so-called positive activities might undermine well-being instead of lifting it. We believe that it is critical to study when, how, and why happiness-increasing activities can actually make people less (rather than more) happy, not just because this phenomenon is counterintuitive, but because well-being scientists can learn a great deal about when such practices will "work" by learning about when they will not work.

For example, if counting too many blessings is found to trigger feelings of disenchantment and alarm, then researchers will be galvanized to test what precise optimal dosage of counting blessings is necessary to trigger feelings of elevation, connectedness, and contentment. By the same token, after learning that expressing gratitude sometimes makes people feel less (rather than more) happy, gratitude scientists may be inspired to design a gratitude practice that could deliver the perfect mix of positive and negative emotions necessary to motivate the individual to be a better person. In previous work (Armenta, Fritz, & Lyubomirsky, 2017), we have proposed that gratitude can stimulate self-improvement (e.g., "Now that I recognize how much my parents have supported me throughout my education, I want to prove myself worthy of their kindness by being the best student possible"). However, this process may operate most successfully when the expression of gratitude produces enough positive emotion (e.g., feeling uplifted and supported by others) to motivate the person to approach goals, but also enough negative emotion (e.g., feeling guilty and indebted) to recognize the need to do so.

This idea, that although the practice of gratitude may sometimes "feel bad," the lingering unpleasant feelings may light a fire of change, suggests that sometimes the backfiring effects of positive activities may actually not be backfiring effects at all, but may instead represent adaptive processes. Indeed, according to evolutionary theorists, occasional negative emotions, combined with mild positive emotions, appear to be the most adaptive combination for humans (see Diener, Kanazawa, Suh, & Oishi, 2015; von Hippel & Gonsalkorale; and Forgas, this volume). Future investigators would do well to establish when, why, and how the apparent well-being-undermining effects of some positive activities under particular conditions may produce beneficial outcomes in the short term or long run.

Finally, but not unimportantly, as McNulty and Fincham eloquently proposed in 2012, well-being scientists should reconsider using the term "positive" to refer to positive activities, positive processes, and positive constructs. The evidence presented here persuasively suggests that positive activities (like expressing gratitude and doing acts of kindness) can have adverse impacts. To call them positive may not only be inaccurate but uninformative.

Our review, however, is clearly only the beginning, highlighting a few areas in which empirical evidence is emerging and many more areas in which it is scarce or lacking. Given mounting evidence suggesting that small and simple self-administered activities can transform people into happier and more flourishing individuals, it is critical to focus more empirical attention on what may not be "positive" about such practices and habits.

Bibliography

Ajzen, I. (1991). The theory of planned behavior. *Organizational Behavior and Human Processes*, *50*, 179–211.

Amichai-Hamburger, Y., & Etgar, S. (2017). Internet and wellbeing. To appear in J. P. Forgas & R. F. Baumeister (Eds.), *The social psychology of living well*. New York, NY: Psychology Press.

Armenta, C. N., Fritz, M., & Lyubomirsky, S. (2017). Functions of positive emotions: Gratitude as a motivator of self-improvement and positive change. *Emotion Review*.

Bandura, A. (1986). *Social foundations of thought and action: A social cognitive theory*. Englewood Cliffs, NJ: Prentice Hall.

Baumeister, R. F., & Tice, D. M. (1984). Role of self-presentation and choice in cognitive dissonance under forced compliance: Necessary or sufficient causes? *Journal of Personality and Social Psychology*, *46*, 5–13.

Boehm, J. K., & Kubzansky, L. D. (2012). The heart's content: The association between positive psychological well-being and cardiovascular health. *Psychological Bulletin*, *138*, 655–691.

Boehm, J. K., Lyubomirsky, S., & Sheldon, K. M. (2011). A longitudinal experimental study comparing the effectiveness of happiness-enhancing strategies in Anglo Americans and Asian Americans. *Cognition & Emotion*, *25*, 1263–1272.

Bolger, N., Zuckerman, A., & Kessler, R. C. (2000). Invisible support and adjustment to stress. *Journal of Personality and Social Psychology*, *79*, 953.

Chancellor, J., Margolis, S. M., Bao, K. J., & Lyubomirsky, S. (2017). *Everyday prosociality in the workplace: The benefits of giving, getting, and glimpsing*. Manuscript under review.

Chida, Y., & Steptoe, A. (2008). Positive psychological well-being and mortality: A quantitative review of prospective observational studies. *Psychosomatic Medicine*, *70*, 741–756.

Cohn, M. A., & Fredrickson, B. L. (2010). In search of durable positive psychology interventions: Predictors and consequences of long-term positive behavior change. *Journal of Positive Psychology*, *5*, 355–366.

Deci, E. L., & Ryan, R. M. (2000). Self-determination theory and the facilitation of intrinsic motivation, social development, and wellbeing. *American Psychologist*, *55*, 68–78.

Dickerhoof, R. M. (2007). Expressing optimism and gratitude: A longitudinal investigation of cognitive strategies to increase wellbeing. *Dissertation Abstracts International*, *68*, 4174 (UMI No. 3270426).

Diener, E. (2000). Subjective well-being: The science of happiness and a proposal for a national index. *American Psychologist*, *55*, 34–43.

Diener, E., Kanazawa, S., Suh, E. M., & Oishi, S. (2015). Why people are in a generally good mood. *Personality and Social Psychology Review*, *19*, 235–256.

Diener, E., Suh, E. M., Smith, H., & Shao, L. (1995). National differences in reported subjective well-being: Why do they occur? *Social Indicators Research*, *34*, 7–32.

Dunn, E. W., Aknin, L. B., & Norton, M. I. (2008). Spending money on others promotes happiness. *Science, 319*, 1687–1688.

Dunn, E. W., & Dwyer, R. J. (2017). The future of happiness. To appear in J. P. Forgas & R. F. Baumeister (Eds.), *The social psychology of living well*. New York, NY: Psychology Press.

Dweck, C. S., & Leggett, E. L. (1988). A social-cognitive approach to motivation and personality. *Psychological Review, 95*, 256–273.

Emmons, R. A., & McCullough, M. E. (2003). Counting blessings versus burdens: An experimental investigation of gratitude and subjective well-being in daily life. *Journal of Personality and Social Psychology, 84*, 377–389.

Fiedler, K., & Arslan, P. (2017). From a hedonic perspective on the good life to an analysis of underlying adaptive principles. To appear in J. P. Forgas & R. F. Baumeister (Eds.), *The social psychology of living well*. New York, NY: Psychology Press.

Fisher, J. D., Nadler, A., & Whitcher-Alagna, S. (1982). Recipient reactions to aid. *Psychological Bulletin, 91*, 27.

Ford, B. Q., & Mauss, I. B. (2014). The paradoxical effects of pursuing positive emotion: When and why wanting to feel happy backfires. In *Positive emotion: Integrating the light sides and dark sides* (1st ed., pp. 363–381). New York, NY: Oxford University Press.

Ford, B. Q., Shallcross, A. J., Mauss, I. B., Floerke, V. A., & Gruber, J. (2014). Desperately seeking happiness: Valuing happiness is associated with symptoms and diagnosis of depression. *Journal of Social and Clinical Psychology, 33*, 890–905.

Forgas, J. P. (2017). Negative affect and the good life: On the cognitive, motivational, and interpersonal benefits of negative mood. To appear in J. P. Forgas & R. F. Baumeister (Eds.), *The social psychology of living well*. New York, NY: Psychology Press.

Fredrickson, B. L. (2017). Biological underpinnings of positive emotions and purpose. To appear in J. P. Forgas & R. F. Baumeister (Eds.), *The social psychology of living well*. New York, NY: Psychology Press.

Fredrickson, B. L., Cohn, M. A., Coffey, K. A., Pek, J., & Finkel, S. M. (2008). Open hearts build lives: Positive emotions, induced through loving-kindness meditation, build consequential personal resources. *Journal of Personality and Social Psychology, 95*, 1045–1062.

Froh, J. J., Sefick, W. J., & Emmons, R. A. (2008). Counting blessings in early adolescents: An experimental study of gratitude and subjective well-being. *Journal of School Psychology, 46*, 213–233.

Gruber, J., Mauss, I. B., & Tamir, M. (2011). The dark side of happiness. *Perspectives on Psychological Science, 6*, 222–233.

Huppert, F. A. (2017). Living life well: The role of mindfulness and compassion. To appear in J. P. Forgas & R. F. Baumeister (Eds.), *The social psychology of living well*. New York, NY: Psychology Press.

Inagaki, T. K., & Orehek, E. (in press). On the benefits of giving social support: When, why, and how support providers gain by caring for others. *Current Directions in Psychological Science*.

Kesebir, P., & Diener, E. (2008). In pursuit of happiness: Empirical answers to philosophical questions. *Perspectives on Psychological Science, 3*, 117–125.

Layous, K., Lee, H., Choi, I., & Lyubomirsky, S. (2013). Culture matters when designing a successful happiness-increasing activity: A comparison of the United States and South Korea. *Journal of Cross-Cultural Psychology, 44*, 1294–1303.

Layous, K., & Lyubomirsky, S. (2014). The how, why, what, when, and who of happiness: Mechanisms underlying the success of positive interventions. In J. Gruber & J. Moscowitz (Eds.), *Positive emotion: Integrating the light sides and dark sides* (pp. 473–495). New York, NY: Oxford University Press.

Layous, K., Nelson, S. K., & Lyubomirsky, S. (2013). What is the optimal way to deliver a positive activity intervention? The case of writing about one's best possible selves. *Journal of Happiness Studies, 14*, 635–654.

Layous, K., Nelson, S. K., Oberle, E., Schonert-Reichl, K., & Lyubomirsky, S. (2012). Kindness counts: Prompting prosocial behavior in preadolescents boosts peer acceptance and well-being. *Plos One, 7*, e51380.

Layous, K., Sweeny, K., Armenta, C., Na, S., Choi, I., & Lyubomirsky, S. (2017). *The proximal experience of gratitude*. Manuscript under review.

Linder, D. E., Cooper, J., & Jones, E. E. (1967). Decision freedom as a determinant of the role of incentive magnitude in attitude change. *Journal of Personality and Social Psychology, 6*, 245–254.

Lyubomirsky, S. (2008). *The how of happiness: A scientific approach to getting the life you want*. New York, NY: Penguin Press.

Lyubomirsky, S. (2011). Hedonic adaptation to positive and negative experiences. In S. Folkman (Ed.), *The Oxford handbook of stress, health, and coping* (pp. 200–224). New York, NY: Oxford University Press.

Lyubomirsky, S., Dickerhoof, R., Boehm, J. K., & Sheldon, K. M. (2011). Becoming happier takes both a will and a proper way: An experimental longitudinal intervention to boost well-being. *Emotion, 11*, 391–402.

Lyubomirsky, S., King, L., & Diener, E. (2005). The benefits of frequent positive affect: Does happiness lead to success? *Psychological Bulletin, 131*, 803–855.

Lyubomirsky, S., & Layous, K. (2013). How do simple positive activities increase well-being? *Current Directions in Psychological Science, 22*, 57–62.

Lyubomirsky, S., Sheldon, K. M., & Schkade, D. (2005). Pursuing happiness: The architecture of sustainable change. *Review of General Psychology, 9*, 111–131.

Maisel, N. C., & Gable, S. L. (2009). The paradox of received social support: The importance of responsiveness. *Psychological Science, 20*, 928–932.

Mauss, I. B., Tamir, M., Anderson, C. L., & Savino, N. S. (2011). Can seeking happiness make people unhappy? Paradoxical effects of valuing happiness. *Emotion, 11*, 807–815.

McClure, M. J., Xu, J. H., Craw, J. P., Lane, S. P., Bolger, N., & Shrout, P. E. (2014). Understanding the costs of support transactions in daily life. *Journal of Personality, 82*, 563–574.

McMahon, D. M. (2008). The pursuit of happiness in history. In M. Eid & R. J. Larsen (Eds.), *The science of subjective well-being* (pp. 80–93). New York, NY: Guilford Press.

McNulty, J. K., & Fincham, F. D. (2012). Beyond positive psychology? Toward a contextual view of psychological processes and well-being. *American Psychologist, 67*, 101–110.

Neff, K. D., & Germer, C. K. (2013). A pilot study and randomized controlled trial of the Mindful Self-Compassion program. *Journal of Clinical Psychology, 69*, 28–44.

Nelson, S. K., Fuller, J. A. K., Choi, I., & Lyubomirsky, S. (2014). Beyond self-protection: Self-affirmation benefits hedonic and eudaimonic well-being. *Personality and Social Psychology Bulletin, 40*, 998–1011.

Nelson, S. K., Layous, K., Cole, S., & Lyubomirsky, S. (2016). Do unto others or treat yourself? The effects of prosocial and self-focused behavior on psychological flourishing. *Emotion, 16*, 850–861.

Oishi, S., Graham, J., Kesebir, S., & Galinha, I. C. (2013). Concepts of happiness across time and cultures. *Personality and Social Psychology Bulletin, 39*, 559–577.

Peters, M. L., Flink, I. K., Boersma, K., & Linton, S. J. (2010). Manipulating optimism: Can imagining a best possible self be used to increase positive future expectancies? *The Journal of Positive Psychology, 5*, 204–211.

Pressman, S. D., Kraft, T. L., & Cross, M. P. (2014). It's good to do good and receive good: The impact of a "pay it forward" style kindness intervention on giver and receiver well-being. *The Journal of Positive Psychology, 10*, 293–302.

Rafaeli, E., & Gleeson, M. E. (2009). Skilled support in intimate relationships. *Journal of Family Theory & Review, 1*, 20–37.

Schueller, S. M. (2010). Preferences for positive psychology exercises. *The Journal of Positive Psychology, 5*, 192–203.

Schwarz, N., Bless, H., Strack, F., Klumpp, G., Rittenauer-Schatka, H., & Simons, A. (1991). Ease of retrieval as information: Another look at the availability heuristic. *Journal of Personality and Social Psychology, 61*, 195–202.

Schwarz, N., Bless, H., Wanke, M., & Winkielman, P. (2003). Accessibility revisited. In G. V. Bodenhausen & A. J. Lambert (Eds.), *Foundations of social cognition: A festschrift in honor of Robert S. Wyer, Jr.* (pp. 51–77). Hillsdale, NJ: Lawrence Erlbaum Associates, Inc.

Sheldon, K. M. (2017). Understanding the good life: Eudaimonic living involves well-doing, not well-being. To appear in J. P. Forgas & R. F. Baumeister (Eds.), *The social psychology of living well*. New York, NY: Psychology Press.

Sheldon, K. M., Abad, N., Ferguson, Y., Gunz, A., Houser-Marko, L., Nichols, C. P., & Lyubomirsky, S. (2010). Persistent pursuit of need-satisfying goals leads to increased happiness: A 6-month experimental longitudinal study. *Motivation and Emotion, 34*, 39–48.

Sheldon, K. M., Boehm, J. K., & Lyubomirsky, S. (2012). Variety is the spice of happiness: The hedonic adaptation prevention (HAP) model. In I. Boniwell & S. David (Eds.), *Oxford handbook of happiness* (pp. 901–914). Oxford: Oxford University Press.

Sheldon, K. M., & Lyubomirsky, S. (2006). How to increase and sustain positive emotion: The effects of expressing gratitude and visualizing best possible selves. *The Journal of Positive Psychology, 1*, 73–82.

Shin, L. J., & Lyubomirsky, S. (2017). *Recalling kind acts for close others vs. strangers in Hong Kong Chinese and European Americans*. Paper to be presented at the annual meeting of the Society for Personality and Social Psychology, San Antonio, TX.

Simpson, J. A., Farrell, A. K., Huelsnitz, C. O., & Eller, J. (2017). Early social experiences and living well: A longitudinal view of adult physical health. To appear in J. P. Forgas & R. F. Baumeister (Eds.), *The social psychology of living well*. New York, NY: Psychology Press.

Sin, N. L., Della Porta, M. D., & Lyubomirsky, S. (2011). Tailoring positive psychology interventions to treat depressed individuals. In S. I. Donaldson, M. Csikszentmihalyi, & J. Nakamura (Eds.), *Applied positive psychology: Improving everyday life, health, schools, work, and society* (pp. 79–96). New York, NY: Routledge.

Sin, N. L., & Lyubomirsky, S. (2009). Enhancing well-being and alleviating depressive symptoms with positive psychology interventions: A practice friendly meta-analysis. *Journal of Clinical Psychology, 65*, 467–487.

von Hippel, W., & Gonsalkorale, K. (2017). Evolutionary imperatives and the good life. To appear in J. P. Forgas & R. F. Baumeister (Eds.), *The social psychology of living well*. New York, NY: Psychology Press.

Weinstein, N., & Ryan, R. M. (2010). When helping helps: Autonomous motivation for prosocial behavior and its influence on well-being for the helper and recipient. *Journal of Personality and Social Psychology, 98*, 222–244.

8

UNDERSTANDING THE GOOD LIFE

Eudaimonic Living Involves Well-Doing, Not Well-Being

Kennon M. Sheldon

Overview

"Eudaimonia" is a philosophical concept, derived from the writings of Aristotle, which concerns the most virtuous, rational, or exemplary ways to live. First imported into psychology by Waterman in the 1990s (Waterman, 1990a, 1990b, 1993), the concept is becoming increasingly popular with positive psychology researchers. A November 2016 PsychInfo search on the terms "eudaimonia, eudaimonic, eudaemonia, eudaemonic" revealed 4 articles in the 1990s, 92 articles in the 2000s, and already 418 articles in the 2010s. A separate search on the terms "eudaimonic well-being, eudaimonic happiness, eudaemonic well-being, eudaemonic happiness" yielded 0 hits in the 1990s, 49 in the 2000s, and 312 so far in the 2010s. Clearly, "eudaimonia" is a growth industry within positive psychology and within well-being psychology. But is it growing too fast?

Expanding on the observations of other well-being researchers in recent years (Diener, 1994; Kashdan, Biswas-Diener, & King, 2008; Kashdan & Steger, 2011; King, 2011), this chapter criticizes psychology's current use of the term "eudaimonia," and in particular, the terms "eudaimonic well-being" and "eudaimonic happiness." I suggest that psychologists have made a serious category mistake in linking the concepts of "eudaimonia" and "well-being," a mistake that Aristotle himself took great pains to avoid (e.g., in *Nicomachean Ethics* 1095b13–23; 1097b1–5; 1098a1–10; 1099a6–25). Eudaimonia, as originally conceived, was not a *feeling*, *psychological condition*, or *type of well-being*; rather, the concept referred to particular *ways of thinking and/or behaving*, ways which might subsequently affect or contribute to well-being. I will show that researchers' failure to make this distinction has contributed to erosion in scientific precision, and lost opportunities for understanding how positive change actually occurs.

In making this critique, my hope is not to eliminate the concept of eudaimonia from psychological research. Instead I hope to point the way toward a more circumscribed (but still very broad) definition of the term, so that it can be more usefully applied within temporal process models of positive functioning and positive personality development. In the latter part of the article I discuss one such process model, the "Eudaimonic Activity Model" (EAM; Sheldon, 2013, 2016). The EAM carefully distinguishes the concept of eudaimonia from the concept of well-being, by treating well-being as an outcome criterion variable that reliably results from truly eudaimonic activities, due to the experiential satisfactions that those activities bring. I will show that the EAM supplies a potentially valuable framework for testing and comparing different eudaimonic theories and constructs.

Problems With the Concept of EWB

As noted above, there has been exponential growth in usage of the term "eudaimonic well-being." But what does EWB mean, theoretically? Many answers have been given to this question, including "living in accordance with one's daemon or true self" (Waterman, 1993); "striving for perfection that represents the realization of one's true potential" (Ryff & Keyes, 1995); "having meaning/value/relevance to a broader context, personal growth/self-realization/maturity, excellence/ethics/quality, and authenticity/autonomy/integration" (Huta & Waterman, 2014; see also Baumeister, this volume); and "being autonomous, competent, and related in life" (Deci & Ryan, 2000). As these quotes illustrate, EWB is seemingly an umbrella term that can accommodate widely varying conceptions of the fully functioning human being, and widely varying conceptions of the nature of the good life.

From an empirical standpoint, the meaning of EWB is even broader and more multifarious. Below is just a partial list of measures that have been used to operationalize EWB. In some cases these measures are taken singly as measures of EWB, whereas in other cases they are combined together to create various aggregate EWB measures. The measures include autonomy, mastery, positive relations, purpose, personal growth, and self-acceptance (i.e., psychological well-being; Ryff & Keyes, 1995; see also Huppert; Fritz & Lyubomirsky; and Shah, this volume); flow, psychological need-satisfaction, and meaning in life (Nelson et al., 2014); self-concordant motivation and elevation (Passmore & Howell, 2014); vitality, personal growth, life-engagement, and self-determination (Lewis et al., 2014); vitality and self-actualization (Thrash, Elliott, Maruskin, & Cassidy, 2010); and feelings of connectedness to nature (Trigwell et al., 2014). Bauer and McAdams (2010) operationalized EWB as Loevingerian ego development (for the reader's information, ego development is scored via content analysis of the complexity of participants' sentence completions). Hansen (2015) operationalized EWB as the combination of meaning in life, vitality, flourishing, and social relationships. Kiaei and Reio (2014) operationalized EWB in terms of a 15-item "goal aspiration" scale that combines goal-related effort intentions, importance, clarity, and inspiration. McMahan and colleagues (McMahan & Estes, 2011; McMahan, Dixon, & King, 2013) operationalized EWB in terms of participant's lay theories about well-being, specifically in terms of the extent people endorse the mere *belief* that well-being is a eudaimonic phenomenon. The 21-item Questionnaire for Eudaimonic Well-Being (QEWB; Waterman et al., 2010) assesses feelings of self-discovery, of fulfilling best potentials, of pursuing excellence, of having meaning in life, of investing significant effort in something, of being involved in life, of having purpose, and being personally expressive (Seaton & Beaumont, 2015). The recent *Handbook of Eudaimonic Well-Being* (Vitterso, 2016) has chapters on the following 12 "elements" of EWB: self-actualization, self-determination, personal expressiveness, flow, intrinsic motivation, meaningful life, flourishing, spirituality (wholeness and holiness), wisdom, positivity, personal growth, and individual orientations.

As these examples illustrate, the category of "eudaimonic well-being constructs" is threatening to become merely synonymous with the category of "positive psychology constructs," a kind of terminological bracket creep (Kashdan & Steger, 2011). Figure 8.1 illustrates the resulting situation, in which the concept of EWB can contain any and every positive-sounding psychological characteristic. The only positive psychology constructs definitely *not* included in the EWB category are positive mood, life-satisfaction, and (low) negative affect. These are the three main components of subjective well-being (SWB), or hedonic well-being (HWB) as it is sometimes labelled. SWB and HWB will be discussed more fully in a later section of the chapter.

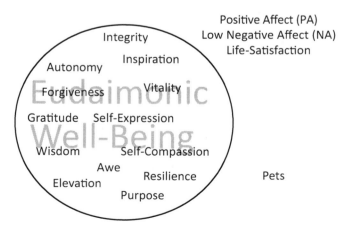

FIGURE 8.1 The Ever-Expanding EWB Category

Of course there are many non-eudaimonic factors that can have effects on well-being. One such factor, illustrated in Figure 8.1, is "pets." Most people are familiar with the *Peanuts* comic phrase, "Happiness is a warm puppy." While we might agree with the sentiment, few of us would make the mistake of thinking that a warm puppy *literally IS* happiness; rather, it is a potential *cause* of happiness, among infinite other potential causes of happiness. Although it is easy (in this context) to see the mistake made by the "happiness is a warm puppy" phrase, it is more difficult to see the mistake when psychological constructs are involved. A central contention of this chapter is that those who use the terms "eudaimonic well-being" or "eudaimonic happiness" are making the "happiness is a warm puppy" mistake, and are thereby losing the distinction between the *causes* of happiness, and happiness *itself*.

Another problem with this state of affairs is that the EWB umbrella is easily extended to cover ideas or constructs that define "the good" in questionable ways (e.g., spiritual ideologies demanding annihilation of nonbelievers, cultural ideologies extolling possession of a perfect body, or political ideologies justifying a permanent underclass). An additional problem is that researchers are faced by an ever greater variety of outcome measures to consider including within their costly intervention studies. What kind of "well-being" should they measure and try to influence—spirituality, wisdom, benevolence, purpose, gratitude, self-regulation, ego development? What if they pick the "wrong" kind or kinds of well-being to study, according to reviewers of their work—will they have missed the boat?

Towards a Solution: Definitional Considerations

Defining Well-Being as Prevailing SWB

In this section I will examine the definitions and meanings of happiness, well-being, and eudaimonia, seeking a plausible way forward. In Merriam-Webster, the first definition of *well-being* is "the state of being happy, healthy, or prosperous." The first definition of *happiness* is "a state of well-being and contentment." The fact that happiness and well-being appear in each other's definitions suggests that they are close synonyms, both referring to a positively valenced feeling or state of mind whose content, stability, and duration are unspecified. In research psychology, the construct hewing closest to these definitions is SWB (mentioned earlier), which typically combines high positive mood, low negative mood, and high global life-satisfaction (Busseri, 2015; Diener, 1984, 1994; Sheldon & Elliott, 1999). SWB reflects the person's evaluation of his or her own psychological feeling-state (Busseri, 2015; Busseri & Sadava, 2011; Diener, 1994), assessed as a resting condition of the person at a particular moment in time. This psychological state may of course be influenced by people's prior or current behavioral activity, but the SWB measure makes no direct reference to such activity, a desirable characteristic as will be shown below.

In common research practice SWB refers not to *momentary* emotions or feelings, but rather, to *a prevailing* psychological state during a particular period of a person's life—a moving average that can be nudged up or down by the varying and changing circumstances people encounter, the various kinds of activities in which people engage, and their varying responses to those circumstances and activities (Lyubomirsky, Sheldon, & Schkade, 2005; Sheldon & Lyubomirsky, 2006). Defining happiness as a relatively stable but also somewhat changeable outcome state allows for scientific investigation of substantive rather than transitory changes in well-being, at the level of individual lives—lives in which people are continually trying out various new activities, goals, friends, work-out programs, positive psychology interventions, and so on, in the effort to craft enjoyable and meaningful lives for themselves. Thus the question arises: "Which of the things people do, say, and think, actually succeed in improving their prevailing SWB?" (Sheldon, 2004). Perhaps ten sessions at the tanning salon will not do it, but ten sessions volunteering at a local shelter *would* do it (or vice versa)? People conduct many such experiments in their lives.

Defining Eudaimonia as a Type or Aspect of Conative Activity

The *Encyclopaedia Britannica* notes that for Aristotle, "eudaimonia was not a state of mind consequent on or accompanying certain activities but is a name for these activities themselves. 'What is eudaimonia?' is then the same question as 'What are the best activities of which man is capable?'" This passage clearly shows that Aristotle did not define eudaimonia as a positive *feeling or state of mind*, as in the dictionary and operational definitions of well-being above; rather, eudaimonia refers to *activity*, specifically, activities that are known (or shown) to be rational, virtuous, ethical, or otherwise commendable (see also Fiedler & Arslan, this volume). The term "activity" here refers to people's values, orientations, motivations, goals, and behaviors (Huta & Waterman, 2014), all of which are expressions of people's answers to Socrates' perennial question: "How shall we live?" This activity-based conception of eudaimonia clearly distinguishes it from feeling-based conceptions of well-being, which, again, involve emotional or evaluative states assessed as a resting condition of a person at a particular moment or period in time.

This conception of eudaimonia also fits well with the classical distinction between the cognitive, affective, and conative components of the human mind (Huitt & Cain, 2005; Little, 1999; Mayer, Chabot, & Carlsmith, 1997; Tallon, 1997). According to Meyer et al. (1997, p. 31),

> Conation (or motivation) includes components that propel or move the organism such as the hunger drive or the need for achievement. In contrast the affect group—in particular, emotion—includes basic feelings such as anger and happiness along with the mental programs for emotional

facial expressions. The cognition group—thought-related processes and mechanisms—includes elements such as working memory, judgment, and reasoning.

In these terms, eudaimonia is a conative concept, specifically attempting to address the "quality" of what the person is doing, or trying to do. In contrast, "well-being" is a construct that is primarily affective and evaluative in nature, concerning how the person feels. Meyer et al. (1997) insisted that clear distinctions should be maintained between these three components of the mind, in order to promote greater theoretical development and integration. Unfortunately the term EWB does the exact opposite, conflating affective, cognitive, and conative facets of the mind.   In my view, eudaimonia is something that is *done*, not felt; in contrast, well-being is something that is *felt*, not done. This difference is important, because it means that the two types of concept are relevant at different phases of a dynamic behavioral process, in which motivated behaviors lead to experiential outcomes, which reinforce or fail to reinforce those behaviors, leading to further behaviors, and so on (Carver & Scheier, 1981; Sheldon, 2011).

Figure 8.2 illustrates a different approach for well-being and positive psychology researchers, in which the concept of well-being is restricted to SWB, and positive activity-based concepts are considered to be "eudaimonic factors," rather than "aspects of EWB." Figure 8.2 also shows that eudaimonic factors and SWB could both be considered as aspects of a broader category of "Flourishing," if

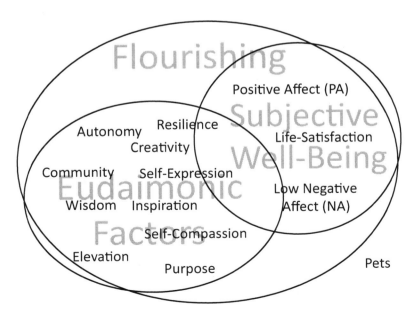

FIGURE 8.2   Distinguishing Eudaimonic Factors From Subjective Well-Being, as Aspects of Flourishing

desired (as suggested by Keyes, 2002; see also Huppert, this volume). After all, they are both attempts to understand the high-functioning human being, and eudaimonic and SWB measures tend to share much overlapping variance (Keyes, 2002).

Subjective Well-Being as an Unbiased Metric for Evaluating the Eudaimonic Quality of Activity

Is there an objective, value-free way to evaluate the happiness-relevant "quality" of an activity? In this section, I will further describe the properties of SWB and discuss several possible advantages of using it as a primary definition and measure of well-being. In the section after that, I will present the Eudaimonic Activity Model (EAM), which takes advantage of these properties to provide a general model for testing eudaimonic theories. Then in the final section of the chapter I will consider further problems in the EWB literature, and show how the EAM handles or resolves these problems.

Advantages of Adopting SWB as a Primary Measure of Well-Being and Thriving

1. SWB Is a Good Indicator of the Overall State of the Personality System

SWB provides a reasonably accurate readout of the current prevailing state of the person's emotional-evaluative system. Right now, in this particular period of his or her life, is the person cheerful, engaged, and satisfied—or is he or she sad, angry, and dissatisfied? Such feelings are biologically grounded, to be point of being hard-wired into the facial musculature (Keltner, 2009; see also von Hippel & Gonsalkorale, this volume). Of course SWB as measured by self-report is necessarily subjective, but this does not mean it is just a "feel good" state with few consequences; on the contrary, SWB predicts a wide variety of positive outcomes including greater job success, physical health, marital longevity, and even lifespan duration (Lyubomirsky, King, & Diener, 2005; Myers, 2000). For example, the well-known nuns study (Danner, Snowdon, & Friesen, 2001) found that positive affect, as coded from the diaries of young nuns in their 20s, predicted the nun's survival (or failure to survive) into their 80s and 90s (see also Fredrickson, this volume).

2. SWB Is Reasonably Unitary and Economical

Researchers working with measures of mood and life-satisfaction typically find that they form a single factor, upon which negative affect loads negatively. Still, the three components can be kept separate for some purposes, to derive more detailed information (Busseri, 2015; Busseri & Sadava, 2011). For example, perhaps some interventions work primarily by reducing negative affect, and other interventions work primarily by increasing positive affect; this could be important information (van Zyl & Rothman, 2014). Overall, the construct of SWB gives researchers a relatively simple and easily administered measure of emotional health that can be used to compare the effects of the wide variety of different attitudes, activities, and practices that humans may adopt. This recommendation does not limit the complexity of our *theories* of well-being, nor does it preclude construing eudaimonic constructs as *outcomes*, rather than as predictors; nor am I saying that researchers should *only* use SWB as an outcome. Instead, I am suggesting that SWB might form the core of a standardized well-being assessment, with additional outcome variables such as performance, social adjustment, or physical health being identified and included based on the researcher's goals.

3. SWB Is Relatively Unbiased Because It Is Mostly Free of Psychosocial Content

As researchers try to conceptualize and compare the various ways that humans think, feel, behave, and live, their concepts and measures inevitably contain what I will call "psychosocial content." Psychosocial content refers to the world of semantic and thematic concepts within which human beings live their lives— what Karl Popper (1978) termed World 2, the world of mental objects and mental events. Psychosocial content can be seen not only in people's minds, but also in the terminology of our psychological theories, as they name and explain the various possible causes of experience and behavior. Psychosocial content can also be seen in various philosophies of life, including eudaimonic philosophies, as these philosophies lay claim to identify the "best" goals, attitudes, practices, and so forth for people to engage in. Psychosocial content always comes within networks of implications, associations, and connotations, including both meanings that are shared across the globe and meanings that can be highly idiosyncratic to individuals and/or to the linguistic or cultural groups to which they belong.

For example, Levontina and Zalizniak (2001) noted that

> the difference between the Russian sčastliv, sčast'e and the English words happy or happiness, is so great that it makes one doubt whether it is right to regard these words as translation equivalents ... unlike the English word happiness which denotes an everyday emotion, the Russian word "schastye" refers to an existential ideal.
>
> *(p. 297)*

It seems there is more psychosocial content bound up with the Russian conception of happiness than in the English conception, content having to do with prescriptive ideals for living. Thus, Americans and Russians might have very different concepts in mind when rating their "happiness," making it impossible to meaningfully compare their scores.

If well-being is conceptualized primarily as SWB, however, then the situation is much simplified. The positive affect negative affect schedule (PANAS) contains single mood adjectives that reference relatively universal emotional states, backed by biological processes (i.e., excited, afraid, ashamed), adjectives that are easy to translate and back-translate across different languages and cultural settings. Ratings on the Satisfaction With Life Scale (SWLS; Diener, Emmons, Larsen, & Griffin, 1985) are also relatively free of psychosocial content, but in a different way: The referent, the participant's overall level of "satisfaction," is quite abstract (e.g., "I am satisfied with my life"; "My life is close to my ideal"). This abstraction entails that measures of global life-satisfaction contain no hints concerning what factors may have brought about the referenced degree of satisfaction; the items are uncontaminated with psychosocial content.

Returning to the English/Russian difference: If researchers were to define well-being as SWB, this would simplify and standardize the definition of well-being, and would facilitate comparison of the effects of the two cultural systems upon their citizens. Perhaps Russians are lower in SWB, because their culture impresses an unattainable ideal of happiness upon them? Or perhaps Russians are instead higher in SWB, because of the inspirational effects of these existential ideals? Such hypotheses and processes can be tested.

4. SWB Already Distinguishes Between Eudaimonic and Non-Eudaimonic Ways of Valuing and Living

In the last 25 years, constructs associated with hedonism (i.e., materialism, narcissism, Machiavellianism) have been found to be negatively associated with SWB, rather than positively associated (Kasser, 2002; Crocker & Canevello, 2012). In contrast, constructs associated with eudaimonia (i.e., purpose, gratitude, forgiveness) are typically positively associated with SWB (Vitterso, 2016). Thus, when purportedly "eudaimonic" (virtuous, commendable) and "hedonic" (self-centered, interpersonally corrosive) ways of living are compared to each other as predictors, SWB is already sufficient to distinguish between them. This means that researchers may not need to invent any additional measures of well-being in order to make the distinctions they want to make; SWB suffices to distinguish between eudaimonic and non-eudaimonic living.

5. SWB Thus Provides a Criterion for Comparing and Winnowing Eudaimonic Theories

Different models or theories of EWB propose varying numbers of basic elements of EWB. For example, Seligman's PERMA model (Seligman, 2011) focuses on five: positive emotions, engagement, positive relationships, meaning, and accomplishment. Ryff's PWB (Psychological Well-Being) model (Ryff & Keyes, 1995) focuses on six: mastery, positive relationships, personal growth, purpose, self-acceptance, and autonomy. Vitterso's edited (2016) EWB book has chapters for 12 different elements of EWB, including self-actualization, self-determination, personal expressiveness, flow, intrinsic motivation, meaningful life, flourishing, spirituality, wisdom, positivity, personal growth, and individual orientations. Chapters in this book illustrate a number of additional possible conceptualizations and definitions of EWB (see, for example, Fiedler & Arslan; Huppert; Gable; Fredrickson; Shah) Considering these lists together raises questions. Which set of elements, if any, is correct? If no single list is correct in its entirety, which particular elements within the sets, if any, belong on a "final" list? Perhaps the ones that appear most frequently across the different sets? (For example, "meaning" made many lists above.) But this would seem to reduce the search for the core features of eudaimonic living to a popularity contest among theorists.

The solution advocated here is to test the multifarious members of these different sets, to determine which elements in the sets may be more or less important than others. Perhaps some eudaimonic-sounding concepts do not actually help people to thrive—how will we know unless we test them? But how can we test and compare them? Again, SWB can provide a relevant comparison standard, allowing any and all purportedly eudaimonic contents, activities, practices, traits, contexts, interventions, or organizational/cultural styles to be compared as to whether they help create positive mental states.

Note—just because SWB *can* be used as a criterion variable (amongst other criteria a researcher might choose) does *not* mean that SWB is an ultimate virtue, or that SWB should be the true goal of all striving. SWB is a convenient outcome that seems to result from "right activity." As King (2011) eloquently put it, "What stronger argument could there be for the central role of happiness . . . than evidence that this variable ('plain old happiness') tracks the engagement of our better natures?" (p. 441). But again, that does not mean that people should pursue SWB directly—that would mistake the symptom for the cause (Sheldon, Corcoran, & Prentice, 2017), would go against Aristotle's recommendation to pursue virtue not happiness, and likely would not work anyway (van Zyl & Rothman, 2014).

The Temptation to Expand the Conception of Well-Being

Why do researchers feel that additional measures or conceptions of well-being are needed, in addition to SWB? There appear to be several reasons. First, there is a fear that SWB misses something important—intuition tells us that "there must be more to a good life than just positive mood and satisfaction." Indeed, this intuition likely explains much of the appeal of Ryff's Psychological Well-Being model (PWB; Ryff, 1989; Ryff & Keyes, 1995) when it first appeared: The model promised to deliver a more nuanced, complex understanding of well-being than what existed before. And in fact, the intuition is correct: There *is* much more to a good life besides SWB; as noted above, SWB is not what people should strive for.

However, in the Aristotelian view, these additional features of a good life are *not* additional features of well-being, because they involve well-*doing*, not well-being; they are conative processes, not affective processes.

A second reason for some researchers' desire to define well-being as involving something more than SWB is what might be called the "myth of the happy hedonist." Believers in this myth feel sure that the world is full of pleasure-seeking, self-centered people who are happier than they should be. Truly virtuous people, in this view, are the ones for whom happiness does not matter; perhaps they even entirely sacrifice their happiness for great causes. Taken to its logical extreme, the myth suggests that measures of eudaimonic living should be *negatively*, not positively, associated with SWB! Again, however, research during the last 20 years has amply demonstrated that people who are more narcissistic, materialistic, self-centered, and pleasure-centered are (on average) less happy, not more happy, than the rest of us (Crocker & Canevello, 2012; Kasser, 2002; Sheldon, 2014; see also Fiedler & Arslan, this volume). Their relationships are not healthy and their personal growth is stalled; their hedonism is an overcompensation for an unfulfilling life (Kasser, 2002; Vansteenkiste & Ryan, 2013).

Yet a third reason the field searches for a different thriving indicator than SWB is because of the misleading equation of SWB with "hedonic" well-being (HWB). A recent search (November 23, 2016) yielded 283 research articles comparing the effects of various interventions, social contexts, or personal practices upon both "hedonic" and "eudaimonic" well-being (Kopperud & Vitterso, 2008). In these articles, HWB (theoretically involving self-indulgence and pleasure) is construed as a less desirable or commendable form of well-being than EWB (theoretically involving virtuous living and self-actualization strivings; see Vitterso, 2013). Very frequently, however, *SWB* serves as the measure of hedonic well-being, because of SWB's reference to positive relative to negative emotions (Church et al., 2014; Nelson, Fuller, Choi, & Lyubomirsky, 2014; Ryff & Singer, 2008; Ryff, 2014). However, as discussed above, SWB is actually predicted by virtuous, eudaimonic activity, not by pleasure- and self-centered activity. Hedonic well-being (HWB) may well be worth studying, but if so, it needs to be defined and measured in ways more commensurate with its connotations of excess, imbalance, and immaturity. I suggest that the concept of HWB should not be operationalized via the SWB measure, because it taints the concept of SWB with content and properties that it does not actually possess.

The Eudaimonic Activity Model

The foregoing reasoning suggests a specific heuristic for testing eudaimonic theories, which can resolve many of the problems discussed above: the "Eudaimonic Activity Model" (EAM). The simplest version of the EAM is depicted below:

Eudaimonic Activities ⟶ SWB

The EAM is based on the assumption that peoples' activities yield experiential results that may or may not bring SWB, and that (actual) eudaimonic activities tend to be the ones that really *do* bring SWB. In my own longitudinal research I have employed the EAM model to study the SWB changes induced by varying types of personal goal pursuits (Sheldon & Elliot, 1999; Sheldon & Kasser, 1998), varying happiness strategies (Sheldon & Lyubomirsky, 2006, 2012), varying value types (Sheldon, 2005; Sheldon, Arndt, & Houser-Marko, 2003), varying role identities and identity characteristics (Sheldon, Gunz, & Schachtman, 2012; Sheldon, Ryan, Rawsthorne, & Ilardi, 1997), and varying types of goal-motive matching (Sheldon & Cooper, 2008; Sheldon & Schuler, 2011). Many other researchers have pursued a similar strategy of treating SWB as a criterion variable for evaluating the effectiveness of particular traits, virtues, or activities (Kahneman, Diener, & Schwartz, 1999; Ryan et al., 2013; see also Huppert; Gable; and Fritz & Lyubomirsky, this volume). Although it is possible to think of some eudaimonic activities that might *not* be associated with well-being (e.g., self-control, self-denial, self-sacrifice), it should still be the case that these activities *do* produce SWB in the long term. In contrast, any purportedly eudaimonic activity that reduces a person's SWB, in both the short and long term, should be viewed with suspicion.

What About Outcome Experiences That Have Psychosocial Content?

Readers may have noticed that the boundary between conative activities (values, orientations, motivations, goals, and behaviors) and well-being (affective and evaluative outcomes) is not always as clear as I have portrayed. Again, I have suggested that conative constructs always come with psychosocial content, while SWB does not. However, there are many positive experiential constructs that are not necessarily conative, which *do* come with psychosocial content—occupying an intermediate zone between intentional activity and evaluative/emotional reactions. Carol Ryff's six PWB subscales—autonomy, mastery, positive relations, personal growth, purpose, and self-acceptance—are a case in point (Ryff & Keyes, 1995).

I suggest that like SWB, the PWB scales should *also* be treated as readouts of the psychological health of the person, with each aspect of PWB having a narrower and more specific content focus compared to SWB, and with each aspect perhaps helping to produce SWB. Of course, the six PWB constructs are not really narrow; Ryff (1989) distilled them from a comprehensive analysis of the entire mental health literature. Still, from the EAM perspective, none of the six types of PWB are well-being itself; instead, they are important categories of satisfying experiences that may potentially cause SWB.

One benefit of recognizing an intermediate category of "satisfying experiences" is that it can help us to explain *why* certain eudaimonic activities produce SWB: namely, because those behaviors bring people rich and rewarding experiences, which both reinforce the behaviors and produce well-being. Self-determination theory (SDT; Deci & Ryan, 1985, 2000) makes extensive use of this idea. As noted above, SDT says that all human beings have basic psychological needs for three specific types of satisfying experiences: autonomy, competence, and relatedness. When people's needs are satisfied, they are enabled to experience wholeness, health, and happiness (Deci & Ryan, 2000). In my own research, psychological need-satisfaction has been shown to mediate the SWB effects of achieving self-concordant versus less concordant goals (Sheldon & Elliott, 1999), the SWB effects of having balanced versus unbalanced time apportionments across the day (Sheldon, Cummins, & Khamble, 2010), the SWB effects of having one's "social character" traits be consistent with one's "unguarded self" traits (Sheldon et al., 2012), the SWB effects of attending a student-centered compared to a traditional law school (Sheldon & Krieger, 2007), the SWB effects of being assigned to pursue motive-congruent (Sheldon & Schuler, 2011) or need-congruent goals (Sheldon, Abad, Ferguson, Gunz, Houser-Marko, Nichols, & Lyubomirsky, 2010) rather than alternative goals, and the SWB effects of being exposed to need-supportive versus unsupportive instructional styles in a game-learning context (Sheldon & Filak, 2008).

The Full Eudaimonic Activity Model

The above reasoning leads to the full EAM, depicted below.

Eudaimonic Activities   —>   Satisfying Experiences   —>   SWB

This is a very simple but abstract model that acknowledges that people have a wide variety of choices they can make regarding what to do, who to associate with, and what to think and believe in their conative life. The chief advantage of making wise (i.e., truly eudaimonic) choices, according to the model, is that such choices will bring many satisfying experiences, which in turn will tend to bring happiness and satisfaction, that is, SWB. As noted above, the EAM also implies that people should not pursue SWB directly (Sheldon et al., 2017). Since SWB is relatively content free, it is very difficult to forecast or predict in advance what will bring positive feelings and satisfaction (Gilbert, 2006; Wilson & Gilbert, 2005). Instead, as discussed earlier, people should pursue "the best activities of which they are capable" (i.e., eudaimonia). People will know that they are succeeding at this when they start to feel deep satisfactions in life. In Keltner's memorable (2009) book title, humans are "born to be good." This means that people are born to *feel* good (i.e., to feel SWB) when they *are* good (i.e., when they behave eudaimonically). We receive emotional rewards when we strive for our best. Notably, the EAM is conceptually similar to the general model of well-being presented by Fritz and Lyubomirsky (this volume), in which various behaviors can potentially produce gains in happiness or well-being, as mediated by various types of high-quality experiences. One difference is that Fritz and Lyubomirsky's model applies more to positive psychology interventions than to motivated activity, and it does not contain the EAM's assumption that only activities that are beneficial for personality development are likely to produce happiness boosts.

Figure 8.3 contains an updated version of Figure 8.2, which distinguishes three aspects of flourishing, not just two. It does this by splitting the "eudaimonic factors" category into two categories: eudaimonic practices and satisfying psychosocial experiences. The satisfying experiences category (Sheldon et al., 2001) potentially contains the three proposed needs of SDT (autonomy, competence, relatedness), as well as Ryff and Keyes' six PWB constructs, as well as other seemingly important experiences such as awe, meaning, or inspiration, which still need to be evaluated in comparison to one another. Figure 8.3 also contains three arrows that depict the full dynamic process model posited by the EAM, illustrating a "virtuous cycle" effect in which, if people can get themselves to behave in eudaimonic ways, they will have satisfying experiences (lower arrow), which will both reinforce the original behaviors (upper arrow), and bring SWB as an outcome (right arrow), which will support further eudaimonic practices.

Importantly, the EAM in some respects merely formalizes a suggestion made by Ryan, Huta, and Deci (2008). Ryan et al. (2008) argued that there are four aspects of eudaimonic living: self-determined motivation, intrinsic value orientation, the practice of mindful self-awareness, and psychological need-satisfaction. Furthermore, Ryan et al. (2008) suggested that psychological need-satisfaction

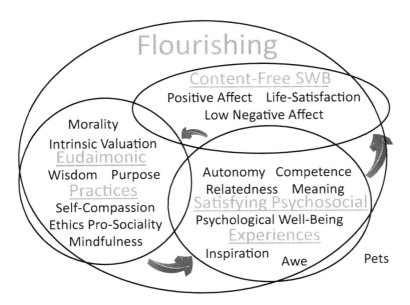

FIGURE 8.3 The Full Eudaimonic Activity Model

is best construed as a mediator, which can explain the effects of the other three aspects of eudaimonia upon positive outcomes such as SWB or physical health. The EAM fully accepts this suggestion but does not restrict the category of eudaimonic activities to only self-determined motivation, intrinsic value orientation, and mindful self-awareness; other eudaimonic constructs besides the three could be proposed and tested.

How the Eudaimonic Activity Model Can Help Solve Other Problems in the EWB Literature

In sum, there are a variety of problems with the concept of eudaimonic well-being, problems which seem to have confused researchers and unduly complicated our understanding of well-being. These problems include a) the problem of mixing up two different aspects of the human mind (conation and affect), and the consequent problem of confusing prescribable behaviors with the experiential results of those behaviors; b) the problem of profound disagreements within the field concerning the definition and measurement of well-being; c) the problem of over-proliferation of eudaimonic theories and constructs, without sufficient winnowing and comparative testing; and d) the problem of value and confirmation bias in positive psychology research and eudaimonia research. The EAM addresses all of these issues, by a) clearly distinguishing between three types of construct—conative activities, satisfying psychosocial experiences, and SWB; b) defining well-being primarily as SWB, thereby preventing contamination of an important criterion variable by the very practices which may produce (or not produce) that criterion; c) providing a powerful process model framework that can afford comparative evaluation and explanation of new eudaimonic concepts and measures; and d) promoting a norm in which eudaimonic theories are expected to be tested as producers of agreed-upon measures of psychological health, in the same way that medical prescriptions are efficacy-tested by their effects on agreed-upon measures of physical health.

Conclusion

In 2009, in their response to Kashdan, Biswas-Diener, and King's (2008) article criticizing the EWB construct, Ryan and Huta (2009) argued in favor of retaining the concept of EWB. They suggested that it is premature to confine well-being to SWB alone, and asserted that it would be more generative for the field to further explore the implications of the EWB concept. My survey of the recent literature suggests that EWB has failed the test: It is making the situation more confusing rather than less confusing. However, there is a relatively simple solution to the problem. Namely, reconceptualize EWB constructs not as forms of well-being, but rather, as *either* "eudaimonic activity" constructs, which can potentially bring satisfying experiences and thus SWB, *or* as "satisfying experience" constructs, which can potentially reinforce eudaimonic activities and mediate their effects upon SWB. I suggest that this reconceptualization could allow the field to make swift new progress concerning many important questions and surmount considerable confusion in the process. Failing this, the field of positive psychology might continue to be a marketing competition as much as a scientific competition, in which the incentives sometimes favor murkiness over clarity.

Although I have painted the picture in somewhat dire terms, in truth, there is more agreement than disagreement here. All eudaimonia researchers would agree that an essential aspect of human nature is people's quest to find better ways to live, so that they, and those around them, can thrive to the maximal extent. And all researchers would agree that some forms of activity and ways of living are more self-centered and short-sighted and unlikely to be as fulfilling as other, more eudaimonic ways of living. The only problem is that eudaimonia researchers have gone somewhat astray by focusing on distinguishing eudaimonic well-being from "mere" SWB, rather than focusing on distinguishing eudaimonic activity from less eudaimonic activity. Instead of *battling* SWB, eudaimonia researchers might instead *use* SWB as one of the most powerful tools for validating their theories of right action.

Note

The study has been funded by the Russian Academic Excellence Project 5–100.

Bibliography

Bauer, J. J., & McAdams, D. P. (2010). Eudaimonic growth: Narrative growth goals predict increases in ego development and subjective well-being 3 years later. *Developmental Psychology, 46*(4), 761–772. doi:10.1037/a0019654

Bauer, J. J., McAdams, D. P., & Pals, J. L. (2008). Narrative identity and eudaimonic well-being. *Journal of Happiness Studies, 9*(1), 81–104. doi:10.1007/s10902-006-9021-6

Bryden, C. I., Field, A. M., & Francis, A. P. (2015). Coping as a mediator between negative life events and eudaimonic well-being in female adolescents. *Journal of Child and Family Studies.* doi:10.1007/s10826-015-0180-0

Busseri, M. A. (2015). Toward a resolution of the tripartite structure of subjective well-being. *Journal of Personality, 83*(4), 413–428. doi:10.1111/jopy.12116

Busseri, M. A., & Sadava, S. W. (2011). A review of the tripartite structure of subjective well-being: Implications for conceptualization, operationalization, analysis, andsynthesis. *Personality and Social Psychology Review, 15*(3), 290–314. doi:10.1177/1088868310391271

Carver, C. S., & Scheier, M. F. (1981). *Attention and self-regulation.* New York: Springer-Verlag.

Church, A. T., Katigbak, M. S., Ibáñez-Reyes, J., de Jesús Vargas-Flores, J., Curtis, G. J., Tanaka-Matsumi, J., . . . Simon, J. R. (2014). Relating self-concept consistency to hedonic and eudaimonic well-being in eight cultures. *Journal of Cross-Cultural Psychology, 45*(5), 695–712. doi:10.1177/0022022114527347

Crocker, J., & Canevello, A. (2012). Consequences of self-image and compassionate goals. In P. Devine, A. Plant, P. Devine, & A. Plant (Eds.), *Advances in experimental social psychology* (Vol. 45, pp. 229–277). San Diego, CA: Academic Press.

Danner, D. D., Snowdon, D. A., & Friesen, W. V. (2001). Positive emotions in early life and longevity: Findings from the nun study. *Journal of Personality and Social Psychology*, *80*, 804–813.

Deci, E. L., & Ryan, R. M. (1985). *Intrinsic motivation and self-determination in human behavior.* New York, NY: Plenum.

Deci, E. L., & Ryan, R. M. (2000). The "what" and "why" of goal pursuits: Human needs and the self-determination of behavior. *Psychological Inquiry*, *11*, 227–268.

Diener, E. (1984). Subjective well-being. *Psychological Bulletin*, *95*, 542–575.

Diener, E. (1994). Assessing subjective well-being: Progress and opportunities. *Social Indicators Research*, *31*, 103–157.

Diener, E., Emmons, R., Larsen, R., & Griffin, S. (1985). The satisfaction with life scale. *Journal of Personality Assessment*, *47*, 1105–1117.

Gilbert, D. (2006). *Stumbling on happiness.* New York, NY: Alfred A. Knopf.

Hansen, K. B. (2015). Exploring compatibility between "subjective well-being" and "sustainable living" in Scandinavia. *Social Indicators Research*, *122*(1), 175–187. doi:10.1007/s11205-014-0684-9

Haybron, D. M. (2008). *The pursuit of unhappiness: The elusive psychology of well-being.* Oxford, UK: Oxford University Press.

Huitt, W., & Cain, S. (2005). An overview of the conative domain. *Educational Psychology Interactive.* Valdosta, GA: Valdosta State University. Retrieved February 13, 2008, from www.edpsycinteractive.org/papers/conative.pdf

Huta, V., & Waterman, A. S. (2014). Eudaimonia and its distinction from hedonia: Developing a classification and terminology for understanding conceptual and operational definitions. *Journal of Happiness Studies*, *15*(6), 1425–1456. doi:10.1007/s10902-013-9485-0

Kahneman, D., Diener, E., & Schwarz, N. (1999). *Well-being: The foundations of hedonic psychology.* New York, NY: Russell Sage Foundation.

Kashdan, T. B., Biswas-Diener, R., & King, L. A. (2008). Reconsidering happiness: The costs of distinguishing between hedonics and eudaimonia. *Journal of Positive Psychology*, *3*, 219–233.

Kashdan, T. B., & Steger, M. F. (2011). Challenges, pitfalls, and aspirations for positive psychology. In K. M. Sheldon, T. B. Kashdan, & M. F. Steger (Eds.), *Designing positive psychology: Taking stock and moving forward* (pp. 9–24). New York, NY: Oxford University Press.

Kasser, T. (2002). *The high price of materialism.* Cambridge, MA: MIT Press.

Keltner, D. (2009). *Born to be good: The science of a meaningful life.* New York, NY: W. W. Norton & Co.

Keyes, C. L. M. (2002). The mental health continuum: From languishing to flourishing in life. *Journal of Health and Social Behavior*, *43*, 207–222.

Kiaei, Y. A., & Reio, T. J. (2014). Goal pursuit and eudaimonic well-being among university students: Metacognition as the mediator. *Behavioral Development Bulletin*, *19*(4), 91–104. doi:10.1037/h0101085

King, L. A. (2011). Are we there yet? What happened on the way to the demise of positive psychology. In K. Sheldon, T. Kashdan, & M. Steger (Eds.), *Designing positive psychology: Taking stock and moving forward* (pp. 439–446). New York, NY: Oxford University Press.

Kopperud, K. H., & Vittersø, J. (2008). Distinctions between hedonic and eudaimonic well-being: Results from a day reconstruction study among Norwegian jobholders. *The Journal of Positive Psychology*, *3*(3), 174–181. doi:10.1080/17439760801999420

Lazarus, R. S. (2003). Does the positive psychology movement have legs? *Psychological Inquiry*, *14*, 93–109.

Levontina, I. B., & Zalizniak, A. A. (2001). Human emotions viewed through the Russian language. In J. Harkins & A. Wierzbicka (Eds.), *Emotions in cross-linguistic perspective*. Berlin: Walter de Gruyter.

Lewis, P., Kimiecik, J., Horn, T., Zullig, K. J., & Ward, R. M. (2014). Can becoming my self influence my health? Exploring the effects of a eudaimonic-enhancement process on psychological indicators of well-being and physical activity. *Applied Research in Quality of Life*, *9*(3), 643–665. doi:10.1007/s11482-013-9263-5

Little, B. R. (1999). Personality and motivation: Personal action and the conative evolution. In L. A. Pervin & O. P. John (Eds.), *Handbook of personality: Theory and research* (2nd ed., pp. 501–524). New York, NY: Guilford Press.

Lyubomirsky, S., King, L. A., & Diener, E. (2005). The benefits of frequent positive affect: Does happiness lead to success? *Psychological Bulletin*, *131*, 803–855.

Lyubomirsky, S., Sheldon, K., & Schkade, D. (2005). Pursuing happiness: The architecture of sustainable change. *Review of General Psychology*, *9*, 111–131.

Mayer, J. D., Chabot, H. F., & Carlsmith, K. M. (1997). Conation, affect, and cognition in personality. *Advances in Psychology*, *124*, 31–63.

McMahan, E. A., Dixon, K. J., & King, L. M. (2013). Evidence of associations between lay conceptions of well-being, conception-congruent behavior, and experienced well-being. *Journal Of Happiness Studies*, *14*(2), 655–671. doi:10.1007/s10902-012-9347-1

McMahan, E. A., & Estes, D. (2011). Hedonic versus eudaimonic conceptions of well-being: Evidence of differential associations with self-reported well-being. *Social Indicators Research*, *103*(1), 93–108. doi:10.1007/s11205-010-9698-0

Meyers, D. (2000). The friends, funds, and faith of happy people. *American Psychologist*, *55*, 56–67.

Nelson, S. K., Fuller, J. K., Choi, I., & Lyubomirsky, S. (2014). Beyond self-protection: Self-affirmation benefits hedonic and eudaimonic well-being. *Personality and Social Psychology Bulletin*, *40*(8), 998–1011. doi:10.1177/0146167214533389

Passmore, H., & Howell, A. J. (2014). Nature involvement increases hedonic and eudaimonic well-being: A two-week experimental study. *Ecopsychology*, *6*(3), 148–154.

Popper, K. (1978). *Three worlds: The Tanner lecture on human values*. Delivered by Karl Popper at The University of Michigan on April 7, 1978.

Ryan, R. M., Huta, V., & Deci, E. L. (2008). Living well: A self-determination theory perspective on eudaimonia. *Journal of Happiness Studies*, *9*, 139–170.

Ryan, R. M., & Deci, E. L. (2001). On happiness and human potentials: A review of research on hedonic and eudaimonic well-being. *Annual Review of Psychology*, *52*, 141–166. doi:10.1146/annurev.psych.52.1.141

Ryan, R. M., & Deci, E. L. (2008). Self-determination theory and the role of basic psychological needs in personality and the organization of behavior. In O. P. John, R. W. Robins, & L. A. Pervin (Eds.), *Handbook of personality: Theory and research* (3rd ed., pp. 654–678). New York, NY: Guilford Press.

Ryan, R. M., & Huta, V. (2009). Wellness as healthy functioning or wellness as happiness: The importance of eudaimonic thinking (Response to the Kashdan et al. and Waterman discussion). *The Journal of Positive Psychology*, *4*(3), 202–204. doi:10.1080/17439760902844285

Ryan, R. M., Huta, V., & Deci, E. L. (2013). Living well: A self-determination theory perspective on eudaimonia. In A. Delle Fave (Eds.), *The exploration of happiness: Present and future perspectives* (pp. 117–139). New York, NY: Springer Science + Business Media.

Ryff, C. D. (1989). Happiness is everything, or is it? Explorations on the meaning of psychological well-being. *Journal of Personality and Social Psychology*, *57*(6), 1069–1081. doi:10.1037/0022–3514.57.6.1069

134 Kennon M. Sheldon

Ryff, C. D. (2014). Psychological well-being revisited: Advances in the science and practice of eudaimonia. *Psychotherapy and Psychosomatics, 83*(1), 10–28. doi:10.1159/000353263
Ryff, C. D., & Keyes, C. L. M. (1995). The structure of psychological well-being revisited. *Journal of Personality & Social Psychology, 69*, 719–727.
Ryff, C. D., & Singer, B. H. (2008). Know thyself and become what you are: A eudaimonic approach to psychological well-being. *Journal of Happiness Studies, 9*(1), 13–39. doi:10.1007/s10902-006-9019-0
Seaton, C. L., & Beaumont, S. L. (2015). Pursuing the good life: A short-term follow-up study of the role of positive/negative emotions and ego-resilience in personal goal striving and eudaimonic well-being. *Motivation and Emotion*. doi:10.1007/s11031-015-9493-y
Seligman, M. E. P. (2011). *Flourish: A visionary new understanding of happiness and well-being.* New York, NY: Free Press.
Sheldon, K. M. (2004). *Optimal human being: An integrated multi-level perspective.* Mahwah, NJ: Lawrence Erlbaum.
Sheldon, K. M. (2005). Positive value change during college: Normative trends and individual differences. *Journal of Research in Personality, 39*, 209–223.
Sheldon, K. M. (2011). Integrating behavioral-motive and experiential-requirement perspectives on psychological needs: A two process perspective. *Psychological Review, 118*(4), 552–569.
Sheldon, K. M. (2013). Individual daimon, universal needs, and subjective well-being: Happiness as the natural consequence of a life well lived. In A. Waterman (Ed.), *The best within us: Positive psychology perspectives on eudaimonic functioning* (pp. 119–137). Washington, DC: American Psychological Association.
Sheldon, K. M. (2014). Becoming oneself: The central role of self-concordant goal selection. *Personality and Social Psychology Review, 18*, 349–365.
Sheldon, K. M. (2016). Putting eudaimonia in its place (On the predictor, not the outcome, side of the equation). In J. Vitterso (Ed.), *Handbook of eudaimonic well-being.* New York, NY: Springer.
Sheldon, K. M., Abad, N., Ferguson, Y., Gunz, A., Houser-Marko, L., Nichols, C., & Lyubomirsky, S. (2010). Persistent pursuit of need-satisfying goals leads to increased happiness: A 6-month experimental longitudinal study. *Motivation and Emotion, 34*, 39–48.
Sheldon, K. M., Arndt, J., & Houser-Marko, L. (2003). In search of the organismic valuing process: The human tendency to move towards beneficial goal choices. *Journal of Personality, 71*, 835–869.
Sheldon, K. M., & Cooper, M. L. (2008). Goal striving within agentic and communal roles: Functionally independent pathways to enhanced well-being. *Journal of Personality, 76*, 415–447.
Sheldon, K. M., Corcoran, M., & Prentice, M. (2017). *Pursuing eudaimonia versus pursuing well-being: The first goal succeeds in its aim, whereas the second does not.* Manuscript under review.
Sheldon, K. M., Cummins, R., & Khamble, S. (2010). Life-balance and well-being: Testing a two-pronged conceptual and measurement approach. *Journal of Personality, 78*, 1093–1134.
Sheldon, K. M., & Elliot, A. J. (1999). Goal striving, need-satisfaction, and longitudinal well-being: The self-concordance model. *Journal of Personality and Social Psychology, 76*, 482–497.
Sheldon, K. M., Elliot, A. J., Kim, Y., & Kasser, T. (2001). What's satisfying about satisfying events? Comparing ten candidate psychological needs. *Journal of Personality and Social Psychology, 80*, 325–339.

Sheldon, K. M., & Filak, V. (2008). Manipulating autonomy, competence, and relatedness in a game-learning context: New evidence that all three needs matter. *British Journal of Social Psychology, 47*, 267–283.

Sheldon, K. M., Gunz, A., & Schachtman, T. (2012). What does it mean to be in touch with oneself? Testing a social character model of self-congruence. *Self and Identity, 11*, 51–70.

Sheldon, K. M., Jose, P. E., Kashdan, T. B., & Jarden, A. (2015). Personality, effective goal-striving, and enhanced well-being: Comparing 10 candidate personality strengths. *Personality and Social Psychology Bulletin, 4*, 575–585.

Sheldon, K. M., & Kasser, T. (1998). Pursuing personal goals: Skills enable progress, but not all progress is beneficial. *Personality and Social Psychology Bulletin, 24*, 1319–1331.

Sheldon, K. M., & Krieger, L. K. (2007). Understanding the negative effects of legal education on law students: A longitudinal test of self-determination theory. *Personality and Social Psychology Bulletin, 33*, 883–897.

Sheldon, K. M., & Lucas, R. L. (Eds.). (2014). *Stability of happiness: Theories and evidence on whether happiness can change.* Elsevier: London.

Sheldon, K. M., & Lyubomirsky, S. (2006). How to increase and sustain positive emotion: The benefits of expressing gratitude and visualizing best possible selves. *Journal of Positive Psychology, 1*, 73–82.

Sheldon, K. M. & Lyubomirsky, S. (2012). The challenge of staying happier: Testing the hedonic adaptation prevention (HAP) model. *Personality and Social Psychology Bulletin, 38*, 670–680.

Sheldon, K. M., Ryan, R. M., Rawsthorne, L., & Ilardi, B. (1997). "True" self and "trait" self: Cross role variation in the big five traits and its relations with authenticity and well-being. *Journal of Personality and Social Psychology, 73*, 1380–1393.

Sheldon, K. M., & Schuler, J. (2011). Needing, wanting, and having: Integrating motive disposition theory and self-determination theory. *Journal of Personality and Social Psychology, 101*, 1106–1123.

Tallon, A. (1997). *Head and heart: Affection, cognition, volition as triune consciousness.* New York, NY: Fordham University.

Thrash, T. M., Elliot, A. J., Maruskin, L. A., & Cassidy, S. E. (2010). Inspiration and the promotion of well-being: Tests of causality and mediation. *Journal of Personality and Social Psychology, 98*(3), 488–506. doi:10.1037/a0017906

Tiberius, V. (2006). Well-being: Psychological research for philosophers. *Philosophy Compass, 1*, 493–505.

Trigwell, J. L., Francis, A. P., & Bagot, K. L. (2014). Nature connectedness and eudaimonic well-being: Spirituality as a potential mediator. *Ecopsychology, 6*(4), 1–11. doi:10.1089/eco.2014.0025

Vansteenkiste, M., & Ryan, R. M. (2013). On psychological growth and vulnerability: Basic psychological need satisfaction and need frustration as a unifying principle. *Journal of Psychotherapy Integration, 23*(3), 263–280. doi:10.1037/a0032359

van Zyl, L. E., & Rothmann, S. (2014). Towards happiness interventions: Construct clarification and intervention methodologies. *Journal of Psychology in Africa, 24*(4), 327–341.

Vittersø, J. (2013). Feelings, meanings, and optimal functioning: Some distinctions between hedonic and eudaimonic well-being. In A. S. Waterman (Eds.), *The best within us: Positive psychology perspectives on eudaimonia* (pp. 39–55). Washington, DC: American Psychological Association. doi:10.1037/14092–003

Vittersø, J. (2016). *Handbook of eudaimonic well-being.* New York, NY: Springer.

Waterman, A. S. (1990a). Personal expressiveness: Philosophical and psychological foundations. *Journal of Mind and Behavior, 11*(1), 47–73.

Waterman, A. S. (1990b). The relevance of Aristotle's conception of eudaimonia for the psychological study of happiness. *Theoretical & Philosophical Psychology*, *10*(1), 39–44. doi:10.1037/h0091489

Waterman, A. S. (1993). Two conceptions of happiness: Contrasts of personal expressiveness (eudaimonia) and hedonic enjoyment. *Journal of Personality and Social Psychology*, *64*(4), 678–691. doi:10.1037/0022–3514.64.4.678

Waterman, A. S. (2013b). *The best within us: Positive psychology perspectives on eudaimonia.* Washington, DC: American Psychological Association. doi:10.1037/14092–000

Waterman, A. S., Schwartz, S. J., Zamboanga, B. L., Ravert, R. D., Williams, M. K., Agocha, V. B., . . . Donnellan, M. B. (2010). The questionnaire for eudaimonic well-being: Psychometric properties, demographic comparisons, and evidence of validity. *The Journal of Positive Psychology*, *5*(1), 41–61. doi:10.1080/17439760903435208

Watson, D., Tellegen, A., & Clark, L. (1988). Development and validation of brief measures of positive and negative affect: The PANAS scales. *Journal of Personality and Social Psychology*, *54*, 1063–1070.

Wilson, T. D., & Gilbert, D. T. (2005). Affective forecasting: Knowing what to want. *Current Directions in Psychological Science*, *14*(3), 131–134. doi:10.1111/j.0963-7214.2005.00355

van Zyl, L. E., & Rothmann, S. (2014). Towards happiness interventions: Construct clarification and intervention methodologies. *Journal of Psychology in Africa*, *24*(4), 327–341.

9

RELIGIOUS ENGAGEMENT AND LIVING WELL

David G. Myers

"Does religion do more harm or good?" In response to this perennial question, posed by *The Economist* for a 2010 debate, partisans offer potent examples of religion's horrors and heroes.

Mindful of yesterday's Crusades today's Islamic State beheadings, and the antigay religious right, one can understand why Richard Dawkins (1997) declared that "Faith is one of the world's great evils" and why Christopher Hitchens would subtitle his *God Is Not Great* as *How Religion Poisons Everything*. From the genocide of Kosovo Muslims to the religion-enabled terror of September 11, 2001, history leaves little doubt: Religion at its worst is toxic.

But then religion's defenders remind us of the worst acts of atheists (as in the genocides of Stalin and Mao) and of religion at its best—of its Martin Luther Kings and Desmond Tutus; of faith-enabled hospitals, orphanages, hospices, and universities; and of the antislavery movement and the beginnings of modern science (Stark, 2014). Moreover, there are the clear justice mandates: Love God and neighbor, even those who persecute you. And the ideals—"the fruit of the Spirit": "love, joy, peace, patience, kindness, generosity, faithfulness, gentleness, and self-control." Religion is "the source of life's deepest perversions," argued theologian Langdon Gilkey (1966), but also "the ground of its only hope."

Historical happenings aside (malevolence and morality, cruelty and compassion, arising from people of all faiths and none), is the religious life, on balance, more heartless or humane? Is religion, as Freud assumed in *The Future of an Illusion*, an "obsessional neurosis" that engenders sexually repressed, guilt-laden, unhappy lives? Or was St. Paul closer to truth in writing that "the kingdom of God is . . . righteousness and peace and joy?"

Setting aside recent research on the virtues embraced by major religions such as forgiveness, humility, and gratitude, let's first glimpse what we have gleaned from extensive studies of religiosity and a) happiness, b) health, and c) prosocial behavior. (Spoiler alert: The associations are mostly positive, across individuals.) Then let's examine a paradoxically reverse finding—negative associations across places (nations or states).

A cautionary note: Studies of religion's associations with things good and bad have no bearing on its truth claims. Are religious people committed to an illusion, perhaps hooked on a mental opiate? Or are they apprehending transcendent truths? This chapter speaks to the debate over whether religion does more harm or good, but not to the debate between theism and atheism.

Happiness

My first exposure to the faith-happiness correlation came from the Gallup Organization's (1984) "Religion in America" surveys. People highest in "spiritual commitment" (who consistently agreed with statements such as "God loves me even though I may not always please him" and "My religious faith is the most important influence in my life") were twice as likely to report being "very happy" as those least spiritually committed.

Ensuing survey research replicated the association:

- In a follow-up Gallup survey, 55 percent of "engaged" U.S. congregation members reported being "completely satisfied with the conditions of my life," as did 25 percent of those "actively disengaged" (Winseman, 2002).
- A slew of 1980s studies, meta-analyzed by Morris Okun and William Stock (1987), found that the two best predictors of well-being among older persons were health and religious engagement.
- In General Social Surveys (tinyurl.com/generalsocialsurvey), 42 percent of Americans who "feel God's presence" daily have reported being "very happy," as have 24 percent of those never feeling God's presence.
- Gallup's newer daily surveys reached 676,080 Americans in 2009 and 2010. "Very religious" adults reported higher overall psychological and physical "well-being" than did those "moderately religious" and nonreligious (Newport, Witters, & Argrawal, 2010, 2012). "Very religious Americans are doing very well," reported the Gallup team. They "have higher overall wellbeing, lead healthier lives, and are less likely to have ever been diagnosed with depression . . ."
- In 2011 surveys (Figure 9.1), Gallup further found that day-to-day positive emotions increased with more frequent religious attendance (and negative emotions decreased).

But of course mere correlations do not indicate which way the traffic flows between religiosity and well-being. Perhaps happiness somehow enhances religiosity (though there is evidence that suffering engenders a quest for religious

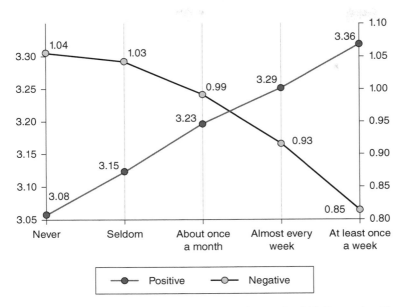

FIGURE 9.1 Average Number of Daily Positive and Negative Life Events, by Church Attendance

Source: Gallup-Healthways Well-Being Index, January 2–December 31, 2011

meaning and solace—see Baumeister, 1992). So one research team mined 20 years of data from a German study that has followed more than 12,000 lives through time (Headey, Schupp, Tucci, & Wagner, 2010). Their finding: "Individuals who become more religious over time record long term gains in life satisfaction, while those who become less religious record long term losses." Thus, they surmised, "Religious beliefs and activities can make a substantial difference to life satisfaction."

If that is so, what explains it? Unpacking "the religious factor," social scientists have noted these ingredients:

1. *Social support.* As von Hippel and Gonsalkorale (this volume) emphasize, humans historically have flourished when "embedded in community." Religious engagement provides, first, a support community—indeed, some 350,000 such communal support systems in, for example, the United States (Hartford, 2016). Supportive faith communities help meet the human need to belong. "The fellowship of kindred spirits," "the bearing of one another's burdens," "the ties of love that bind" are intrinsic to faith communities. As John Winthrop (1630/1965, p. 92) explained to his Puritan followers before they disembarked to their New World, "We must delight in each other, make others' conditions our own, rejoice together, mourn together, labor, and suffer

together, always having before our eyes our community as members of the same body."

2.   *Meaning and purpose.* Faith also offers many people a sense of what Baumeister (this volume) calls "a meaningful life." And with a sense of life's meaning and purpose comes a sense of coherence, identity, and behavioral guidance (Canada, Murphy, Fitchett, & Stein, 2016; Park, Edmondson, & Hale-Smith, 2013). Faith satisfies "the most fundamental human need of all," wrote Rabbi Harold Kushner (1987). "That is the need to know that somehow we matter, that our lives mean something, count as something more than just a momentary blip in the universe."

3.   *Impulse control.* All the health and well-being measures predicted by religious engagement are also predicted by self-control and self-regulation, observed Michael McCullough and Brian Willoughby (2009). Indeed, they document, religiosity promotes self-monitoring and self-control, which promotes positive self-regulation.

4.   *Self-acceptance.* Theologian Paul Tillich (1988) speculated that believing that God loves you, just as you are, provides a foundation for self-worth (independent of achievements or others' approval). "*Simply accept the fact that you are accepted!* . . . If that happens to us, we experience grace."

5.   *Terror management.* Writing from a place called Hope, I am mindful that some religious worldviews encourage an ultimate hope, especially when confronting the "terror" that accompanies our awareness of our vulnerability and impending death (Solomon, Greenberg, & Pyszczynski, 2015). Most faiths offer a hope that, no matter what adversity may strike, in the end—the very end—"all shall be well and all shall be well and all manner of thing shall be well" (Julian of Norwich, 1395/2016, p. 49). Such hope empowered Martin Luther King, Jr. (1964), even when facing the terror of threats on his life, to say, "If physical death is the price that I must pay to free my white brothers and sisters from a permanent death of the spirit, then nothing can be more redemptive."

By controlling for these and other mediating influences, could we squeeze the juice out of the religion factor and conclude that religiosity is "nothing but" the combined effect of social support, meaning, impulse control, and so forth? Psychologically speaking, yes, albeit in the same sense that a hurricane's effect is nothing more than the effect of its subfactors, such as wind, rain, and storm surge. Control for such and there's no real "hurricane effect" per se (much as there is no religiosity effect per se). Religiosity and hurricanes are package variables, with multiple subfactors.

Health

Throughout history, religion and medicine have collaborated, sometimes through the same person. In the 12th century, the Jewish philosopher Maimonides was also both a rabbi and physician. Hospitals often began in monasteries and were spread by missionaries. The Catholic Church remains one of the largest global health care providers, with 5,246 hospitals and 15,208 houses for the chronically ill and those with disabilities (Brown, 2014).

As medical science matured, religion and medicine diverged. With vaccines to spare children from smallpox and antibiotics to relieve fever, people turned to medicine before prayer. Now, in the 21st century, religion and medicine have reconnected. In a Medline search, the word root "religio" appeared in 6,751 abstracts in the 35 years from 1965 to 1999, and in 16,562 abstracts in the fewer 16+ years from 2000 to 2016.

Are there fires (solid findings) beneath all this smoke? Several epidemiological studies, each tracking thousands of lives through years of time, reveal an association between religious engagement and health or longevity.

- *Kibbutz communities.* Jeremy Kark and his co-researchers (1996) compared the 16-year death rates of those in religiously Orthodox or matched nonreligious Israeli collective settlements. Their finding: "Belonging to a religious collective was associated with a strong protective effect" (roughly equal to the gender mortality difference) that was unexplained by age or economic differences.
- *Men's and women's longevity.* The religiosity-longevity correlation occurs among men, and even more strongly among women—and so is not merely a result of women's being both more religious and longer-lived (McCullough, Hoyt, Larson, Koenig, & Thoresen, 2000; McCullough & Laurenceau, 2005; VanderWeele, 2017). Three examples:

  - When 5,286 Californians were followed over 28 years (with controls for gender, age, ethnicity, and education), frequent religious attendees were 36 percent less likely to have died in any year (Oman, Kurata, Strawbridge, & Cohen, 2002; Strawbridge, Cohen, & Shema, 1997).
  - A U.S. Centers for Disease Control and Prevention-financed National Health Interview Survey similarly followed 21,204 adults over eight years. After controlling for gender, age, race, and region, religious non-attenders were 1.9 times more likely to have died than were weekly attenders (Hummer, Rogers, Nam, & Ellison, 1999). This translated into an eight-year life-expectancy difference from age 20.
  - Among 74,534 women assessed in 1992 in the Nurses' Health Study, the most regular religious attenders were—after controlling for various health risk factors—33 percent less likely to die in the ensuing 20 years (Li et al., 2016).

- *Suicide risk.* In 1996, Tyler VanderWeele and his colleagues (2016) recorded religious attendance among 89,708 women participants in the Nurses' Health Study. In the ensuing 14+ years, those reporting weekly or more attendance had a dramatically lower suicide rate than did non-attenders (1 versus 7 per 100,000 person years). More religious countries also have less suicide (Pelham & Nyiri, 2008).

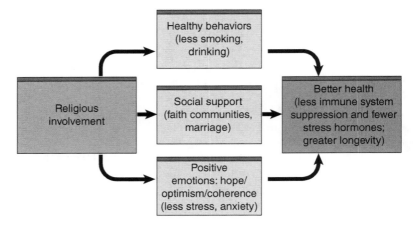

FIGURE 9.2 Possible Explanations for the Religiosity-Longevity Association

Source: From Myers & DeWall, 2016

Harvard epidemiologist and biostatistician Tyler VanderWeele (2017) con-cludes that "religious participation . . . is a powerful social determinant of health." Again we wonder: Why? What explains these consistent findings?

- *Healthier behaviors.* Religiously engaged people smoke and drink alcohol less (Lyons, 2002; Strawbridge, Shema, Cohen, & Kaplan, 2001).
- *Social support.* As with happiness, social support contributes to health— and also to healthy behaviors (George, Ellison, & Larson, 2002). Moreover, religious engagement encourages marriage, which is another predictor of health and longevity. As Gable (this volume) demonstrates, close relation-ships matter.
- *Stress protection and enhanced well-being.* Even after controlling for unhealthy behaviors, social ties, gender, and preexisting health problems, much of the religiosity-associated mortality reduction remains (George, Larson, Koenig, & McCullough, 2000; Powell, Schahabi, & Thoresen, 2003). Researchers have speculated, for example, that a coherent worldview, a sense of hope, happi-ness, and meditation practices may reduce stress (Figure 9.2). As Fredrickson (this volume) documents, positive well-being has an underlying biology.

Helping Behaviors

Even nontheists have clashing presumptions regarding whether religion under-mines or enhances prosociality. Religion, argued Christopher Hitchens (2007, p. 56), "is violent, irrational, intolerant, allied to racism and tribalism and bigotry, invested in ignorance and hostile to free inquiry, contemptuous of women and coercive toward children." But then evolutionists such as David Sloan Wilson (2003, 2007), E.O. Wilson (1998) and their interpreters (Robert Wright and Nicholas Wade), have argued the opposite—that religion is widespread because it is socially adaptive. It fosters morality, social cohesion, and group survival. Religious conviction, noted E.O. Wilson (p. 244), "is largely beneficent. [It] nourishes love, devotion, and above all, hope."

In their surveys of Israeli Jews, Spanish Catholics, Greek Orthodox, Dutch Calvinists, and German Lutherans and Catholics, Shalom Schwartz and Sipke Huismans (1995) found that, in each case, those religiously engaged people expressed less hedonism and self-orientation. Religions "exhort people to pursue causes greater than their personal desires." Such interfaith self-sacrificial compassion was memorably illustrated by the World War II Protestant, Catholic, and Jewish "Four Chaplains," who, with their torpedoed ship sinking into icy waters, each gave away their life jackets and were last seen, with arms linked, saying their final prayers (fourchaplains.org). In the United States, the General Social Survey (tinyurl.com/generalsocialsurvey) found that "volunteering tied to community service" was felt to be an "important obligation" by 16 percent of adults attending religious services less than annually, and by 38 percent of those attending weekly or more.

Other studies also have found "that religious belief is positively associated with moral concern" (Jack, Friedman, Boyatzis, & Taylor, 2016). But talk is cheap. Will religiously engaged folks enact the compassion and love they espouse? Luke Galen (2012) thinks not. Religious people, he argues, display ingroup bias (favoring their own religion) and offer less support for public (government) charity.

Volunteerism. Religious people *do*, however, exhibit elevated levels of volunteerism and of charitable giving. In repeated U.S. Gallup surveys (1984, 2013; Colasanto, 1989; Wuthnow, 1994), religiously engaged or "highly spiritually committed" people have reported substantially greater volunteerism, such as among the infirm, the poor, or the elderly. And in European Values Surveys and World Values Surveys of 117,007 people, "People who attend church twice a week are more than 5 times more likely to volunteer than people who never visit church," reported Stijn Ruiter and Nan Dirk De Graaf (2006).

Dwarfing other surveys, however, are the Gallup World Poll's big data from more than a quarter million respondents (Pelham & Crabtree, 2008). In every world region, highly religious people were substantially more likely to report volunteering in the past month (Figure 9.3).

Charitable giving. Repeated surveys reveal that the jest, "When it comes to giving, some people stop at nothing," is seldom true of religiously engaged Americans. In one Gallup survey, repeated in follow-up years, the 24 percent of people who were weekly attenders gave 48 percent of all charitable contributions (Center for Global Prosperity, 2007; Hodgkinson & Weitzman, 1992; Hodgkinson, Weitzman, & Kirsch, 1990). Newer, global data confirm the faith-philanthropy association (Figure 9.4).

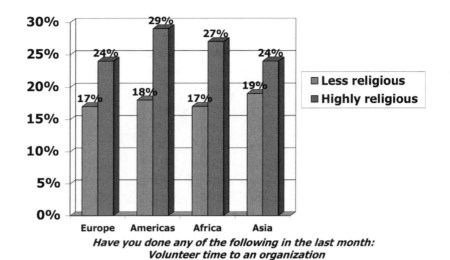

FIGURE 9.3   Religiosity and Volunteerism

Source: Gallup World Poll, 2000+ people from each of 140 countries, 2006 to 2008

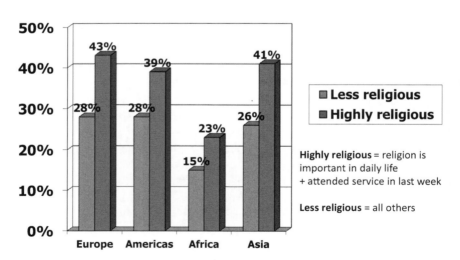

FIGURE 9.4   Religiosity and Charitable Contributions

Source: Gallup World Poll, 2000+ people from each of 140 countries, 2006 to 2008

Robert Putnam and David Campbell's (2010) national survey data concur with earlier surveys:

> Religiously observant Americans are more generous with time and treasure than demographically similar secular Americans. This is true for secular causes (especially help to the needy, the elderly, and young people) as well as for purely religious causes. It is true even for most random acts of kindness. . . . And the pattern is so robust that evidence of it can be found in virtually every major national survey of American religious and social behavior. Any way you slice it, religious people are simply more generous.
>
> *(pp. 453–454)*

Is the greater giving by those "highly religious" enabled by their greater income? To the contrary, reported the Gallup World Poll researchers (Pelham & Crabtree, 2008). Those highly religious tend to have *lower* incomes. Thus, they concluded, "The data presented here offer compelling evidence of the role of religious dedication in helping to encourage supportive, community-oriented behaviors. . . ." In experiments, priming religious cognition (such as by unscrambling sentences with words such as *God*, *spirit*, and *sacred*) also has increased participants' generosity (Pichon, Boccato, & Saroglou, 2007; Shariff & Norenzayan, 2007).

But this research story is unfinished. To further explore the religiosity-prosociality relationship, perhaps we could ask:

- Who is most likely to adopt children and provide foster care?
- Who mentors at-risk children, ex-prisoners, and immigrants?
- Who provides disaster relief, by volunteering time and resources after catastrophes?
- Who seeks prosocial careers, as in human service work and teaching?
- Who includes a substantial charitable component in their estate planning?
- Who is most at risk for antisociality (crime and delinquency)?

The Religious Engagement Paradox

I began by noting that, historically, religions have at times exemplified the love, peace, and justice they profess, and at other times quite the opposite. Extrinsically motivated religion has even, at times, provided self-justification—by thinking God is on one's side—for ingroup bias, opposition to equal rights for women and sexual minorities, and war. Yet religious engagement, especially in the relatively religious Western countries such as the United States, correlates positively with happiness, health, and helping behaviors.

But now the plot thickens, for these positive associations between religious engagement and the good life are *reversed* when comparing more versus less religious *places* (nations or states) rather than individuals. Said differently, religious engagement correlates *positively* with well-being across *individuals* and *negatively* across *places*. Simply put, religious individuals and irreligious places are generally flourishing.

Before reflecting on this startling assertion, consider the evidence. For starters, I harvested Gallup World Poll data from 152 countries and discovered a striking *negative* correlation between these countries' population percentage declaring that religion is "important in your daily life" and their average life satisfaction score (Figure 9.5). Ergo, despite the religiosity/good life associations noted above, at the aggregate (country) level, religious engagement is associated with the bad life.

Emotional well-being. Turning to U.S. data (Figures 9.6 and 9.7), I observed that, across states, religious attendance rates predict modestly *lower* emotional well-being. (The attendance data come from Gallup surveys of 706,888 Americans [Newport, 2010] and the emotional health data from Gallup-Healthway surveys asking people if yesterday they felt treated with respect all day, smiled and laughed

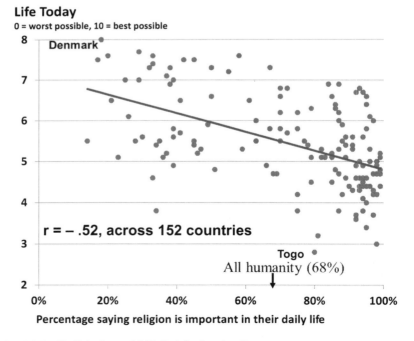

FIGURE 9.5   Religiosity and Life Satisfaction, by Country

Source: Gallup World Poll, 2000+ people from each of 140 countries, 2006 to 2008

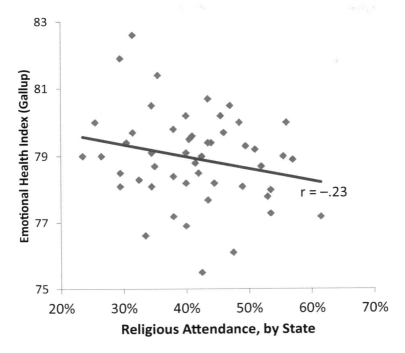

FIGURE 9.6   Religious Attendance and Emotional Health, by U.S. State

Source: Gallup-Healthways, 2008 to 2009

a lot, learned or did something interesting, and experienced enjoyment, worry, sadness, stress, anger, happiness, and depression.) Yet across individuals, religious attendance predicts substantially *greater* happiness (tinyurl.com/generalsocialsurvey; see also Inglehart, 1990, and Australian Centre on Quality of Life, 2008, for data from other countries).

Life expectancy. Across states, religious engagement predicts *shorter* life expectancy (Figure 9.8; life expectancy data from SSRC, 2009). But across individuals, as we've previously noted, epidemiological studies reveal that religious engagement predicted *longer* life expectancy (Figure 9.9; meta-analytic data from Hummer et al., 1999).

Smoking. Life expectancy differences are influenced by smoking rates, which are somewhat greater in most religiously engaged states, but lower among the most religiously engaged individuals (Figures 9.10 and 9.11).

Crime. Across states, religious engagement predicts higher crime rates (Figure 9.12, from the FBI Uniform Crime Report of property + violent crime). But across individuals, it predicts *lower* arrest rates (Figure 9.13, from tinyurl.com/generalsocialsurvey).

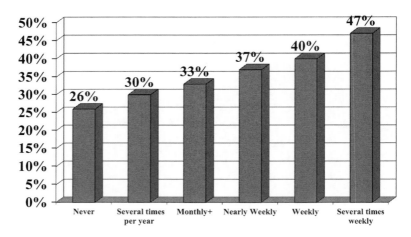

FIGURE 9.7 Religious Attendance and Percent "Very Happy" (n = 57,226, NORC, 1972–2016)

Source: General Social Survey of 57,226 Americans, 1972 to 2016

Teen pregnancy and birth rates. Across states, religious engagement predicts higher teen pregnancy and birth rates (Figures 9.14 and 9.15, data from Henshaw & Carlin, 2010). Using an eight-item measure of adult religious belief and practice from the Pew Forum's U.S. Religious Landscapes Survey, another research team found a stronger .73 correlation between state-level religiosity and teen (ages 15 to 19) birth rates (Strayhorn & Strayhorn, 2009).

Across *individual* teens, however, religious engagement predicts more support for "waiting till married," less sexual activity, and modestly *fewer* teen births (Figures 9.16, 9.17, and 9.18). These data come from the National Survey on Youth and Religion (a survey of a nationally representative sample of 13- to 17-year-olds [Regnerus, 2007]) and the National Longitudinal Study of Adolescent Health (Nonnemaker, McNeely, & Blum, 2003). The latter study also found that among sexually active teens, religious engagement was not a predictor of birth control use. If religiously engaged teens are a) more sexually restrained, and b) equally likely to use birth control when sexually active, then they should have somewhat fewer pregnancies. Indeed, religiously engaged teens have a slightly reduced risk of "ever being pregnant" (National Longitudinal Study of Adolescent Health: r = −.22) and of premarital pregnancy (a meta-analytic review of 87 studies of adolescent religiosity and sexuality: r = −.16 [Lucero, Kusner, Speace, & O'Brien, 2008]).

Reflections on the Religious Engagement Paradox

So we are presented with strikingly paradoxical results. Various measures reveal a positive association between religious engagement and human flourishing across individuals, and a negative association across aggregate places. If you were to be

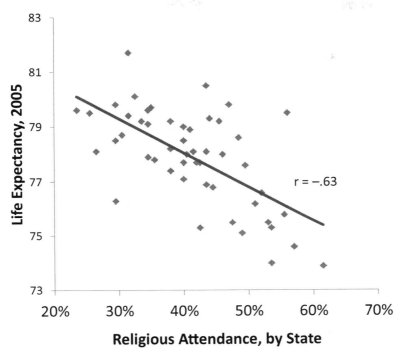

FIGURE 9.8 Religious Attendance and Life Expectancy, by U.S. State

Source: Attendance data from Gallup surveys, 2008 to 2009

plucked from where you live now and dropped into another country or state, and if you want your new place to embody the good life—the healthy, happy, crime-free life—then hope for a secular place. Pray that it will be secular Denmark rather than religious Pakistan, or secular Vermont rather than religious Mississippi. Yet survey data from many countries (though especially the more religious countries) reveal that actively religious individuals are happier, live longer, smoke less, commit fewer crimes, have lower risk of teen pregnancy, and so forth. For religion's apologists and critics, there is a practical lesson here: If you want to make religion look good, cite individual data. If you want to make it look bad, cite aggregate data.

Angus Deaton and Arthur Stone (2013) have been independently struck by these paradoxical findings: "Why might there be this sharp contradiction between religious people being happy and healthy, and religious places being anything but?"

And consider this: Similarly stunning individual versus aggregate paradoxes appear in other realms as well. As Ed Diener and I explain (Myers & Diener, 2018), these realms include:

- *Politics. Low*-income states and *high*-income individuals have voted Republican in recent U.S. presidential elections (tinyurl.com/PoliticalParadox).

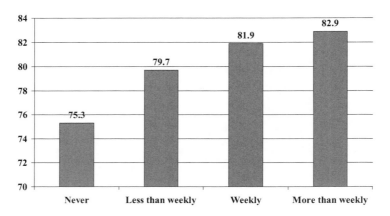

FIGURE 9.9 Worship Attendance and Life Expectancy at Age 20 (21,204 Americans in Nation Health Interview Survey)

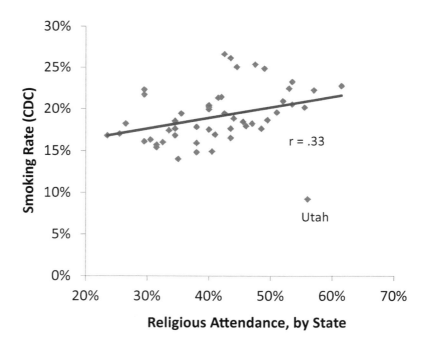

FIGURE 9.10 Religious Attendance and Smoking Rate, by U.S. State

Source: Gallup, 2008–2009

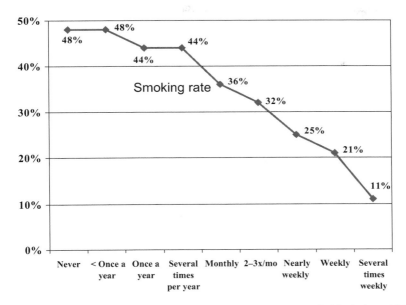

FIGURE 9.11   Religious Attendance and Smoking Rate, U.S. Individuals (n = 16,276, NORC, 1972–2010)

Source: From General Social Surveys

- *Happy liberal countries and unhappy liberal individuals.* Liberal countries and conservative individuals express greater well-being (Okulicz-Kozaryn, Holmes, & Avery, 2014).
- *Google sex searches.* Highly religious U.S. states, and less religious individuals, do more Google "sex" searching (MacInnis & Hodson, 2015, 2016; Rasmussen & Bierman, 2016).
- *Meaning in life.* Self-reported meaning in life is greatest in poor countries and among rich individuals (Oishi & Diener, 2014; King, Heintzelman, & Ward, 2016).

Sociologist W.S. Robinson (1950) long ago appreciated that "An ecological correlation is almost certainly not equal to its individual correlation." But that leaves us wondering *why* religiosity correlates negatively with the good life across countries and positively across individuals. Surely there are some complicating factors.

Consider marriage, for example. Religiously active people are more likely to be married. And married people are happier and healthier. So is religion merely a proxy for the "real" marriage factor? (Or should we say that religion's encouragement of marriage is one of the social support mechanisms that mediates its effect?) Earlier I noted that the religiosity-longevity association occurs both with women and with men (and so is not just a tendency for women, who are more religious,

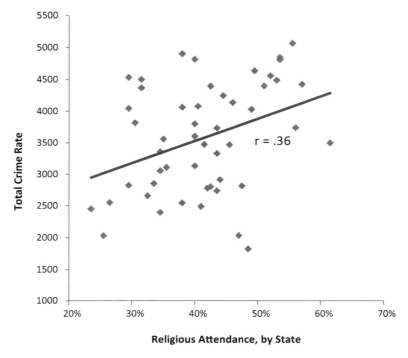

FIGURE 9.12 Religious Attendance (Gallup) and Crime Rate (FBI), by U.S. State

Source: Gallup, 2008–2009

to outlive men). Similarly, the religiosity-happiness association exists both among married and unmarried people.

With these preliminary observations, I leave the full unraveling of the religious engagement paradox to others from higher statistical pay grades. There is surely more sleuthing to come. Solving the paradox will likely involve controlling for those complicating (confounded) factors.

One such factor is income. We might ask, for example, if the religiosity-happiness association is mediated by a third factor—income—which has some association with happiness. Looking first at individuals:

1. Richer individuals are happier than poor individuals.
2. Religiously engaged individuals tend to have *lower* incomes.
3. Despite their generally lower incomes, religious people express greater happiness.

Ergo, across individuals, income seems not to explain the religiosity-happiness correlation (religiously engaged folks tend to be happier, though poorer).

But what about the comparisons of religious versus more irreligious places (countries and states)? Less religious places also tend to be *affluent* places (think

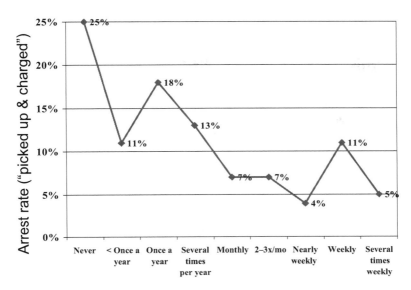

FIGURE 9.13   Religious Attendance and Arrest Rate, U.S. Individuals (n = 12,217, NORC, 1972–2014)

Source: From General Social Surveys

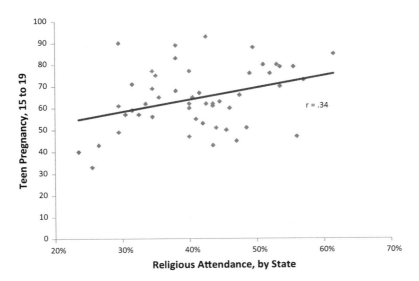

FIGURE 9.14   Religious Attendance and Teen Pregnancy Rate, by U.S. State

Source: Gallup, 2008–2009

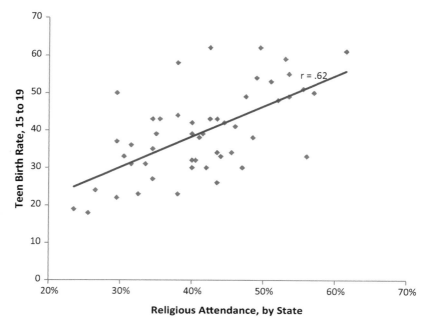

FIGURE 9.15   Religious Attendance and Teen Birth Rate, by U.S. State

Source: Gallup, 2008–2009

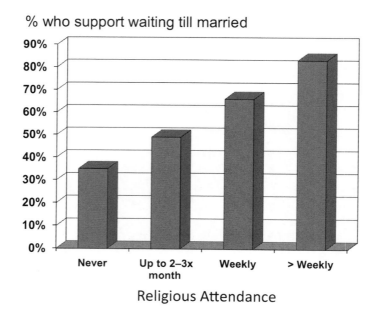

FIGURE 9.16   Religious Attendance and Teen Support for Sexual Abstinence

Source: National Survey of Religion and Youth

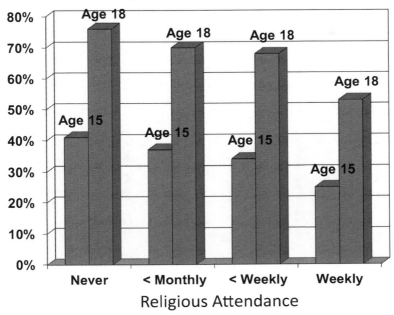

FIGURE 9.17   Religious Attendance and Sexual Abstinence

Source: National Longitudinal Study of Adolescent Health

Denmark and Vermont). More religious places tend to be poorer places (think Pakistan and Mississippi). Thus, when we compare less versus more religious places, we also are comparing richer versus poorer places. And as Ed Diener, Louis Tay, & I (2011) observed from Gallup World Poll data, controlling for objective life circumstances, such as income, eliminates, or even slightly reverses the negative religiosity–well-being correlation across countries. Thus lower incomes do help explain the lower life quality in highly religious places.

Finally, a question to ponder: Which data—aggregate or individual level—tell the more important or the truer story? If wondering whether rich people are relatively more or less likely to vote Republican, should we take our clue more from the aggregate data (where poor states vote Republican) or the individual data (where Republican support is greater among rich folks)? Ditto for the data on religious engagement and human flourishing: Is the more important story told by the aggregate or individual data?

In the meantime, we have a moral to our story. When reporting and interpreting data on predictors of the good life, be aware: Aggregate and individual data may point to radically differing conclusions. Conclusions drawn from aggregate

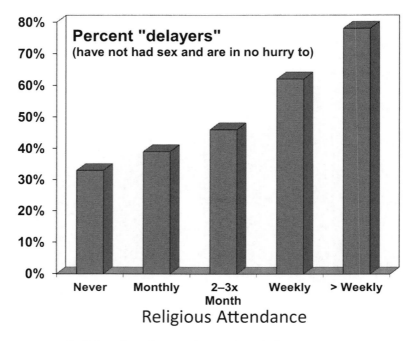

FIGURE 9.18 Religious Attendance and Teen Sexual Abstinence

Source: National Survey of Youth and Religion

data—comparing nations and states—may offer different predictors of the good life than data drawn from where life is lived—at the level of the individual.

Bibliography

Australian Centre on Quality of Life. (2008). *The Australian unity wellbeing index*. Deakin University. Retrieved from http://acqol.deakin.edu.au/index_wellbeing/Survey_18.2.pdf

Baumeister, R. F. (1992). *Meanings of life*. New York, NY: Guilford.

Brown, P. J. (2014). Religion and global health. In E. Idler (Ed.), *Religion as a determinant of public health*. New York, NY: Oxford University Press.

Canada, A. L., Murphy, P. E., Fitchett, G., & Stein, K. (2016). Re-examining the contributions of faith, meaning, and peace to quality of life: A report from the American Cancer Society's studies of cancer survivors-II (SCS-II). *Annals of Behavioral Medicine*, *50*, 79–86.

Center for Global Prosperity. (2007). *The index of global philanthropy*. Washington, DC: Center for Global Prosperity.

Colasanto, D. (1989, November). Americans show commitment to helping those in need. *Gallup Report*, (290), 17–24.

Dawkins, R. (1997, January/February). Is science a religion? *The Humanist*, 26–29.

Deaton, A., & Stone, A. A. (2013). Two happiness puzzles. *American Economic Review*, *103*(3), 591–597.

Diener, E., Tay, L., & Myers, D. G. (2011). The religion paradox: If religion makes people happy, why are so many dropping out? *Journal of Personality and Social Psychology*, *101*(6), 1278–1290.

Galen, L. W. (2012). Does religious belief promote prosociality? *Psychological Bulletin*, *138*, 876–906.

Gallup. (2013, December 13). *Most Americans practice charitable giving, volunteerism.* Retrieved from www.gallup.com

Gallup, G., Jr. (1984, March). Religion in America. *The Gallup Report*, Report No. 222.

George, L. K., Ellison, C. G., & Larson, D. B. (2002). Explaining the relationships between religious involvement and health. *Psychological Inquiry*, *13*, 190–200.

George, L. K., Larson, D. B., Koenig, H. G., & McCullough, M. E. (2000). Spirituality and health: What we know, what we need to know. *Journal of Social and Clinical Psychology*, *19*, 102–116.

Gilkey, L. (1966). *The Shantung compound: The story of men and women under pressure.* New York, NY: Harper & Row.

Hartford Institute for Religion Research. (2016, July 16). *Fast facts about American religion: How many religious congregations are there in the United States?* Retrieved from hirr.hart sem.edu/research/fastfacts/fast_facts.html#numcong

Headey, B., Schupp, J., Tucci, I., & Wagner, G. G. (2010). Authentic happiness theory supported by impact of religion on life satisfaction: A longitudinal analysis with data for Germany. *The Journal of Positive Psychology*, *5*(1), 73–82.

Henshaw, K. K., & Carlin L. (2010). *U.S. teenage pregnancies, births and abortions: National and state trends by race and ethnicity.* Retrieved from www.guttmacher.org/pubs/UST Ptrends.pdf

Hitchens, C. (2007). *God is not great: How religion poisons everything.* New York, NY: Twelve.

Hodgkinson, V. A., & Weitzman, M. S. (1992). *Giving and volunteering in the United States.* Washington, DC: Independent Sector.

Hodgkinson, V. A., Weitzman, M. S., & Kirsch, A. D. (1990). From commitment to action: How religious involvement affects giving and volunteering. In R. Wuthnow, V. A. Hodgkinson & Associates (Eds.), *Faith and philanthropy in America: Exploring the role of religion in America's voluntary sector.* San Francisco, CA: Jossey-Bass.

Hummer, R. A., Rogers, R. G., Nam, C. B., & Ellison, C. G. (1999). Religious involvement and U.S. adult mortality. *Demography*, *36*, 273–285.

Inglehart, R. (1990). *Culture shift in advanced industrial society.* Princeton, NJ: Princeton University Press.

Jack, A. I., Friedman, J. P., Boyatzis, R. E., & Taylor, S. N. (2016). Why do you believe in God? Relationships between religious belief, analytic thinking, mentalizing and moral concern. *PLoS One*, *11*(3).

Julian of Norwich. (1395/2016). *Revelation of divine love.* Mineola, NY: Dover.

Kark, J. D., Shemi, G., Friedlander, Y., Martin, O., Manor, O., & Blondheim, S. H. (1996). Does religious observance promote health? Mortality in secular vs. religious kibbutzim in Israel. *American Journal of Public Health*, *86*, 341–346.

King, L. A., Heintzelman, S. J., & Ward, S. J. (2016). Beyond the search for meaning: A contemporary science of the experience of meaning in life. *Current Directions in Psychological Science*, *25*, 211–216.

King, Jr., M. L. (1964, June 5). *On learning of physical threats on his life.* St. Augustine, FL. (quoted in *New York Times* obituary, April 5, 1968, by Murray Schumach.)

Koenig, H. G., King, D. E., & Carson, V. B. (2012). *Handbook of religion and health* (2nd ed.). New York, NY: Oxford University Press.

Kushner, H. (1987, December). You've got to believe in something. *Redbook*, 92–94.

Li, S., Stampfer, M. J., Williams, D. R., & VanderWeele, T. J. (2016). Association of religious service attendance with mortality among women. *JAMA Internal Medicine, 176,* 777–785.

Lucero, S., Kusner, K., Speace, E., & O'Brien, W. (2008, May). *Religiosity and adolescent sexual behavior: A meta-analytic study.* Paper presented at the 20th annual meeting of the Association for Psychological Science, Chicago.

Lyons, L. (2002, June 25). Are spiritual teens healthier? *Gallup Tuesday Briefing,* Gallup Organization. Retrieved from www.gallup.com/poll/tb/religValue/20020625b.asp

MacInnis, C. C., & Hodson, G. (2015). Do American states with more religious or conservative populations search more for sexual content on Google? *Archives of Sexual Behavior, 44*(1), 137–147.

MacInnis, C. C., & Hodson, G. (2016). Surfing for sexual sin: Relations between religiousness and viewing sexual content online. *Sexual Addiction and Compulsivity, 23*(2–3), 196–210.

McCullough, M. E., Hoyt, W. T., Larson, D. B., Koenig, H. G., & Thoresen, C. (2000). Religious involvement and mortality: A meta-analytic review. *Health Psychology, 19,* 211–222.

McCullough, M. E., & Laurenceau, J-P. (2005). Religiousness and the trajectory of self-rated health across adulthood. *Personality and Social Psychology Bulletin, 31,* 560–573.

McCullough, M. E., & Willoughby, B. L. B. (2009). Religion, self-regulation, and self-control: Associations, explanations, and implications. *Psychological Bulletin, 135*(1), 69–93.

Myers, D. G., & DeWall, C. N. (2016). *Psychology, 11th Edition.* New York: Worth Publishers

Myers, D. G., & Diener, E. (2018). The scientific pursuit of happiness. *Perspectives on Psychological Science* (invited article—soon in press).

Newport, F., Witters, D., & Agrawal, S. (2010, December 23). Very religious Americans lead healthier lives. *Gallup.* Retrieved from www.gallup.com/poll/145379/religious-americans-lead-healthier-lives.aspx

Newport, F., Witters, D., & Agrawal, S. (2012, February 16). Religious Americans enjoy higher well-being. *Gallup.* Retrieved from www.gallup.com/poll/152723/religious-americans-enjoy-higher-wellbeing.aspx

Nonnemaker, J. M., McNeely, C. A., & Blum, R. W. (2003). Public and private domains of religiosity and adolescent health risk behaviors: Evidence from the national longitudinal study of adolescent health. *Social Science and Medicine, 57,* 2049–2054.

Oishi, S., & Diener, E. (2014). Residents of poor nations have a greater sense of meaning in life than residents of wealthy nations. *Psychological Science, 25,* 422–430.

Okulicz-Kozaryn, A., Holmes, IV, O., & Avery, D. R. (2014). The subjective well-being political paradox: Happy welfare states and unhappy liberals. *Journal of Applied Psychology, 99*(6), 1300–1308.

Okun, W. A., & Stock, M. J. (1987). Correlates and components of subjective well-being among the elderly. *Journal of Applied Gerontology, 6,* 95–112.

Oman, D., Kurata, J. H., Strawbridge, W. J., & Cohen, R. D. (2002). Religious attendance and cause of death over 31 years. *International Journal of Psychiatry in Medicine, 32,* 69–89.

Park, C. L., Edmondson, D., & Hale-Smith, A. (2013). Why religion? Meaning as motivation. In *APA handbook of psychology, religion, and spirituality (Vol. 1): Context, theory, and research.* (pp. 157–171). Washington, DC: American Psychological Association.

Pelham, B., & Crabtree, S. (2008, October 8). Worldwide, highly religious more likely to help others. *Gallup.* Retrieved from www.gallup.com/poll/111013/worldwide-highly-religious-more-likely-help-others.aspx

Pelham, B., & Nyiri, Z. (2008, July 3). In more religious countries, lower suicide rates. *Gallup.* Retrieved from www.gallup.com/poll/108625/morereligious-countries-lower-suicide-rates.aspx

Pichon, I., Boccato, G., & Saroglou, V. (2007). Nonconscious influences of religion on prosociality: A priming study. *European Journal of Social Psychology, 37*(5), 1032–1045.

Powell, L. H., Schahabi, L., & Thoresen, C. E. (2003). Religion and spirituality: Linkages to physical health. *American Psychologist, 58*, 36–52.

Putnam, R. D., & Campbell, D. E. (2010). *American grace: How religion divides and unites us.* New York, NY: Simon & Schuster.

Rasmussen, K., & Bierman, A. (2016). How does religious attendance shape trajectories of pornography use across adolescence? *Journal of Adolescence, 49*, 191–203.

Regnerus, M. (2007). *Forbidden fruit.* New York, NY: Oxford University Press.

Robinson, W. S. (1950). Ecological correlations and the behavior of individuals. *American Sociological Review, 15*, 351–357.

Ruiter, S., & De Graaf, N. D. (2006). National context, religiosity, and volunteering: Results from 53 countries. *American Sociological Review, 71*(2), 191–210.

Schwartz, S. H., & Huismans, S. (1995). Value priorities and religiosity in four Western religions. *Social Psychology Quarterly, 58*, 88–107.

Shariff, A. F., & Norenzayan, A. (2007). God is watching you: Priming God concepts increases prosocial behavior in an anonymous economic game. *Psychological Science, 18*(9), 803–809.

Solomon, S., Greenberg, J., & Pyszczynski, T. (2015). *The worm at the core: On the role of death in life.* New York, NY: Random House.

SSRC. (2009). *American human development report 2008–2009.* Brooklyn, NY: Social Science Research Council.

Stark, R. (2014). *How the West won: The neglected story of the triumph of modernity.* Wilmington, DE: ISI Books.

Strawbridge, W. J., Cohen, R. D., & Shema, S. J. (1997). Frequent attendance at religious services and mortality over 28 years. *American Journal of Public Health, 87*, 957–961.

Strawbridge, W. J., Shema, S. J., Cohen, R. D., & Kaplan, G. A. (2001). Religious attendance increases survival by improving and maintaining good health behaviors, mental health, and social relationships. *Annals of Behavioral Medicine, 23*, 68–74.

Strayhorn, J. M., & Strayhorn, J. C. (2009). Religiosity and teen birth rate in the United States. *Reproductive Health, 6*(14). www.reproductive-health-journal.com/content/6/1/14

Tillich, P. (1988). *Shaking the foundations.* Gloucester, MA: Peter Smith Publishers.

VanderWeele, T. J. (2017). Religion and health: A synthesis. In J. R. Peteet & M. J. Balboni (Eds.), *Spirituality and religion within the culture of medicine.* New York, NY: Oxford University Press.

VanderWeele, T. J., Li, S., Tsai, A. C., & Kawachi, I. (2016). Association between religious service attendance and lower suicide rates among US women. *JAMA Psychiatry, 73*, 845–851.

Wilson, D. S. (2003). *Darwin's cathedral: Evolution, religion, and the nature of society.* Chicago: University of Chicago Press.

Wilson, D. S. (2007, July 4). Beyond demonic memes: Why Richard Dawkins is wrong about religion. *eSkeptic.* Retrieved from www.skeptic.com/skeptic/07-07-04.html

Wilson, E. O. (1998). *Consilience*. New York: Knopf.

Winseman, A. L. (2002, February 26). Congregational engagement index: Life satisfaction and giving. *Gallup Poll*.

Winthrop, J. (1630/1965). A model of Christian charity. In E. S. Morgan (Ed.), *Puritan political ideas, 1558–1794*. Indianapolis: Bobbs-Merrill.

Wuthnow, R. (1994). *God and mammon in America*. New York: Free Press.

PART III

Affective and Cognitive Aspects of Living Well

10

BIOLOGICAL UNDERPINNINGS OF POSITIVE EMOTIONS AND PURPOSE

Barbara L. Fredrickson

A life lived well, arguably, is one that includes being healthy and living long. A host of social psychological constructs have been related to physical health and longevity, among them positive emotions and purpose (e.g., Chida & Steptoe, 2008; Hill & Turiano, 2014). These two constructs are also positively correlated (Baumeister, this volume; Keyes, Shmotkin, & Ryff, 2002; Sheldon, this volume; Waterman, 1993). Whereas some scholars take this positive association to indicate that positive emotions and purpose are fundamentally confounded (Brown, Macdonald, Samanta, Friedman, & Coyne, 2014; Coyne, 2013), I see them as distinct and interacting in complex and dynamic ways. Positive emotions, for instance, have been found to prospectively predict and cause increases in purpose, as indicated by the likelihood of detecting meaning in life (Hicks, Schlegel, & King, 2010; Hicks, Trent, Davis, & King, 2012; King & Hicks, 2009; King, Hicks, Krull, & Del Gaiso, 2006). In addition, studies have shown that purpose-laden experiences and activities, such spirituality and meditation, predict and cause increases in positive emotions (Fredrickson, Cohn, Coffey, Pek, & Finkel, 2008; Van Cappellen, Way, Isgett, & Fredrickson, 2016). Reciprocal causality can thus be expected here, such that positive emotions and purpose augment and are augmented by each other in an upward spiral dynamic.

Positive emotions and purpose are not merely subjective experiences. Each appears to shape and be shaped by an individual's biological attributes. Evidence suggests that, barring major neurological disorders, the capacities to experience positive emotions and purpose are human universals (Fredrickson, 1998, 2013), which is consistent with the logic that these capacities have been sculpted over millennia by the discerning chisel of natural selection (von Hippel & Gonsalkorale, this volume). Natural selection of any human quality, including the capacities for positive emotions and purpose, by definition depends on those qualities having a genetic and biological basis. As such, investigations of the biological underpinnings of positive emotions and purpose stand to shed light on the adaptive value that these experiences held for our human ancestors, as well as the impact they may have on the physical health and longevity of present-day humans. With these considerations in mind, in this chapter I draw on recent discoveries from my *Positive Emotions and Psychophysiological Laboratory* (a.k.a. the *PEP Lab*) to build a bottom-up, data-driven model for how individual variation in immunological, parasympathetic, and oxytocin profiles underpins individual differences in the capacities to experience positive emotions and purpose.

Let's first agree on terminology. Positive emotions, as I use the term here, include a range of discernible pleasant affective states, including joy, gratitude, serenity, interest, hope, pride, amusement, inspiration, awe, and love. This list is not exhaustive. Rather it covers a set of positive emotions that research suggests people experience with some frequency in daily life (Fredrickson, 2013). Like all emotions, positive emotions are brief, multisystem activation patterns related to changes in the way people make sense of their current circumstances. When these multisystem activation patterns register that an individual's circumstances are somehow bad for the self, an unpleasant affective state is experienced; when it registers good prospects or good fortune, a pleasant affective state is experienced (Fredrickson, 2013; von Hippel & Gonsalkorale, this volume). The particulars of an individual's past experiences and current situation ultimately shape the emotion(s) that will be experienced. Despite the wide range of positive emotions, at times this construct is measured as a single dimension of positive affect or hedonia.

Purpose, as characterized here, also includes a range of discernible psychological constructs. Holding these constructs together is the shared feature of transcending immediate self-gratification—be it sensory, emotional, or material—to connect the self to something larger. Defined as such, purpose includes experiences of meaning, spirituality, or a calling, or feeling connected and "in tune" with others or with nature. It also includes eudaimonia, a term at times used to rope these various transcendent experiences together (see also Sheldon, this volume; Vittersø, 2016). For the present chapter, however, I use the term "purpose" as an umbrella term to encompass these various forms of self-transcendence, for both its accessibility and its alliteration with positive emotions.

The *broaden-and-build theory* (Fredrickson, 1998, 2013) provides a theoretical backdrop for the present exploration of the biological underpinnings of positive emotions and purpose. In brief, the broaden-and-build theory posits that various positive emotions momentarily broaden people's awareness in ways that, over time, incrementally build their resources and resilience (for a compatible treatment of the complex emotion of nostalgia, see Sedikides, Wildschut, & Stephan, this volume). Ample empirical evidence now supports this theory (for a review, see Fredrickson, 2013). As just one example, longitudinal randomized controlled trials (Fredrickson et al., 2008; Kok et al., 2013) have demonstrated that an intervention that helps people to subtly increase their day-to-day positive emotions—based on the purpose-laden practice of meditation—in turn builds people's resources. These increased resources are wide-ranging, including those that are social (e.g., feeling connected to others; Fredrickson et al., 2008; Kok et al., 2013), psychological (e.g., purpose in life, mindfulness; Fredrickson et al., 2008), and biological (e.g., cardiac vagal tone; Kok et al., 2013).

Greater resources, in turn, predict greater emotional well-being (Cohn, Fredrickson, Brown, Mikels, & Conway, 2009; Fredrickson et al., 2008), in part through upward spiral dynamics (Fredrickson & Cohn, 2008). My team and I have identified a subset of the resources built through experiences of positive emotions as potentially potent in promoting good lives. Following Pluess and Belsky (2013), we call these *vantage resources* to the extent that they render people more sensitive to subsequent positive experiences (Van Cappellen, Rice, Catalino, & Fredrickson, 2017). That is, just as malleable risk factors (e.g., pessimism, inflammation) can deter health and well-being by altering affective processes, malleable vantage resources (e.g., purpose in life, cardiac vagal tone) can support health and well-being by amplifying (moderating) positive emotions experienced in day-to-day living, creating an upward spiral dynamic. Such recursive, upward spiral processes offer a systems-level perspective on the dynamic and reciprocal causality among affective, social psychological, and biological constructs. (For related evidence on the links between social relationships and physical health, see Gable, this volume, and Simpson et al., this volume; for evidence regarding the benefits of negative affect, see Forgas, this volume; for evidence and discussion of the ways that technology interferes with social connectedness, see Dunn & Dwyer, this volume, and Amichai-Hamburger & Etgar, this volume, respectively.)

To sum, positive emotions and purpose, theory and evidence suggest, are not merely facets of living well, but rather they function as active ingredients that help to maintain and strengthen biological systems that support upward spirals of well-being. The following three sections focus in turn on three distinct biological vantage resources that may—through dynamic and reciprocal processes—underpin people's experiences of positive emotions and purpose.

Leukocyte Gene Expression

The close association between positive emotions and purpose has made it a challenge for researchers to discern which is more directly associated with biological health benefits. To unravel this mystery, my team and I gathered self-reports of positive emotions (assessed as hedonia) and purpose (assessed as eudaimonia), each via the Mental Health Continuum-Short Form (Keyes, 2002; Keyes & Annas, 2009; Lamers, Westerhof, Bohlmeijer, Ten Klooster, & Keyes, 2011). In addition to these self-report measures, we drew a blood sample from each participant to examine profiles of gene expression within their circulating white blood cells.

This approach to using functional genomics as a window onto physical health status was inspired by the work of my collaborator Steve Cole. Across a series of studies, Cole and his collaborators had linked adverse psychological and social conditions to a pattern of altered gene expression within circulating leukocytes (Cole, 2012, 2013; Irwin & Cole, 2011). This profile, termed the *conserved transcriptional response to adversity*, is marked by higher expression of genes involved in inflammation (e.g., pro-inflammatory cytokines such as *IL-1B*, *IL-6*, *IL-8*, and *TNF*) and lower expression of genes involved in type I IFN antiviral responses (e.g., *IFI-*, *OAS-*, and *MX-* family genes) and IgG1 antibody synthesis (e.g., *IGJ*; Cole, 2012, 2013; Irwin & Cole, 2011; Slavich & Cole, 2013). Studies of non-human primates show that experimental imposition of threatening or unstable social conditions can causally induce this adversity-related profile of gene expression (Cole et al., 2012; Tung et al., 2012). The conserved transcriptional response to adversity profile is thought to have evolved to help human ancestors' immune systems anticipate and counter changing patterns of microbial threat recurrently associated with changing environmental conditions. These could be increased risk of wound-related bacterial infection associated with experienced threat, social conflict, or isolation, or increased risk of socially mediated viral infection associated with frequent and positive social contact (Cole, Hawkley, Arevalo, & Cacioppo, 2011; Irwin & Cole, 2011). In modern environments, however, to the extent that social or psychological threats yield chronic activation of this gene expression profile, it may produce inflammation-mediated chronic diseases and impair host resistance to viral infections.

Given that various forms of psychosocial adversity had been convincingly linked with the conserved transcriptional response to adversity profile, together with Cole, my team and I investigated whether positive emotions and purpose—either singly or in combination—would oppose this gene expression profile, as represented across a set of 53 genes selected *a priori* based on Cole and colleagues' past results in studies of psychosocial adversity. An opposing leukocyte gene expression profile would be marked by a *lower* expression of pro-inflammatory genes, coupled with a *higher* expression of antiviral and antibody synthesis genes. Such a molecular signature is arguably supportive of a healthy functioning immune system, although that assumption remains to be tested empirically.

Taking this empirical approach my team and I have published two empirical reports, based on three studies. Because two of those studies used identical measures, here I discuss the results obtained when pooling their respective data sets (N = 198, as presented in Fredrickson et al., 2015, Discovery and Confirmation studies combined). Mixed effect linear models predicted participants' gene expression profiles, as observed within their circulating white blood cells, from their self-reports of positive emotions and purpose. Although correlated, these two subjective measures captured distinct constructs. When both positive emotions and purpose are simultaneously entered as predictor variables (alongside an *a priori* set of demographic and health-related control variables), only purpose emerges as significantly associated with the inverse of the adversity-related gene expression profile. The association for positive emotions, in this same analysis, is of the opposite sign (i.e., it shows a *positive* association with the adversity-related gene expression profile), albeit not statistically significant. This inverse association between purpose and the adversity-related gene expression profile has also emerged in three additional, independent studies that used different and more robust assessments of purpose (Cole et al., 2015; Fredrickson et al., 2015, Generalization Study; Kitayama, Akutsu, Uchida, & Cole, 2016). Together, this accumulating evidence supports the conclusion that purpose may be most directly related to the inverse of the adversity-related pattern of leukocyte gene expression.

This does not necessarily mean that positive emotions play no role in fostering human health and longevity. Indeed, these findings need be interpreted in light of (1) existing evidence that positive emotions prospectively predict and cause increases in purpose (described above) and (2) that the variance that positive emotions share with purpose has been statistically removed (for a similar approach, see Baumeister, this volume). Even if the elements of positive emotions that are devoid of association with the transcendent experiences of purpose, meaning, contribution, and interconnectedness may function as "empty calories" with respect to physical health, the overall construct of positive emotions may be a vital contributing factor to the subsequent detection of meaning and the emergence of purpose. If so, positive emotions may well contribute *indirectly* to a purportedly healthy pattern of gene expression as a result of their direct relationship with purpose.

To test this possibility, my team reanalyzed and extended one of our prior studies (i.e., Fredrickson et al., 2015, Confirmation Study) to test whether positive emotions (assessed by the hedonic items of the Mental Health Continuum-Short Form or by seven consecutive daily reports of ten distinct positive emotions, via the modified Differential Emotions Scale [mDES], Fredrickson, 2013) predicted the inverse of the adversity-related gene expression profile. It did. When either index of positive emotions was the sole predictor of this gene expression profile, it showed a negative association with it, consistent with the idea that positive emotions support health. Further tests suggested that purpose (indexed by the eudaimonic items of the Mental Health Continuum-Short Form), accounted for (mediated) this relation. That is, to the extent that positive emotions are positively associated with purpose, positive emotions are indirectly related to a (presumably) health-supportive pattern of gene expression—one marked by reduced expression of pro-inflammatory genes and increased expression of antiviral and antibody synthesis genes (Isgett, Boulton, Cole, & Fredrickson, 2016). It is worth noting that this same indirect path between positive emotions and the inverse of the conserved transcriptional response to adversity profile (mediated by purpose) has also been demonstrated within a nationally representative sample (Cole et al., 2015). Purpose, the data suggest, appears to be one of the many durable resources that positive emotions function to build. Although purpose may be more directly tied to the molecular shifts that support physical health, positive emotions may be the springboards that lead to increments in purpose. Positive emotions and purpose, then, are dynamically intertwined, and each appears to play a vital role in shaping leukocyte gene expression, a plausible biological underpinning of a good life.

Cardiac Vagal Tone

Another biological resource with which my research team and I have seen positive emotions and purpose interrelate is cardiac vagal tone (Kok & Fredrickson, 2010). Cardiac vagal tone represents the functioning of the vagus nerve, a key cranial nerve that connects the brain to the heart (and to other internal organs). In contrast to a "fight or flight" autonomic response, which is orchestrated by the body's sympathetic nervous system, the vagus nerve has been implicated in a "calm and connect" autonomic response, which is orchestrated by the parasympathetic nervous system. It is thus centrally involved in autonomic flexibility, or the body's ability to flexibly and efficiently respond to changing circumstances. Like muscle tone, higher levels of cardiac vagal tone are better than lower levels. Cardiac vagal tone is inferred from heart rate variability, which can be indexed using one of a handful of data reduction techniques, including, among others, respiratory sinus arrhythmia, which incorporates a measure of respiration frequency, and spectral analysis of heart rate variability at various frequencies, with a high-frequency heart rate variability (e.g., 0.12–0.4 Hz) emerging as a frequent choice among researchers. Although researchers continue to debate which data reduction technique is superior, my research team's approach has become to report results using multiple techniques.

Cardiac vagal tone is a compelling biological attribute because it too relates both to physical health and to social psychological individual differences. Within the domains of physical health, individuals with higher levels of cardiac vagal tone have been found to have better regulated cardiovascular systems (Thayer & Lane, 2007), better regulated inflammatory processes (Thayer & Sternberg, 2006), and better regulated blood glucose levels (Carnethon, Golden, Folsom, Haskell, & Liao, 2003). Plus, for those who have life-threatening cardiac events, such as myocardial infarctions, physicians look to indices of cardiac vagal tone to estimate patient prognoses (Bibevski & Dunlap, 2011). Within social psychological domains, individuals with higher levels of cardiac vagal tone are better able to regulate their attention (Suess, Porges, & Plude, 1994) and their emotions (Demaree, Robinson, Everhart, & Schmeichel, 2004; Porges, Doussard-Roosevelt, & Maiti, 1994), and perhaps because of these superior regulatory abilities, they show better social skills (Fabes, Eisenberg, & Eisenbud, 1993). Cardiac vagal tone, then, is a health marker that also shapes consequential intrapersonal social psychological abilities and skills.

Connecting these various intrapersonal abilities and skills to positive emotions and purpose, my team and I have studied the degree to which cardiac vagal tone relates to individuals' quotidian experiences of connection to others. One investigation, led by Suzannah ("Zan") Isgett, measured the cardiac vagal tone of 73 midlife adults alongside their reports on the last time they had engaged in a variety of common activities (e.g., eating a meal, spending time outdoors, commuting). For each activity, participants reported (a) whether anyone else was present with them; (b) the degree to which they considered that particular activity to be social; and (c) the degree to which they experienced ten positive emotions during it (again indexed by the mDES; Fredrickson, 2013). The pattern of results suggested two distinct associations between cardiac vagal tone and purpose, here indexed as being in connection with others. The first was that higher levels of cardiac vagal tone were associated with more frequently being in the presence of others, a finding consistent with Porges' (2011) prediction the vagus nerve modulates affiliative behavior. The second was that, to the extent that participants viewed these ordinary activities as social, these activities were associated with greater intensities of positive emotions, a finding consistent with the hypothesis that cardiac vagal tone amplifies the positive emotion yield of activities that involve social connection (Isgett, Kok, et al., 2017). These data suggest that cardiac vagal tone functions as a biological vantage resource, one that amplifies the positive emotions experienced during moments of social connection.

Approaching these same ideas from another angle, Bethany Kok and I examined how individuals' cardiac vagal tone related to their day-to-day experiences of positive emotions, as well as to interpersonal experiences that transcend the self and bring feelings of social connectedness. We drew on another sample of 73 individuals who, as part of a larger study (described below), provided daily reports of their emotion experiences (again using the modified Differential Emotions Scale; Fredrickson, 2013) and rated how "close" and "in tune" they felt with others with whom they interacted that day (items adapted from the UCLA Loneliness Scale; Russell, 1996). Before and after the nine weeks of daily reporting, we assessed participants' cardiac vagal tone. The data revealed that participants with higher initial levels of cardiac vagal tone were more likely to increase week by week in their experiences of positive emotions and perceived social connectedness, which here served as our index of self-transcendence or purpose. In addition, those who showed greater increases in positive emotions and purpose were more likely to exhibit increases over the nine weeks in their cardiac vagal tone, a pattern consistent with an upward spiral dynamic of reciprocal causality (Kok & Fredrickson, 2010).

These same participants were part of a larger investigation on the effects of increasing people's daily experiences of positive emotions and purpose. Accordingly, study participants were randomly assigned to learn loving-kindness meditation or to serve in a monitoring waitlist control group. Loving-kindness meditation involves the intentional cultivation of compassionate and caring sentiments for the self and others and thus can be taken as a recurrent, purpose-laden behavior (see Huppert, this volume). Indeed, field and laboratory experiments have found the practice of loving-kindness meditation to reduce depressive symptoms (Fredrickson et al., 2008), increase compassion and altruistic behavior (Hutcherson, Seppala, & Gross, 2008; Jazaieri et al., 2013; Klimecki, Leiberg, Lamm, & Singer,

2013; Leiberg, Klimecki, & Singer, 2011; Weng et al., 2013), and yield functional neural plasticity in brain circuits associated with positive affect and empathy (Klimecki et al., 2013; Weng et al., 2013).

The analyses reported above (i.e., Kok & Fredrickson, 2010) statistically controlled for experimental condition (loving-kindness meditation or waitlist) and in doing so revealed that upward spiral relations between changes in positive emotions (or purpose, indexed as social connectedness) and changes in cardiac vagal tone emerged across all participants, regardless of group assignment. Thus, dynamic reciprocal relations between biological attributes and social psychological well-being appear normative within nonclinical samples.

Might people be able to nudge this reciprocal dynamic to experience even greater biopsychosocial benefit? The larger intervention study had been designed to address this question. Whereas across the entire sample, participants who started the study with higher cardiac vagal tone tended to show larger increases in positive emotion and perceived social connectedness, slowly—week by week—those who were randomized to learn loving-kindness meditation began to show even larger increases. The significantly steeper increases in positive emotions and purpose that loving-kindness meditation produced were in turn associated with larger improvements in cardiac vagal tone (Fredrickson & Kok, in press; Kok et al., 2013; see also Kok & Fredrickson, 2015). The overall pattern of results suggests that a preexisting biopsychosocial reciprocal dynamic within individuals can be further stimulated by an ancient wellness practice that infuses daily life with emotional warmth and interpersonal tenderness.

Importantly, the effect of the loving-kindness meditation intervention on cardiac vagal tone was indirect. Model fit was best with changes in positive emotions and, sequentially, changes in perceived social connectedness were included as statistical mediators. Here again we see that experiences of positive emotions appear to serve as springboards for experiences of purpose, here indexed as feeling close and "in tune" with others. Social connectedness, the data suggest, appears to be one of the many durable resources that positive emotions function to build. In addition, the work described earlier in the present section (Isgett, Kok, et al., 2017) suggests that cardiac vagal tone functions as a biological vantage resource that amplifies the positive emotions felt during moments of connection. Finally, akin to the work described in the previous section on gene expression (Isgett, Boulton, et al., 2016), self-transcendent experiences of feeling connected to others appear to be more directly tied to improvements in physical health, as indexed by cardiac vagal tone. Here again, positive emotions and purpose appear to be intertwined in an upward spiral dynamic: Each may shape and be shaped by cardiac vagal tone in ways that reveal another facet of the biological underpinnings of living well.

Oxytocin

Oxytocin is another biological resource with which my research team and I have found positive emotions and purpose to interrelate. Oxytocin is a polypeptide synthesized in the hypothalamus, which can be released into the bloodstream as well as to the forebrain. The link between oxytocin and physical health is supported by both animal and human studies. Such studies have provided evidence for a bidirectional link between oxytocin and inflammatory and immune activity. For instance, oxytocin suppresses inflammation (Clodi et al., 2008; Jankowski et al., 2010; Petersson, Wiberg, Lundeberg, & Uvnäs-Moberg, 2001) and oxytocin receptor mRNA transcription is influenced by pro-inflammatory cytokines, IL-1B and IL-6 (Rauk & Friebe-Hoffmann, 2000; Rauk, Friebe-Hoffmann, Chiao, Rauk, & Winebrenner, 2001; Schmid, Wong, & Mitchell, 2001). Oxytocin also has known cardiovascular effects, with higher levels linked to enhanced cardiac vagal tone and reduced hypertension (Barbaris & Tribollet, 1996; Gutkowska, Jankowski, Mukaddam-Daher, & Mccann, 2000; Holt-Lunstad, Birmingham, & Light, 2008; Jankowski et al., 2000).

My own foray into this research area was inspired by data from human and non-human animals alike, which has suggested that oxytocin may specifically heighten the salience of social information (for reviews, see Bartz, Zaki, Bolger, & Ochsner, 2011; Shamay-Tsoory & Abu-Akel, 2016). Oxytocin in rodent mothers, for instance, appears to tune the auditory cortex to detect vocalizations from rodent pups but has no impact on the detection of non-social auditory stimuli (Marlin, Mitre, D'amour, Chao, & Froemke, 2015). Similarly, oxytocin appears to tune the olfactory cortex to social odors, but not general odors (Choe et al., 2015). My team and I reasoned that oxytocin might also amplify the affective rewards gained from benign or benevolent social interactions. To test this idea, our empirical approach has been to triangulate the oxytocin system from multiple angles: We have (a) assayed people's tonic, endogenous levels of oxytocin through bodily fluids; (b) classified individuals based on common variants of genes related to oxytocin signaling; and (c) administered a synthetic form of oxytocin exogenously in a randomized, double-blind experimental design. This section describes what my team and I have thus far learned through each of these approaches.

One investigation, led by Zan Isgett, capitalized on the long-standing evidence that social interaction is a reliable behavioral determinant of positive emotions (see also Baumeister, this volume; Fritz & Lyubomirsky, this volume; von Hippel & Gonsalkorale, this volume). We examined whether individuals' tonic, endogenous levels of oxytocin moderated the link between sociality and positive emotions. In the same study (described earlier) in which cardiac vagal tone was found to amplify the positive emotions individuals experienced during social activities (i.e., Isgett, Kok, et al., 2017), we also measured these 73 participants' tonic levels of oxytocin. We did this by assaying urine each participant gathered over a 24-hour period. Results revealed that, as for cardiac vagal tone, tonic oxytocin moderated the association between the perceived sociality of an activity and the positive emotions experienced during it. Unlike cardiac vagal tone, however, tonic oxytocin did not predict the frequency of being in the presence of others. This pattern of results suggests that oxytocin and cardiac vagal tone may be linked to positive social experiences in somewhat distinct ways. Indeed, we found them to be uncorrelated ($r = .04$; CI $[-.19, .27]$; $p = .74$). Even so, each appears to function as a biological vantage resource that renders people more responsive, in terms of positive emotions, to quotidian opportunities for social connection (Isgett, Kok, et al., 2017). Thus, like cardiac vagal tone, oxytocin appears to underpin, to an extent, the affective rewards that come from transcending the self to connect with others.

Another investigation, again led by Zan Isgett, tested whether common genetic polymorphisms related to oxytocin signaling might also modulate the positive emotions that people experience in contexts characterized by a high degree of benevolent sociality. Such findings would provide additional evidence that the oxytocin system functions as a biological vantage resource that underpins positive emotions and purpose. Midlife adults ($N = 122$) were randomly assigned to learn one of two forms of meditation, each taught over a six-week period, while also reporting on their emotions daily (again using the modified Differential Emotions Scale). One meditation practice was loving-kindness meditation (described in the previous section), which centers on cultivating benevolent attitudes toward other people. The comparison practice was mindfulness meditation, which centers on stabilizing attention, without any particular focus on others. Study participants also provided blood samples, from which assays identified two genes important to oxytocin functioning, namely *OXTR* and *CD38*. Results revealed that individuals homozygous for one allele of *OXTR* (i.e., the G allele in single-nucleotide polymorphism rs1042778) experienced gains in daily positive emotions with training in loving-kindness meditation (but not mindfulness meditation), whereas individuals with the other allele did not experience gains in positive emotions with either training. These findings are among the first to show that a common genetic difference in oxytocin signaling may amplify or mute the positive emotions that individuals experience when they adopt a benevolent social focus (Isgett, Algoe, Boulton, Way, & Fredrickson, 2016; see also, Algoe & Way, 2014).

Our third study of the effects of oxytocin, led by Patty Van Cappellen, examined the links between oxytocin and spirituality, which is central to the experiences of purpose and meaning in life for millions of people worldwide (for a discussion of religiosity and health, see Myers, this volume). In keeping with past research, we define spirituality as one's personal affirmation of and relationship to a Higher Power, or to the sacred. Because the oxytocin system has been implicated in social bonding, we reasoned that it may also, to an extent, undergird spirituality. Although correlational studies had offered initial support for such an association (Holbrook, Hahn-Holbrook, & Holt-Lunstad, 2015; Kelsch et al., 2013), experimental evidence was lacking. To provide such evidence, we randomly assigned 83 midlife males to receive intranasal oxytocin or a placebo, using a double-blind experimental design. For exploratory analyses, participants were also genotyped for *OXTR* and *CD38*. Analyses revealed that oxytocin increased participants' self-reports of spirituality that same day, as well as one week later. Oxytocin also boosted the positive emotions participants experienced during an initial exposure to meditation practice, either loving-kindness or mindfulness. This effect was particularly pronounced for the self-transcendent positive emotions of awe, gratitude, inspiration, and love (Van Cappellen et al., 2016). So here again oxytocin functions as a biological vantage resource, one that enhances the affective rewards of meditation, which for many people is perceived as laden with meaning and purpose. Our confidence in this result is strengthened because it emerged through both explicit and implicit measures of positive affect. Mediational analyses also suggested that increases in spirituality accounted for the more positive affective responses to meditation that emerged in the oxytocin condition. Finally, our inference that the effects observed are indeed due to action within the oxytocin system is supported by exploratory analyses, which found genetic variation in *CD38* and, to a lesser extent, *OXTR* to moderate the effects of intranasal oxytocin administration (Van Cappellen et al., 2016). So here again we find that oxytocin functions as a biological vantage resource, one that boosts self-transcendent experiences of spirituality as well as the affective rewards of a purpose-laden activity (i.e., meditation).

Integration and Implications

Across this range of studies, my collaborators and I have uncovered evidence for multiple pathways by which biological attributes underpin positive emotions and purpose. Integrating this range of evidence, I speculate here about one possible overarching model, as illustrated in the accompanying Figure 10.1. First, we know

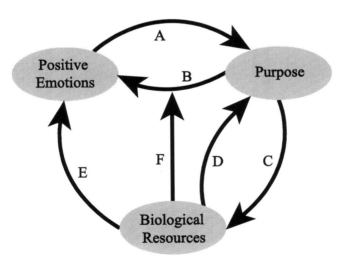

FIGURE 10.1   Evidence-Based Overarching Model of the Pathways Through Which Individuals' Biological Resources Underpin the Reciprocal Dynamic Between Positive Emotions and Purpose

from past research that positive emotion and purpose are themselves intertwined in an upward spiral dynamic. That is, positive emotions have been found to predict and cause increases in purpose (Path A; Hicks et al., 2010; Hicks et al., 2012; King & Hicks, 2009; King et al., 2006), and likewise, aspects of purpose have been found to predict and cause increases in positive emotions (Path B; Fredrickson et al., 2008; Yamasaki, Uchida, & Katsuma, 2009). In research described in the present chapter, my team and I have uncovered evidence for Path C, that purpose shows an association with biological attributes, namely leukocyte gene expression profiles (Fredrickson et al., 2015; Fredrickson et al., 2013) and cardiac vagal tone (Kok et al., 2013), that is more direct than the link between positive emotions and these same biological attributes (along Path A, then Path C; Isgett, Boulton, et al., 2016; Kok et al., 2013). We've also found that cardiac vagal tone predicts (Isgett, Kok, et al., 2016) and oxytocin causes (Van Cappellen et al., 2016) increases in purpose (Path D). In addition, we found these same biological attributes to predict and cause positive emotions, either directly (Path E; Kok et al., 2013; see also Kok & Fredrickson, 2015), or indirectly (Path D to Path B; Van Cappellen et al., 2016). Finally, we also find evidence that biological attributes function as vantage resources: that is, the association between purpose and positive emotions (Path B) is strengthened (moderated) by biological attributes (Path F), namely cardiac vagal tone (Isgett, Kok, et al., 2017) and oxytocin (Isgett, Algoe, et al., 2016; Isgett, Kok, et al., 2016).

The emergent overarching model thus implies two distinct ways that individuals' biological attributes may underpin the upward spiral dynamic between positive emotions and purpose (Paths A and B). First, biological attributes may join in this upward spiral dynamic such that positive emotions, purpose, and certain biological attributes mutually build on one another, either directly (Paths C, D, and E) or indirectly (along Path A then Path C). Second, biological attributes may also function as vantage resources that augment the affective rewards of purpose-laden activities (Path F). Taken as a whole, this model implies that positive emotions and purpose serve to build healthier levels of various biological attributes, either directly or indirectly, and that these accumulating biological resources advantage individuals further by amplifying the positive emotion yield of purpose-laden activities, which in turn accelerates the hypothesized biopsychosocial upward spiral dynamic even more so. (The model sketched here shares features in common with my upward spiral theory of lifestyle change [Fredrickson, 2013; Van Cappellen, Rice, et al., 2017], namely the acceleration factor represented by the outer loop of the upward spiral theory of lifestyle change. The inner loop dynamics of each model, however, are articulated at different levels of analysis.) Whether and to what extent the model depicted in Figure 10.1 faithfully describes how biological attributes underpin positive emotions and purpose merits further testing, with particular emphasis on longitudinal and experimental research designs.

For decades, scientists have known that psychological and physical health are related. Yet the specific physiological mechanisms that account for this mind-body connection are less understood. This chapter sheds light on plausible biological pathways by which positive mind states, such as positive emotions and purpose, over time become linked to physical health. Integrating disparate findings from the PEP Lab's recent biological investigations, I offer a provisional model (portrayed in Figure 10.1) to specify how various biological attributes—ranging from leukocyte gene expression profiles to cardiac vagal tone and oxytocin—function as mechanisms (mediators) and moderators that undergird both positive emotions and purpose. Insight into how, when, and for whom psychological and physical health interrelate and mutually enhance one another can reveal how, when, and for whom practitioners might best intervene to help more people to live well (for theory and evidence regarding well-being interventions, see Fritz & Lyubomirsky, this volume; see also Crano & Donaldson, this volume, and Simpson et al., this volume).

Author Note

The author expresses appreciation for her coauthors on the papers reported herein, especially Suzannah Isgett, Bethany Kok, and Patty Van Cappellen. The author also thanks Ann Firestine for her assistance with the research process and in preparing the reference section. Special thanks go to Garrett Chappell for rendering the figure. Support for the author's time and many of the studies described herein came from three research grants awarded by the U.S. National Institutes of Health (NIH) to Principal Investigator Barbara L. Fredrickson. These were a National Institute for Nursing Research Grant (R01NR012899), an award supported by the NIH Common Fund, which is managed by the NIH Office of the Director/Office of Strategic Coordination; a National Cancer Institute Research Grant (R01CA170128); and a National Center for Complementary and Integrative Health Research Grant (R01AT007884). These funding agencies played no role in study design, data collection, data analysis, decision to publish, or preparation of the manuscript.

Bibliography

Algoe, S. B., & Way, B. M. (2014). Evidence for a role of the oxytocin system, indexed by genetic variation in *cd38*, in the social bonding effects of expressed gratitude. *Social Cognitive and Affective Neuroscience, 9*(12), 1855–1861. doi:10.1093/scan/nst182

Amichai-Hamburger, Y., & Shir, E. (in press). Internet and wellbeing. In J. P. Forgas & R. F. Baumeister (Eds.), *The social psychology of living well*. New York, NY: Psychology Press.

Barbaris, C., & Tribollet, E. (1996). Vasopressin and oxytocin receptors in the central nervous system. *Critical Review of Neurobiology, 10*, 119–154.

Bartz, J. A., Zaki, J., Bolger, N., & Ochsner, K. N. (2011). Social effects of oxytocin in humans: Context and person matter. *Trends in Cognitive Sciences, 15*(7), 301–309.

Baumeister, R. F. (in press). Meaningfulness and happiness. In J. P. Forgas & R. F. Baumeister (Eds.), *The social psychology of living well*. New York, NY: Psychology Press.

Bibevski, S., & Dunlap, M. E. (2011). Evidence for impaired vagus nerve activity in heart failure. *Heart Failure Reviews, 16*(2), 129–135. doi:10.1007/s10741-010-9190-6

Brown, N. J. L., Macdonald, D. A., Samanta, M. P., Friedman, H. L., & Coyne, J. C. (2014). A critical reanalysis of Fredrickson et al.'s study of genomics and well-being. *Proceedings of the National Academy of Sciences, 111*(35), 12705–12709.

Carnethon, M. R., Golden, S. H., Folsom, A. R., Haskell, W., & Liao, D. (2003). Prospective investigation of autonomic nervous system function and the development of type 2 diabetes: The atherosclerosis risk in communities study, 1987–1998. *Circulation, 107*(17), 2190–2195. doi:10.1161/01.CIR.0000066324.74807.95

Chida, Y., & Steptoe, A. (2008). Positive psychological well-being and mortality: A quantitative review of prospective observational studies. *Psychosomatic medicine, 70*(7), 741–756. doi:10.1097/PSY.0b013e31818105ba

Choe, H. K., Reed, M. D., Benavidez, N., Montgomery, D., Soares, N., Yim, Y. S., & Choi, G. B. (2015). Oxytocin mediates entrainment of sensory stimuli to social cues of opposing valence. *Neuron, 87*(1), 152–163. doi:10.1016/j.neuron.2015.06.022

Clodi, M., Vila, G., Geyeregger, R., Riedl, M., Stulnig, T. M., Struck, J., . . . Luger, A. (2008). Oxytocin alleviates the neuroendocrine and cytokine response to bacterial endotoxin in healthy men. *American Journal of Physiology-Endocrinolology and Metabolism, 295*(3), E686–691. doi:10.1152/ajpendo.90263.2008

Cohn, M. A., Fredrickson, B. L., Brown, S. L., Mikels, J. A., & Conway, A. M. (2009). Happiness unpacked: Positive emotions increase life satisfaction by building resilience. *Emotion, 9*(3), 361–368. doi:10.1037/a0015952

Cole, S. W. (2012). Social regulation of gene expression in the immune system. In S. Segerstrom (Ed.), *Handbook of psychoneuroimmunology* (pp. 254–273). New York, NY: Oxford University Press.

Cole, S. W. (2013). Social regulation of human gene expression: Mechanisms and implications for public health. *American Journal of Public Health, 103*(Suppl 1), S84–S92. doi:10.2105/AJPH.2012.301183

Cole, S. W., Conti, G., Arevalo, J. M. G., Ruggiero, A. M., Heckman, J. J., & Suomi, S. J. (2012). Transcriptional modulation of the developing immune system by early life social adversity. *Proceedings of the National Academy of Sciences, 109*(50), 20578–20583. doi:10.1073/pnas.1218253109

Cole, S. W., Hawkley, L. C., Arevalo, J. M. G., & Cacioppo, J. T. (2011). Transcript origin analysis identifies antigen-presenting cells as primary targets of socially regulated gene expression in leukocytes. *Proceedings of the National Academy of Sciences of the United States of America, 108*(7), 3080–3085. doi:10.1073/pnas.1014218108

Cole, S. W., Levine, M. E., Arevalo, J. M. G., Ma, J., Weir, D. R., & Crimmins, E. M. (2015). Loneliness, eudaimonia, and the human conserved transcriptional response to adversity. *Psychoneuroendocrinology, 62*, 11–17.

Coyne, J. C. (2013). Highly correlated hedonic and eudaimonic well-being thwart genomic analysis. *Proceedings of the National Academy of Sciences of the United States of America, 110*(45), E4183. doi:10.1073/pnas.1315212110

Crano, W., & Donaldson, C. D. (in press). The role of positive parenting in living well: Preventing adolescent substance use. In J. P. Forgas & R. F. Baumeister (Eds.), *The social psychology of living well.* New York: Psychology Press.

Demaree, H. A., Robinson, J. L., Everhart, D. E., & Schmeichel, B. J. (2004). Resting RSA is associated with natural and self-regulated responses to negative emotional stimuli. *Brain Cogn, 56*(1), 14–23. doi:10.1016/j.bandc.2004.05.001

Dunn, E. W., & Dwyer, R. (in press). The future of happiness. In J. P. Forgas & R. F. Baumeister (Eds.), *The social psychology of living well*. New York, NY: Psychology Press.

Fabes, R. A., Eisenberg, N., & Eisenbud, L. (1993). Behavioral and physiological correlates of children's reactions to others in distress. *Developmental psychology, 29*(4), 655–663. doi:10.1037/0012–1649.29.4.655

Forgas, J. P. (in press). Negative affect and the good life: On the cognitive, motivational and interpersonal benefits of negative mood. In J. P. Forgas & R. F. Baumeister (Eds.), *The social psychology of living well*. New York, NY: Psychology Press.

Fredrickson, B. L. (1998). What good are positive emotions? *Review of General Psychology, 2*(3), 300–319. doi:10.1037/1089-2680.2.3.300

Fredrickson, B. L. (2013). Positive emotions broaden and build. *Advances in Experimental Social Psychology, 47*, 1–53. doi:10.1016/B978-0-12-407236-7.00001-2

Fredrickson, B. L., & Cohn, M. A. (2008). Positive emotions. In M. Lewis, J. M. Haviland-Jones, & L. F. Barrett (Eds.), *Handbook of emotions* (3rd ed., pp. 777–796). New York, NY: Guilford Press.

Fredrickson, B. L., Cohn, M. A., Coffey, K. A., Pek, J., & Finkel, S. M. (2008). Open hearts build lives: Positive emotions, induced through loving-kindness meditation, build consequential personal resources. *Journal of Personality and Social Psychology, 95*(5), 1045–1062. doi:10.1037/a0013262

Fredrickson, B. L., Grewen, K. M., Algoe, S. B., Firestine, A. M., Arevalo, J. M. G., Ma, J., & Cole, S. W. (2015). Psychological well-being and the human conserved transcriptional response to adversity. *Plos One, 10*(3), e0121839. doi:10.1371/journal.pone.0121839

Fredrickson, B. L., Grewen, K. M., Coffey, K. A., Algoe, S. B., Firestine, A. M., Arevalo, J. M. G., ... Cole, S. W. (2013). A functional genomic perspective on human well-being. *Proceedings of the National Academy of Sciences of the United States of America, 110*(33), 13684–13689. doi:10.1073/pnas.1305419110

Fredrickson, B. L., & Kok, B. E. (in press). The upward spiral stands steady: Response to nickerson (2017). Invited commentary for *Psychological Science*.

Gable, S. L. (in press). Capitalization: The good news about close relationships. In J. P. Forgas & R. F. Baumeister (Eds.), *The social psychology of living well*. New York, NY: Psychology Press.

Gutkowska, J., Jankowski, M., Mukaddam-Daher, S., & Mccann, S. M. (2000). Oxytocin is a cardiovascular hormone. *Brazilian Journal of Medical and Biological Research, 33*, 625–633.

Hicks, J. A., Schlegel, R. J., & King, L. A. (2010). Social threats, happiness, and the dynamics of meaning in life judgments. *Personality and Social Psychology Bulletin, 36*(10), 1305–1317. doi:10.1177/0146167210381650

Hicks, J. A., Trent, J., Davis, W. E., & King, L. A. (2012). Positive affect, meaning in life, and future time perspective: An application of socioemotional selectivity theory. *Psychology and Aging, 27*(1), 181–189. doi:10.1037/a0023965

Hill, P. L., & Turiano, N. A. (2014). Purpose in life as a predictor of mortality across adulthood. *Psychological Science, 25*(7), 1–5. doi:10.1177/0956797614531799

Holbrook, C., Hahn-Holbrook, J., & Holt-Lunstad, J. (2015). Self-reported spirituality correlates with endogenous oxytocin. *Psychology of Religion and Spirituality, 7*(1), 46–50. doi:10.1037/a0038255

Holt-Lunstad, J., Birmingham, W. A., & Light, K. C. (2008). Influence of a "warm touch" support enhancement intervention among married couples on ambulatory blood pressure, oxytocin, alpha amylase, and cortisol. *Psychosomatic Medicine*, 70(9), 976–985. doi:10.1097/PSY.0b013e318187aef7

Huppert, F. A. (in press). Living life well: The role of mindfulness and compassion. In J. P. Forgas & R. F. Baumeister (Eds.), *The social psychology of living well*. New York, NY: Psychology Press.

Hutcherson, C. A., Seppala, E. M., & Gross, J. J. (2008). Loving-kindness meditation increases social connectedness. *Emotion*, 8(5), 720–724. doi:10.1037/a0013237

Irwin, M. R., & Cole, S. W. (2011). Reciprocal regulation of the neural and innate immune systems. *Nature Reviews Immunology*, 11(9), 625–632. doi:10.1038/nri3042

Isgett, S. F., Algoe, S. B., Boulton, A. J., Way, B., & Fredrickson, B. L. (2016). Common variant in *OXTR* predicts growth in positive emotions from loving-kindness training. *Psychoneuroendocrinology*, 73, 244–251. doi:10.1016/j.psyneuen.2016.08.010

Isgett, S. F., Boulton, A. J., Cole, S. W., & Fredrickson, B. L. (2016). *Day-to-day positive emotions, mediated by eudaimonic well-being, predict leukocyte gene expression profiles*. Manuscript in preparation.

Isgett, S. F., Kok, B. E., Baczkowski, B., Algoe, S. B., Grewen, K. M., & Fredrickson, B. L. (2017). Influences of oxytocin and respiratory sinus arrhythmia on social behavior and emotions in daily life. *Emotion*, 17, 1156–1165. doi:10.1037/emo0000301

Jankowski, M., Bissonauth, V., Gao, L., Gangal, M., Wang, D., Danalache, B., . . . Gutkowska, J. (2010). Anti-inflammatory effect of oxytocin in rat myocardial infarction. *Basic Research in Cardiology*, 105(2), 205–218. doi:10.1007/s00395-009-0076-5

Jankowski, M., Wang, D., Hajjar, F., Mukaddam-Daher, S., Mccann, S. M., & Gutkowska, J. (2000). Oxytocin and its receptors are synthesized in the rat vasculature. *Proceedings of the National Academy of Sciences of the United States of America*, 97(11), 6207–6211.

Jazaieri, H., Jinpa, G. T., Mcgonigal, K., Rosenberg, E. L., Finkelstein, J., Simon-Thomas, E., . . . Goldin, P. R. (2013). Enhancing compassion: A randomized controlled trial of a compassion cultivation training program. *Journal of Happiness Studies*, 14(4), 1113–1126. doi:10.1007/s10902-012-9373-z

Kelsch, C. B., Ironson, G., Szeto, A., Kremer, H., Schneiderman, N., & Mendez, A. J. (2013). The relationship of spirituality, benefit finding, and other psychosocial variables to the hormone oxytocin in hiv/aids. *Research in the Social Scientific Study of Religion*, 24, 137–162.

Keyes, C. L. M. (2002). The mental health continuum: From languishing to flourishing in life. *Journal of Health and Social Behavior*, 43(2), 207–222. doi:10.2307/3090197

Keyes, C. L. M., & Annas, J. (2009). Feeling good and functioning well: Distinctive concepts in ancient philosophy and contemporary science. *The Journal of Positive Psychology*, 4(3), 197–201. doi:10.1080/17439760902844228

Keyes, C. L. M., Shmotkin, D., & Ryff, C. D. (2002). Optimizing well-being: The empirical encounter of two traditions. *Journal of Personality and Social Psychology*, 82(6), 1007–1022. doi:10.1037//0022-3514.82.6.1007

King, L. A., & Hicks, J. A. (2009). Detecting and constructing meaning in life events. *The Journal of Positive Psychology*, 4(5), 317–330. doi:10.1080/17439760902992316

King, L. A., Hicks, J. A., Krull, J. L., & Del Gaiso, A. K. (2006). Positive affect and the experience of meaning in life. *Journal of Personality and Social Psychology*, 90(1), 179–196. doi:10.1037/0022-3514.90.1.179

Kitayama, S., Akutsu, S., Uchida, Y., & Cole, S. W. (2016). Work, meaning, and gene regulation: Findings from a japanese information technology firm. *Psychoneuroendocrinology*, 72, 175–181.

Klimecki, O. M., Leiberg, S., Lamm, C., & Singer, T. (2013). Functional neural plasticity and associated changes in positive affect after compassion training. *Cereb Cortex*, 23(7), 1552–1561. doi:10.1093/cercor/bhs142

Kok, B. E., Coffey, K. A., Cohn, M. A., Catalino, L. I., Vacharkulksemsuk, T., Algoe, S. B., . . . Fredrickson, B. L. (2013). How positive emotions build physical health: Perceived positive social connections account for the upward spiral between positive emotions and vagal tone. *Psychological Science, 24*(7), 1123–1132. doi:10.1177/0956797612470827

Kok, B. E., & Fredrickson, B. L. (2010). Upward spirals of the heart: Autonomic flexibility, as indexed by vagal tone, reciprocally and prospectively predicts positive emotions and social connectedness. *Biological Psychology, 85*(3), 432–436. doi:10.1016/j.biopsycho.2010.09.005

Kok, B. E., & Fredrickson, B. L. (2015). Evidence for the upward spiral stands steady: A response to heathers, brown, coyne, and friedman (2015). *Psychological Science, 26*(7), 1144–1146.

Lamers, S. M. A., Westerhof, G. J., Bohlmeijer, E. T., Ten Klooster, P. M., & Keyes, C. L. M. (2011). Evaluating the psychometric properties of the mental health continuum-short form (mhc-sf). *Journal of Clinical Psychology, 67*(1), 99–110. doi:10.1002/jclp.20741

Leiberg, S., Klimecki, O., & Singer, T. (2011). Short-term compassion training increases prosocial behavior in a newly developed prosocial game. *Plos One, 6*(3), e17798. doi:10.1371/journal.pone.0017798

Lyubomirsky, S., & Fritz, M. S. (in press). Wither happiness? When, how, and why positive activities might undermine versus boost well-being. In J. P. Forgas & R. F. Baumeister (Eds.), *The social psychology of living well*. New York, NY: Psychology Press.

Marlin, B. J., Mitre, M., D'amour, J. A., Chao, M. V., & Froemke, R. C. (2015). Oxytocin enables maternal behaviour by balancing cortical inhibition. *Nature, 520*(7548), 499–504. doi:10.1038/nature14402

Myers, D. G. (in press). Religious engagement and the good life. In J. P. Forgas & R. F. Baumeister (Eds.), *The social psychology of living well*. New York, NY: Psychology Press.

Petersson, M., Wiberg, U., Lundeberg, T., & Uvnäs-Moberg, K. (2001). Oxytocin decreases carrageenan induced inflammation in rats. *Peptides, 22*(9), 1479–1484.

Pluess, M., & Belsky, J. (2013). Vantage sensitivity: Individual differences in response to positive experiences. *Psychological Bulletin, 139*(4), 901–916. doi:10.1037/a0030196

Porges, S. W. (2011). *The polyvagal theory: Neuropsychological foundations of emotions, attachment, communication, & self-regulation*. New York, NY: Norton.

Porges, S. W., Doussard-Roosevelt, J. A., & Maiti, A. K. (1994). Vagal tone and the physiological regulation of emotion. *Monographs of the Society for Research in Child Development, 59*(2/3), 167–186. doi:10.2307/1166144

Rauk, P. N., & Friebe-Hoffmann, U. (2000). Interleukin-1β down-regulates the oxytocin receptor in cultured uterine smooth muscle cells. *American Journal of Reproductive Immunology, 43*(2), 85–91. doi:10.1111/j.8755–8920.2000.430204.x

Rauk, P. N., Friebe-Hoffmann, U., Chiao, J.-P., Rauk, P. N., & Winebrenner, L. D. (2001). Interleukin-6 up-regulates the oxytocin receptor in cultured uterine smooth muscle cells. *American Journal of Reproductive Immunology, 45*(3), 148–153. doi:10.1111/j.8755-8920.2001.450305.x

Russell, D. W. (1996). Ucla loneliness cale (version 3): Reliability, validity, and factor structure. *Journal of Personality Assessment, 66*(1), 20–40.

Schmid, B., Wong, S., & Mitchell, B. F. (2001). Transcriptional regulation of oxytocin receptor by interleukin-1beta and interleukin-6. *Endocrinology, 142*(4), 1380–1385. doi:10.1210/endo.142.4.8107

Sedikides, C. (in press). Nostalgia potentiates a positive and attainable future. In J. P. Forgas & R. F. Baumeister (Eds.), *The social psychology of living well*. New York, NY: Psychology Press.

Shamay-Tsoory, S. G., & Abu-Akel, A. (2016). The social salience hypothesis of oxytocin. *Biological Psychiatry*, *79*(3), 194–202.

Sheldon, K. M. (in press). Happiness is not a warm puppy: Using the eudaimonic activity model to sort out the well-being literature. In J. P. Forgas & R. F. Baumeister (Eds.), *The social psychology of living well*. New York, NY: Psychology Press.

Simpson, J. A., Huelsnitz, C., & Jones, R. E. (in press). Early social experiences and living well: A longitudinal view of adult physical health. In J. P. Forgas & R. F. Baumeister (Eds.), *The social psychology of living well*. New York: Psychology Press.

Slavich, G. M., & Cole, S. W. (2013). The emerging field of human social genomics. *Clinical Psychological Science*, *1*(3), 331–348. doi:10.1177/2167702613478594

Suess, P. E., Porges, S. W., & Plude, D. J. (1994). Cardiac vagal tone and sustained attention in school-age children. *Psychophysiology*, *31*(1), 17–22. doi:10.1111/j.1469-8986.1994.tb01020.x

Thayer, J. F., & Lane, R. D. (2007). The role of vagal function in the risk for cardiovascular disease and mortality. *Biological Psychology*, *74*(2), 224–242. doi:10.1016/j.biopsycho.2005.11.013

Thayer, J. F., & Sternberg, E. (2006). Beyond heart rate variability: Vagal regulation of allostatic systems. *Annals of the New York Academy of Sciences*, *1088*, 361–372. doi:10.1196/annals.1366.014

Tung, J., Barreiro, L. B., Johnson, Z. P., Hansen, K. D., Michopoulos, V., Toufexis, D., . . . Gilad, Y. (2012). Social environment is associated with gene regulatory variation in the rhesus macaque immune system. *PNAS Proceedings of the National Academy of Sciences of the United States of America*, *109*(17), 6490–6495. doi:10.1073/pnas.1202734109

Van Cappellen, P., Rice, E. L., Catalino, L. I., & Fredrickson, B. L. (2017). Positive affective processes underlying positive health behavior change. *Psychology and Health*. Advance online publication. http://dx.doi.org/10.1080/08870446.2017.1320798

Van Cappellen, P., Way, B., Isgett, S. F., & Fredrickson, B. L. (2016). Effects of oxytocin administration on spirituality and emotional responses to meditation. *Social Cognitive and Affective Neuroscience*, 1–9. doi:10.1093/scan/nsw078

Vitterso, J. (2016). *The handbook of eudaimonic wellbeing*. New York: Springer.

Von Hippel, W., & Gonsalkorale, K. (in press). What can evolutionary theory tell us about how to live the good life? In J. P. Forgas & R. F. Baumeister (Eds.), *The social psychology of living well*. New York: Psychology Press.

Waterman, A. S. (1993). Two conceptions of happiness: Contrasts of personal expressiveness (eudaimonia) and hedonic enjoyment. *Journal of Personality and Social Psychology*, *64*(4), 678–691. doi:10.1037/0022-3514.64.4.678

Weng, H. Y., Fox, A. S., Shackman, A. J., Stodola, D. E., Caldwell, J. Z., Olson, M. C., . . . Davidson, R. J. (2013). Compassion training alters altruism and neural responses to suffering. *Psychol Sci*, *24*(7), 1171–1180. doi:10.1177/0956797612469537

Yamasaki, K., Uchida, K., & Katsuma, R. (2009). An intervention study of the effects of the coping strategy of "finding positive meaning" on positive affect and health. *International Journal of Psychology*, *44*(4), 249–256. doi:10.1080/00207590701750912

11

NOSTALGIA SHAPES AND POTENTIATES THE FUTURE

Constantine Sedikides, Tim Wildschut, and Elena Stephan

On Nostalgia

Nostalgia is "a sentimental longing or wistful affection for the past" (Pearsall, 1998, p. 1266). This dictionary definition aligns well with lay conceptions (i.e., prototype analysis; cf. Rosch, 1978). Laypeople (Hepper, Ritchie, Sedikides, & Wildschut, 2012) across 18 cultures (Hepper et al., 2014) think of the construct "nostalgia" as encompassing fond, rose-colored, and personally important (i.e., self-defining) memories of one's childhood or relationships, but also as encompassing pining and wishing for momentary returns to the past. They think of it, then, as a bittersweet (albeit more positive than negative) emotion that is relevant to the self and close others. Both content analyses of nostalgic narratives (Abeyta, Routledge, Roylance, Wildschut, & Sedikides, 2015; Holak & Havlena, 1998; Wildschut, Sedikides, Arndt, & Routledge, 2006, Studies 1–2) and in vivo manipulations of nostalgia (Baldwin, Biernat, & Landau, 2015; Wildschut et al., 2006, Studies 5–7; Stephan, Sedikides, & Wildschut, 2012) have corroborated these properties of the emotion.

The most salient property of nostalgia, however, is its reference to the past: The emotion comprises recollections of meaningful events from one's life. Partly because of this reference, nostalgia has often been considered an escapist reaction to the demands of the present. For example, it has been labeled "a regressive manifestation" (Castelnuovo-Tedesco, 1980, p. 110), that may arise from a subconscious desire to return to one's fetal state (Fodor, 1950), and has been equated with living in times past (Best & Nelson, 1985; Hertz, 1990; Holbrook, 1994). The standard conceptualization of nostalgia has portrayed it as a retreat from the world—often into an idealized yesteryear, as a quest for solace in daydream, and as anxiety if not fear of the future (Flinn, 1992; Nawas & Jerome, 1965; see also for reviews: Batcho, 2013; Sedikides, Wildschut, & Baden, 2004.)

Implications of Nostalgia for One's Future

There have been a few dissenting voices, however. Foremost among them is that of the sociologist Fred Davis (1977). He opined (p. 420):

> It [nostalgia] reassures us of past happiness and accomplishment; and, since these still remain on deposit, as it were, in the bank of our memory, it simultaneously bestows upon us a certain worth, irrespective of how present circumstances may seem to question or obscure this. And current worth, as our friendly bank loan officer assures us, is titled to at least some claim on the future as well.

This bright outlook on nostalgia, depicting it as a resource that can be used to maximize future well-being, served as an impetus for our research into how nostalgia shapes and potentiates one's future.

In this chapter, we cover experimental work in which nostalgia is typically manipulated with the Event Reflection Task (ERT; Sedikides et al., 2015). Participants are randomly assigned to the experimental or control condition. In the experimental condition, they are usually provided with the dictionary definition of nostalgia ("a sentimental longing or wistful affection for the past") and are then instructed to recollect a nostalgic event from their lives and write a brief narrative about it. In the control condition, participants are instructed to recollect an ordinary (i.e., regular or everyday) event from their lives and also write a brief narrative about it. (Sometimes the control condition involves a positive past event, and we indicate so.) Subsequently, participants note down five keywords that purport to capture the gist of the relevant event; alternatively, they note down five keywords and describe the event in writing (for five minutes). Following a three-item manipulation check (e.g., "I feel nostalgic at the moment"; Routledge et al., 2011, Study 2; Wildschut et al., 2006, Studies 5–7), participants complete the measures pertaining to the putative mediators or the dependent variables. We note that the effects of nostalgia we report are independent of positive affect (or positive mood).

How Nostalgia Shapes the Future

We argue that nostalgia shapes one's future and well-being by sparking approach orientation, increasing optimism, and evoking inspiration.

Approach Orientation

We obtained an early lead that nostalgia entails an approach orientation (see also Shah, this volume) by content-analyzing nostalgic episodes, examining the presence of two narrative sequences (McAdams, Reynolds, Lewis, Patten, & Bowman, 2001). In one, *redemption*, the episode progresses from an affectively unpleasant situation to an affectively pleasant one ("The bad is redeemed, salvaged, mitigated, or made better in light of the ensuing good"; McAdams et al., p. 474). In the other, *contamination*, the episode follows the reverse order ("The good is spoiled, ruined, contaminated, or undermined by what follows it"; McAdams et al., p. 474). Specifically, we content-analyzed stories submitted to the periodical *Nostalgia* by its readers (Wildschut et al., 2006, Study 1) and descriptions generated by participants under a nostalgia-writing prompt (Wildschut et al., 2006, Study 2, p. 979). This prompt instructed them to ". . . think of an important part of your past (e.g., event or episode) that makes you feel *most nostalgic*. Please bring this nostalgic experience to mind and think it through," to write about their nostalgic experience "in all its vivid detail," and to "be as detailed, thorough, and descriptive" as possible. In both studies, nostalgic episodes more frequently followed a redemption than a contamination sequence. As Davis (1979, p. 14) put it, in nostalgia "the component of sadness serves only to heighten the quality of recaptured joy" and, as Chaplin (2000) emphasized, nostalgia reflects appreciation, if not re-enjoyment, of past experiences. In all, although nostalgic episodes often start badly, they acquire momentum as they move along, ending with a bang. This trajectory is a mark of an approach orientation.

We suggest that nostalgia sparks an approach orientation to test. Having manipulated nostalgia with the ERT, we assessed the fundamental action tendency of approach orientation (Stephan et al., 2014, Study 3). This tendency is sensitive to signals of reward, facilitating goals and behavior that are likely to lead to desirable outcomes such as hope or happiness (Carver, 2006; Carver & White, 1994; see also Shah, this volume). We assessed approach orientation with the 13-item Behavioral Activation System (BAS) subscale of the BIS/BAS Scales (Carver & White, 1994). This subscale measures approach behavioral tendencies in three domains: Drive (e.g., "I go out of my way to get things I want"), Fun Seeking (e.g., "I will often do things for no other reason than that they might be fun"), and Reward Responsiveness (e.g., "It would excite me to win a contest"). Nostalgic (relative to control) participants manifested stronger approach orientation: They scored higher on Drive and Fun Seeking. Nostalgic and control participants, however, did not differ on Reward Responsiveness. Prior work (Carver & White, 1994) has suggested that Drive and Fun Seeking are characterized by excitability and euphoria (and are thus more dependent on intrinsic processes), whereas Reward Responsiveness is characterized by maintaining behavior previously associated with reward (and is thus more dependent on environmental contingencies). Drive and Fun Seeking, then, being tuned toward desirable goals, may reflect a more faithful operationalization of approach motivation. Overall, then, the results (Stephan et al., 2014, Study 3) do suggest that nostalgia sparks approach motivation.

Findings from other laboratories are consistent with this suggestion. Abeyta and Routledge (2016) tested whether nostalgia induces perceptions of youthfulness, arguably an indirect indicator of approach orientation. They manipulated nostalgia either with the ERT (Studies 2–3) or with YouTube-based song selection (Study 1). In the latter case, participants in the nostalgia condition were provided with the relevant dictionary definition and instructed to ". . . search for and listen to a song that makes you feel nostalgic. This should be a song that reminds you of a fond memory," whereas participants in the control condition were instructed to "search for and listen to a song that you heard for the first time recently. This should be a song that you recently discovered and enjoyed listening to" (p. 360). Participants then answered the question "At times, people feel older or younger than they actually are. At this moment, what age do you feel?" (Study 1, p. 360) or the question "At this time, how youthful do you feel?" (Study 2, p. 362, and also Study 3). In addition, participants (Study 3—sample of older adults) responded to four adjectives associated with feeling young ("energetic," "alert," "happy-go-lucky," "rejuvenated") and to four subjective health items (Hays, Sherbourne, & Mazel, 1993; Warner, Schwarzaer, Schüz, & Tesch-Römer, 2012) reflecting a sense of youthfulness ("I am as healthy as anyone I know," "My health is excellent," "I seem to get sick a little easier than other people" [reverse-scored], "If you compare yourself with an average person of your sex and age, how healthy are you?"). Across studies, nostalgic (relative to control) participants felt younger than their chronological age, felt more invigorated, and reported having better subjective health.

Baldwin and Landau (2014) tested whether nostalgia promotes perceptions of psychological growth ("the potential to cultivate inner potentialities, seek out optimal challenges, and integrate new experiences into the self-concept," p. 163), arguably an indirect indicator of approach orientation as well (see also Fredrickson, this volume). In two experiments, these researchers manipulated nostalgia with the ERT and found that it promoted psychological growth, operationalized in terms of self-expansion, curiosity, and inclination toward new experiences.

Optimism

We first wondered whether nostalgic episodes reflect optimism (i.e., expectation of positive, rather than negative, outcomes; Scheier & Carver, 1985). They do (Cheung et al., 2013, Study 1). We manipulated nostalgia with the ERT, and subjected the ensuing narratives to Linguistic Inquiry and Word Count (LIWC; Pennebaker, Booth, & Francis, 2007) analyses. LIWC has an internal dictionary of approximately 4,500 words and calculates the proportion of word categories. The LIWC was successful at classifying 77.06% of words, a ratio typical of relevant studies (Pennebaker & Graybeal, 2001). We analyzed the proportion of optimism-related words, a category consisting of 70 words (e.g., optimism, hope, determined). LIWC arrived at this proportion by dividing the number of optimism-related words by the total word count for a given narrative. Nostalgic (relative to ordinary) episodes included a higher proportion of optimism-related words. We next examined the causal relation between nostalgia and optimism.

Nostalgia Increases Optimism

In an experimental foray into the topic, we (Cheung et al., 2013, Study 2) manipulated nostalgia with the ERT and measured subsequent optimism with four
items: "optimistic about my future," "like the sky is the limit," "hopeful about my
future," "ready to take on new challenges." Nostalgia increased optimism. We
confirmed the same result pattern in an exact replication (Cheung, Sedikides, &
Wildschut, 2016).

We obtained this pattern showing that nostalgia improves optimism, and indirectly well-being, in two additional studies. In one, we manipulated nostalgia with
nomothetically derived song lyrics (Cheung et al., 2013, Study 3). First, participants listened to a nostalgic or control song. Whether a given song was nostalgic
or not was confirmed in a pretest through normative ratings. Next, participants
completed a brief measure of optimism (i.e., "optimistic about the future," "hopeful about the future"). Nostalgic (compared to control) songs increased optimism.
In the following study, participants read idiosyncratically derived nostalgic versus
control song lyrics (Cheung et al., 2013, Study 4). More precisely, participants
designated in a preliminary session three songs that made them feel nostalgic,
and, three weeks later, received randomly the lyrics of one of these three songs.
Each "nostalgia lyrics" participant was yoked to a "control lyrics" participant, who
received the same song lyrics (that she or he had not designated before as nostalgic). Afterwards, all participants reported their level of optimism on the six-item
Revised Life Orientation Test (Scheier, Scheier, Carver, & Bridges, 1994; e.g., "In
uncertain times, I usually expect the best"). Participants who read nostalgic lyrics
were more optimistic than those who read control lyrics.

In another study, we measured scent-induced nostalgia and optimism (Reid,
Green, Wildschut, & Sedikides, 2015). During a pretest, participants sampled at
random 33 pleasantly or neutrally scented oils and reported how nostalgic each
made them feel. We retained the 12 scents with the highest item-total correlations (e.g., Chanel #5, fresh-cut roses, eggnog, apple pie) for the subsequent
experiment in which participants sampled (also at random) each of the 12 scents,
presented in glass test tubes. Participants rated each scent for nostalgia (i.e., "How
nostalgic does this scent make you feel?") and reported their optimism (i.e., "optimistic about my future," "ready to take on new challenges"). Higher levels of
scent-evoked nostalgia predicted greater levels of optimism.

Other laboratories have produced parallel findings. Following an ERT-based
nostalgia induction in a sample of older adults, Abeyta and Routledge (2016,
Study 3) assessed health-related optimism with three items (Hays et al., 1993;
Warner et al., 2012): "How do you estimate the likelihood that your health status
will worsen in the near future?", "If you compare yourself with an average person
of your sex and age, how likely is it for you that your health will worsen in the near
future?", "I expect my health to get worse." Nostalgic participants reported higher

health-related optimism than controls. Similarly, Kersten, Cox, and Van Enkevort (2016, Experiment 1) manipulated nostalgia with the ERT and assessed health-related optimism with a 16-item scale (Aspinwall & Brunhart, 1996; e.g., "If I did get a serious illness, I would recover from it sooner than most other people"). Nostalgia increased health-related optimism. Finally, Abeyta, Routledge, and Juhl (2015, Experiment 1) manipulated nostalgia with the ERT and assessed how likely participants felt it was they would achieve their relationship goals. Nostalgic (relative to control) participants expressed higher optimism about the attainment of such goals, confirming nostalgia's broadly beneficial effects for well-being.

Nostalgia Increases Optimism by Elevating Self-Esteem

How does nostalgia increase optimism? Davis (1977), as quoted above, implied that it does so by raising self-esteem ("current worth"). When nostalgizing, people recollect mostly positive and meaningful events from their past. Such recollection is likely to boost their self-esteem (Peetz & Wilson, 2008; Wilson & Ross, 2003), and, as a consequence, to make them feel more optimistic. Preliminary findings are consistent with the nostalgia–self-esteem link. Experimentally manipulated nostalgia elevates self-esteem (Baldwin & Landau, 2014, Experiment 2; Hepper et al., 2012, Study 7; Wildschut et al., 2006, Studies 5–6), regardless of whether it is assessed in terms of bespoke items (e.g., "feel good about myself," "value myself") or the ten-item Rosenberg self-esteem scale (Rosenberg, 1965; e.g., "I feel that I'm a person of worth, at least on an equal plane with others"). Also, preliminary findings are consistent with the self-esteem–optimism link. Self-esteem is positively associated with optimism (Chemers, Watson, & May, 2000; Mäkikangas, Kinnunen, & Feldt, 2004).

We (Cheung et al., 2013, Study 3) tested the full sequence (nostalgia ⇒ self-esteem ⇒ optimism) in an experiment in which we manipulated nostalgia with nomothetically derived song lyrics, as described above. Nostalgia increased optimism (i.e., "optimistic about the future," "hopeful about the future") via self-esteem (i.e., "feel good about myself," "satisfied with myself"). This mediational pattern was replicated in a study where participants read idiosyncratically derived nostalgic versus control song lyrics (Cheung et al., 2013, Study 4), as described above. Here, we measured self-esteem with four items ("feel good about myself," "I like myself better," "I like myself more," and "I have many positive qualities"), and, as a reminder, optimism was measured with the Revised Life Orientation Test. Lastly, the same mediational pattern was replicated in a study in which we (Cheung et al., 2016) manipulated nostalgia with the ERT and measured self-esteem and optimism with four items (*self-esteem*: "feel good about myself," "I like myself better," "I like myself more," and "I have many positive qualities"; *optimism*: "optimistic about my future," "like the sky is the limit," "hopeful about my future," "ready to take on new challenges"). In sum, improved self-esteem functions as the mechanism through which nostalgia increases optimism.

Nostalgia Increases Optimism by Fostering Social Connectedness, Which Elevates Self-Esteem

But how does nostalgia elevate self-esteem in the first place? Social connectedness, a sense of belongingness or acceptance, is a prime candidate, according to insights and evidence from several influential theories (sociometer theory: Leary & Baumeister, 2000; contingencies of self-worth: Crocker & Wolfe, 2001; terror-management theory: Pyszczynski, Greenberg, Solomon, Arndt, & Schimel, 2004; see also Gable; and Simpson et al., this volume). Nostaglia is a social emotion. Nostalgic episodes reflect momentous and mostly social occasions from one's life (e.g., weddings, graduations, vacations, Thanksgiving dinners). Although in those episodes the self is the master of ceremonies, the self is almost invariably surrounded by close others (e.g., family, friends, romantic partners). Nostalgia then should engender social connectedness. Indeed it does, as experimental tests have demonstrated. During nostalgic reverie, the person feels loved, protected, socially supported, able to trust others, empathetic towards others, and more emotionally supportive of others (Hepper et al., 2012, Study 7; Wildschut et al., 2006, Studies 5–7; Wildschut, Sedikides, Routledge, Arndt, & Cordaro, 2010, Study 5; Zhou, Sedikides, Wildschut, & Gao, 2008; Zhou, Wildschut, Sedikides, Shi, & Feng, 2012, Studies 1–4).

We (Cheung et al., 2013, Study 4) proceeded to test the idea that nostalgia-induced social connectedness leads to higher self-esteem, which in turn leads to greater optimism (nostalgia ⇒ social connectedness ⇒ self-esteem ⇒ optimism). We induced nostalgia with idiosyncratically derived lyrics (see above), and then assessed social connectedness (i.e., "connected to loved ones," "protected," "loved," "trust others"), self-esteem ("feel good about myself," "I like myself better," "I like myself more," "I have many positive qualities"), and optimism (Revised Life Orientation Test). Nostalgia fostered social connectedness, which subsequently elevated self-esteem, which in turn increased optimism. Cheung et al. (2016) replicated this mediational sequence, although they found it to be more pronounced among individuals high (rather than low) on nostalgia proneness, that is, on the dispositional tendency to engage frequently in nostalgia and to ascribe personal importance to nostalgia (Barrett et al., 2010; Routledge, Arndt, Sedikides, & Wildschut, 2008—see below).

Inspiration

Does nostalgia evoke inspiration, and, if so, how? The experience of inspiration entails transcending the mundane while becoming aware of more attractive possibilities or ideas and intending to act upon them (Thrash & Elliot, 2003, 2004). We (Stephan et al., 2015, Study 1) began by examining the natural covariance between nostalgia and inspiration. We assessed nostalgia with the Nostalgia Inventory (Batcho, 1995) and the Southampton Nostalgia Scale (Barrett et al., 2010; Routledge et al., 2008). For the Nostalgia Inventory, participants rate how nostalgic they feel for 18 facets of their past (e.g., "My family," "My pets," "TV shows," "Having someone to depend on"). For the Southampton Nostalgia Scale, participants respond to four items that apply to frequency of nostalgia proneness (e.g., "How often do you experience nostalgia?", "How prone are you to feeling nostalgia?"), and to three items that apply to personal relevance of nostalgic engagement (e.g., "How important is it for you to bring to mind nostalgic experiences?", "How valuable is nostalgia for you?"). The two nostalgia scales were highly correlated, and so we created a composite that we used in data analyses. We assessed inspiration with five items from the Inspiration Scale (Thrash & Elliot, 2003): "I feel inspired," "I experience inspiration," "Something I encounter or experience inspires me," "I am inspired to do something," "I am filled with inspiration." Participants rated each item on both frequency ("How often does this happen?") and intensity ("How deeply or strongly [in general]?"). Nostalgia was positively associated with inspiration frequency and intensity. Further, given that frequency and intensity were highly correlated, we formed an overall inspiration index. Unsurprisingly, nostalgia was positively associated with that index as well. Having shown that nostalgia and inspiration covary naturally, we proceeded to test their causal relation.

Nostalgia Evokes Inspiration

In the first experiment addressing this relation, we (Stephan et al., 2015, Study 2) manipulated nostalgia with the ERT and assessed general inspiration with a three items ("feel inspired," "inspires me to do something," "fills me with inspiration"), two of which we adapted from Thrash and Elliott (2003) and one which we created. Nostalgia evoked general inspiration. We obtained the same finding in an exact replication (Stephan et al., 2015, Study 6). Further, we replicated this finding in an experiment that manipulated nostalgia with idiosyncratically derived song lyrics (as in Cheung et al., 2013, Study 4), and in an experiment that manipulated nostalgia with the ERT but used a positive event condition ("... bring to mind a lucky event in your life. Specifically, try to think of a positive past event that was brought on by chance rather than through your own actions;" p. 1402) rather than an ordinary event condition (Stephan et al., 2015, Studies 4 and 5, respectively). Finally, we replicated this finding by manipulating nostalgia with the ERT but assessing specific, rather than general, inspiration with a five-item scale ("meet new people," "travel overseas this summer," "go to a modern art museum," "try skydiving or some other adventurous activity," "explore some place that I have never been before"—adapted from Green & Campbell, 2000). In all, nostalgia evokes inspiration.

Nostalgia Evokes Inspiration by Elevating Self-Esteem

We wondered next about the mechanism through which nostalgia might evoke (general) inspiration. Self-esteem, once again, may qualify as such. Thrash and

Elliot (2003) reported that high self-esteem plays a critical role in the evocation of inspiration. Also, as we have seen earlier, nostalgia elevates self-esteem (Baldwin & Landau, 2014, Experiment 2; Hepper et al., 2012, Study 7; Wildschut et al., 2006, Studies 5–6). We thus tested the above implied mediational model (nostalgia $\Rightarrow$ self-esteem $\Rightarrow$ inspiration) and found support for it in three experiments. As mentioned above, one assessed nostalgia with the ERT (nostalgic vs. ordinary event; Stephan et al., 2015, Study 6), another with a revised version of the ERT (nostalgic vs. positive event; Stephan et al., 2015, Study 5), and a third with idiosyncratically derived song lyrics (Stephan et al., 2015, Study 4).

Nostalgia Evokes Inspiration by Fostering Social Connectedness, Which Elevates Self-Esteem

We capitalized on a rich source of evidence that points to social connectedness as a solid basis for self-esteem (Crocker & Wolfe, 2001; Leary & Baumeister, 2000; Pyszczynski et al., 2004), and tested the extended mediational sequence (nostalgia $\Rightarrow$ social connectedness $\Rightarrow$ self-esteem $\Rightarrow$ inspiration). We found support for it in three experiments. The first assessed nostalgia via the ERT (nostalgic vs. ordinary event; Stephan et al., 2015, Study 6), the second via a revised ERT (nostalgic vs. positive event; Stephan et al., 2015, Study 5), and the third via idiosyncratically derived song lyrics (Stephan et al., 2015, Study 4). In summary, nostalgia fosters social connectedness, which elevates self-esteem, which then evokes inspiration.

How Nostalgia Potentiates the Future

Having discussed how nostalgia shapes one's future and potentially influences well-being, we now turn to the issue of how the emotion potentiates it. We argue that it does so by strengthening motivation for goal pursuit, boosting creativity, and guiding overt behavior.

Motivation for Goal Pursuit

We have found that nostalgia sparks an approach orientation, increases optimism, and evokes creativity. Nostalgia, then, has motivational potential, as do other affective states as well (see Forgas, this volume). Does such potential materialize in the concrete case of goal pursuit?

Nostalgia Strengthens Motivation for Goal Pursuit

We addressed the causal relation between nostalgia and motivation for goal pursuit in three experiments. We (Sedikides et al., 2017, Experiment 1) started by manipulating nostalgia with the ERT and assessing motivation for goal pursuit with a procedure that we adapted from Milyavskaya, Ianakieva, Foxen-Craft, Colantuoni, and Koestner (2012). In particular, participants listed five important goals and designated the most important one. Afterwards, they reported how motivated they were to pursue their most important goal. Nostalgia strengthened participants' motivation to pursue their most important goal. We (Stephan et al., 2015, Study 6) obtained the same finding in an experiment where we manipulated nostalgia with the ERT and measured motivation for goal pursuit with the adapted Milyavskaya et al. (2012) procedure. In addition, we asked two independent judges to code the types of goals that participants listed. The judges identified three themes: agentic goals (e.g., graduating with good grades), hedonistic goals (e.g., enjoying life), and social goals (e.g., having a family). Ancillary analyses revealed that nostalgia strengthened goal pursuit on all three goal domains. Research by Abeyta, Routledge, and Juhl (2015) also indicated that nostalgia strengthens social, and in particular, relationship goals (e.g., connecting with friends).

In an effort to specify the effect of nostalgia on goal pursuit, we (Sedikides et al., 2017, Experiment 2) manipulated nostalgia via the ERT and assessed goal pursuit with another modification of the Milyavskaya et al. (2012) procedure. Specifically, we asked participants to respond to five statements, such as "I am motivated to pursue this goal," but this time with regard to both their most important goal and least important goal (presented at random). Nostalgia strengthened participants' most important goal, but not their least important goal. This suggests that nostalgia has a specific influence on focal goal pursuit, galvanizing a person's cherished goals.

We identified two mechanisms through which nostalgia strengthens motivation for goal pursuit. One is its effect on meaning in life. The other is a protracted causal sequence going from nostalgia-induced social connectedness to self-esteem to inspiration.

Nostalgia Strengthens Motivation for Goal Pursuit by Imbuing Life With Meaning

As we discussed, nostalgia pertains to recollections of time spent with close others (e.g., family, partners, friends) during momentous life events (e.g., vacations, graduations, Thanksgiving dinners). Also, nostalgia fosters social connectedness. Close others (Lambert et al., 2010), and social connectedness more generally (Stavrova & Luhmann, 2016), are key sources of giving meaning to life (see also Baumeister, this volume). Indeed, research has established that nostalgia augments perceptions of life as meaningful (Hepper et al., 2012; Reid et al., 2015; Routledge et al., 2011; Routledge, Wildschut, Sedikides, Juhl, & Arndt, 2012). Meaning in life, in turn, has been linked to motivational constructs (i.e., approach orientation, curiosity, exploration; Steger, Kashdan, Sullivan, & Lorentz, 2008), albeit not to motivational goal pursuit per se.

We (Sedikides et al., 2017) tested whether nostalgia evokes motivation for goal pursuit through promoting meaning in life (nostalgia ⇒ meaning in life ⇒

motivation for goal pursuit). We manipulated nostalgia with the ERT, assessed meaning in life, and then assessed motivation to pursue one's goals (Experiment1) or motivation to pursue one's most important goal (Experiment 2), as mentioned above. We assessed meaning in life with the items "life is meaningful," "life has a purpose," "there is a greater purpose to life," and "life is worth living" (Hepper et al., 2012; Wildschut et al., 2006). Increased meaning in life emerged as a mechanism through which nostalgia strengthens motivation for goal pursuit, particularly in relation to one's most important goal.

Nostalgia Strengthens Motivation for Goal Pursuit Through an Extended Causal Sequence Involving Social Connectedness, Self-Esteem, and Inspiration

We focused on an additional, serial mechanism via which nostalgia might strengthen pursuit of one's goals. We built on prior findings (Stephan et al., 2015, Studies 1–5) in which we had documented an extended mediational pathway through which nostalgia evokes inspiration (nostalgia ⇒ social connectedness ⇒ self-esteem ⇒ inspiration). We asked whether the end point of this pathway, inspiration, might strengthen goal pursuit, given that inspiration entails intent to act (Thrash & Elliot, 2003, 2004). This was indeed the case (Stephan et al., 2015, Study 6). Put otherwise, nostalgia strengthens motivation to pursue one's goals, and in particular one's most important goal, by fostering social connectedness, which raises self-esteem, which in turn leads to inspiration.

Creativity

It seems to be a cultural meme that nostalgia boosts creativity (both original and useful ideas; Feist, 1998), or at least literary creativity. Indeed, nostalgia has been duly implicated in explanations of creative works (Austin, 2003; Cook, 2009; Flinn, 1992). The link between nostalgia and creativity is plausible, given that nostalgia sparks approach orientation, evokes inspiration, and strengthens motivation to pursue one's important goal(s). We (Van Tilburg, Sedikides, & Wildschut, 2015) examined the nostalgia-creativity link in several experiments.

Nostalgia Boosts Creativity

We wondered whether nostalgia boosts self-reported creativity (Van Tilburg et al., 2015, Experiment 3). After manipulating nostalgia with the ERT, we instructed participants to fill out a 12-item creativity scale (Ivcevic, 2007). Sample items are: "My strategy towards challenging tasks is to . . ." (1 = *creative and novel solutions*, 6 = *traditional and familiar solutions*), "When solving challenging tasks I tend to propose strategies that are . . ." (1 = *innovative and risky*, 6 = *cautious and dependable*, reversed). Nostalgia boosted self-reported creativity.

But does nostalgia also boost actual creativity? We (Van Tilburg et al., 2015, Experiment 1) manipulated nostalgia with the ERT and asked participants to write a story about a princess, a cat, and a race car in 30 minutes (Proulx, 2012; Proulx & Inzlicht, 2012). We proceeded with content coding (Thrash, Maruskin, Cassidy, Fryer, & Ryan, 2010). Specifically, we asked two independent judges, familiar with the concept of creativity, to code the stories ("How creative do you consider the story to be?"). Judges' ratings were highly correlated, and we thus formed and analyzed a composite. Nostalgia boosted actual creativity.

We (Van Tilburg et al., 2015, Experiment 2) tested the replicability of this effect with an alternate procedure. After manipulating nostalgia with the ERT, we instructed participants to write a story (in 30 minutes) that began with the sentence: "One cold winter evening, a man and a woman were alarmed by a sound coming from a nearby house" (Thrash et al., 2010). Content coding followed, which, again, produced highly consistent codings between the judges. As in the prior experiment, nostalgia boosted actual creativity.

Finally, we (Van Tilburg et al., 2015, Experiment 4) tested the replicability of this effect with a different nostalgia manipulation and a different creativity task. The manipulation was a revised ERT using a positive (i.e., lucky) event condition in lieu of an ordinary event one. The task was a linguistic creativity measure (Zhu et al., 2009) in which we instructed participants to "try to write a creative sentence about each keyword," followed by ten common words (beautiful, eating, fun, money, pain, sea, sun, tasty, warm, water; www.kuleuven.be/semlab/; De Deyne & Storms, 2008). Evaluative coding followed, producing high inter-judge agreement. In replication, nostalgia boosted creativity.

Nostalgia Boosts Creativity Though Openness to Experience

How does nostalgia boost creativity? A likely mechanism is increased openness to experience (henceforth: openness), which reflects "an interest in varied experience for its own sake" (McCrea, 1987, p. 1259). Nostalgia is likely to influence openness, as it promotes states associated with openness such as inspiration (Thrash & Elliot, 2003) and approach orientation (Niholson, Soane, Fenton-O'Creevy, & Willman, 2005). Also, openness is likely to be related to creativity, as a meta-analysis (Feist, 1998) indicated.

After manipulating nostalgia with the ERT, we (Van Tilburg et al., 2015, Experiment 3) assessed openness with the 10-item Openness to Experience subscale of the 44-item Big Five Inventory (Benet-Martínez & John, 1998). Sample items are: "I see myself as someone who is curious about many different things," "I see myself as someone who has an active imagination," "I see myself as someone who is inventive." Subsequently, we asked participants to complete a 12-item self-reported creativity scale (Ivcevic, 2007). Openness mediated the effect of nostalgia on self-reported creativity. We replicated this pattern with actual creativity. After manipulating nostalgia with a revised ERT (i.e., featuring a positive ordinary event as control), we (Van Tilburg et al., 2015, Experiment 4), assessed openness with the 10-item Openness to Experience subscale (Benet-Martínez & John, 1998) and assessed creativity with the linguistic creativity measure (Zhu et al., 2009). Nostalgia's effect on actual creativity was mediated by openness.

Overt Behavior

Finally, nostalgia potentiates the future and directly influences well-being by also guiding overt behavior. This behavior takes the form of prosociality and engagement in physical activity.

Prosociality

One index of prosociality is *physical proximity*. An example of this index is how close a person sets her or his chair to that of a prospective interaction partner (i.e., reduced seating distance; Macrae, Bodenhausen, Milne, & Jetten, 1994). We (Stephan et al., 2014, Study 4) manipulated nostalgia with the ERT, and then informed participants of an impending social interaction (i.e., conversation) they would have with an unacquainted participant who was waiting in a nearby cubicle. In preparation for this conversation, the experimenter first asked participants to position two chairs (one for them, one for the interaction partner) in the room, and then left the scene under a pretext. Participants in the nostalgia condition positioned the chairs closer to each other than participants in the control condition. Nostalgia induced physical proximity.

A more direct index of prosociality is *monetary donations to charity*. In our study (Zhou et al., 2012, Study 5), participants (all Chinese nationals) first completed various laboratory tasks for which they were paid 7 renminbi (in 1 renminbi notes). Subsequently, participants were randomly assigned to two conditions. They were presented with printed charity appeals for "Half the Sky Foundation." We used a nostalgic appeal in the experimental condition and a future-oriented appeal in the control condition. The two appeals looked the same (e.g., illustrated children's photographs or children engaged in leisure activities), but differed in an important way. The experimental-condition appeal consisted of nostalgic cues, such as the headline "Those Were the Days: Restoring the Past for Children in Wenchuan." The control-condition appeal, on the other hand, consisted of cues to the future, such as the headline "Now Is the Time: Build the Future for Children in Wenchuan." We proceeded to discreetly alert participants to a collection box near the laboratory exit and casually mention that they could privately donate as much or as little money as they wished. Participants in the experimental condition donated more money than control participants. (We returned this money to participants and donated the pooled sum to charity.)

An even more direct index of prosociality is *helping*. Having manipulated nostalgia with the ERT, we (Stephan et al., 2014, Study 5) staged a mishap. An experimenter (unaware of conditions) walked into the room holding a folder of papers and a box of pencils, made an awkward move, and spilled the pencils on the floor. We counted the number of pencils that participants picked up, a validated measure of helping (Vohs, Mead, & Goode, 2008). Nostalgic participants helped more than controls.

Physical Activity

Kersten, Cox, and Van Enkevort (2016, Study 3) manipulated nostalgia with the ERT three times over the course of two weeks. At the end of this two-week period, the researchers assessed health optimism with Aspinwall and Brunhart's (1996) 16-item measure. Importantly, the researchers also assessed behavior, namely, physical activity operationalized as steps taken (counted by a wireless fitness tracker, *Fitbit One*). Step count is a valid measure of physical activity (Takacs et al., 2014). Nostalgic participants exhibited more intense physical activity (i.e., took more steps) than controls. This effect was mediated by health optimism.

Coda

Nostalgia has been regarded an ossifying, escapist emotion for too long. Yet these adjectives only served to caricature the emotion. Nostalgia may refer to the past, but it points to the future, as it has implications for the "good life" (Baumeister, this volume; Sheldon, this volume). Nostalgia allows one to visit the past, but not remain in it. We have shown here that this visit bestows vigor and insight for forging ahead. Through a variety of mechanisms, nostalgia shapes the future, as it sparks approach orientation, increases optimism, and evokes inspiration. And through a variety of mechanisms, nostalgia potentiates the future, as it strengthens motivation for goal pursuit, boosts creativity, and guides behavior. Ultimately, nostalgia is an emotion that plays an important and adaptive role in triggering positive life strategies and so promoting well-being.

Bibliography

Abeyta, A. A., & Routledge, C. (2016). Fountain of youth: The impact of nostalgia on youthfulness and implications for health. *Self and Identity, 15*, 356–369. doi:10.1080/1 5298868.2015.1133452

Abeyta, A. A., Routledge, C., & Juhl, J. (2015). Looking back to move forward: Nostalgia as a psychological resource for promoting relationship goals and overcoming relationship challenges. *Journal of Personality and Social Psychology, 109*, 1029–1044. doi:10.1037/ pspi0000036

Abeyta, A., Routledge, C., Roylance, C., Wildschut, R. T., & Sedikides, C. (2015). Attachment-related avoidance and the social and agentic content of nostalgic memories. *Journal of Social and Personal Relationships, 32*, 406–413. doi:10.1177/026540751453377

Aspinwall, L. G., & Brunhart, S. M. (1996). Distinguishing optimism from denial: Optimistic beliefs predict attention to health threats. *Personality and Social Psychology Bulletin, 22,* 993–1003. doi:10.1177/01461672962210002

Austin, L. M. (2003). Children of childhood: Nostalgia and the romantic legacy. *Studies in Romanticism, 42,* 75–98.

Baldwin, M., Biernat, M., & Landau, M. J. (2015). Remembering the real me: Nostalgia offers a window to the intrinsic self. *Journal of Personality and Social Psychology, 108,* 128–147. doi:10.1037/a0038033

Baldwin, M., & Landau, M. J. (2014). Exploring nostalgia's influence on psychological growth. *Self and Identity, 13,* 162–177. doi:10.1080/15298868.2013.772320

Barrett, F. S., Grimm, K. J., Robins, R. W., Wildschut, T., Sedikides, C., & Janata, P. (2010). Music-evoked nostalgia: Affect, memory, and personality. *Emotion, 10,* 390–403. doi:10.1037/a0019006

Batcho, K. I. (1995). Nostalgia: A psychological perspective. *Perceptual and Motor Skills, 80,* 131–143. doi:10.2466/pms.1995.80.1.131

Batcho, K. I. (2013). Nostalgia: The bittersweet history of a psychological concept. *History of Psychology, 16,* 165–176. doi:10.1037/a0032427

Benet-Martínez, V., & John, O. P. (1998). Los Cinco Grandes across cultures and ethnic groups: Multitrait-multimethod analyses of the Big Five in Spanish and English. *Journal of Personality and Social Psychology, 75,* 729–750. doi:10.1037/0022-3514.75.3.729

Best, J., & Nelson, E. E. (1985). Nostalgia and discontinuity: A test of the Davis hypothesis. *Sociology and Social Research, 69,* 221–233.

Carver, C. S. (2006). Approach, avoidance, and the self-regulation of affect and action. *Motivation and Emotion, 30,* 105–110. doi:10.1007/s11031-006-9044-7

Carver, C. S., & White, T. L. (1994). Behavioral inhibition, behavioral activation and affective responses to impending reward and punishment: The BIS/BAS scales. *Journal of Personality and Social Psychology, 67,* 319–333. doi:10.1037/0022-3514.67.2.319

Castelnuovo-Tedesco, P. (1980). Reminiscence and nostalgia: The pleasure and pain of remembering. In S. I. Greenspan & G. H. Pollack (Eds.), *The course of life: Psychoanalytic contributions toward understanding personality development* (Vol. III: Adulthood and the aging process, pp. 104–118). Washington, DC: U.S: Government Printing Office.

Chaplin, S. (2000). *The psychology of time and death.* Ashland, OH: Sonnet Press.

Chemers, M. M., Watson, C. B., & May, S. T. (2000). Dispositional affect and leadership effectiveness: A comparison of self-esteem, optimism, and efficacy. *Personality and Social Psychology Bulletin, 26,* 267–277. doi:10.1177/0146167200265001

Cheung, W. Y., Sedikides, C., & Wildschut, T. (2016). Induced nostalgia increases optimism (via social connectedness and self-esteem) among individuals high, but not low, in trait nostalgia. *Personality and Individual Differences, 90,* 283–288. doi:10.1016/j.paid.20215.11.028

Cheung, W. Y., Wildschut, T., Sedikides, C., Hepper, E. G., Arndt, J., & Vingerhoets, A. J. J. M. (2013). Back to the future: Nostalgia increases optimism. *Personality and Social Psychology Bulletin, 39,* 1484–1496. doi:10.1177/0146167213499187

Cook, P. C., Jr. (2009). Here we go again (again): The Eighties nostalgia movement in contemporary popular culture. *ProQuest Dissertations and Theses.*

Crocker, J., & Wolfe, C. T. (2001). Contingencies of self-worth. *Psychological Review, 108,* 593–623. doi:10.1037//0033-295X.108.3.593

Davis, F. (1977). Nostalgia, identity, and the current nostalgia wave. *Journal of Popular Culture, 11,* 414–425. doi:10.1111/j.0022-3840.1977.00414.x

Davis, F. (1979). *Yearning for yesterday: A sociology of nostalgia*. New York, NY: The Free Press.

De Deyne, S., & Storms, G. (2008). Word associations: Network and semantic properties. *Behavior Research Methods*, *40*, 213–231. doi:10.3758/BRM.40.1213

Feist, G. J. (1998). A meta-analysis of personality in scientific and artistic creativity. *Personality and Social Psychology Review*, *2*, 290–309. doi:10.1207/s15327957pspr0204_5

Flinn, C. (1992). *Strains of utopia: Gender, nostalgia, and Hollywood film music*. Princeton, NJ: Princeton University Press.

Fodor, N. (1950). Varieties of nostalgia. *Psychoanalytic Review*, *37*, 25–38.

Green, J. D., & Campbell, W. K. (2000). Attachment and exploration in adults: Chronic and contextual accessibility. *Personality and Social Psychology Bulletin*, *26*, 452–461. doi:10.1177/0146167200266004

Hays, R. D., Sherbourne, C. D., & Mazel, R. M. (1993). The RAND 36-item survey 1.0. *Health Economics*, *3*, 217–227.

Hepper, E. G., Ritchie, T. D., Sedikides, C., & Wildschut, T. (2012). Odyssey's end: Lay conceptions of nostalgia reflect its original Homeric meaning. *Emotion*, *12*, 102–119. doi:10.1037/a0025167

Hepper, E. G., Wildschut, T., Sedikides, C., Ritchie, T. D., Yung, Y.-F., Hansen, N., . . . Zhou, X. (2014). Pancultural nostalgia: Prototypical conceptions across cultures. *Emotion*, *14*, 733–747. doi:10.1037/a0036790

Hertz, D. G. (1990). Trauma and nostalgia: New aspects of the coping of aging holocaust survivors. *Israeli Journal of Psychiatry and Related Sciences*, *27*, 189–198.

Holak, S. L., & Havlena, W. J. (1998). Feelings, fantasies, and memories: An examination of the emotional components of nostalgia. *Journal of Business Research*, *42*, 217–226. doi:10.1016/S0148-2963(97)00119-7

Holbrook, M. B. (1994). Nostalgia proneness and consumer tastes. In J. A. Howard (Ed.), *Buyer behavior in marketing strategy* (2nd ed., pp. 348–364). Englewood Cliffs, NJ: Prentice-Hall.

Ivcevic, Z. (2007). Artistic and everyday creativity: An act-frequency approach. *Journal of Creative Behavior*, *41*, 271–290. doi:10.1002/j.2162–6057.2007.tb01074.x

Kersten, M., Cox, C. R., & Van Enkevort, E. A. (2016). An exercise in nostalgia: Nostalgia promotes health optimism and physical activity. *Psychology and Health*, *10*, 1166–1181. doi:10.1080/08870446.2016.11855

Lambert, N. M., Stillman, T. F., Baumeister, R. F., Fincham, F. D., Hicks, J. A., & Graham, S. M. (2010). Family as a salient source of meaning in young adulthood. *Journal of Positive Psychology*, *5*, 367–376. doi:10.1080/17439760.2010.516616

Leary, M. R., & Baumeister, R. F. (2000). The nature and function of self-esteem: Sociometer theory. *Advances in Experimental Social Psychology*, *32*, 1–62.

Macrae, C. N., Bodenhausen, G. V., Milne, A. B., & Jetten, J. (1994). Out of mind but back in sight: Stereotypes on the rebound. *Journal of Personality and Social Psychology*, *67*, 808–817. doi:10.1037/0022–3514.67.5.808

Mäkikangas, A., Kinnunen, U., & Feldt, T. (2004). Self-esteem, dispositional optimism, and health: Evidence from cross-lagged data on employees. *Journal of Research in Personality*, *38*, 556–575. doi:10.1016/j.jrp.2004.02.001

McAdams, D. P., Reynolds, J., Lewis, M., Patten, A. H., & Bowman, P. J. (2001). When bad things turn good and good things turn bad: Sequences of redemption and contamination in life narratives and their relation to psychosocial adaptation in midlife adults and in students. *Personality and Social Psychology Bulletin*, *27*, 474–485. doi:10.1177/0146167201274008

McCrea, R. R. (1987). Creativity, divergent thinking, and openness to experience. *Journal of Personality and Social Psychology*, *52*, 1258–1265. doi:10.1037/0022–3514.52.6.1258

Milyavskaya, M., Ianakieva, I., Foxen-Craft, E., Colantuoni, A., & Koestner, R. (2012). Inspired to get there: The effects of trait and goal inspiration on goal progress. *Personality and Individual Differences*, *52*, 56–60. doi:10.1016/j.paid.2011.08.031

Nawas, M. M., & Platt, J. J. (1965). A future-oriented theory of nostalgia. *Journal of Individual Psychology*, *21*, 51–57.

Niholson, N., Soane, E., Fenton-O'Creevy, M., & Willman, P. (2005). Personality and domain-specific risk taking. *Journal of Risk Research*, *8*, 157–176. doi:10.1080/136698 7032000123856

Pearsall, J. (1998). *The new Oxford dictionary of English*. Oxford, UK: Oxford University Press.

Peetz, J., & Wilson, A. E. (2008). The temporally extended self: The relation of past and future selves to current identity, motivation, and goal pursuit. *Social and Personality Psychology Compass*, *2*, 2090–2106. doi:10.1111/j.1751–9004.2008.00150.x

Pennebaker, J. W., Booth, R. J., & Francis, M. E. (2007). *Linguistic inquiry and word count: LIWC2007: Operator's manual*. Austin, TX: LIWC.net

Pennebaker, J. W., & Graybeal, A. (2001). Patterns of natural language use: Disclosure, personality, and social integration. *Current Directions in Psychological Science*, *10*, 90–93. doi:10.1111/1467-8721.00123

Proulx, T. (2012, May). *New Directions in the Psychology of Meaning*. Invited Symposium. Association for Psychological Science, Chicago.

Proulx, T., & Inzlicht, M. (2012). The five 'A's of meaning maintenance: Making sense of the theories of sense-making. *Psychological Inquiry*, *23*, 317–335. doi:10.1080/10478 40X.2012.702372

Pyszczynski, T., Greenberg, J., Solomon, S., Arndt, J., & Schimel, J. (2004). Why do people need self-esteem? A theoretical and empirical review. *Psychological Bulletin*, *130*, 435–468. doi: 10.1037/0033–2909.130.3.435

Reid, C. A., Green, J. D., Wildschut, T., & Sedikides, C. (2015). Scent-evoked nostalgia. *Memory*, *23*, 157–166. doi:10.1080/09658211.2013.876048

Rosch, E. (1978). Principles of categorization. In E. Rosch & B. B. Lloyd (Eds.), *Cognition and categorization* (pp. 27–48). Hillsdale, NJ: Erlbaum.

Rosenberg, M. (1965). *Society and the adolescent self-image*. Princeton, NJ: Princeton University Press.

Routledge, C., Arndt, J., Sedikides, C., & Wildschut, T. (2008). A blast from the past: The terror management function of nostalgia. *Journal of Experimental Social Psychology*, *44*, 132–140. doi:10.1016/j.jesp.2006.11.001

Routledge C., Arndt, J., Wildschut, T., Sedikides, C., Hart, C., Juhl, J., . . . Scholtz, W. (2011). The past makes the present meaningful: Nostalgia as an existential resource. *Journal of Personality and Social Psychology*, *101*, 638–652. doi:10.1037/a0024292

Routledge, C., Wildschut, T., Sedikides, C., Juhl, J., & Arndt, J. (2012). The power of the past: Nostalgia as a meaning-making resource. *Memory*, *20*, 452–460. doi:10.1080/096 58211.2012.677452

Scheier, M. F., & Carver, C. S. (1985). Optimism, coping, and health: Assessment and implications of generalized outcome expectancies. *Health Psychology*, *4*, 219–247. doi:10.1037/0278–6133.4.3.219

Scheier, M. F., Carver, C. S., & Bridges, M. W. (1994). Distinguishing optimism from neuroticism (and trait anxiety, self-mastery, and self-esteem): A re-evaluation of the Life Orientation Test. *Journal of Personality and Social Psychology*, *67*, 1063–1078. doi:10.1037/0022–3514.67.6.1063

Sedikides, C., Cheung, W. Y., Wildschut, T., Hepper, E. G., Baldursson, E., & Pedersen, B. (2017). *Nostalgia motivates goal pursuit by increasing meaning in life*. Manuscript under review, University of Southampton.

Sedikides, C., Wildschut, T., & Baden, D. (2004). Nostalgia: Conceptual issues and existential functions. In J. Greenberg, S. Koole, & T. Pyszczynski (Eds.), *Handbook of experimental existential psychology* (pp. 200–214). New York, NY: Guilford Press.

Sedikides, C., Wildschut, T., Routledge, C., Arndt, J., Hepper, E. G., & Zhou, X. (2015). To nostalgize: Mixing memory with affect and desire. *Advances in Experimental Social Psychology*, *51*, 189–273. doi:10.1016/bs.aesp.2014.10.001

Stavrova, O., & Luhmann, M. (2016). Social connectedness as a source and consequence of meaning in life. *The Journal of Positive Psychology*, *11*, 470–479.

Steger, M. F., Kashdan, T. B., Sullivan, B. A., & Lorentz, D. (2008). Understanding the search for meaning in life: Personality, cognitive style, and the dynamic between seeking and experiencing meaning. *Journal of Personality*, *76*, 199–228. doi:10.1111/j.1467-6494.2007.00484.x

Stephan, E., Sedikides, C., & Wildschut, T. (2012). Mental travel into the past: Differentiating recollections of nostalgic, ordinary, and positive events. *European Journal of Social Psychology*, *42*, 290–298. doi:10.1002/ejsp.1865

Stephan, E., Sedikides, C., Wildschut, T., Cheung, W. Y., Routledge, C., & Arndt, J. (2015). Nostalgia-evoked inspiration: Mediating mechanisms and motivational implications. *Personality and Social Psychology Bulletin*, *41*, 1395–1410. doi:10.1177/0146167215596985

Stephan, E., Wildschut, T., Sedikides, C., Zhou, X., He, W., Routledge, C., . . . Vingerhoets, A. J. J. M. (2014). The mnemonic mover: Nostalgia regulates avoidance and approach motivation. *Emotion*, *14*, 545–561. doi:10.1037/a0035673

Takacs, J., Pollock, C. L., Guenther, J. R., Bahar, M., Napier, C., & Hunt, M. A. (2014). Validation of the fitbit one activity monitor device during treadmill walking. *Journal of Science and Medicine in Sport*, *17*, 496–500. doi:10.1016/j.jsams.2013.10.241

Thrash, T. M., & Elliot, A. J. (2003). Inspiration as a psychological construct. *Journal of Personality and Social Psychology*, *84*, 871–889. doi:10.1037/0022–3514.84.4.871

Thrash, T. M., & Elliot, A. J. (2004). Inspiration: Core characteristics, component processes, antecedents and function. *Journal of Personality and Social Psychology*, *87*, 957–937. doi:10.1037/0022–3514.87.6.957

Thrash, T. M., Maruskin, L. A., Cassidy, S. E., Fryer, J. W., & Ryan, R. M. (2010). Mediating between the muse and the masses: Inspiration and the actualization of creative ideas. *Journal of Personality and Social Psychology*, *98*, 469–487. doi:10.1037/a0017907

Van Tilburg, W. A. P., Sedikides, C., & Wildschut, T. (2015). The mnemonic muse: Nostalgia fosters creativity through openness to experience. *Journal of Experimental Social Psychology*, *59*, 1–7. doi:10.1016//j.jesp.2015.02.002

Vohs, K. D., Mead, N. L., & Goode, M. R. (2008). Merely activating the concept of money changes personal and interpersonal behavior. *Science*, *314*, 1154–1156. doi:10.1111/j.1467–8721.2008.00576.x

Warner, L. M., Schwarzer, R., Schüz, B., Wurm, S., & Tesch-Römer, C. (2012). Health-specific optimism mediates between objective and perceived physical functioning in older adults. *Journal of Behavioral Medicine*, *35*, 400–406. doi:10.1007/s10865–011–9368-y

Wildschut, T., Sedikides, C., Arndt, J., & Routledge, C. (2006). Nostalgia: Content, triggers, functions. *Journal of Personality and Social Psychology*, *91*, 975–993. doi:10.1037/0022–3514.91.5.975

Wildschut, T., Sedikides, C., Routledge, C., Arndt, J., & Cordaro, F. (2010). Nostalgia as a repository of social connectedness: The role of attachment-related avoidance. *Journal of Personality and Social Psychology*, *98*, 573–586. doi:10.1037/a0017597

Wilson, A., & Ross, M. (2003). The identity function of autobiographical memory: Time is on our side. *Memory*, *11*, 137–149. doi: 10.1080/741938210

Zhou, X., Sedikides, C., Wildschut, C., & Gao, D.-G. (2008). Counteracting loneliness: On the restorative function of nostalgia. *Psychological Science*, *19*, 1023–1029. doi:10.1111/j.1467–9280.2008.02194.x

Zhou, X., Wildschut, T., Sedikides, C., Shi, K., & Feng, C. (2012). Nostalgia: The gift that keeps on giving. *Journal of Consumer Research*, *39*, 39–50. doi:10.1086/662199

Zhu, X., Xu, Z., & Khot, T. (2009). How creative is your writing? A linguistic creativity measure from computer science and cognitive psychology perspectives. In *Proceedings of the Workshop on Computational Approaches to Linguistic Creativity* (pp. 87–93). Association for Computational Linguistics.

12

NEGATIVE AFFECT AND THE GOOD LIFE

On the Cognitive, Motivational and Interpersonal Benefits of Negative Mood

Joseph P. Forgas

Introduction

How to live well? Fluctuating mood states are obviously a critically important aspect of living a good life. We also know that human beings are an amazingly moody species. Our daily lives are accompanied by an ever-shifting spectrum of affective reactions, and such fluctuating affective states subtly colour and filter everything we think and do during our waking hours. We still don't know enough about the role of affective states in guiding our reactions to the manifold challenges of everyday life. In particular, the possible adaptive benefits of temporary experiences of mild negative mood states are poorly understood. Yet in terms of evolutionary theories, we would do well to assume that all affective reactions serve important adaptive functions, operating in essence like preordained functional 'mind modules' that spontaneously spring into action in response to various environmental contingencies (Forgas, Haselton & von Hippel, 2007; Frijda, 1986; Tooby & Cosmides, 1992; see also Fiedler & Arslan, and von Hippel & Gonsalkorale, this volume).

This chapter will advocate a somewhat unusual answer to the question of how to live well. Rather than seeking unrelenting happiness, the 'good life' is more readily attainable if we accept, and learn to handle and benefit from, occasional negative affective states. In support of this position, the chapter will describe extensive empirical evidence documenting the often surprising cognitive and behavioural benefits of mild negative moods.

On Positive and Negative Affect

Advocating the acceptance rather than the elimination of negative affect might at first sight appear counterintuitive. Negative affective states are by necessity unpleasant, and not enjoyable (but see Sedikides, Wildschut & Stephan, this volume, on nostalgia for an exception). And yet, human beings evolved a very wide range of negative affective reactions to various environmental challenges, and so it is plausible to assume that even aversive affective states serve some beneficial adaptive purpose, as functional algorithms promoting appropriate responses. In the case of some of the intense, distinct emotions such as anger, fear or disgust, we do know what their adaptive purpose is—to overcome obstacles, to avoid dangers and to reject harmful stimuli, respectively. Yet what can we make of the purpose of perhaps the most ubiquitous and problematic negative affect, sadness?

In contemporary Western culture, experiences of sadness are often considered unnecessary and dysfunctional. Most bookshops have shelves full of self-help books promoting the benefits of positive thinking, positive attitudes and positive behaviors. We tend to consign negative affect in general, and sadness in particular, to the category of undesirable 'problem emotions' that need to be controlled or eliminated if possible.

Much of clinical and counselling psychology is devoted to managing negative affectivity and alleviating sadness. Yet, it seems that some degree of sadness and melancholia has been far more accepted in previous historical epochs than is the case today (Sedikides, Wildschut, Arndt & Routledge, 2006; see also Sedikides, Wildschut & Stephan, this volume). From the classic philosophers through Shakespeare to the works of Chekhov, Ibsen and the great novels of the 19th century, exploring the landscape of sadness, longing and melancholia has long been considered instructive, and indeed ennobling. It is only in the last few decades that a veritable industry promoting the cult of positivity has managed to eliminate this earlier and more balanced view of the landscape of human affectivity. Even though sadness is probably the most common of all our negative affective states, it is also the one whose possible adaptive functions still remain puzzling and poorly understood (Ciarrochi, Forgas & Mayer, 2006).

Of course, in historical terms negative emotions have always been with us, and it may be instructive to consider how other cultures at other times handled negative affect. We find that many of the greatest achievements of the human mind and spirit were actually borne out of sadness, dysphoria and even enduring depression. Many of the classic works of Western culture and civilization in particular also deal with the evocation, rehearsal and even cultivation of negative feelings and emotions. Greek tragedies famously had as their cultural objective to expose, and train their audiences in accepting and dealing with, inevitable misfortune. There are more Greek tragedies than there are comedies, and Shakespeare's greatest works are also tragedies rather than comedies. It seems that hilarity generally comes a distant second to seriousness and themes of adversity and sadness in most great literature and art. One of the possible benefits of negative affect may have to do with its interpersonal functions. Evolutionary psychologists, puzzled by the ubiquity of dysphoria, have speculated that negative affect may provide hidden social benefits by possibly arousing interpersonal sympathy and reducing the likelihood of interpersonal challenges and competition (Forgas, Haselton & von Hippel, 2007; Tooby & Cosmides, 1992).

Philosophical Antecedents

It seems then that dealing with negative affect and what it tells us about the human condition has long been the focus of many artists and writers. Yet a far more obvious and less subtle interest has been the explicit search for happiness; the philosophy of hedonism has also been an enduring theme in human affairs.

Hedonism, the seeking of pleasure and avoidance of pain, is one of the most influential simple and sovereign principles in all of psychology; the reinforcement principle is just one reincarnation of this ancient idea (Allport, 1985). Siduri in the *Epic of Gilgamesh*, perhaps the first literary work ever, argued that seeking happiness is the universal task of humans. Democritus and the Cyrenaic school developed a hedonistic philosophy suggesting seeking the good life involves exercising wise judgment to obtain such pleasures through love, friendship, altruism and justice. Perhaps the most influential exponent of hedonism was Epicurus (*c.* 341–*c.* 270 BC), who thought that living well involves using knowledge and judgment to seek modest, sustainable "pleasure" and tranquility and freedom from anxiety (see also Fiedler & Arslan, this volume). His advice about how to live well is still part of modern psychology, as several chapters here illustrate.

Hedonism reappears in 18th-century philosophy as utilitarianism, an ethical system that argues that the value of all actions can be determined by assessing their consequences in terms of contributing to human happiness or decreasing suffering. Although measuring hedonistic outcomes is far from simple, as Jeremy Bentham (1838/1962) recognized, there are contemporary ideas to adopt similar principles to inform social policy.

Hedonism in our very own age is rather different in that rather than focusing on stable, rational and achievable long-term happiness, we often emphasize the importance of easy, simple and readily obtainable pleasure. Obviously the requirements of advertising and marketing promoting instantly available material consumption—offering the illusion of purchasable happiness—have a great deal to do with this. This incessant individual and cultural pursuit of easy happiness, driven in no small measure by manipulative advertising and marketing messages, creates hedonistic expectations that are probably impossible to fulfil and possibly cause more grief than happiness (Diener & Seligman, 2004).

Whereas hedonism emphasizes contentment and happiness as a means of living well, a complementary philosophical approach, *Stoicism*, sets an alternative goal: to learn to anticipate and accept inevitable negative outcomes in our lives. The message of Stoicism, accepting inevitable negativity, is philosophically close to the main message of this chapter. Stoics such as Zeno emphasized the development of insight and self-control as a means of living well. By clear and unbiased thinking, humans can learn to recognize and accept the natural order of the world and so remain content even in the face of adversity. Stoicism also emphasizes the importance of internal control and rational thinking. It is a philosophy of acceptance, and remained popular throughout the ancient world for centuries. Its teachings are still part of contemporary thinking and bear strong resemblance to various Eastern philosophies emphasizing self-control and mindfulness that nowadays are also part of the message of positive psychology.

Affect, Cognition and Well-Being

Within our own discipline, social psychology, the study of affect remained relatively neglected until quite recently. Of the historical tripartite division of the human mind into cognition, affect and conation, affect was the last to be explored. This may be partly due to the ancient idea going back to Plato that affect represents a more primitive, dangerous and invasive force that is incompatible with rational thinking and behaviour. Another reason for the neglect of affect is the absence of suitable methods for reliably inducing and studying affective states. Freud's psychoanalytic speculations further entrenched the view of affect as a dangerous, primeval force that needs to be controlled. Fortunately, the last few decades saw a radical revision of this view. Steady advances in neuroscience confirmed that affect is often an essential component of responding adaptively to environmental challenges (Adolphs & Damasio, 2001; Forgas, 1995, 2002; Frijda, 1986).

The evidence to be considered here will show that negative affect in general and sadness in particular also have important adaptive consequences by spontaneously triggering cognitive, motivational and behavioural strategies that are well suited to dealing with the requirements of demanding social situations (Frijda, 1986). Of course, positive affect also has many adaptive and beneficial consequences, such as promoting flexibility, creativity, confidence, cooperation, and life satisfaction (Forgas, 1994, 1998a,b, 2002; Forgas & George, 2001; Fredrickson, this volume). However, many empirical studies now also demonstrate that moods such as sadness may often recruit a more attentive, accommodating thinking style that produces superior outcomes when detailed, externally oriented, inductive thinking is required (Bless & Fiedler, 2006; Forgas & Eich, 2012; see also Kalkstein, Hubbard & Trope, this volume). This prediction is broadly consistent with evolutionary, functionalist theories of affect that argue that affective states "exist for the sake of signalling states of the world that have to be responded to" (Frijda, 1988, p. 354; see also von Hippel & Gonsalkorale, this volume).

In this research program we focused on mild temporary moods effects rather than on distinct emotions, as moods are more common, context-free and enduring and also produce more robust and reliable cognitive and behavioural effects than do context-specific emotions (Forgas, 2002, 2006). Moods may be defined as low-intensity, diffuse and relatively enduring affective states without a salient antecedent cause and therefore little conscious cognitive content. In contrast, emotions are more intense, short-lived and usually have a definite cause and conscious cognitive content (Forgas, 1995, 2002). We will begin with a brief review of theoretical approaches linking affect and cognition before turning to a review of a number of experiments demonstrating the beneficial effects of negative affective states for cognition and behaviour. The role of different information processing strategies in mediating these effects will receive special attention.

Theoretical Frameworks

Contemporary theories show that affect can influence cognition and ultimately social behaviours such as interpersonal communication or fairness towards others (see our experiments described later) through two kinds of mechanisms: (1) *informational effects* (such as affect congruence) occur when affect colours the valence of information, and (2) *processing effects* occur when affect influences the way information is processed.

Informational Effects

The informational influence of affect on the valence of cognition may be due to *affect priming* or *affect-as-information* mechanisms. According to the *affect-priming account* (Bower, 1981), affect is linked to an associative network of memory associations and may selectively prime affect-congruent contents and ideas. For example, a positive mood improves the selective recall of mood-congruent details from the past (Bower, 1981). Greater access to mood-congruent constructs can also influence the valence of constructive social judgments and impressions (Forgas, Bower & Krantz, 1984; Forgas & Bower, 1987). However, as predicted by the affect Infusion Model (Forgas, 1995, 2002) and confirmed by numerous studies, affect priming is most likely to occur when a task requires open, constructive processing (e.g. Bower & Forgas, 2001; Forgas, 2002; Forgas & Eich, 2012).

A complementary *affect-as-information* (AAI) model was outlined by Schwarz and Clore (1988; Clore, Schwarz & Conway, 1994), suggesting that "rather than computing a judgment on the basis of recalled features of a target, individuals may ... ask themselves: 'how do I feel about it?' [and] in doing so, they may mistake feelings due to a pre-existing state as a reaction to the target" (Schwarz, 1990, p. 529). In those terms, affect congruence is caused by an inferential error, when people misattribute a pre-existing affective state as relevant to an unrelated social stimulus. This prediction mirrors earlier conditioning theories (Clore & Byrne, 1974). Such affective misattribution is most likely when "the task is of little personal relevance, when little other information is available, when problems are too complex to be solved systematically, and when time or attentional resources are limited" (Fiedler, 2001, p. 175), as is the case, for example, when people are asked to perform personally uninvolving off-the-cuff judgments (Forgas & Bower, 1987; Schwarz & Clore, 1988).

Processing Effects

Affect may also influence *information processing styles*, that is, *how* people think (Clark & Isen, 1982; Fiedler & Forgas, 1988; Forgas, 2002). Positive mood was first thought to lead to less effortful processing (Clark & Isen, 1982; Sinclair & Mark, 1992), while negative mood was assumed to promote more effortful and vigilant processing (Schwarz, 1990; Schwarz & Bless, 1991), consistent with affective states functioning as evolutionary signals indicating the degree of effort and vigilance required in a given situation, or perhaps because in a good mood people avoid cognitive effort (mood maintenance; Clark & Isen, 1982).

An integrative explanation for processing effects was offered by Bless and Fiedler (2006), who argue that different moods have an evolutionary function recruiting qualitatively different processing *styles*. Following Piaget, they suggest that negative moods call for *accommodative, bottom-up* processing, focused on the details of the external world. In contrast, positive moods recruit *assimilative, top-down* processing and greater reliance on existing schematic knowledge and heuristics (Bless, 2000; Bless & Fiedler, 2006; Fiedler, 2001). This affectively induced assimilative/accommodative processing dichotomy received extensive support in recent years.

Several studies suggest (e.g. Fiedler at al., 1991) that people experiencing a positive mood are more likely to engage in constructive processing and are more influenced by prior priming manipulations when forming judgments, while negative mood reduced this tendency. Further, negative affect can reduce top-down judgmental mistakes such as the fundamental attribution error (Forgas, 1998a), reduce halo effects and primacy effects in impression formation (Forgas, 2011a,b), improve the quality and efficacy of persuasive arguments (Forgas, 2007), and also improve eyewitness memory (Fiedler et al., 1991; Forgas et al., 2005), as the following review will show. Thus, *both* positive and negative moods can produce processing advantages in response to different situations.

Cognitive Benefits of Dysphoria on Memory and Judgments

In this section we will briefly review evidence suggesting that more accommodative processing triggered by negative affect can produce a variety of cognitive benefits, improving memory and reducing various judgmental errors (Forgas & Eich, 2012). For example, remembering causally encountered everyday scenes can be of crucial importance in everyday life, as well as in forensic and legal practice

(Loftus, 1979; Neisser, 1982). In one field study we used a small suburban shop (Forgas, Goldenberg & Unkelbach, 2009) to investigate how well happy and sad people will remember various incidental details about objects we placed near the checkout counter. We used a natural mood induction, carrying out the experiment on rainy, unpleasant (negative affect) or sunny, warm (pleasant affect) days (Schwarz & Clore, 1988). These mood effects were further reinforced by playing sad and depressing or cheerful and upbeat background music in the store. We unobtrusively observed whether customers spent enough time in front of the checkout counter, and after they left the shop, a research assistant asked them to first recall, and then recognize, the objects they saw (Forgas et al., 2009). As predicted, negative mood (on rainy days) produced significantly better memory compared to positive mood (Figure 12.1).

Can negative mood also protect against the common tendency for people to incorporate later, incorrect details into their *eyewitness memories* (Fiedler et al., 1991; Loftus, 1979; Wells & Loftus, 2003)? Although Fiedler, Asbeck and Nickel (1991) suggested over 20 years ago that we need to examine "the mediating role of mood in eyewitness testimony" (p. 376), this was not done before. In a series of experiments, we exposed participants to complex scenes (photos of a traffic accident, observing an altercation in a lecture; Forgas, Vargas & Laham, 2005).

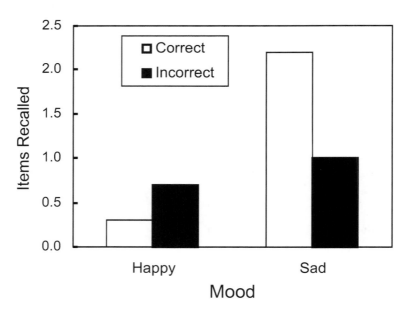

FIGURE 12.1 The Effects of Good or Bad Mood, Induced by the Weather, on Correct and Incorrect Recall of Items Casually Seen in a Shop

Source: After Forgas et al., 2009

Some time later, they were induced into happy or sad moods before receiving questions about the scenes that either did or did not contain misleading, false information (e.g. "Did you see the woman in the brown coat force her way into the lecture?"—the woman wore a black coat). After a further interval of up to one week, eyewitness memory for the original target events was tested. In all experiments, negative mood reduced, and positive mood increased, the tendency to incorporate misleading information into eyewitness memories (Figure 12.2).

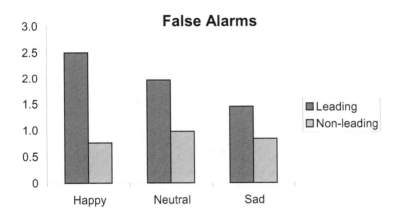

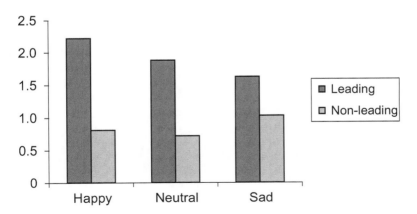

FIGURE 12.2   Mood Effects on the Tendency to Incorporate Misleading Information Into Eyewitness Memory: Negative Mood Reduced, and Positive Mood Increased, Eyewitness Distortions Due to Misleading Information (False Alarms)

Source: After Forgas, Vargas & Laham, 2005, Experiment 2

A signal detection analysis confirmed that negative mood indeed improved the ability to accurately discriminate between correct and false details. These results suggest the counterintuitive effect that negative mood can improve memory performance and protect against subsequent eyewitness distortions, consistent with a more assimilative/accommodative processing style it promotes (Bless, 2001; Fiedler & Bless, 2001; Forgas, 1995, 2002).

If negative mood recruits more attentive processing, this could help to eliminate top-down biases such as *halo effects and primacy effects* and improve the accuracy of impression formation judgments in general (Forgas & Laham, 2017). In one study we asked happy or sad participants to form impressions about the writer of a brief philosophical essay—who was shown in an attached photo as either a young, unorthodox-looking female or a middle-aged, bespectacled male (Forgas, 2011b). It turned out that those in a negative mood were indeed significantly less influenced by the appearance of the writer (a halo effect) than were judges in a positive mood (Figure 12.3). Another top-down judgmental bias occurs when judges pay disproportionate attention to early information, and neglect later details (a primacy effect; Asch, 1946; Luchins, 1958). We predicted that primacy effects should also be reduced by negative mood that recruits more attentive, accommodative thinking style (Forgas, 2011a,b). In this study, participants received a mood induction before forming impressions about a target character, Jim, based on two descriptive paragraphs (Luchins, 1958), describing him first as an extravert, and then as an introvert, or in the reverse order. We found a significant overall primacy effect—but negative mood completely eliminated this

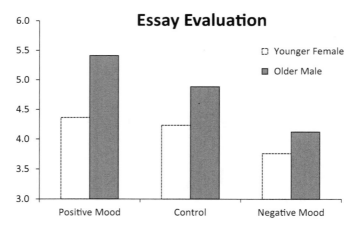

FIGURE 12.3 Mood Moderates the Incidence of Halo Effects on the Evaluation of an Essay: Positive Mood Increased, and Negative Mood Eliminated, the Halo Effect Associated With the Appearance of the Writer

Source: After Forgas, 2011b

common judgmental bias. Conversely, primacy effects were consistently greater in a positive mood (Figure 12.4). In a more recent experiment, we found negative mood can also reduce the influence of perceptual salience and cognitive fluency on impression formation (Forgas, 2015). Consistent with prior evidence, we found that persons presented with high visibility (large, colour photographs) were judged as more influential than the same person when shown in a small, black-and-white photo. However, this salience effect was eliminated when judges were induced into a negative affective state.

Another common judgmental error is the tendency to infer dispositions from observed behaviours—the *fundamental attribution error* (FAE). By promoting more accommodative processing, negative affect might also reduce the incidence of the FAE by directing more careful attention to external, situational information (Forgas, 1998a). For example, when happy or sad participants were asked to read and make attributions about the writer of an essay that was either assigned or was freely chosen (e.g. Jones & Harris, 1967), negative affect reduced the FAE of inferring internal causation about coerced essays. By analysing subsequent recall data, we also found more direct evidence for the expected mood-induced processing differences (Forgas, 1998a, Exp. 3). Judges in a negative mood had better memory for essay details, consistent with their more accommodative processing style. A mediational analysis confirmed that processing style was a significant mediator of mood effects on judgmental accuracy.

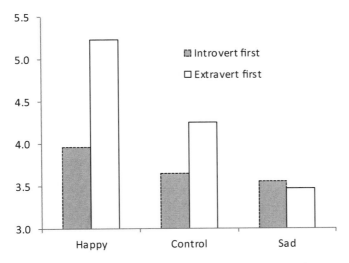

FIGURE 12.4   The Effects of Mood and Primacy on the Evaluation of a Target Person: Positive Mood Increases, and Negative Mood Reduces, the Primacy Effect on Evaluative Judgments (Vertical Axis)

Source: After Forgas, 2011

As negative affect seems to improve attention to stimulus details, it may also improve people's ability to *detect deception* (e.g. Lane & De Paulo, 1999). To explore this possibility, we asked happy or sad participants to detect deception in the videotaped statements of people accused of theft, who were either guilty or not guilty (Forgas & East, 2008b). Those in a negative mood were indeed significantly better able at correctly distinguish between truthful and deceptive statements from the videotapes (Forgas & East, 2008b).

By triggering more attentive and externally oriented processing, negative affect may well function as a general defence against *excessive gullibility*. Most information we receive is second-hand; rejecting valid information as false (excessive scepticism) is just as dangerous as accepting invalid information as true (excessive gullibility). In one experiment, happy or sad participants were asked to judge the likely truth of a number of urban legends and rumours such as 'power lines cause leukaemia' or 'the CIA murdered Kennedy' (Forgas & East, 2008a). Negative mood increased scepticism and reduced gullibility, but only for new and unfamiliar claims that judges had no pre-formed opinions about. In a follow-up experiment, the familiarity of ambiguous claims taken from trivia games was explicitly manipulated. Once again, negative mood increased scepticism about unfamiliar items, consistent with a more externally focused and accommodative thinking style. In a similar way, when we asked happy or sad participants to judge the genuineness of positive, neutral and negative facial expressions, those in a negative mood were significantly less likely to accept facial expressions as genuine

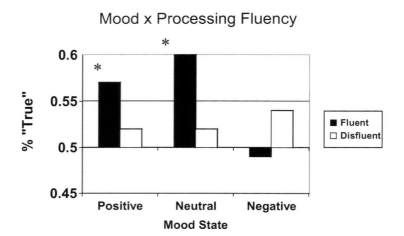

FIGURE 12.5 The Interactive Effects of Mood and Perceptual Fluency on Truth Judgments: Negative Mood Significantly Reduced the Tendency for People to Rely on Visual Fluency as a Truth Cue (differences marked by asterisks are statistically significant)

Source: After Koch & Forgas, 2012

than were people in the neutral or happy condition. Negative mood apparently reduced, and positive mood increased, people's tendency to accept facial displays as genuine, consistent with the more attentive and accommodative processing style associated with negative moods.

The previous studies suggest that the perceived *truth or falsehood* of ambiguous information may be influenced by various heuristics, such as the 'truth effect', when more cognitively fluent information is more likely to be judged as true than disfluent information. Thus, ease of processing, or *fluency*, is one of the implicit cues people seem to use in truth judgments. To evaluate this possibility, in one study we asked happy or sad participants to judge the truth of 30 ambiguous statements presented with high or low visual fluency (against a high- or low-contrast background). Judges in a neutral and positive mood rated fluent (high-contrast) claims as more true—however, negative affect eliminated this effect (see Figure 12.5). Thus, affect can moderate people's reliance on fluency cues in truth judgments, an important effect, as in real-life situations truth judgments (such as believing or disbelieving rumours, false news on the Internet, or even one's part-ner) often occur in affect-rich contexts.

Behavioural and Motivational Benefits of Mild Dysphoria

As we have seen, mild dysphoria seems to produce a range of subtle cognitive and judgmental benefits, consistent with a more attentive and externally focused information processing style. Can these effects extend to actual, behavioural con-sequences in interpersonal situations? We now turn to this issue.

For example, greater attention to external information in negative mood may also improve interpersonal effectiveness, such as *social influence strategies*. Although there has been long-standing interest in how people respond to persuasive mes-sages and the effects of moods on the quality and effectiveness of *producing* per-suasive messages attracted little attention (but see Bohner & Schwarz, 1993). In one series of studies, we asked participants who first received a mood induction to write persuasive messages on current topics such as increasing student fees (Forgas, 2007). The arguments were rated by trained raters for overall quality, persuasiveness, concreteness and valence (positive–negative). Those in a negative mood produced higher-quality and more persuasive arguments, and a mediational analysis confirmed that it was especially mood-induced variations in argument *concreteness* that influenced argument quality, with those in a negative mood pro-ducing more concrete arguments (see Figure 12.6; Bless, 2001; Bless & Fiedler, 2006; Fiedler, 2001; Forgas, 2002).

Further, we found that the arguments produced by sad participants were actu-ally more effective in changing attitudes when presented to a naive audience of undergraduate students whose attitudes on the target issues were previously assessed. Similar effects were also observed in a more realistic situation when happy and sad people were asked to persuade a 'partner' in an email exchange

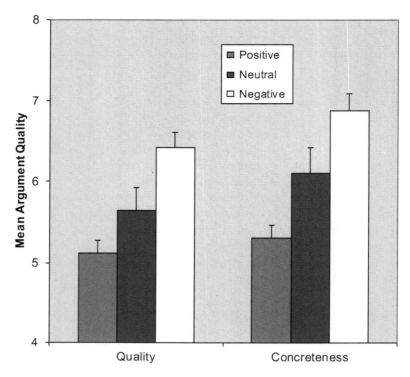

FIGURE 12.6 Mood Effects on the Quality and Concreteness of the Persuasive Messages Produced: Negative Affect Increases the Degree of Concreteness of the Arguments Produced, and Arguments Produced in Negative Mood Were Also Rated as More Persuasive

Source: After Forgas, 2007, Experiment 2

(Forgas, 2007; see also Amichai-Hamburger & Etgar, this volume). In other words, negative affect improved the quality and effectiveness of persuasive arguments by recruiting a more accommodative thinking style leading to more concrete and effective arguments. It appears then that mild negative affect (Forgas, 1998a,b; Forgas et al., 2005) can deliver marked benefits for the effectiveness of social influence strategies.

We obtained further recent evidence indicating the adaptive influence of negative affect on *language processing*. In three experiments (Koch, Forgas & Matovic, 2013), we predicted and found that participants in a negative mood communicated more effectively and complied significantly better with Grice's normative maxims in conversational situations than did participants in a positive mood when using natural language to describe previously observed social events (Figure 12.7). Negative mood actually improved the quality of language production, and this

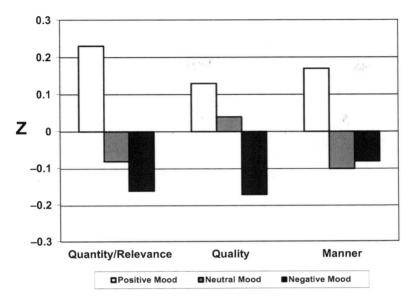

FIGURE 12.7   Mood Effects on Adherence to Grice's (1975) Conversational Maxims (Z-Scores): Negative Mood Produces Fewer Overall Violations of the Cooperative Principle in Spoken Language Compared With Positive Mood

Source: After Koch, Forgas & Matovic, 2013, Experiment 1

effect was not merely due to improvements in the encoding (Exp. 2) and retrieval (Exp. 3) of the relevant information.

These beneficial negative mood effects may apply not only to language *production*, but may also improve people's ability to *monitor and understand* language. In two experiments (Matovic, Koch & Forgas, 2014), we found that mild negative affect improved people's ability to correctly identify 'bad' sentences that are ambiguous and lack clear meaning (ambiguous anaphora; Figure 12.8). An analysis of response latencies (Studies 1 & 2) further confirmed that negative mood produced longer and more attentive processing, which mediated mood effects on language comprehension. These results are conceptually consistent with negative affect selectively promoting a more concrete and externally focused processing style.

In ambiguous and potentially uncertain interpersonal situations, negative affect could provide a further benefit by priming more cautious, careful and pessimistic interpretations, resulting in more polite, hesitant and considerate interpersonal strategies (Bower & Forgas, 2001; Forgas, 1995, 2002). One such situation is *requesting*, a complex communicative task that is characterized by uncertainty. Requests should be formulated with just the right degree of assertiveness versus politeness so as to maximize compliance without risking rejection. While positive

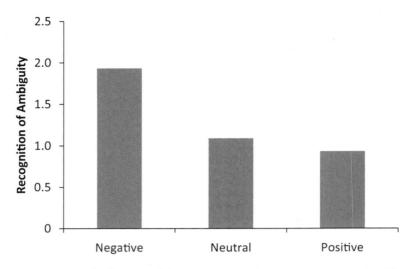

FIGURE 12.8   Mood Effects on Ability to Detect Ambiguous Communication: Negative Mood Promoted the More Accurate Recognition of Ambiguity in Communicative Sentences Compared to Positive Mood

Source: After Matovic, Koch, & Forgas, 2014

mood may prime a more optimistic and confident strategy and lead to more assertive and less polite requests, sad mood should promote more polite and considerate requests (Forgas, 1999a). We found support for this prediction; negative mood resulted in preference for more polite and cautious requests in both easy and difficult social situations (Forgas, 1999a, Exps. 1, 2). We found similar mood effects on requesting in a real-life interaction (Forgas, 1999b, Exp. 2), when happy and sad participants were asked to make a request for a file in a neighbouring office. Their words were surreptitiously recorded and analysed, showing that negative mood resulted in significantly more polite, elaborate and hedging request forms, whereas those in a positive mood used more direct and less polite strategies (Figure 12.9).

Why do these effects occur? In this instance, affect can selectively prime access to more affect-congruent interpretations of complex situations that will eventually influence behaviours. Of course, negative affect will not always result in more effective behaviours. We know, for example, that it is those in a positive mood who are often more confident and effective negotiators (Forgas, 1998a), respond more positively to requests directed at them (Forgas, 1998b), are better at managing interpersonal self-disclosure (Forgas, 2011c) and may be more effective in some organizational situations (Forgas & George, 2001; see also Fredrickson, this volume). The point is that in some situations where more caution, tact and consideration is required, it may be negative rather than positive affect that promotes more effective interpersonal behaviours.

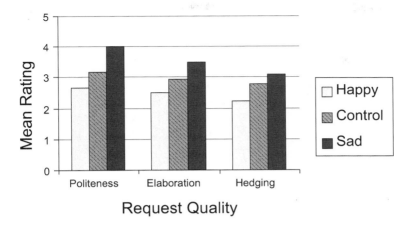

FIGURE 12.9   Mood Effects on Naturally Produced Requests: Positive Mood Decreases, and Negative Mood Increases, the Degree of Politeness, Elaboration and Hedging in Strategic Communications

Source: After Forgas, 1999b

Another interpersonal domain we studied where mood may make a difference to social behaviour is *selfishness versus fairness* to others. These experiments used strategic interactions such as the dictator game and the ultimatum game to explore mood effects. Economic games offer a reliable and valid method to study interpersonal strategies such as fairness, selfishness, trust and cooperation. In the *dictator game* an allocator has the power to allocate a scarce resource (e.g. money, etc.) between him or herself and another person in any way he or she sees fit. In the *ultimatum game*, the allocator faces a responder who has a veto power to accept or reject the offer. If rejected, neither side gets anything. Affective state may influence such decisions in at least two ways. As those in a negative mood tend to access more negative information, they might construct more careful, cautious, pessimistic and socially constrained responses. Secondly, affect can also influence *processing tendencies*, as negative affect may recruit more *accommodative*, externally focused processing, resulting in greater attention to external norms of fairness as against internal desires for selfishness. In several experiments we used the dictator game (Tan & Forgas, 2010) and asked happy or sad allocators to divide scarce resources (raffle tickets) between themselves and another person. Happy allocators were more selfish and kept more raffle tickets to themselves than did sad players. Similar patterns were observed in a series of sequential allocations to different partners, as those in a sad mood were again fairer and less selfish (Figure 12.10).

These surprising mood effects also endured in the more complex decisional environment faced by players in the *ultimatum game*, where the partner can accept or reject the offers (Forgas & Tan, 2013). As hypothesized, those in a negative

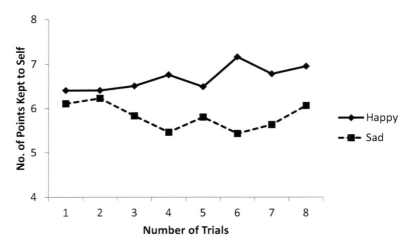

FIGURE 12.10 The Effects of Mood on Selfishness vs. Fairness: Happy Persons Kept More Rewards to Themselves, and This Effect Is More Pronounced in Later Trials

mood allocated significantly more resources to others than did happy individuals, confirming the predicted mood effects on selfishness/fairness. The latency of their decisions was also recorded, confirming that these mood effects could be directly linked to differences in processing style, as sad individuals took longer to make allocation decisions, consistent with a more accommodative and attentive processing. We also found that even *responders* were more concerned with fairness when in a negative mood, and they were more likely to *reject* unfair offers even if that meant not receiving anything (Forgas & Tan, 2013). Overall, 57% of those in negative mood rejected unfair offers compared to only 45% in the positive condition. These results challenge the common assumption in much of applied, organizational, clinical and health psychology that positive affect has universally desirable social and interpersonal consequences. Rather, our findings suggest that negative affect often produces adaptive and more socially sensitive outcomes.

Affect can also have a profound influence on *motivation*. In an influential paper, Clark and Isen (1982) suggested that positive affect motivates strategies designed to maintain, and negative affect triggers strategies designed to improve the affective states. This kind of *mood repair versus mood maintenance* hypothesis is also consistent with affect theories based on evolutionary ideas (Frijda, 1986; Schwarz, 1990). Thus, paradoxically, negative mood, although unpleasant, may sometimes increase engagement and motivation. In contrast, positive affect may not only 'feel good', but it may also produce disengagement, reducing motivation and attention to the outside world (Forgas, 2007).

Several of our experiments now provide support for such dichotomous motivational effects. In particular, positive moods sometimes reduce, and negative moods increase, perseverance and ambition. If a person is already in a positive affective state, this may result in the *discounting* of the expected hedonistic value of possible future success, reducing perseverance and motivation (*hedonistic discounting*). In contrast, present negative affect may result in a higher evaluation of the expected hedonistic benefit of success on an achievement task, improving present effort and motivation.

In one experiment (Goldenberg & Forgas, 2016), we predicted that negative affect produced beneficial motivational consequences and increased perseverance on an effortful cognitive problem-solving task. As expected, participants in the positive mood condition spent significantly less time working on the task compared to those in a negative mood—they attempted to solve fewer items and scored fewer correct answers. A mediational analysis confirmed that it was mood-induced differences that resulted in the relative devaluation of the expected value of future positive outcomes when already in a happy mood—a hedonistic discounting effect that mediated mood effects on perseverance.

Another motivated strategy that may interfere with optimal performance is *self-handicapping* (Jones & Berglas, 1978), when people create artificial handicaps when success is uncertain to protect against damaging attributions due to possible failure. When we investigated mood effects on people's tendency to *self-handicap* (Alter & Forgas, 2007), we found that positive mood increased, and negative mood decreased defensive self-handicapping. Self-handicapping was assessed in terms of participants' preference for a performance-inhibiting or performance-enhancing tea when facing an uncertain outcome. The possible beneficial consequences of negative affect on achievement are only now beginning to be explored. Such effects may be particularly important in everyday situations and especially in organizational settings (Forgas & George, 2001). It now appears that, in some circumstances, negative affect may deliver greater perseverance and a reduction in dysfunctional self-handicapping behaviours (Alter & Forgas, 2007; Goldenberg & Forgas, 2016).

Summary and Conclusion

Overall, the series of experiments reviewed here provide a compelling case showing that, in many everyday situations, mild negative affective states can provide distinct adaptive advantages. In particular, the functional benefits of mild dysphoria—sadness—have not been intensively investigated before. These results are broadly consistent with recent evolutionary theories that suggest that the human affective repertoire has been largely shaped by processes of natural selection, and all mood states function as evolutionary algorithms that promote appropriate responses (see also von Hippel & Gonsalkorale, this volume). Consequently, all of our affective states—including the unpleasant ones—can potentially function as efficient 'mind modules' that produce real benefits in some circumstances (Tooby & Cosmides, 1992).

In terms of answering the central question of this book, how to live well, the practical message of these studies is that we ought to understand and accept temporary states of dysphoria as a normal part of our affective repertoire (see also Fiedler & Arslan, this volume). These sets of findings stand in stark contrast with the overwhelming and unilateral emphasis on the benefits of positive affect in the recent literature, as well as in much of our popular culture (Forgas & George, 2001). We should accept that positive affect, although often beneficial (see Fredrickson, this volume), is *not* universally desirable and should not always be preferred to dysphoria. As we have found here, people in a negative mood are less prone to judgmental errors (Forgas, 1998a, 2015), are more resistant to eyewitness distortions (Forgas et al., 2005), are more motivated (Goldenberg & Forgas, 2016), are fairer and more sensitive to social norms (Forgas, 1999b), and are better at producing and decoding linguistic messages (Forgas, 2007; Koch et al., 2013; Matovic et al., 2014). Given the consistency of the results across a number of different experiments, tasks and mood inductions, these effects appear robust and reliable.

However, it is obviously not claimed here that negative affect is *always* beneficial, or that positive affect does not have important adaptive consequences as well. Negative affective states that are intense, enduring and debilitating such as depression clearly have very negative consequences and require clinical intervention. What we were mostly concerned with here are the cognitive, motivational and interpersonal consequences of mild, temporary mood states, of the kind that we all regularly experience in everyday life. These experiments are broadly consistent with the idea that, over evolutionary time, affective states became adaptive, functional triggers that automatically promote motivational and information processing patterns that are appropriate and helpful in a given situation.

Interpersonal behaviour is necessarily a complex and demanding task that requires a high degree of elaborate processing (Forgas, 1995, 2002). The empirical studies presented here suggest that, in many demanding situations, negative affect such as sadness may increase, and positive affect decrease, the quality and efficacy of cognitive processes and interpersonal behaviours. When considering what kind of advice social psychologists might give to the general public about how to live well, we should pay greater attention to potential benefits of negative affective states. Accepting the entire range of affective reactions, including the negative ones, may be more conducive to well-being than focusing on the pursuit of positive affective states alone.

Author's Note

Support from the Australian Research Council is gratefully acknowledged.

Bibliography

Adolphs, R., & Damasio, A. (2001). The interaction of affect and cognition: A neurobiological perspective. In J. P. Forgas (Ed.), *The handbook of affect and social cognition* (pp. 27–49). Mahwah, NJ: Lawrence Erlbaum Associates, Inc.

Allport, G. W. (1985). The historical background of social psychology. In G. Lindzey & E. Aronson (Eds.), *The handbook of social psychology*. New York, NY: McGraw Hill.

Alter, A. L., & Forgas, J. P. (2007). On being happy but fearing failure: The effects of mood on self-handicapping strategies. *Journal of Experimental Social Psychology, 43*, 947–954.

Asch, S. E. (1946). Forming impressions of personality. *Journal of Abnormal and Social Psychology, 41*, 258–290.

Atkinson, J. W. (1957). Motivational determinants of risk-taking behaviour. *Psychological Review, 64*(6, Pt. 1), 359–372.

Bentham, J. (1838/1962). *The works of Jeremy Bentham* (John Bowring, Ed.). London, 1838–1843; Reprinted New York, 1962.

Bless, H. (2000). The interplay of affect and cognition: The mediating role of general knowledge structures. In J. P. Forgas (Ed.), *Feeling and thinking: The role of affect in social cognition*. (pp. 201–222). New York, NY: Cambridge University Press.

Bless, H. (2001). Mood and the use of general knowledge structures. In L. L. Martin (Ed.), *Theories of mood and cognition: A user's guidebook* (pp. 9–26). Mahwah, NJ: Lawrence Erlbaum Associates, Inc.

Bless, H., & Fiedler, K. (2006). Mood and the regulation of information processing and behavior. In: J. P. Forgas (Ed.), *Affect in social thinking and behavior* (pp. 65–84). New York, NY: Psychology Press.

Bodenhausen, G. V. (1993). Emotions, arousal, and stereotypic judgments: A heuristic model of affect and stereotyping. In D. M. Mackie & D. L. Hamilton (Eds.), *Affect, cognition, and stereotyping* (pp. 13–37). San Diego: Academic Press, Inc.

Bohner, G., & Schwarz, N. (1993). Mood states influence the production of persuasive arguments. *Communication Research, 20*, 696–722.

Bower, G. H. (1981). Mood and memory. *The American Psychologist, 36*, 129–148.

Bower, G. H., & Forgas, J. P. (2001). Mood and social Memory. In J. P. Forgas (Ed.), *The handbook of affect and social cognition* (pp. 95–120). Mahwah, NJ: Erlbaum.

Ciarrochi, J. V., Forgas, J. P., & Mayer, J. D. (Eds.). (2006). *Emotional intelligence in everyday life* (2nd ed.). Philadelphia: Psychology Press.

Clark, M. S., & Isen, A. M. (1982). Towards understanding the relationship between feeling states and social behavior. In A. H. Hastorf & A. M. Isen (Eds.), *Cognitive social psychology* (pp. 73–108). New York, NY: Elsevier-North Holland.

Clore, G. L., & Byrne, D. (1974). The reinforcement affect model of attraction. In T. L. Huston (Ed.), *Foundations of interpersonal attraction* (pp. 143–170). New York, NY: Academic Press.

Clore, G. L., Schwarz, N., & Conway, M. (1994). Affective causes and consequences of social information processing. In R. S. Wyer & T. K. Srull (Eds.), *Handbook of social cognition* (2nd ed.). Mahwah, NJ: Erlbaum.

Diener, E., & Seligman, M. E. P. (2004). Beyond money: Toward an economy of well-being. *Psychological Science in the Public Interest, 5*(1), 1–31.

Ekman, P., & O'Sullivan, M. (1991). Who can catch a liar? *American Psychologist, 46*, 913–920.

Feather, N. T. (1992). Values, valences, expectations, and actions. *Journal of Social Issues, 48*(2), 109–124.

Feshbach, S., & Singer, R. D. (1957). The effects of fear arousal and suppression of fear upon social perception. *Journal of Abnormal and Social Psychology, 55*, 283–288.

Fiedler, K. (2001). Affective influences on social information processing. In J. P. Forgas (Ed.), *The handbook of affect and social cognition* (pp. 163–185). Mahwah, NJ: Lawrence Erlbaum Associates, Inc.

Fiedler, K., Asbeck, J., & Nickel, S. (1991). Mood and constructive memory effects on social judgment. *Cognition and Emotion, 5*, 363–378.

Fiedler, K., & Bless, H. (2001). The formation of beliefs in the interface of affective and cognitive processes. In N. Frijda, A. Manstead, & S. Bem (Eds.), *The influence of emotions on beliefs.* New York, NY: Cambridge University Press.

Fiedler, K. & Forgas, J. P. (Eds.) (1988) *Affect, cognition and social behavior.* Toronto: Hogrefe International.

Forgas, J. P. (1994). Sad and guilty? Affective influences on explanations of conflict episodes. *Journal of Personality and Social Psychology, 66*, 56–68.

Forgas, J. P. (1995). Mood and judgment: The Affect Infusion Model (AIM). *Psychological Bulletin, 116*, 39–66.

Forgas, J. P. (1998a). Happy and mistaken? Mood effects on the fundamental attribution error. *Journal of Personality and Social Psychology, 75*, 318–331.

Forgas, J. P. (1998b). On feeling good and getting your way: Mood effects on negotiation strategies and outcomes. *Journal of Personality and Social Psychology, 74*, 565–577.

Forgas, J. P. (1999a). Feeling and speaking: Mood effects on verbal communication strategies. *Personality and Social Psychology Bulletin, 25*, 850–863.

Forgas, J. P. (1999b). On feeling good and being rude: Affective influences on language use and requests. *Journal of Personality and Social Psychology, 76*, 928–939.

Forgas, J. P. (2002). Feeling and doing: Affective influences on interpersonal behavior. *Psychological Inquiry, 13*, 1–28.

Forgas, J. P. (2003). Why don't we do it in the road . . .? Stereotyping and prejudice in mundane situations. *Psychological Inquiry, 14*, 249–255.

Forgas, J. P. (Ed.). (2006). *Affect in social thinking and behavior.* New York, NY: Psychology Press.

Forgas, J. P. (2007). When sad is better than happy: Negative affect can improve the quality and effectiveness of persuasive messages and social influence strategies. *Journal of Experimental Social Psychology, 43*, 513–528.

Forgas, J. P. (2011a). Can negative affect eliminate the power of first impressions? Affective influences on primacy and recency effects in impression formation. *Journal of Experimental Social Psychology, 47*, 425–429.

Forgas, J. P. (2011b). She just doesn't look like a philosopher . . .? Affective influences on the halo effect in impression formation. *European Journal of Social Psychology, 41*, 812–817.

Forgas, J. P. (2011c). Affective influences on self-disclosure strategies. *Journal of Personality and Social Psychology, 100*(3), 449–461.

Forgas, J. P. (2015). Why do highly visible people appear more important? Affect mediates visual fluency effects in impression formation. *Journal of Experimental Social Psychology, 58*, 136–141.

Forgas, J. P., & Bower, G. H. (1987). Mood effects on person perception judgements. *Journal of Personality and Social Psychology, 53*, 53–60.

Forgas, J. P., Bower, G. H. & Krantz, S. (1984). The influence of mood on perceptions of social interactions. *Journal of Experimental Social Psychology, 20*, 497–513.

Forgas, J. P., & East, R. (2008a). How real is that smile? Mood effects on accepting or rejecting the veracity of emotional facial expressions. *Journal of Nonverbal Behavior, 32*, 157–170.

Forgas, J. P., & East, R. (2008b). On being happy and gullible: Mood effects on scepticism and the detection of deception. *Journal of Experimental Social Psychology, 44*, 1362–1367.

Forgas, J. P., & Eich, E. E. (2012). Affective influences on cognition: Mood congruence, mood dependence, and mood effects on processing strategies. In A. F. Healy & R. W.

Proctor (Eds.), *Experimental psychology*. Volume 4 in I. B. Weiner (Editor-in-Chief), *Handbook of Psychology* (pp. 61–82). New York, NY: Wiley.

Forgas, J. P., & George, J. M. (2001). Affective influences on judgments and behavior in organizations: An information processing perspective. *Organizational Behavior and Human Decision Processes, 86,* 3–34.

Forgas, J. P., Goldenberg, L., & Unkelbach, C. (2009). Can bad weather improve your memory? A field study of mood effects on memory in a real-life setting. *Journal of Experimental Social Psychology, 54,* 254–257.

Forgas, J. P., Haselton, M. G., & von Hippel, W. (Eds.). (2007). *Evolution and the social mind.* New York, NY: Psychology Press.

Forgas, J. P. & Laham, S. (2017). Halo effects. In: Pohl, R. (Ed.) *Cognitive Illusions* (pp. 276–291). New York: Psychology Press.

Forgas, J. P., & Tan, H. B. (2013). To give or to keep? Affective influences on selfishness and fairness in computer-mediated interactions in the dictator game and the ultimatum game. *Computers and Human Behavior, 29,* 64–74.

Forgas, J. P., Vargas, P., & Laham, S. (2005). Mood effects on eyewitness memory: Affective influences on susceptibility to misinformation. *Journal of Experimental Social Psychology, 41,* 574–588.

Frijda, N. (1986). *The emotions.* Cambridge, UK: Cambridge University Press.

Frijda, N. (1988). The laws of emotion. *American Psychologist, 43,* 349–358.

Goldenberg, L., & Forgas, J. P. (2016). *Mood effects on perseverance: Positive mood reduces motivation according to the hedonistic discounting hypothesis.* Manuscript, University of New South Wales, Sydney, Australia.

Grice, H. P. (1975). Logic and Conversation. In: P. Cole & J. Morgan (Eds.) Syntax and Semantics, Vol. 3, pp. 22–40. New York: Academic Press.

Jones, E. E., & Berglas, S. (1978). Control of attributions about the self through self-handicapping strategies: The appeal of alcohol and the role of underachievement. *Personality and Social Psychology Bulletin, 4,* 200–206.

Jones, E. E., & Harris, V. A. (1967). The attribution of attitudes. *Journal of Experimental Social Psychology, 3,* 1–24.

Koch, A. S., & Forgas, J. P. (2012). Feeling good and feeling truth: The interactive effects of mood and processing fluency on truth judgments. *Journal of Experimental Social Psychology, 48,* 481–485.

Koch, A. S., Forgas, J. P., & Matovic, D. (2013). Can negative mood improve your conversation? Affective influences on conforming to Grice's communication norms. *European Journal of Social Psychology, 43,* 326–334.

Lane, J. D., & DePaulo, B. M. (1999). Completing Coyne's cycle: Dysphorics' ability to detect deception. *Journal of Research in Personality, 33,* 311–329.

Loftus, E. F. (1979). *Eyewitness testimony.* Cambridge, MA: Harvard University Press.

Luchins, A. H. (1958). Definitiveness of impressions and primacy—recency in communications. *Journal of Social Psychology, 48,* 275–290.

Matovic, D., Koch, A., & Forgas, J. P. (2014). Can negative mood improve language understanding? Affective influences on the ability to detect ambiguous communication. *Journal of Experimental Social Psychology, 52,* 44–49.

Neisser, U. (1982). *Memory observed: Remembering in natural contexts.* San Francisco, CA: Freeman.

Petty, R. E., DeSteno, D., & Rucker, D. (2001) The role of affect in attitude change. In J. P. Forgas (Ed.), *The handbook of affect and social cognition* (pp. 212–236). Mahwah, NJ: Lawrence Erlbaum.

Schwarz, N. (1990). Feelings as information: Informational and motivational functions of affective states. In E. T. Higgins & R. Sorrentino (Eds.), *Handbook of motivation and cognition* (Vol. 2, pp. 527–561). New York, NY: Guildford Press.

Schwarz, N., & Bless, H. (1991). Happy and mindless, but sad and smart? The impact of affective states on analytic reasoning. In J. P. Forgas (Ed.), *Emotion and social judgments* (pp. 55–71). Oxford: Pergamon Press.

Schwarz, N., & Clore, G. L. (1988). How do I feel about it? The informative function of affective states. In K. Fiedler & J. P. Forgas (Eds.), *Affect, cognition, and social behavior* (pp. 44–62). Toronto: Hogrefe.

Sedikides, C., Wildschut, T., Arndt, J., & Routledge, C. (2006). Affect and the self. In J. P. Forgas (Ed.), *Affect in social thinking and behavior* (pp. 197–216). New York, NY: Psychology Press.

Sinclair, R. C., & Mark, M. M. (1992). The influence of mood state on judgment and action. In L. L. Martin & A. Tesser (Eds.), *The construction of social judgments* (pp. 165–193). Mahwah, NJ: Lawrence Erlbaum.

Tan, H. B., & Forgas, J. P. (2010). When happiness makes us selfish, but sadness makes us fair: Affective influences on interpersonal strategies in the dictator game. *Journal of Experimental Social Psychology, 46*, 571–576.

Tooby, J., & Cosmides, L. (1992). The psychological foundations of culture. In J. H. Barkow & L. Cosmides (Eds.), *The adapted mind: Evolutionary psychology and the generation of culture* (pp. 19–136). London: Oxford University Press.

Wells, G. L., & Loftus, E. F. (2003). Eyewitness memory for people and events. In A. M. Goldstein (Ed.), *Handbook of psychology: Forensic psychology* (Vol. 11, pp. 149–160). New York, NY: John Wiley & Sons, Inc.

13

EXPANSIVE AND CONTRACTIVE LEARNING EXPERIENCES

Mental Construal and Living Well

David Kalkstein, Alexa Hubbard, and Yaacov Trope

As a species, humans enjoy an exceptionally rich learning environment due to the ability to communicate with and learn from one another. With each new social interaction, an individual has the potential to gain vicarious experience with contexts, situations, or events that are foreign to him or herself, but are known by another person. As a result, our sociality extends the scope of our learning environments as far as our social networks reach. Over time, that reach has been continually expanded through the development of transportation and communication technologies that serve to connect people across greater spans of distance and with a wider array of others. For example, airplanes make it possible for scholars to travel to international conferences and learn from the ideas of peers living in distant locations. Writing and the printing press make it possible for historians to learn from the experiences of people who lived in times past. More recently, advances in Internet technologies and social media have enabled people to connect with and learn from more distant and diverse others than ever before (see also Amichai-Hamburger & Etgar, and Dunn & Dwyer, this volume). Taken together, these developments have contributed to the expansion of modern-day learning environments by increasing the scope of possible social interaction and the sheer number of others from whom one can learn.

Increasing the number and diversity of interaction partners available to any given person creates more varied opportunities for learning since it exposes individuals to a wider range of ideas, experiences, and situations than they would otherwise encounter. However, ideas that originate in disparate contexts may not necessarily be directly applicable to one's own context. For example, if we were learning about shelter design from people who live in a different environment, we might not have access to all the materials they use, but we could still learn something general about the form and structure of their designs. Because of this increase in scope and diversity of social interactions, the ability to extract general lessons from exposure to the experiences of diverse others—that is, to effectively navigate this expansive social landscape—is an essential skill for maintaining over-all psychological well-being and life satisfaction.

In this chapter, we explore the psychological mechanisms that allow people to learn and acquire meaningful knowledge from others across such diverse and divergent contexts. In the first part of the chapter, we explore a parallel between the challenges people face today in learning from others in highly variable con-texts and the challenges our species faced surviving extended periods of environ-mental variability (see also von Hippel & Gonsalkorale, this volume). We propose that the human capacity for abstract thought is adaptive in modern times for learning across variable contexts and was adaptive evolutionarily for humans' con-tinued survival through variable environmental conditions. In the second part of the chapter, we focus more specifically on abstraction in social learning and discuss its role in allowing people to learn from distant others occupying diverse and dissimilar contexts.

An Evolutionary Perspective

Recent theories of hominid evolution have focused on how the degree of vari-ability in the natural climate may have impacted which characteristics were adaptive for survival (e.g., Potts, 1998). We propose that the psychological chal-lenge presented by communicating and learning across highly varied contexts is analogous to the selection pressures encountered by species evolving in times of marked environmental variability. Furthermore, we suggest that in both cases, the most adaptive strategy for success relies on the capacity for generalization of skills, knowledge, and adaptations.

Selection Pressures in Constant Versus Variable Evolutionary Environments

According to the variability selection hypothesis (Potts, 1996, 1998), over long periods of time, different degrees of variability in a species' external environ-ment exert different selection pressures on that species. An environment with low degrees of variability will exert selection pressures that are consistent and unidirectional across time. The most adaptive response to such constancy of conditions would be continual refinement of habitat-specific characteristics over successive generations. Ultimately, because the same characteristics are selected for over the course of many generations, low variability in an evolutionary envi-ronment will tend to yield species that are highly specialized to navigate and survive in a specific context. For example, organisms evolving in consistently hot environments may develop a physical specialization in the form of longer appendages, because the greater surface area allows heat to escape more easily;

whereas consistently cold climates may lead to increasingly shorter appendages that more easily retain heat.

On the other hand, a highly variable evolutionary environment would exert selection pressures that are variable over successive generations. In this case, adaptations that are specific to a given habitat may yield only short-term benefits since the species' habitat is liable to change. A more advantageous adaptation in these conditions would be to evolve characteristics that allow for flexible responding to a variety of environments. While such adaptations may leave a given species less efficient in any one particular environment, in the long term they would allow the species to thrive and prosper even as their external environment undergoes rapid change. In short, an evolutionary environment that remains constant over successive generations tends to promote adaptations that are highly specific and specialized, whereas a highly variable evolutionary environment promotes adaptations that are general and versatile. Returning to the previous example, a species that is adapting to variable climates may develop more average appendages that are neither extremely long nor extremely short. This average physical characteristic is not ideally specialized, but it will survive more readily across several types of climates.

Psychological Challenges of Social Learning Across Constant and Variable Contexts

As we have outlined, environments with different degrees of variability impose different selection pressures. We argue that there is a parallel process in social learning. We conceptualize social learning as the process of acquiring new information about the world through social interactions (see Bandura, 1977). Social interactions can consist of actors who come from similar or dissimilar contexts. The degree of similarity between the contexts of social interaction partners is an external constraint to which people need to adapt. When one's interaction partner is close to the self, an individual is gaining exposure to information acquired from another person's experience in an external environment that is likely highly consistent with one's own. In this way, learning from proximal others is analogous to a species evolving in an unchanging environment, since both entail accruing experience within a constant external context. Just as the characteristics that are adaptive for one generation remain applicable and adaptive for subsequent generations in conditions of environmental constancy, much of the information gained through exposure to close others' experiences may be directly applicable and useful in one's own circumstance. Extending the analogy further, just as a constant evolutionary environment encourages continual refinement of habitat-specific characteristics, we propose that a constant learning environment encourages specialization and the development of context-specific expertise.

However, as one's interaction partners become more distant from the self, the challenge of learning from their experience is exacerbated by the fact that it is increasingly possible that their experience occurred in external settings that are highly discrepant from one's own. Hence, learning from more distant others is analogous to a species evolving in a highly variable environment—both entail accruing experience across diverse external contexts. Just as characteristics that are adapted for any specific environment may be useless when the external environment changes, aspects of the information gained through distant others' experience that are specific to their context will be inapplicable to the extent that their external surroundings differ from one's own. In this case, just as success in a highly variable evolutionary environment depends on the evolution of general and versatile adaptations, we propose that social learning across highly variable contexts depends on the ability to extract general information that is relevant across a diverse array of contexts.

Navigating Diverse Contexts

The ability to effectively navigate diverse contexts and environmental constraints was critical to survival in human evolution and remains critical for living well in today's ever-expanding social world. Humans' evolutionary history is marked by success and thriving during extended periods of environmental fluctuation (Potts, 1996; 1998), and in modern social life people are increasingly exposed to ideas and experiences originating in diverse and highly variable contexts. We propose that the capacity for abstract thought is a psychological adaptation that evolved in response to the pressures of environmental variability, and that continues to be critical for living well in modern daily life as a way to navigate increasingly diverse social contexts in today's interconnected world.

Abstraction

Any target (object, event, action, situation, etc.) can be construed at varying levels of abstraction ranging from low to high (Rosch, Mervis, Gray, Johnson, & Boyes-Braem, 1976; Trope & Liberman, 2010; Vallacher & Wegner, 1987). Low-level construals are concrete and contextualized as they focus on the peripheral, specific, and subordinate features of the target. Higher-level construals are more abstract and decontextualized as they focus more on central, general, and superordinate features of the target. For example, a low-level construal of "exercising" may identify a specific means of exercising, like "swimming". A higher-level construal of the same action may focus instead on the superordinate goal that the action is a means to, such as "being healthy" (Vallacher & Wegner, 1987). As this example illustrates, lower-level construals incorporate more contextual features into their representation (e.g., being in water is likely included in one's representation of swimming) whereas higher-level construals are more context independent (e.g., the goal being healthy does not connote any specific contextual setting). In general, a primary function of higher-level construals is to allow people to construct mental representations of goals, events, or stimuli that are divorced from any specific context in which they may occur.

By omitting specific details that bind a given target to a particular context and focusing instead on its superordinate and central features, moving to a higher level of construal identifies a wider variety of objects or events that are equivalent for some purpose, an important skill in managing one's life well (e.g., Gilead, Trope, & Liberman, forthcoming; Rosch et al., 1976). For example, construing a bike as an example of a "vehicle" represents a higher-level construal that renders the bike equivalent to any other target that fulfills the goal of transportation (e.g., a car). On the other hand, by focusing on increasingly specific details, moving to a lower-level construal functions to distinguish a given target from other potentially similar targets. Construing that same bike at a lower level such as "mountain bike" places the item in a narrower category of objects characterized by a more specific function. Overall, higher-level construals encapsulate a wider variety of possible instantiations of a target than do lower-level construals. That is, there are more possible manifestations of the abstract concept of "vehicle" than there are of "mountain bike".

Abstraction as an Evolutionary Adaptation

How might the ability to engage in abstract thought have conferred a selective evolutionary advantage to humans? As mentioned earlier, humans evolved throughout periods of high degrees of environmental instability. This inconsistency in environmental pressures over the course of many generations would have created selection pressures that encouraged the replacement of highly habit-specific adaptations with ones that promote flexibility in responding to a variety of environmental contexts. We argue that a key adaptation for this challenge was the emerging capacity of increasingly abstract thought. The primary adaptive benefit of abstract thought is that it frees human cognition from any specific environmental context and allows people to establish psychological continuity across discrepant contexts. This ability to identify commonalities across divergent contexts grants humans a unique flexibility to respond to diverse environmental conditions and to develop response algorithms that are functional over a wider range of situational challenges.

To see this, imagine that there are two species competing for survival in an idealized environment. Suppose in this environment there are various sources of nutrition that are all equally plentiful, but of which blueberries are the most nutritious. Further imagine that one species has a highly specialized cognitive system oriented around the specific goal of finding blueberries, whereas the other has a more abstract cognitive system oriented to the goal of finding food. If the environment were to remain stable, an organism with a cognitive system specifically oriented to blueberries would enjoy high levels of fitness, while the more abstract-thinking "food finders" may find themselves lagging behind such specialists. However, if the environment were to change and blueberries went extinct, the blueberry finders would be at a serious disadvantage, while the food finders would easily be able to accommodate such a change, due to their capacity to hold a more abstract goal and substitute any other source of nutrition as an equivalent means. Thus, over the course of variable climates, the generalist "food finders" would attain higher rates of survival.

More generally, the ability to conceive of a goal that is superordinate to the means of obtaining it would have prevented early hominids from getting locked into a specific means of accomplishing their goals, that is, into a specified behavioral pattern. In other words, thinking at higher levels of abstraction allows for the generation of goal hierarchies, which render subgoals interchangeable in service of superordinate goals. For example, from the relatively low-level goal of eating blueberries, an abstract thinker can generate a higher-level goal of getting nutrition; this goal in turn makes the subgoal to eat blueberries one in a set of possibilities. In contrast, the inability to recognize higher-level goals makes an organism dependent on environmental constraints to dictate behavior (e.g., having an environment with blueberries), and thus more vulnerable to shifts in the environment.

Supporting the idea that abstraction evolved out of selection pressures created by evolving through variable conditions, Potts (1996, 1998) presents evidence showing that several key hominid adaptations—including biological changes such as highly encephalized brains, technological developments like the creation and use of stone tools, and behavioral patterns such as increased sociality—emerged during periods of heightened environmental variability. Many of these adaptations are likely related to the basic cognitive adaptation to engage in increasing levels of abstract thought. Increased brain size and encephalization are likely to have been associated with increased cognitive processing and capacity for abstract thought (e.g., Roth & Dicke, 2005; see also von Hippel & Gonsalkorale, this volume). The creation and use of tools is a hallmark of abstract thought since it implies the capability to conceive of a general, superordinate goal (e.g., kill an animal for meat) and the ability to work backwards from this goal to develop a specific means of achieving it. Finally, as we will argue below, the ability to engage in social communication and social learning is made possible by the capacity for abstract thought.

Overall, the evidence presented suggests that humans evolved the capacity for increasing levels of abstract thought in response to the selection pressures created by evolving through highly variable environmental contexts. This conclusion has important implications for our understanding of the kinds of cognitive skills required to live life well in contemporary societies. While abstraction arose out of environmental changes that occurred gradually and over the course of thousands of years, the flexibility it affords for navigating diverse external contexts is functional within modern daily life for navigating the diverse contexts of the other people we interact with and learn from in today's interconnected world. How might the ability to engage in varying levels of abstract thought facilitate social learning across an expansive social landscape of the kind we face in our current social and cultural environment?

The Role of Abstraction in Social Learning

Construal Level Theory and Social Learning

Drawing on construal level theory (CLT; Liberman & Trope, 2008; Trope & Liberman, 2010), we propose that people are able to expand their social scope to learn from increasingly distant and dissimilar others by engaging in higher levels of construal, or more abstract thought (see Kalkstein, Kleiman, Wakslak, Trope, & Liberman, 2016). The main hypothesis of CLT is that higher-level construals allow people to expand their mental horizons and traverse psychological distance to consider targets that are experienced as existing outside of the egocentric here and now (Ledgerwood, Trope, & Liberman, 2015; Liberman & Trope, 2014). Applied to social learning, the basic idea is that by constructing mental representations of an object or event that are decontextualized and encapsulating of a variety of instantiations, higher-level construals allow people to extract information from the experiences of others across greater psychological distances, and across increasingly diverse contexts, that is stable and applicable to their own circumstances. These stable construals allow for adaptive flexibility in rapidly changing social environments.

Fundamental to the integration of CLT with social learning is the concept of psychological distance. Psychological distance is a general term to refer to all of the ways that an event, object, or situation can be removed from the egocentric here and now (Trope & Liberman, 2010). It can be spatial (i.e., occurring in a different place), temporal (i.e., occurring in the past or the future), social (i.e., someone unfamiliar or dissimilar), or hypothetical (i.e., not occurring in reality). Since the experience of another person is always located beyond the self, social learning always requires the traversing of some psychological distance. The amount of psychological distance traversed in social learning will vary depending on who the person that one is learning from is (e.g., a close friend vs. a distant stranger), and when and where the other person's experience took place (e.g., recently in proximal location vs. long ago in a faraway land). The farther removed another person's experience is along any of the four dimensions (spatial, temporal, social, or hypothetical) from one's immediate egocentric context, the more psychologically distant it is.

Learning From Proximal and Distal Others

Within social learning, psychological distance operates as a cue to the degree of potential discrepancy between the learner's own immediate circumstance and the context of the other person's experience. For the learner, increasing psychological proximity to another person's experience constrains the range of possibilities for what the context of that experience may have been to be more similar one's own context. The closer another person is to oneself, the more similar the context of their experience is likely to be to one's own context. In this case, the learner will be able to extract relevant and useful information from exposure to their partner's experience with relatively low-level construals. For example, in learning from a neighbor how to construct a shelter, the geographic proximity and similarity of contexts in terms of resources available would allow the learner to focus on relatively specific details such as the type and quantity of material used to build the walls.

A major advantage of learning from closer others is that it affords the opportunity to gain expertise in a specific context. The development of expertise entails a mastery of the low-level mechanics of how to complete an action or goal (e.g., Vallacher & Wegner, 1987). The low-level mechanics of how to complete an action are often contextually bound. For example, the specific actions involved in driving a car differ depending on whether one is driving in the mountains on icy roads or is driving in a city with heavy traffic. To the extent that the context of the other person's experience overlaps with one's own, construing their behavior at a lower level will facilitate the development of context-specific skills and expertise. Thus, a person living in the mountains would be able to learn more specialized driving skills from another person living in the mountains than from a more distant city driver. In this way, the ability to tune one's learning to the more concrete features of proximal others contributes to living well as it promotes the acquisition of knowledge about the most effective and efficient means for navigating one's own immediate environment.

As the experience that one is learning from becomes more distant from the self, the learner will tend to have less information about the context of the experience. From the learner's perspective, the experience could have occurred in any of a highly variable set of contexts that includes contexts that are very different from one's own. To accommodate a wide range of possibilities, people learning from distant others benefit by adopting a higher-level construal that captures all possible manifestations of the object or event.

Furthermore, in cases where information about the context of another person's experience is provided, thus reducing the learner's uncertainty about the nature of the context, it may still be irrelevant. For example, learning about the building materials used in igloos would not be relevant for a person learning to construct a shelter in a tropical climate. In cases where psychological distance is related to a discrepancy in the contexts of one person's experience and that of the learner, higher-level construals will allow the learner to extract meaningful information from the exchange in spite of irrelevant contextual details. Thus, that same tropical learner could still benefit from learning from the igloo builder by learning about the higher-level structural properties that make an igloo a viable shelter. Similarly, one may be able to learn abstract lessons about power structures from a distant culture, even if the specific status-related rituals in that distant culture are not relevant across contexts. Overall, higher-level construals are extremely functional within social learning as they allow people to extract useful information from more distant others and across more discrepant contexts. This ability to engage with and learn from distant and dissimilar others promotes living well as it allows people to take advantage of the vast learning opportunities in today's interconnected world.

As a result of this functional relationship between the psychological distance to a given target and its level of construal, people possess a general cognitive association between psychological distance and construal level (Trope & Liberman, 2010). The more psychologically distant a target is the higher level people will tend to construe it. While this association is likely borne out of an ecological relationship between psychological distance and availability/applicability of low-level features of a target, its employment in everyday experience is independent of this ecological reality. Rather, the association is overgeneralized so that even when people have the same amount of low-level information available (and it is equally applicable), people will still tend to construe the target at a higher level when experienced as more psychologically distant. In terms of social learning, this overgeneralization hypothesis suggests that even when the amount and applicability of information provided remains the same, people will still tend to learn from others at a higher level of construal when the source of the information feels more psychologically distant from the self.

Empirical Evidence

At the most basic level, the above logic suggests that given the same information, people should represent it and learn it at a higher level when it is acquired socially through observation of another person's experience than when it is acquired through direct experience. This is because learning from another person's experience entails learning from a more distant source than learning from one's own direct experience. Research has shown that people learn new information at a higher level when they learn it socially than through direct experience (Kalkstein et al., 2016). Specifically, when learning to categorize novel objects into separate groups, people who learned socially were more likely to later categorize objects based on their global configuration (rather than their local components) than were participants who learned through direct experience.

Extending this further, research shows that within social learning, when people are learning from others, they tend learn at a higher level when learning from a more psychologically distant source (Hansen, Alves, & Trope, 2016; Kalkstein et al., 2016). Importantly, this entails that people not only construe the incoming information at a higher level when it is learned from a more distant source, but that this higher-level construal influences the way they internalize it and subsequently act upon that learned information. As discussed above, when learning a new skill from another person, people should attend to and subsequently emulate the specific means of accomplishing a given task more when the person they are learning from is psychologically proximal. On the other hand, when learning from a more distant source, people should learn from the model more in terms of the ultimate goal of the task while adhering less rigidly to the specific means of achieving it.

To test these assertions, Hansen and colleagues (2016) designed a series of studies wherein they presented participants with a novel task that they were to learn how to complete by watching someone else perform it. The two tasks used across this set of studies were one wherein participants had to fold a towel into the shape of a dog and another that was a simpler task of folding paper into various shapes. People learned these tasks by watching a video of either a psychologically distant model (e.g., a video of someone from 20 years ago) or a more proximal model (e.g., a video of someone from earlier that year) perform the task. The results of these studies showed that participants imitated the model's specific steps in completing the task more precisely when the model was psychologically proximal than when the model was more distant (see also Bandura, Ross, & Ross, 1963). When the model was distant, people tended to emulate the model more at the level of the higher-order goal of the task (e.g., fold a sheet of paper into a kite) while omitting the specific steps demonstrated by the model.

The direction of influence explored thus far is how the psychological distance to the person one is learning from influences the level at which the shared information is learned. However, the direction of influence can also be reversed. CLT posits that the relationship between construal level and psychological distance is bidirectional; so, not only do people tend to construe more distant targets at a higher level, but higher-level construals promote the consideration of more distant targets (Trope & Liberman, 2010; Ledgerwood et al., 2015). In terms of social learning, this implies that higher-level construals expand one's social horizons and encourage people to consider a more diverse array of others as potential sources of information. Given the abundance of potential sources of information available to people in today's information-rich world, considering a broader array of sources to find information is greatly beneficial for living well and expanding one's knowledge.

Expansive and Contractive Social Scopes

Higher-level construals are functional for expanding people's social horizons because they represent objects and events in a decontextualized manner that renders them stable and applicable across diverse contexts. For example, an individual wanting to learn about higher-level abstract ideas—such as basic theories within an academic discipline—could look to a wide array of others including those who are distant and dissimilar from one's self. Put differently, higher-level "why?" questions can be answered by others in more variable contexts including those distant and dissimilar from one's own. Indeed, people often turn to very distant sources for guidance on questions that are critical to maintaining personal well-being, such as those about purpose and meaning (see also Baumeister; Fiedler & Arslan, this volume). As a classic example, one of the world's most popular sources for answering "why?" questions are religious texts that were written hundreds, if not thousands, of years ago (see also Myers, this volume). By allowing people to formulate questions that can be answered by people who occupy divergent contexts, higher-level construals function to expand people's social scope, and thus their overall learning environments.

Whereas higher-level construals function to expand one's social horizons, lower-level construals serve to contract people's mental horizons and aid immersion into one's immediate egocentric context. By focusing on contextually bound specifics of an event or object, lower-level construals orient people to proximal others occupying the same or a similar context. A common example of this in the world is the practice of apprenticeships. Typically, apprenticeships are about developing expertise in a specific domain, and typically apprenticeships involve working in close proximity with a teacher. We argue that the reason people apprentice in such close proximity to a teacher is because the concreteness of the skills they want to learn leads them to contract their mental horizons and orient them toward someone inhabiting a similar context to themselves. For example, a medical student learning to become a surgeon would be better served by physically observing a more practiced surgeon operate than he or she would be by reading a book recounting a previous operation. Oftentimes, learning how to do something requires careful attention to details that are not available or applicable across distant and diverse contexts. Thus, we argue that low-level construals contract the scope of others that one will look to for learning because they encourage the formulation of context-specific questions that are best answered by proximal others with experience in that same specific context.

Supporting the idea that higher-level construals serve to expand one's social horizons while lower-level construals contract them, a series of studies conducted by Kalkstein and colleagues (2016) show that when people are asked who they would choose as a model to learn from, they were more likely to select distant others when the content of what they were learning was more abstract (it is perhaps for this reason that when seeking spiritual enlightenment, faraway gurus are more sought after than your neighbor). For example, in one study, people chose models across a relatively broad range of social distances when asked from whom they would learn if they were to learn about a general trait that they admired. In contrast, when asked to whom they would look in order to learn about a specific behavior, people expressed a strong preference for learning from proximal others. Similarly, in another study, participants expressed relatively equal interest in learning about *why* it is important to adopt certain healthy behaviors from an article written months ago and an article written that day. Again, in contrast, when learning about *how to* adopt that healthy behavior, people expressed a significant preference for learning from the more recent article.

It is important to clarify that while higher-level construals expand people's social horizons, they do not necessarily lead people to prefer distant others to near others as sources of information. Rather, by construing the learning content in a more decontextualized way that is applicable across a wide diversity of contexts, high-level construals lead people to be less biased by context. The data from the last two studies support this account by showing that higher-level construals led people to express relatively equal interest in and likelihood of learning from distant others and close others. Whereas low-level construals bias people toward learning from proximal others, that high-level construals expand the breadth of others that one is willing to consider learning from to include distant others *in addition to* more proximal others. From this expanded scope, it only stands to reason that people then select whomever they deem to be the best possible model, regardless of context, given whatever it is that they are trying to learn.

Overall, this research supports the idea that higher-level construals are functional for allowing people to learn from others across more variable contexts, including those that are distant and dissimilar from one's own. While lower-level construals are functional for allowing people to learn specific information from people close to themselves within highly similar contexts, higher-level construals are functional for allowing people to learn more abstract information from people across a wide variety of contexts. Thus, in today's interconnected world where digital communication is increasingly important, the ability to learn from others at a higher, more abstract level grants people the flexibility to learn meaningful things from the broad variety of sources made possible by modern technology (see also Amichai-Hamburger & Etgar, and Dunn & Dwyer, this volume).

Summary and Conclusions

In this chapter, we explored the psychological mechanisms that allow people to navigate today's complex social world and take advantage of the richness of today's social learning environment as a means of improving their adaptability, achieving positive outcomes, and optimizing their life satisfaction. Drawing an analogy to the selection pressures created by different degrees of variability in evolutionary environments, we argued that different degrees of variability between the external environments of another person and oneself create different opportunities and challenges for social learning. In both cases, constancy in external environments affords the opportunity for specialization in that specific context, whereas variability in external environments challenges species and individuals to engage mechanisms that are more general and flexible. We further presented evidence that abstract thought evolved to meet the challenges of survival across variable external conditions and that it remains adaptive for social learning in modern times by allowing people to learn from others across distant and divergent contexts.

Within social learning, we presented evidence that people strategically employ different levels of construal in order to take advantage of the various opportunities created by learning from near and distant others. We reviewed evidence showing that when people are learning from others in circumstances highly similar to their own (typically close others), they tend to focus on more concrete specific details of the shared content in efforts to gain mastery over a specific environment. However, when people learn from others who they perceive to live in highly dissimilar contexts (e.g., distant others), they increasingly focus on the more abstract qualities of the shared information in efforts to acquire general knowledge that is stable across contexts and relevant when applied to one's own circumstance. This functional account echoes a more general theme that different levels of construal may promote life satisfaction in different ways and in different settings (see also Fiedler & Arslan; Sheldon; Fritz & Lyubomirsky; Shah, this volume).

In this chapter we are building on CLT by suggesting that contextual variability plays a mediating role in the link between psychological distance and higher-level construals. We argue that people treat increased psychological distance to another person's experience as a cue for the potential discrepancy between the context of that experience and one's own. In turn, we propose that the potential for the experience to have occurred in a highly discrepant context prompts people to adopt a higher-level construal of information acquired from more distant others in efforts to render it applicable to their own circumstance. We leave it to future work to explore the role of perceived context variability in the relationship between psychological distance and construal level, and how this relationship promotes subjective well-being and life satisfaction.

Finally, to bring the argument full circle and relate the social learning more directly to humans' evolutionary history, we join a growing viewpoint within social sciences arguing that the ability to engage in social learning is perhaps one of humans' greatest adaptations, and is responsible for our continued success on this earth (see Boyd, Richerson, & Henrich, 2011; Henrich, 2015; see also von Hippel & Gonsalkorale; Fiedler & Arslan, this volume). Through social learning, humans enjoy a richer and more expansive learning environment than any other known species ever. Our contribution to this viewpoint is to highlight the basic cognitive mechanisms that give rise to our ability to share ideas, experiences, and thoughts with each other. Specifically, we propose that it is the ability of both learners and communicators to develop higher-level shared representation of the world that enables social learning and the expansion of our learning environments as far as our social connections reach. By enabling expansive social connections, and allowing people from all over the globe and from all walks of life to come together to share ideas, the use of abstract thought in social learning is essential to developing and maintaining "the good life".

Bibliography

Amit, E., Algom, D., & Trope, Y. (2009). Distance-dependent processing of pictures and words. *Journal of Experimental Psychology: General, 138*, 400–415.

Amit, E., Wakslak, C. J., & Trope, Y. (2013). The use of visual and verbal means of communication across psychological distance. *Personality and Social Psychology Bulletin, 39*, 826–838.

Bandura, A. (1977). *Social learning theory.* Engelwood Cliffs, NJ: Prentice Hall.

Bandura, A., Ross, D., & Ross, S. A. (1963). Imitation of film-mediated aggressive models. *Journal of Abnormal and Social Psychology, 66*, 3–11.

Boyd, R., Richerson, P. J., & Henrich, J. (2011). The cultural niche: Why social learning is essential for human adaptation. *Proceedings of the National Academy of Science of the United States of America, 108*, 10918–10925.

Gilead, M., Trope, Y., & Liberman, N. (forthcoming). *Above and beyond the concrete: The diverse representational substrates of the prospective mind.*

Grice, H. P. (1975). Logic and conversation. In P. Cole & J. L. Morgan (Eds.), *Syntax and semantics: Vol. 3. Speech acts* (pp. 41–58). New York, NY: Academic Press.

Hansen, J., Alves, H., & Trope, Y. (2016). Psychological distance reduces literal imitation: Evidence from an imitation-learning paradigm. *Journal of Experimental Psychology: Human Perception and Performance, 42*, 320–330.

Henrich, J. (2015). *The secret of our success: How culture is driving human evolution, domesticating our species, and making us smarter.* Princeton, NJ: Princeton University Press.

Joshi, P., & Wakslak, C. J. (2014). Communicating with the crowd: Speakers use abstract messages when addressing larger audiences. *Journal of Experimental Psychology: General, 143*, 351–362.

Joshi, P. D., Wakslak, C. J., Raj, M., & Trope, Y. (2016). Communicating with distant others: The functional use of abstraction. *Social Psychological and Personality Science, 7*, 37–44.

Kalkstein, D. A., Kleiman, T., Wakslak, C. J., Liberman, N., & Trope, Y. (2016). Social learning across psychological distance. *Journal of Personality and Social Psychology, 110*, 1–19.

Ledgerwood, A., Trope, Y., & Liberman, N. (2015). Construal level theory and regulatory scope. In *Emerging Trends in the Social and Behavioral Sciences.* Hoboken, NJ: John Wiley and Sons.

Liberman, N., & Trope, Y. (2008). The psychology of transcending the here and now. *Science, 322*, 1201–1205.

Liberman, N., & Trope, Y. (2014). Traversing psychological distance. *Trends in Cognitive Sciences, 18*, 364–369.

Potts, R. (1996). Evolution and climate variability. *Science, 273*, 922–923.

Potts, R. (1998). Variability selection in hominid-evolution. *Evolutionary Anthropology, 7*, 81–96.

Rosch, E., Mervis, C. B., Gray, W. D., Johnson, D. M., & Boyes-Braem, P. (1976). Basic objects in natural categories. *Cognitive Psychology, 8*, 382–439.

Roth, G., & Dicke, U. (2005). Evolution of the brain and intelligence. *Trends in Cognitive Sciences, 9*, 250–257.

Trope, Y., & Liberman, N. (2010). Construal level theory of psychological distance. *Psychological Review, 117*, 440–463.

Vallacher, R. R., & Wegner, D. M. (1987). What do people think they're doing? Action identification and human behavior. *Psychological Review, 94*(1), 3–15.

PART IV

Social and Cultural Factors in Living Well

14

SATISFYING AND MEANINGFUL CLOSE RELATIONSHIPS

Shelly L. Gable

There are some things that people just cannot live without—at least for very long—things like air, food, and water. The human body and mind are designed to ensure these necessities are obtained. Hunger is experienced when food is needed, thirst is felt when water is required, panic sets in when air supplies are cut off, and bodies shiver when their temperatures drop. A question that has long been pondered by songwriters and scholars alike is whether people need close relationships in the same way they need air, food, water, and shelter. Was Janis Joplin right when she said she needed relationships just the same as she needed air to breathe?[1] Can people live without relationships? Can they live well?

Psychologists have considered the existence of a motive for social bonds in one way or another for many years. In 1938 Henry Murray proposed a list of needs; among them was the need for affiliation. This need, along with two others (achievement and power) has been the focus of a good deal of psychological research. Today, few psychologists dispute the fact that humans are social creatures. An early view was that our social nature was a by-product of other basic needs. For example, Freud saw our need for relationships as a consequence of the ever-present sexual drive. And behaviorists viewed our fondness for relationships to be a product of learned associations resulting from repeated instances in which other people were paired with rewards, such as parents who provided food. In the 1950s this view began to crumble in the face of contradictory evidence, such as the evidence from laboratories of scientists like Harry Harlow (1958), who reported that during times of stress infant monkeys preferred their soft cloth monkey "mothers" that provided no reward except comfort to their wire monkey "mother" that provided food and water.

It is fair to say that current scientific thinking readily acknowledges that the act of forming bonds with people can motivate our behavior, rather than viewing human sociality solely as a derivative of other basic needs. It is also clear from the evolutionary historical record that our species evolved to live in small groups, such that our ancestors' probability of survival greatly increased when they shared benevolent ties with those around them (e.g., Beckes & Coan, 2011; Tooby & Cosmides, 1990). In this volume, von Hippel and Gonsalkorale argue that evolution has linked the feeling of happiness and well-being to social bonds through natural selection. Other (more recent) historical evidence supports this. Donald Grayson's (1990) analysis of the ill-fated Donner Party[2] from 1846 revealed that having social connections within the traveling party increased the chance of surviving the winter on the desolate mountain pass. Although the very young, the very old, and men were at greater risk, even in these groups those without family and social ties in the group were the most likely to perish under these harsh conditions. And Durkheim's (1897) careful observation of church records concluded that lack of social connections was a risk factor for suicide, and in doing so he helped found the field of empirical sociology.

However, the question of whether people actually need to bond with others in order to survive and thrive was systematically addressed in a comprehensive review by Baumeister and Leary (1995). The authors first laid out a list of criteria that would have to be met in order for something to be considered a basic and fundamental need like the needs for air, food, water, and shelter. An important criterion was that we should expect to see negative health and well-being consequences if social needs were not met, especially in the long term. At the time of that review, and during the years since that review, a increasing mountain of evidence that *social ties are strongly associated with well-being and physical health* has been built (e.g., Akerlind, Hörnquist, & Hansson, 1987; House, Landis, & Umberson, 1988; Holt-Lunstad, Smith, & Layton, 2010).

Social Relationships and Physical Health

Although the main focus of this chapter is on the role that social relationships play in psychological well-being, clearly one aspect of a *good life* is the existence of that life (i.e., mortality) and physical health and disease occurrence. On the topic of mortality, it has long been known that having social bonds (versus not having bonds) is near the top of the list of sources of variance in mortality (e.g., Berkman & Syme, 1979). In their early review, House, Landis, and Umberson (1988) found that a lack of strong social ties had a similar-sized association with mortality as smoking and high blood pressure. A similar conclusion was reached in a striking recent review of the epidemiological literature by Holt-Lunstad and her colleagues that enumerated the substantial association that social bonds have on mortality (Holt-Lunstad, Smith, & Layton, 2010). Specifically, in their meta-analysis they reviewed 148 longitudinal epidemiological studies. The studies included measures of the existence and/or quality of social bonds and measures of mortality (excluding studies that examined death by suicide or injury). Across the studies reviewed, the time between the assessment of relationship predictors and later mortality ranged from three months to 58 *years*, with an average of 7.5 years of time between assessments. Echoing these effects, Simpson and colleagues (this volume) present evidence that early parenting quality predicts physical health 30 years later, suggesting that relationship quality even in early life may have a long-term impact on health.

The quantitative meta-analysis results revealed a strong link between having social connections with others, especially high-quality connections, and mortality. Although the effect sizes ranged systematically depending upon the indicator of social ties (i.e., whether the study had a rough estimate of social ties such as marital status, or a rich estimate of social ties such as quality of one's network), there is no doubt that social ties are powerful. To put the social ties associations into context, the average effect sizes were as robust predictors of death (or in most cases, more robust) as other well-established mortality risks such as excessive alcohol use, obesity, and failure to treat hypertension. Moreover, of the studies that included complex measures of social integration (e.g., loneliness), those who perceived a lack of social ties were 40% more likely to be dead at follow-up than those who reported feeling connected to others (Holt-Lunstad, Smith, & Layton, 2010).

Although the next generation of research questions is focusing on illuminating pathways that link relationship quality to health outcomes, some clues already appear in the literature. For example, Uchino, Cacioppo, and Kiecolt-Glaser (1996) reviewed 81 studies on social support and social integration and found a consistent association between social ties and increased positive physiological functioning of the cardiovascular, endocrine, and immune systems. Dickerson and Kemeny (2004) conducted a meta-analysis showing that physiological reactions to a laboratory stressor via a heightened cortisol response were most pronounced when the individual was socially threatened. Cole and colleagues (2007) found that chronically lonely individuals had elevated pro-inflammatory activity, a profile associated with increased risk for inflammatory disease.

The picture linking social ties to health and mortality is not all rosy. That is, what is also clear from this work is the realization that only high-quality and rewarding social ties predict outcomes. The majority of social relationships are rewarding, thankfully; however, there are dark sides to our social ties in that there are many potential negative consequences of interpersonal relationships (e.g., Rook, 1984). Potential drawbacks of intimate social ties include threat of abandonment, exploitation, and conflict; and these qualities predict decrements in health (e.g., Kiecolt-Glaser & Newton, 2001; Miller, Rohleder, & Cole, 2009). For example, hostile conflict and negative emotionality in marriage is associated with increased cardiac death (Eaker et al., 2007; Wilcox, Kasl, & Berkman, 1994); and caustic interaction in dyads are associated with increased dysregulation of immune functioning and unhealthy cardiovascular reactivity (Kiecolt-Glaser, 1999; Uchino, Holt-Lunstad, Uno, & Flinders, 2001). It should also be noted that social relationships can pose direct threat to physical health and mortality in the form of abusive relationships and intimate partner violence (e.g., Ellsberg et al., 2008). Thus, although the empirical record makes clear that social isolation and a lack of connections bode poorly for physical health and mortality, that same literature also indicates that low-quality, hostile, and caustic social bonds are harmful as well. Of course, any close relationship can have both rewarding and costly components (see Uchino et al., 2013) and can exert positive and negative forces on health (see also Gable & Gosnell, 2013).

Social Relationships and Well-Being

More central to the theme of the current volume, the literature has also found that social relationships are a consistent, and often the top, source of psychological health (see Berscheid & Reis, 1998, for a review). In the clinical field, research has consistently documented an association between social isolation/ loneliness and mood disturbances (e.g., depression) and disorders such as schizophrenia, personality disorders, and substance abuse (e.g., Akerlind, Hörnquist, & Hansson, 1987; Overholser, 1992; Neeleman & Power, 1994). Turning from research on clinical disorders and toward work focused more broadly on psychological well-being, there is ample evidence that loneliness and well-being are consistently and strongly negatively correlated (e.g., Helliwell & Putnam, 2004; Vanderweele, et al., 2011). Studies routinely find having rewarding social and family relationships to be the best predictors of overall life satisfaction compared to other domains of human activity, such as career, financial attainment, and so forth (e.g., Campbell, Converse, & Rodgers, 1976). Of course, these strong associations do not tell us whether lower mental health (or lower well-being) leads to interpersonal disruptions or vice versa; however, longitudinal studies clearly show evidence that both pathways (e.g., depression leading to later loneliness and loneliness leading to later depression) occur (e.g., Cacioppo, Hughes, Waite, Hawkley, & Thisted, 2006; Whisman & Bruce, 1999).

Similarly, studies have found that a clear characteristic distinguishing those who are very happy (i.e., upper 25%) from those who are less happy (i.e., lowest 25%) is the existence of social ties and the quality of those ties (e.g., Diener & Seligman, 2002; Vanderweele, et al., 2011). What is also remarkable is that the link between social relationships and well-being has been noted at every stage of the human development—children, adolescent, young adults, and older adults (e.g., Chen & Feeley, 2014; Sherman, Lansford, & Volling, 2006; Rönkä et al., 2014; Bradshaw, Hoelscher, & Richardson, 2007). The ubiquitous evidence of the strong association between relationships and well-being across the life span is reflected in theories of well-being as well. Models of eudaimonic well-being include social relationship quality or social connectedness as an integral component (e.g., Deci & Ryan, 2000; Ryff, 1995).

Mirroring the literature on social ties and physical health, the literature on social ties and psychological well-being also makes it clear that quality matters and that there are potential risks to well-being inherent in our relationships. Potential costs such as fears of, and experiences with, rejection and abandonment have well-documented (negative) associations with psychological health (e.g., Baron et al., 2007; Downey, Feldman, & Ayduk, 2000; Mikulincer, 1998). Hostility and conflict in interactions with relationship partners contributes to psychopathological symptoms such as depression, anxiety, and substance abuse (e.g., Davila, Bradbury, Cohan, & Tochluk, 1997; Whisman, 2001; Whisman, Uebelacker, & Settles, 2010). Similarly, a lack of trust and security in relationships has a profound effect on self-esteem and well-being (e.g., Holmes, 2002).

In summary, a lack of social connections is associated with well-being deficits but the existence of social relationships alone does not automatically coincide with higher well-being; these relationships need to be characterized by minimal hostility and insecurity and high warmth. Researchers have argued as to whether overall well-being influences the likelihood that people will form and maintain social relationships or whether high-quality relationships influence well-being. The short conclusion is that there is evidence for both directions of influence. Importantly for the current chapter, there is sufficient longitudinal evidence and analogue experimental studies to conclude that high-quality social relationships contribute substantially to an individual's overall well-being (e.g., Holt-Lunstad et al., 2010; Hawkley et al., 2009). The questions of how and through what pathways social ties contribute to well-being are the focus of the remainder of this chapter. To this end, three components of well-being will be examined: reduced negative affect, increased positive affect, and the experience of life as having meaning and purpose. I will consider each potential pathway separately.

Relationships and Reduced Negative Affect

Negative emotions are critical for our survival. Feelings such as fear, anger, sadness, and guilt are appropriate reactions to environmental stimuli and social situations, and can facilitate adaptive responding in various contexts, as outlined by Forgas and colleagues (this volume). Thus the experience of negative emotions is not antithetical to well-being. However, the experience of negative emotions out of proportion in size or time with the situation, or experiencing negative emotion in absence of actual negative stimuli, is not conducive to well-being. One of the main challenges in life is the regulation of emotional experience (e.g., Gross, 1998), especially the regulation of negative emotional experience. Processes known broadly as social support have emerged as a potential explanation for the reason that social relationships are linked tightly with well-being. It is well known that relationship partners (family, friends, and romantic partners) help mitigate the detrimental effect that negative events and stress have on well-being (e.g., Hawkley et al., 2009).

Social Support

Some of the most consistent findings in the literature are that perceptions of the availability of support are closely tied to relationship quality and well-being (e.g., Kaul & Lakey, 2003). In fact many theories of relationship health include the importance of perceptions that the partner will respond to our needs when we are under stress (e.g., Reis, Clark, & Holmes, 2004). And we also know that people who feel insecure and dissatisfied in close relationships also perceive that others will not be reliably available to them in times of need (e.g., Blain, Thompson, Whiffen, 1993; Rholes, Simpson, Campbell, & Grich, 2001). Lonely people are also less likely to perceive that others will be there for them in times of stress (Russell, 1996) than people who are not lonely. In short, perceptions of the availability of social support are closely tied to both relationship functioning and well-being.

However, the consistency in findings is limited to studies that link perceptions of future available support to well-being and relationship health. When we turn to finding support that is actually enacted by others, called enacted or received support, the findings are more mixed (e.g., Barbee, Derlega, Sherburne, & Grimshaw, 1998; Dakof & Taylor, 1990). That is, the receipt of support from others is sometimes associated with decreases in negative emotions and other times it is associated with increased negative emotion, and other times there is no association between the two. A striking example of this was a pair of prospective studies of mortality in people by Krause (1997a) in which greater perceived availability of support was associated with decreased mortality risk, but receiving actual support was associated with a smaller but significant increase in mortality risk. Another paper by Krause (1997b) showed a similar pattern in predicting depression. The author hypothesized that receiving support can have a detrimental effect on health because of potential inadvertent consequences of receiving support (a point that has been borne out in later research and covered below) even while contributing to the perceptions of future support availability. However, one difficult confound to tease apart is that stress and health status are likely linked, such that those who are in worse health or under more stress may receive more support. However, studies that are able to tease apart these factors still show that received support has a negative impact on outcomes beyond its co-occurrence with poor health (e.g., Forster & Stoller, 1992; Rini, Schetter, Hobel, Glynn, & Sandman; 2006). More central to the current theme is that sometimes receipt of support is associated with reductions in stress and negative emotions and sometimes it is not, and this is independent of the effects of perception of the availability of support (Gleason, Iida, Bolger, & Shrout, 2008).

Researchers have proposed some possible reasons for the apparent risks of enacted support. One set of explanations revolves around the unintended consequences of received support; receiving support from others can bring costs because it may be a blow to one's self-esteem because a vulnerability or weakness has been made salient, or it may draw more attention to the problem (e.g., Bolger et al., 2000). Relatedly, receiving support may lead the recipient to feel overly indebted, incompetent, or weak (Gleason et al., 2003; Shrout, Herman, & Bolger, 2006). So, while receiving support may be helpful for reducing negative emotions (e.g., by helping solve the problem), that same support may also increase negative emotions and insecurities in the recipient.

Evidence for these ideas was found in Bolger and colleagues' (2000) work on invisible support. The authors hypothesized that support that is most effective at reducing distress is support that is not recognized as support by the recipient. For example, Bolger and colleagues (2000) conducted a study examining the effects of actual support interactions. They found that stressed individuals reported better outcomes (e.g., lower anxiety) on days that their partner reported providing support but they did not report receiving support themselves (which the researchers called "invisible support") compared to days the stressed recipient reported receiving support from the partner (called "visible support"). One explanation for these intriguing findings is that invisible support avoids the unintended risks of support provision while maximizing the potential gains.

Another reason that received support may not always reduce negative emotions is that it is actually very difficult to provide high-quality support. A good deal of support that is intended to be helpful can miss the mark or not be delivered in a skilled manner and as such is unhelpful and perhaps even harmful to the recipient (e.g., Dunkel-Schetter & Bennett, 1990; Lehman, Ellard, & Wortman, 1986; Rafaeli & Gleason, 2009). Support that is higher in quality or responsive to the recipient's needs is more likely to be associated with a reduction in distress for the recipient. Rini and colleagues (2006) found a linear association between the effectiveness of enacted support and outcomes, essentially indicating that more effective support was associated with lower anxiety and less effective support was associated with greater anxiety and distress than not receiving support at all. Maisel and Gable (2009) showed that effective support is support that conveys understanding, validation, and caring to the recipient. This quality of an interaction is known as responsiveness and is discussed in more detail in later sections of this chapter. However, we know that while not always effective at reducing negative emotions and distress, social support from close others has the potential to help regulate negative emotions in the recipient.

Relationships and Increased Positive Emotions

Although most work on emotion regulation has focused on the reduction of negative affect, there is good reason to examine the experience of positive emotions. It is often in the context of relationship that we experience positive emotions, and social partners can help regulate positive emotions by maintaining or increasing positive affective states in others. The role that close relationships play in positive affective states is particularly important given the strong links between positive emotions and health and well-being (Fredrickson, this volume; Sheldon, this volume). In the next sections I consider three processes through which social relationships and positive emotions are intertwined.

Capitalization

It is an unpleasant fact that negative events occur in everyone's life. A more pleasant fact of life is that positive events happen too, and in greater frequency than negative events. Mirroring the vast literature on social support showing that people turn to others to help them cope with negative events, research on *capitalization* has shown that people often turn to others to help them make the most of their good news (e.g., Gable, Reis, Impett, & Asher, 2004). The initial research on capitalization (Gable et al., 2004) found that people derive additional benefits, such as increased daily positive affect and daily well-being, when they share positive events with other people. The effects observed were above and beyond the benefits associated with the positive event itself. More importantly, these early studies made it clear that positive events were shared almost exclusively with close relationship partners, such as friends, siblings, parents, roommates, or romantic partners; only occasionally did people share their events with non-close others, such as coworkers and acquaintances.

This near exclusive involvement of close others in capitalization disclosures suggests that the process is dyadic. Consistent with this observation, research on capitalization has found that the response of the person with whom the event is shared plays a critical role in the outcomes for the discloser. Research has found that responses to capitalization attempts vary along two dimensions, the active to passive dimension and the constructive to destructive dimension (Gable et al., 2004; Gable et al., 2006). Thus, there are four prototypes of responses to capitalization attempts: active-constructive responses, passive-constructive responses, active-destructive responses, and passive-destructive responses. When a responder provides an active-constructive response, he expresses excitement or enthusiasm about the positive event and is actively involved in the interaction. The responder likely asks questions about the event, elaborates on the implication of the event for the discloser, and talks about the meaning of the event to the discloser in particular. When a responder provides a passive-constructive response, he also expresses a positive reaction to the event, but this reaction is restrained. The passive-constructive responder says little about the event but conveys quiet positive support during the exchange. When a responder provides an active-destructive response, his response is similar to an active-constructive response in terms of its level of involvement, but the feedback is predominantly negative. An active-destructive responder may point out possible negative consequences of the event, or interpret the event less kindly than the discloser, or even minimize the importance of the event. Finally, when a responder provides a passive-destructive response, he simply fails to acknowledge the positive event being disclosed, either by changing the subject to discuss something else or bringing up his own positive event.

The research has shown that active-constructive and not passive or destructive responses to capitalization attempts are associated with more positive personal outcomes as well as higher relationship quality, as indicated by a variety of measures (e.g., positive affect, well-being, relationship satisfaction, trust, liking; see Gable & Anderson, 2016 for a review). Research has also found that active-constructive responses provide signals that the responder understands the discloser and values his or her abilities, talents, motivation, or even luck associated with the positive event. In addition, active-constructive responses convey caring for the discloser. Passive or destructive responses signal a lack of understanding, valuing, and concern for the discloser (see Maisel & Gable, 2009; Gable et al., 2012). This combination of understanding, validation, and caring is referred to as responsiveness to the self (Reis, Clark, & Holmes, 2004) and has been shown to be a consistent mediator of the interpersonal and intrapersonal outcomes associated with capitalization (e.g., Gable et al., 2006; Maisel & Gable, 2009; Maisel, Gable, & Strachman, 2008). Additionally, work on capitalization processes suggests that these interactions provide an important opportunity for people in relationships to foster intimacy and closeness through supportive exchanges without the drawback of risking one's self-esteem or self-worth, as one might do when seeking support for a negative event (e.g., Bolger, Zuckerman, & Kessler, 2000; Rafaeli & Gleason, 2009).

Gratitude

Empirical research on gratitude has largely focused on gratitude as an intrapersonal emotion and examined associations with personal outcomes (see McCullough, Emmons, & Tsang, 2002, for a review). For example, research in the "counting blessings" tradition (e.g., Emmons & McCullough, 2003) focused on individuals taking time to reflect on and to be grateful for life's gifts as a solitary exercise. However, Algoe and colleagues (Algoe & Haidt, 2009; Algoe, Haidt, & Gable, 2008; Algoe, Gable, & Maisel, 2010; Algoe, Fredrickson, & Gable, 2013) focused on the fact that gratitude often arises when a benefactor provides some type of benefit for the recipient; and there is often some type of relationship between benefactor and recipient. Taking a social-functional perspective on gratitude, Algoe (2012) theorized that gratitude promotes relationship formation and maintenance. For example, in terms of relationship formation, Algoe and Haidt (2009) found that participants who were assigned to recall events that evoked feelings of gratitude were more likely to report that they noticed new positive qualities about the person who provided the benefit (i.e., the benefactor) and that they wanted to spend more time with their benefactors in the future than those who recalled events that evoked happiness (only) with another person. In terms of relationship maintenance, in a daily experience study of cohabiting couples, participants reported on their emotions and behaviors (Algoe, Gable, & Maisel, 2010), and the receipt of thoughtful benefits predicted gratitude in both men and women. Importantly, participants' gratitude on one day predicted an increase in relationship satisfaction the following day, for both the recipient of the thoughtful benefit and his or her partner. Algoe et al. (2013) found evidence that the cross–partner effects were attributable to the expression of gratitude. Algoe (2012) refers to the function of gratitude in relationships as find, remind, and bind.

Love

Love is a topic that has been of interest to poets, musicians, and playwrights for as long as there have been poems, songs, and plays.[3] However, love as an emotion or emotional state has been a topic of study in fits and starts in empirical psychology over time. Harlow's (1958) seminal observation that maternal love was something beyond secondary reinforcement in his cloth and wire monkey experiments was an early milestone in the field. Bowlby (1969) also theorized that love and attachment bonds were part of the mind's architecture and critical to human development. Beyond parent-child accounts of love, work on love in adults has proposed that several different types of love exist (e.g., Sternberg, 1986). However, the bulk of the empirical work has centered on just two kinds: passionate love and companionate love (e.g., Berscheid, 2010). The intense excitement and attraction we feel for someone else is referred to as passionate love, whereas the affection and liking we have for someone else is referred to as companionate love.

Several theorists have argued that passionate love functions to foster attraction and relationship initiation (e.g., Keltner & Haidt, 1999). Researchers have argued and provided empirical evidence for the idea that passion's primary role is to disrupt one from one's current activities to direct energies to initiate a new relationship while companionate love's function is to motivate the maintenance of an existing relationship (e.g., Gonzaga et al., 2006). Consistent with these hypotheses, research has shown that the experience of intense passionate love, such as that experienced in the beginning of a new relationship (e.g., Aron et al., 2005), is associated with changes in the self-concept and self-esteem (Aron, Paris, & Aron, 1995). Also consistent with these functional approaches, companionate love has been associated with commitment and intimacy and is a central feature of communal relationships—relationships characterized by mutual expectations that each will respond to the other's needs (Clark, Mills & Powell, 1986). Companionate love has also been found to be highly predictive of long-term romantic relationship satisfaction and maintenance (e.g., Huston et al., 2001). In short, both passionate love and companionate love are important positive emotional states that are central features of adult close relationships.

Relationships and the Regulation of Emotion More Broadly

Social support and capitalization processes are examples of how social partners can help regulate emotions. However, this work is likely only the tip of the iceberg in terms of how social partners can regulate others' emotion. That is, the work on social support and capitalization focuses on a very limited segment of possible emotion regulation strategies. In contrast, Gross (1998) described a wide array of strategies employed that range from the selection of situations that have a high probability of eliciting certain emotions (e.g., attending an exciting concert or putting on earphones to listen to jazz) to the suppression of the outward signals of an emotion once it is experienced (e.g., keeping anger from showing on your face or smiling during a stressful speech). This process model of emotion regulation separates emotion regulation strategies that are focused on the antecedents of an emotional experience—situation selection, situation modification, attentional deployment, cognitive change—from the strategies employed in response to the experience of the emotion—experiential modulation, behavior change, physiological modulation (Gross, 1998).

In these terms social support and capitalization are strategies largely aimed at cognitive change and possibly experiential modulation. Similarly, a major limitation of the theoretical and empirical work on adult emotion regulation is that it has treated emotion regulation as almost exclusively an intrapersonal process and not an interpersonal process (e.g., Zaki & Williams, 2013). Thus an area of future research is to more carefully and fully examine how individuals employ members of the close social networks to regulate their own emotions across the temporal spectrum of emotion regulation described by Gross (1998). Moreover, a virtually untouched area of research lies in how social partners might attempt to regulate another's emotional experience with or without that target's explicit awareness. By more fully understanding these processes, researchers will provide a clearer picture of how close others contribute to well-being through emotion regulation.

Relationships and Meaning and Purpose in Life

Recent work on meaning has shown that people who feel that their lives have a sense of meaning (purpose, significance, and coherence; King, Heintzelman, & Ward, 2016) also feel that they are connected to others, feel as if they belong, and feel supported by others in their social networks (Hicks & King, 2007), whereas when people are ostracized or socially excluded they feel their lives lack meaning (e.g., Stillman et al., 2009; Zadro, Williams, & Richardson, 2004). This recent work on the concept of meaning dovetails nicely with earlier findings reporting that people routinely cited close relationships among their most important life goals and aspirations (e.g., Emmons, 1999). When describing the factors that give life meaning, most people mention close relationships more than other domains of activity (e.g., Klinger, 1977). How exactly close relationships might contribute to a sense of meaning has not been given a great deal of attention. However, work on the role that close relationships play in personal growth may shed some light on these links.

Self-Growth

In the close relationships literature, two of the lines of research which have focused on the role that close relationships play in personal growth are self-expansion theory and the Michelangelo Phenomenon. Self-expansion in relationships (e.g., Aron, Aron, Tudor, & Nelson, 1991) refers to idea that we include a close other's characteristics (e.g., resources, traits, perspectives) in our conception of the self. The theory of self-expansion is supported by empirical evidence such that in close relationships, mental models of the self and other are closely tied and seem to overlap with one other. Moreover, the closer the relationship the greater this degree of overlap, which renders a partner's personal qualities and resources less distinguishable from the personal qualities and resources of the self. It is also likely that self-expansion contributes to relationship quality. Studies have demonstrated that creating opportunities for self-expansion in the lab leads to increases in relationship satisfaction (Aron et al., 2000). Aron and colleagues (2000) have also found that romantic partners' participation in novel, arousing experiences together in their day-to-day life is associated with increases in relationship satisfaction, presumably because these experiences offer opportunities for continued expansion. Evidence for self-expansion exists not only in romantic couples but also in less close ties (e.g., Fraley & Aron, 2004). Interestingly, other work has shown the interpersonal closeness can motivate self-expansion processes (e.g., Slotter & Gardner, 2009). In this work Slotter and Gardner (2009) found that when people anticipate (or desire) closeness with another person they more readily integrate aspects of the other person into their own self-concept. It remains to be seen if and how the desire for closeness in established relationships may facilitate self-expansion.

The other line of research focusing on self-growth in the context of relationships is work on the Michelangelo Phenomenon (e.g., Drigotas, Rusbult, Weiselquist, & Whitton, 1999, Drigotas, 2002; Rusbult, Kumashiro, Kubacka, & Finkel, 2009). This research posits that close relationship partners are active participants in one another's personal development and that close partners can promote (or hinder) one's pursuit of the ideal self. Rusbult and her colleagues used the term Michelangelo Phenomenon to elegantly invoke Michelangelo Buonarroti's description of the sculptor's release of an ideal figure from a block of stone (Rusbult et al., 2005). One's personal ideal can be an explicit, clearly defined set of goals, or a vaguer collection of dreams or aspirations. Empirical work on the Michelangelo Phenomenon has shown that relationship partners help (or hinder) the growth toward the ideal self by treating their partners as if they (already) are that ideal self and eliciting aspects of the ideal self from the partner through their interactions (Rusbult et al., 2009). Partner affirmations are associated with the partner feeling more similar to his or her ideal self and higher personal well-being and relationship quality (Drigotas, 2002; Drigotas et al., 1999; Rusbult et al., 2009).

Conclusions

Social relationships are closely linked to our social connections. When people have abundant and satisfying social ties, they report higher well-being. Indeed, many theories of well-being contain social relationships as a necessary ingredient for well-being. In this chapter I reviewed evidence in support of this link. In addition, I reviewed the likely reasons for this. Social bonds can help regulate stress. They are also a primary vehicle for the experience of positive emotions. Finally, social relationships are part of meaning and purpose, and relationships' role in personal growth may be a large part of this link. In sum, you cannot live the good life without good relationships.

Notes

1 "*. . . I need a man to love. I gotta find him, I gotta have him like the air I breathe. One lovin' man to understand can't be too much to need*" ~ Janis Joplin, from "I Need a Man to Love."
2 The Donner Party was a group of about 90 pioneers who set out to travel west from Illinois to California by covered wagon in 1846. They became snowbound for the winter of 1846–47 and ran out of provisions; only half of them survived.
3 The oldest surviving love poem is Sumerian, a verse from a bride to a bridegroom, written on a clay tablet around 3500 BC.

Bibliography

Akerlind, I., Hörnquist, J. O., & Hansson, B. (1987). Loneliness correlates in advanced alcohol abusers: I. Social factors and needs. *Scandinavian Journal of Social Medicine, 15*(3), 175–183.

Algoe, S. B. (2012). Find, remind, and bind: The functions of gratitude in everyday relationships. *Social and Personality Psychology Compass, 6*(6), 455–469.

Algoe, S. B., Fredrickson, B. L., & Gable, S. L. (2013). The social functions of the emotion of gratitude via expression. *Emotion, 13*(4), 605.

Algoe, S. B., Gable, S. L., & Maisel, N. C. (2010). It's the little things: Everyday gratitude as a booster shot for romantic relationships. *Personal Relationships, 17*(2), 217–233.

Algoe, S. B., & Haidt, J. D. (2009). Witnessing excellence in action: The "other-praising" emotions of elevation, gratitude, and admiration. *Journal of Positive Psychology, 4*, 105–127.

Algoe, S., Haidt, J., & Gable, S. L. (2008). Beyond reciprocity: Gratitude and relationships in everyday life. *Emotion, 8*, 425–429.

Aron, A., Aron, E. N., Tudor, M., & Nelson, G. (1991). Close relationships as including other in the self. *Journal of Personality and Social Psychology, 60*(2), 241–253.

Aron, A., Fisher, H., Mashek, D. J., Strong, G., Li, H., & Brown, L. L. (2005). Reward, motivation, and emotion systems associated with early-stage intense romantic love. *Journal of Neurophysiology, 94*(1), 327–337.

Aron, A., Norman, C. C., Aron, E. N., McKenna, C., & Heyman, R. (2000). Couples' shared participation in novel and arousing activities and experienced relationship quality. *Journal of Personality and Social Psychology, 78*(2), 273–283.

Aron, A., Paris, M., & Aron, E. N. (1995). Falling in love: Prospective studies of self-concept change. *Journal of Personality and Social Psychology, 69*(6), 1102.

Barbee, A. P., Derlega, V. J., Sherburne, S. P., & Grimshaw, A. (1998). Helpful and unhelpful forms of social support for HIV-positive individuals. In V. J. Derlega & A. P. Barbee (Eds.), *HIV and social interaction* (pp. 83–105). Thousand Oaks, CA: Sage.

Baron, K. G., Smith, T. W., Butner, J., Nealey-Moore, J., Hawkins, M. W., & Uchino, B. N. (2007). Hostility, anger, and marital adjustment: Concurrent and prospective associations with psychosocial vulnerability. *Journal of Behavioral Medicine*, *30*(1), 1e10. http://dx.doi.org/10.1007/s10865-006-9086

Baumeister, R. F., & Leary, M. R. (1995). The need to belong: Desire for interpersonal attachments as a fundamental human motivation. *Psychological Bulletin*, *117*(3), 497–529.

Beckes, L., & Coan, J. A. (2011). Social baseline theory: The role of social proximity in emotion and economy of action. *Social and Personality Psychology Compass*, *5*(12), 976–988.

Berkman, L. F., & Syme, S. L. (1979). Social networks, host resistance and mortality: A nine-year follow-up of Alameda County residents. *American Journal of Epidemiology*, *109*, 186–204.

Berscheid, E. (2010). Love in the fourth dimension. *Annual review of psychology*, 61, 1–25.

Berscheid, E., & Reis, H. T. (1998). Attraction and close relationships. In D. T. Gilbert, S. T. Fiske, & G. Lindzey (Eds.), *The handbook of social psychology* (Vols. 1–2, pp. 193–281). New York, NY: McGraw-Hill.

Blain, M. D., Thompson, J. M., & Whiffen, V. E. (1993). Attachment and perceived social support in late adolescence: The interaction between working models of self and others. *Journal of Adolescent Research*, *8*(2), 226–241.

Bolger, N., Zuckerman, A., & Kessler, R. C. (2000). Invisible support and adjustment to stress. *Journal of Personality and Social Psychology*, *79*(6), 953–961.

Bowlby, J. (1969). *Attachment: Attachment and loss*. New York: Basic Books.

Bradshaw, J., Hoelscher, P., & Richardson, D. (2007). An index of child well-being in the European Union. *Social Indicators Research*, *80*(1), 133–177.

Brown, S. L., Nesse, R. M., Vinokur, A. D., & Smith, D. M. (2003). Providing social support may be more beneficial than receiving it: Results from a prospective study of mortality. *Psychological Science*, *14*(4), 320–327.

Cacioppo, J. T., Hughes, M. E., Waite, L. J., Hawkley, L. C., & Thisted, R. A. (2006). Loneliness as a specific risk factor for depressive symptoms: Cross-sectional and longitudinal analyses. *Psychology and Aging*, *21*(1), 140–151.

Campbell, A., Converse, P. E., & Rodgers, W. L. (1976). *The quality of American life: Perceptions, evaluations, and satisfactions*. New York, NY: Russell Sage Foundation.

Chen, Y., & Feeley, T. H. (2014). Social support, social strain, loneliness, and well-being among older adults: An analysis of the health and retirement study. *Journal of Social and Personal Relationships*, *31*(2), 141–161.

Clark, M. S., Mills, J., & Powell, M. C. (1986). Keeping track of needs in communal and exchange relationships. *Journal of Personality and Social Psychology*, *51*(2), 333–345.

Cole, S. W., Hawkley, L. C., Arevalo, J. M., Sung, C. Y., Rose, R. M., & Cacioppo, J. T. (2007). Social regulation of gene expression in human leukocytes. *Genome Biology*, *8*(9), R189.

Dakof, G. A., & Taylor, S. E. (1990). Victims' perceptions of social support: What is helpful from whom? *Journal of Personality and Social Psychology*, *58*(1), 80.

Davila, J., Bradbury, T. N., Cohan, C. L., & Tochluk, S. (1997). Marital functioning and depressive symptoms: Evidence for a stress generation model. *Journal of Personality and Social Psychology*, *73*(4), 849.

Deci, E. L., & Ryan, R. M. (2000). The "what" and "why" of goal pursuits: Human needs and the self-determination of behavior. *Psychological Inquiry*, *11*(4), 227–268.

Dickerson, S. S., & Kemeny, M. E. (2004). Acute stressors and cortisol responses: A theoretical integration and synthesis of laboratory research. *Psychological Bulletin*, *130*(3), 355.

Diener, E., & Seligman, M. E. P. (2002). Very happy people. *Psychological Science*, *13*(1), 81–84.

Downey, G., Feldman, S., & Ayduk, O. (2000). Rejection sensitivity and male violence in romantic relationships. *Personal Relationships*, *7*(1), 45–61.

Drigotas, S. M. (2002). The Michelangelo phenomenon and personal well-being. *Journal of Personality*, *70*, 59–77.

Drigotas, S. M., Rusbult, C. E., Wieselquist, J., & Whitton, S. (1999). Close partner as sculptor of the ideal self: Behavioral affirmation and the Michelangelo phenomenon. *Journal of Personality and Social Psychology*, *77*, 293–323.

Dunkel-Schetter, C., & Bennett, T. L. (1990). Differentiating the cognitive and behavioral aspects of social support. In B. R. Sarason, I. G. Sarason, & G. R. Pierce (Eds.), *Social support: An interactional view* (pp. 267–296). Oxford, UK: John Wiley & Sons.

Durkheim, E. (1897). *Le suicide: Etude de sociologie* [English translation 1951 *Suicide*]. New York, NY: Free Press.

Eaker, E. D., Sullivan, L. M., Kelly-Hayes, M., D'Agostino Sr, R. B., & Benjamin, E. J. (2007). Marital status, marital strain, and risk of coronary heart disease or total mortality: The Framingham offspring study. *Psychosomatic Medicine*, *69*(6), 509–513.

Elliot, A. J., & Covington, M. V. (2001). Approach and avoidance motivation. *Educational Psychology Review*, *13*(2), 73–92.

Ellsberg, M., Jansen, H. A., Heise, L., Watts, C. H., & Garcia-Moreno, C. (2008). Intimate partner violence and women's physical and mental health in the WHO multi-country study on women's health and domestic violence: An observational study. *The Lancet*, *371*(9619), 1165–1172.

Emmons, R. A. (1999). *The psychology of ultimate concerns: Motivation and spirituality in personality*. New York, NY: Guilford Press.

Emmons, R. A., & McCullough, M. E. (2003). Counting blessings versus burdens: An experimental investigation of gratitude and subjective well-being in daily life. *Journal of Personality and Social Psychology*, *84*(2), 377.

Forster, L. E., & Stoller, E. P. (1992). The impact of social support on mortality: A seven-year follow-up of older men and women. *Journal of Applied Gerontology*, *11*(2), 173–186.

Fraley, B., & Aron, A. (2004). The effect of a shared humorous experience on closeness in initial encounters. *Personal Relationships*, *11*(1), 61–78.

Fredrickson, B. L. (1998). What good are positive emotions? *Review of General Psychology*, *2*(3), 300–319.

Gable, S. L., & Anderson, J. F. (2016). Capitalization: The good news about close relationships. Chapter to appear in C. Knee & H. Reis (Eds.), *Positive approaches to optimal relationship development* (pp. 103–123) Cambridge, UK: Cambridge University Press.

Gable, S. L., Gonzaga, G. C., & Strachman, A. (2006). Will you be there for me when things go right? Supportive responses to positive event disclosures. *Journal of Personality and Social Psychology*, *91*(5), 904–917.

Gable S. L., Gosnell C. L., (2013). Approach and avoidance behavior in interpersonal relationships. *Emotion Review*, *5*(3), 269–274.

Gable, S. L., Gosnell, C. G., Maisel, N., & Strachman, A. N. (2012). Safely testing the alarm: Responses to personal events. *Journal of Personality and Social Psychology*, *103*(6), 949–962.

Gable, S. L., Reis, H. T., Impett, E. A., & Asher, E. R. (2004). What do you do when things go right? The intrapersonal and interpersonal benefits of sharing positive events. *Journal of Personality and Social Psychology, 87*(2), 228–245.

Gleason, M. E., Iida, M., Bolger, N., & Shrout, P. E. (2003). Daily supportive equity in close relationships. *Personality and Social Psychology Bulletin, 29*(8), 1036–1045.

Gleason, M. E., Iida, M., Shrout, P. E., & Bolger, N. (2008). Receiving support as a mixed blessing: Evidence for dual effects of support on psychological outcomes. *Journal of Personality and Social Psychology, 94*(5), 824.

Gonzaga, G. C., Turner, R. A., Keltner, D., Campos, B., & Altemus, M. (2006). Romantic love and sexual desire in close relationships. *Emotion, 6*(2), 163.

Grayson, D. K. (1990). Donner Party deaths: A demographic assessment. *Journal of Anthropological Research, 46*(3), 223–242.

Gross, J. J. (1998). The emerging field of emotion regulation: An integrative review. *Review of General Psychology, 2*(3), 271–283.

Harlow, H. F. (1958). The nature of love. *American psychologist, 13*(12), 673–685.

Hawkley, L. C., Thisted, R. A., & Cacioppo, J. T. (2009). Loneliness predicts reduced physical activity: cross-sectional & longitudinal analyses. *Health Psychology, 28*(3), 354.

Helliwell, J. F., & Putnam, R. D. (2004). The social context of well-being. *Philosophical Transactions-Royal Society of London Series B Biological Sciences, 359*(1449), 1435–1446.

Hicks, J. A., & King, L. A. (2007). Meaning in life and seeing the big picture: Positive affect and global focus. *Cognition and Emotion, 21*(7), 1577–1584.

Holmes, J. G. (2002). Interpersonal expectations as the building blocks of social cognition: An interdependence theory perspective. *Personal Relationships, 9*(1), 1–26.

Holt-Lunstad, J., Smith, T. B., & Layton, J. B. (2010). Social relationships and mortality risk: A meta-analytic review. *PLoS Med, 7*(7).

House, J. S., Landis, K. R., & Umberson, D. (1988). Social relationships and health. *Science, 241*(4865), 540–545.

Huston, T. L., Caughlin, J. P., Houts, R. M., Smith, S. E., & George, L. J. (2001). The connubial crucible: newlywed years as predictors of marital delight, distress, and divorce. *Journal of personality and social psychology, 80*(2), 237.

Kaul, M., & Lakey, B. (2003). Where is the support in perceived support? The role of generic relationship satisfaction and enacted support in perceived support's relation to low distress. *Journal of Social and Clinical Psychology, 22*(1), 59–78.

Keltner, D., & Haidt, J. (1999). Social functions of emotions at four levels of analysis. *Cognition & Emotion, 13*(5), 505–521.

Kiecolt-Glaser, J. K. (1999). Stress, personal relationships, and immune function: Health implications. *Brain, Behavior and Immunity, 13*(1), 61–72.

Kiecolt-Glaser, J. K., & Newton, T. L. (2001). Marriage and health: His and hers. *Psychological Bulletin, 127*(4), 472–503.

King, L. A., Heintzelman, S. J., & Ward, S. J. (2016). Beyond the search for meaning: A contemporary science of the experience of meaning in life. *Current Directions in Psychological Science, 25*(4), 211–216.

Klinger, E. (1977). *Meaning and void: Inner experience and the incentives in peoples lives.* Minneapolis: University of Minnesota Press.

Krause, N. (1997a). Anticipated support, received support, and economic stress among older adults. *The Journals of Gerontology Series B: Psychological Sciences and Social Sciences, 52*(6), P284–P293.

Krause, N. (1997b). Received support, anticipated support, social class, and mortality. *Research on Aging, 19*(4), 387–422.

Lehman, D. R., Ellard, J. H., & Wortman, C. B. (1986). Social support for the bereaved: Recipients' and providers' perspectives on what is helpful. *Journal of Consulting and Clinical Psychology*, *54*(4), 438.

Maisel, N. C., & Gable, S. L. (2009). The paradox of received social support: The importance of responsiveness. *Psychological Science*, *20*(8), 928–932.

Maisel, N., Gable, S. L., & Strachman, A. (2008) Responsive behaviors in good times and in bad. *Personal Relationships*, *15*, 317–338.

McCullough, M. E., Emmons, R. A., & Tsang, J. (2002). The grateful disposition: A conceptual and empirical topography. *Journal of Personality and Social Psychology*, *82*(1), 112–127.

Mikulincer, M. (1998). Attachment working models and the sense of trust: An exploration of interaction goals and affect regulation. *Journal of Personality and Social Psychology*, *74*, 1209–1224.

Miller, G., Rohleder, N., & Cole, S. W. (2009). Chronic interpersonal stress predicts activation of pro-and anti-inflammatory signaling pathways six months later. *Psychosomatic Medicine*, *71*(1), 57–62.

Murray, H. A. (1938). *Explorations in personality: A clinical and experimental study of fifty men of college age.* York: Oxford Press

Neeleman, J., & Power, M. J. (1994). Social support and depression in three groups of psychiatric patients and a group of medical controls. *Social Psychiatry and Psychiatric Epidemiology*, *29*(1), 46–51.

Overholser, J. C. (1992). Interpersonal dependency and social loss. *Personality and Individual Differences*, *13*(1), 17–23.

Rafaeli, E., & Gleason, M. E. (2009). Skilled support within intimate relationships. *Journal of Family Theory & Review*, *1*(1), 20–37.

Reis, H. T., Clark, M. S., & Holmes, J. G. (2004). Perceived partner responsiveness as an organizing construct in the study of intimacy and closeness. In D. J. Mashek & A. P. Aron (Eds.), *Handbook of closeness and intimacy* (pp. 201–225). Mahwah, NJ: Lawrence Erlbaum Associates, Publishers.

Rholes, W. S., Simpson, J. A., Campbell, L., & Grich, J. (2001). Adult attachment and the transition to parenthood. *Journal of Personality and Social Psychology*, *81*(3), 421.

Rini, C., Schetter, C. D., Hobel, C. J., Glynn, L. M., & Sandman, C. A. (2006). Effective social support: Antecedents and consequences of partner support during pregnancy. *Personal Relationships*, *13*(2), 207–229.

Rönkä, A. R., Rautio, A., Koiranen, M., Sunnari, V., & Taanila, A. (2014). Experience of loneliness among adolescent girls and boys: Northern Finland Birth Cohort 1986 study. *Journal of Youth Studies*, *17*(2), 183–203.

Rook, K. S. (1984). The negative side of social interaction: Impact on psychological well-being. *Journal of Personality and Social Psychology*, *46*(5), 1097–1108.

Rusbult, C. E., Kumashiro, M., Kubacka, K. E., & Finkel, E. J. (2009). "The part of me that you bring out": Ideal similarity and the Michelangelo phenomenon. *Journal of Personality and Social Psychology*, *96*(1), 61–82.

Rusbult, C. E., Kumashiro, M., Stocker, S. L., & Wolf, S. T. (2005). The Michelangelo Phenomenon in close relationships. In A. Tesser, J. V. Wood, & D. A. Stapel (Eds.), *On building, defending and regulating the self: A psychological perspective* (pp. 1–29). New York: Psychology Press.

Russell, D. W. (1996). UCLA loneliness scale (Version 3): Reliability, validity, and factor structure. *Journal of Personality Assessment*, *66*(1), 20–40.

Ryff, C. D. (1995). Psychological well-being in adult life. *Current Directions in Psychological Science*, *4*(4), 99–104.

Sherman, A. M., Lansford, J. E., & Volling, B. L. (2006). Sibling relationships and best friendships in young adulthood: Warmth, conflict, and well-being. *Personal Relationships*, *13*(2), 151–165.

Shrout, P. E., Herman, C. M., & Bolger, N. (2006). The costs and benefits of practical and emotional support on adjustment: A daily diary study of couples experiencing acute stress. *Personal Relationships*, *13*(1), 115–134.

Slotter, E. B., & Gardner, W. L. (2009). Where do you end and I begin? Evidence for anticipatory, motivated self—other integration between relationship partners. *Journal of Personality and Social Psychology*, *96*(6), 1137.

Stevens, N., & van Tilburg, T. (2000). Stimulating friendship in later life: A strategy for reducing loneliness among older women. *Educational Gerontology. Special Issue: International Research and Practice*, *26*(1), 15–35.

Stillman, T. F., Baumeister, R. F., Lambert, N. M., Crescioni, A. W., DeWall, C. N., & Fincham, F. D. (2009). Alone and without purpose: Life loses meaning following social exclusion. *Journal of Experimental Social Psychology*, *45*, 686–694.

Sternberg, R. J. (1986). A triangular theory of love. *Psychological Review*, *93*(2), 119–135.

Tooby, J., & Cosmides, L. (1990). The past explains the present: Emotional adaptations and the structure of ancestral environments. *Ethology and Sociobiology*, *11*(4–5), 375–424.

Uchino, B. N., Bosch, J. A., Smith, T. W., Carlisle, M., Birmingham, W., Bowen, K. S., . . . O'Hartaigh, B. (2013). Relationships and cardiovascular risk: Perceived spousal ambivalence in specific relationship contexts and its links to inflammation. *Health Psychology*, *32*, 1067–1075.

Uchino, B. N., Cacioppo, J. T., & Kiecolt-Glaser, J. K. (1996). The relationship between social support and physiological processes: A review with emphasis on underlying mechanisms and implications for health. *Psychological Bulletin*, *119*(3), 488–531.

Uchino, B. N., Holt-Lunstad, J., Uno, D., & Flinders, J. B. (2001). Heterogeneity in the social networks of young and older adults: prediction of mental health and cardiovascular reactivity during acute stress. *Journal of Behavioral Medicine*, *24*(4), 361–382.

VanderWeele, T. J., Hawkley, L. C., Thisted, R. A., & Cacioppo, J. T. (2011). A marginal structural model analysis for loneliness: Implications for intervention trials and clinical practice. *Journal of Consulting and Clinical Psychology*, *79*(2), 225–235.

Whisman, M. A. (2001). The association between depression and marital dissatisfaction. In S. R. H. Beach (Ed.), *Marital and family processes in depression: A scientific foundation for clinical practice* (pp. 3–24). Washington, DC: American Psychological Association.

Whisman, M. A., & Bruce, M. L. (1999). Marital dissatisfaction and incidence of major depressive episode in a community sample. *Journal of Abnormal Psychology*, *108*(4), 674–678.

Whisman, M. A., Uebelacker, L. A., & Settles, T. D. (2010). Marital distress and the metabolic syndrome: Linking social functioning with physical health. *Journal of Family Psychology*, *24*(3), 367.

Wilcox, V. L., Kasl, S. V., & Berkman, L. F. (1994). Social support and physical disability in older people after hospitalization: a prospective study. *Health Psychology*, *13*(2), 170–179.

Zadro, L., Williams, K. D., & Richardson, R. (2004). How low can you go? Ostracism by a computer is sufficient to lower self-reported levels of belonging, control, self-esteem, and meaningful existence. *Journal of Experimental Social Psychology*, *40*(4), 560–567.

Zaki, J., & Williams, W. C. (2013). Interpersonal emotion regulation. *Emotion*, *13*(5), 803.

15

EARLY SOCIAL EXPERIENCES AND LIVING WELL

A Longitudinal View of Adult Physical Health

Jeffry A. Simpson, Allison K. Farrell,
Chloe O. Huelsnitz, and Jami Eller

Several chapters in this volume highlight the importance of psychological well-being for living the good life (see, for example, the chapters by Baumeister, Dunn & Dwyer, Forgas, Fredrickson, Gable, Huppert, Fritz & Lyubomirsky, and Myers). Physical well-being, however, is also important in order to enjoy and appreciate life, especially as people age. Aristotle suggested that bodily excellences were constituent parts of happiness, and research now supports this assertion. Perceptions of physical health, for example, are positively associated with reports of subjective well-being (Okun & George, 1984), especially among older individuals (Okun & Stock, 1987). In order to live the good life, therefore, individuals need to have and maintain good physical health.

The seeds of good health may be planted much earlier in life than was once presumed (see also Crano & Donaldson, this volume). Our work with the Minnesota Longitudinal Study of Risk and Adaptation (MLSRA; Sroufe, Egeland, Carlson, & Collins, 2005), a 40-year ongoing prospective study of development, is finding that certain social experiences encountered in early childhood not only have lasting effects on our minds, but also on our bodies. Building on the well-established literature showing the importance of close relationships for mental well-being across the lifespan (Reis, Collins, & Berscheid, 2000), we are examining whether and how higher-quality functioning in the first close relationship—the early mother-child relationship—has lasting effects on different markers of physical health measured decades later in adulthood. Our research is grounded on the concept of biological programming, which suggests that exposure to certain kinds of events during sensitive periods early in development program the body to react more vigorously to potential health threats, resulting in more health-related problems later in life.

We begin the chapter by describing the biological programming model that has guided our research and by indicating the type of evidence that is needed to test whether certain early life variables may have produced biological programming effects. We then discuss three physical health studies that have been conducted with the MLSRA sample. In doing so, we highlight the roles that early attachment security, the quality of early caregiving, and the amount of early life stress play in forecasting health outcomes approximately three decades later in adulthood. We also highlight the crucial role that the quality of early maternal care assumes in protecting individuals who experienced higher levels of stress earlier in life from experiencing health problems years later. We conclude by pointing out some promising avenues for future research.

A Biological Programming Model

In recent years, attention has turned to the role that childhood socioeconomic disadvantage may have in setting up health problems years later in adulthood. One of the most prominent models, shown in Figure 15.1, is the biological programming model proposed by Miller and Chen (2013). According to this model,

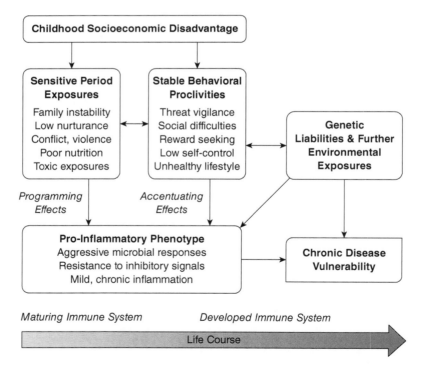

FIGURE 15.1 Miller and Chen's (2013) Biological Programming Model

greater socioeconomic disadvantage in childhood generates both "programming effects" and "accentuating effects," each of which may influence vulnerability to chronic disease later in life. Miller and Chen (2013) propose that programming effects result from exposure to certain events or agents during sensitive periods early in life, such as high levels of family instability, poor parental care, witnessing intense conflict or violence, receiving poor nutrition, or being exposed to toxins in the home, school, or neighborhood. Over time, exposure to these events/agents produces a "pro-inflammatory phenotype" whereby individuals develop hyperaggressive responses to microbial agents (e.g., bacteria, viruses) and become resistant to signals that typically down-regulate such responses in most people. The net result is chronic inflammation, which over time causes cell damage and, ultimately, vulnerability to chronic disease.

The second pathway in the model involves "accentuating effects," which emerge in response to the behavioral tendencies commonly associated with childhood socioeconomic disadvantage. Children who grow up disadvantaged, for instance, often display tendencies or engage in behaviors that may further compromise their long-term health, such as being hypervigilant to threats, having interpersonal problems and chronically low social support, seeking immediate, health-damaging rewards (e.g., smoking, excessive alcohol use, drug use), having poor self-control, or living an unhealthy lifestyle (e.g., having a poor diet, irregular sleep patterns) (Miller, Chen, & Parker, 2011). Each of these tendencies and behaviors should also increase pro-inflammatory phenotypes, eventually resulting in greater vulnerability to chronic disease. This biological programming model also assumes that genetic liabilities and other environmental factors might exacerbate (or in some cases attenuate) these effects and outcomes.

Our research focuses on the possible programming effects of early exposure to certain social experiences, such as greater family stress, less parental nurturance, and heightened family instability/conflict (see also Forgas, and von Hippel & Gonsalkorale, this volume). What kind of data and evidence are needed to document early programming effects? First, one needs to follow individuals prospectively across their lives, ideally starting at birth. Second, one must collect theoretically relevant measures at multiple periods of development. Third, one should attempt to demonstrate that the programming effects of certain early life variables forecast adult health outcomes years later in adulthood while statistically controlling for variables also known to correlate with health outcomes, such as current levels of life stress and other potential confounds.

The Minnesota Longitudinal Study of Risk and Adaptation

To test for possible biological programming effects, we have examined the lives of approximately 170 individuals who have been continuously studied from before birth into middle adulthood as part of the Minnesota Longitudinal Study of Risk and Adaptation (MLSRA: see Sroufe et al., 2005, for a description of the project). Between 1975 and 1977, a sample of low-income women who were receiving free health care in Minneapolis, Minnesota, were recruited into the study during their third trimester of pregnancy. Their first-born child (the current participants, all of whom have been followed longitudinally) were thus born into lower socio-economic and potentially higher-risk environments. Approximately half of the participants in the MLSRA are male and half are female. The racial composition is roughly 65% white, 11% African-American, 18% mixed race, and 6% undetermined (due to missing father information).

Beginning with their mothers prior to birth, the lives of participants have been assessed approximately every three to four years, with more frequent assessments occurring during the first six years of life. Up until the participants were 17 years old, many of the assessments were focused on the birth mothers, concentrating on variables that could affect the development of their child (e.g., socioeconomic status [SES], life stress). However, we also assessed the nature and quality of the relationship between each mother and her child by videotaping each dyad at different ages as the two interacted in well-validated structured tasks that were designed to assess the attachment pattern of each dyad and the quality of care each mother gave to her child. From age 17 onward, all of the assessments focused on the participants themselves. Some of the assessments focused on each partici-pant's attachment representations of childhood (i.e., memories and interpretations of being raised by his or her parents). When they were 32 and 37 years old, we assessed each participant's health status by measuring his or her self-reported qual-ity of physical health, whether he or she had experienced any diagnosed health problems in the recent past, and a set of standard biomarkers (e.g., BMI, inflam-mation in the blood) indexing his or her current health status.

We now overview three recent MLSRA studies that have investigated whether and how three theoretically relevant early life events—being securely versus inse-curely attached to one's mother in infancy, receiving higher versus lower maternal care in childhood, and being exposed to more versus less life stress while grow-ing up—longitudinally predict various health outcomes in middle adulthood (at ages 32 and 37).

Study 1: Child Attachment Insecurity and Adult Health

In the first study (Puig, Englund, Simpson, & Collins, 2013), we examined whether being securely versus insecurely attached to one's mother during the first 12 to 18 months of life uniquely predicts having more versus less health problems in middle adulthood. Several prior studies have indicated that exposure to a larger number of adverse life experiences across development is associated with poorer health outcomes during adulthood (e.g., Barker et al., 1993; Felitti et al., 1998). In addition, retrospective studies have found that people who report having had higher-quality relationships earlier in life experience better health outcomes as adults than people who report having had lower-quality relationships (e.g., Coan, Schaefer, & Davidson, 2006; Kiecolt-Glaser, Glaser, Cacioppo, & Malarkay 1998).

Very little longitudinal research, however, has investigated links between the quality of early relationships and adult physical health status. Nearly all of the existing research on relationship functioning and adult health has focused on concurrent measures taken at a single time-point. Furthermore, the small number of longitudinal studies addressing this topic (e.g., Christakis & Fowler, 2007; House, Landis, & Umberson, 1988) have examined time periods only in adulthood. Incorporating prospective assessments of relationship functioning from very early in development may provide both a less biased and more enriched understanding of how the quality of relationships in the opening years of life impacts adult health.

Bowlby (1969) and Boyce (1985) were among the first to hypothesize that the nature of the attachment relationship between primary caregivers and their children should play a pivotal role in shaping health outcomes, not only during childhood, but across the life course as well. When early parent-child relationships are secure, parents serve as: (a) a safe haven within which the child feels protected and learns to regulate his or her emotions constructively when the child is distressed, and (b) a secure base from which the child can confidently explore the surrounding world (see also Gable, this volume). Whether early attachment relationships are secure or insecure depends in part on the quality of care that infants receive from their caregivers (Ainsworth, Blehar, Waters, & Wall, 1978). More supportive and responsive care usually results in secure parent-child attachments, whereas inconsistent or rejecting care typically culminates in insecure attachments (van IJzendoorn, 1995).

Across development, the nature and quality of care that a child receives is internalized into secure or insecure working models (i.e., schemas), which then guide his or her interpersonal functioning during adolescence and adulthood (Bowlby, 1973; Simpson & Rholes, 2012). Based on their positive interpersonal experiences, securely attached children become adept at giving and receiving high-quality care and support from their significant others (Waters, Merrick, Treboux, Crowell, & Albersheim, 2000), which helps them regulate negative emotions more effectively. Insecurely attached children, on the other hand, do not give and receive care and support well, which impedes their emotion regulation abilities in later relationships (e.g., Simpson, Collins, Tran, & Haydon, 2007). Although secure and insecure attachment patterns can and sometimes do change as individuals encounter new events and new attachment figures later in life (Fraley & Brumbaugh, 2004), early attachment security versus insecurity is believed to lay the groundwork for the functioning of later relationships (Fearon & Belsky, 2016).

Some research suggests that infant attachment relationships are associated with certain aspects of health during childhood, which in turn could be associated with health later in life (e.g., Anderson & Whitaker, 2011). However, prospective studies testing the actual association between the security of early attachment relationships and adult physical health have not been conducted. To fill this gap, Puig and her colleagues (2013) prospectively examined the link between the security of mother-child attachment relationships during the first two years of life (assessed in the Strange Situation) and the health problems of participants in adulthood from the MLSRA sample. The principal hypothesis was that individuals who were rated as securely attached in the Strange Situation during infancy would be less likely to report physical health problems in middle adulthood than those rated as insecurely attached in infancy.

Measures and Methods

Early attachment status was assessed by the Strange Situation Procedure (SSP) when each MLSRA participant was 12 and 18 months old. The SSP is a 20-minute videotaped laboratory procedure in which young children are exposed to a series of stressful separations from, followed by reunions with, their primary caregiver (Ainsworth et al., 1978). Raters classified each participant's attachment relationship with his or her primary caregiver (always the mother in the MLSRA) at 12 and 18 months. Classifications were made according to how each participant responded to the separations and reunions. At both 12 and 18 months, approximately 60% of the participants were secure and 40% were insecure. To create a more reliable attachment measure, we summed the number of times each participant was rated as secure in the 12- and 18-month SSP assessments. Children with a score of 2 were rated as being secure at both time-points (41% of the sample), children with a score of 1 were secure at one time-point (33%), and those with a score of 0 were insecure at both time-points (26%).

Thirty years later, when participants were 32 years old, they completed the Adult Health Survey (Blum, Resnick, & Bergeisen, 1989). They were asked to indicate whether they had experienced any of several chronic diagnosed physical illnesses within the preceding year. Because 60% of the sample reported *no* chronic physical illness within the past year, we created a binary variable on which participants who reported having one or more illnesses were coded 1, and those who reported no illnesses were coded 0.

To rule out the possibility that the hypothesized early attachment security → better adult health link was confounded with participants' current life circumstances, we also statistically controlled for their gender, current socioeconomic status, body mass index (BMI), current observer-rated life stress, current self-reported neuroticism, and current perceived support that was available, all of which were assessed at age 32 with well-validated measures. Each of these variables tends to correlate with adult health outcomes (Puig et al., 2013).

Findings

As hypothesized, the security of early mother-child attachment relationships significantly predicted the likelihood that individuals reported having a chronic physical illness within the past year, even controlling for the possible confounds listed above. Specifically, individuals who had been securely attached to their mothers early in life (at 12 and 18 months) were significantly *less* likely to report having a chronic illness compared to those who were insecurely attached during infancy. The effect sizes were small to moderate in magnitude.

These findings are among the first to document the important role that early attachment status may play in setting the stage for physical health outcomes in adulthood. In related research, Miller and colleagues (2011) have found that retrospective reports of the quality of maternal nurturance early in life mediate the relation between lower SES and more health problems in middle adulthood. Early attachment security could affect adult health through any of several possible pathways, such as by facilitating higher-quality relationships with romantic partners in adulthood (Simpson et al., 2007), increasing medical treatment adherence (Ceichanowski, Walker, Katon, & Russo, 2002), or maintaining better health-promoting behaviors (Scharfe & Eldredge, 2001).

Study 2: Early Maternal Care, Adult Attachment Insecurity, and Adult Health

Research indicates that a primary precursor of attachment security is the quality of care that children receive from their primary caregivers in the home (Ainsworth et al., 1978; van IJzendoorn, 1995). Realizing this fact, we next turned our attention to how the quality of early maternal care forecasts health outcomes in middle adulthood.

Growing evidence suggests that "risky" family environments can impact both biological functioning and health quality in adulthood (e.g., Repetti, Taylor, & Seeman, 2002; see also Fredrickson, this volume). Risky families tend to have greater conflict and lower-quality caregiving, which ought to disrupt psychosocial and biological functioning, leading to elevated risk for early onset of diseases (Miller & Chen, 2013). Consistent with this view, children who receive less warmth, support, and responsiveness from their parents tend to have higher inflammation, higher blood pressure, and greater overall allostatic load than children who receive more warmth, support, and responsiveness. Allostatic load reflects the general amount of wear and tear on the body in response to encountering repeated or chronic stressors. More specifically, it represents the physiological consequences of chronic exposure to high or fluctuating neural or neuroendocrine responses owing to repeated or chronic stress. Such health outcomes are precursors to cardiovascular problems (Bell & Belsky, 2008; Carroll et al., 2013; Lehman et al., 2009; Tobin et al., 2015). Brody and colleagues (2014) have recently shown that these effects extend beyond childhood, with harsher parenting in childhood predicting higher levels of inflammation in adolescence.

At present, we do not know whether these effects extend beyond adolescence into adulthood. However, we do know that adults who report having received lower-quality parenting during childhood tend to have higher allostatic load and more health problems as adults (e.g., Russek & Schwartz, 1997; Slopen et al., 2015; see also Crano & Donaldson, this volume). Relying on retrospective reports of parenting is problematic, as individuals may not accurately remember their childhood experiences (Rubin, Rahhal, & Poon, 1998), especially those early in life when maternal care might be more impactful (cf. Meaney & Szyf, 2005). Moreover, confounding third variables may lead people to exaggerate either their early life experiences or the severity of their current health problems, artificially inflating associations between the two.

Only one study to our knowledge has investigated the link between early parenting quality and adult health outcomes prospectively. Using the data from the Dunedin Multidisciplinary Health and Development Study, Danese and colleagues (2007) found that childhood maltreatment (indexed by maternal rejection, harsh discipline, changes in primary caregivers, and physical/sexual abuse before age 10) predicts higher incidence of age-related disease risk in adulthood, including elevated inflammation and other biological health-risk markers. The Dunedin study, however, did not begin assessing participants until they were 3 years old, and their maltreatment composite contains a mix of coder ratings and retrospective self-reports.

If poorer parenting early in life is systematically tied to more health problems in adulthood, we need to understand how these early experiences "get under the skin" and are carried forward to affect health decades later. Chen and her colleagues (2011) have proposed that more nurturant caregiving communicates to children that the world is a relatively safe place and that people can typically be trusted and counted upon. This realization may allow children—even those from disadvantaged socioeconomic backgrounds—to perceive less threat in their daily lives, which ought to reduce the wear and tear that chronic vigilance can have on endocrine and other health-relevant systems. Nurturant care might also help children—even disadvantaged ones—learn better coping skills and more effective emotion-regulation strategies, which, over time, should reduce stress and aggressive biological responses to it. This emphasis on instilling feelings of safety and trust, reducing threat, and developing more constructive emotion-regulation strategies insinuates that the attachment system should be a key psychosocial mediator of the purported link between the quality of early parenting and adult health outcomes (see also Gable, this volume).

There is, in fact, some preliminary evidence supporting this possibility. As we have seen, higher-quality parenting early in life is associated with attachment security in childhood and beyond (e.g., van IJzendoorn, 1995; Zayas et al., 2011). Moreover, some of the cardinal features of attachment insecurity—over-perception of stressors, poorer self-regulation, less effective support-seeking, and poorer relationship functioning—typically produce over-activation of the biological stress system and, therefore, elevated health risks due to repeated exposure to stress hormones (Farrell & Simpson, 2017; Pietromonaco, Uchino, & Dunkel-Schetter, 2013). Indeed, across different types of relationships, insecure attachment is associated with greater biological stress reactivity (Fagundes et al., 2011), more inflammation (Gouin et al., 2008; Kidd et al., 2014), and higher incidence of cardiovascular disease (McWilliams & Bailey, 2010).

Given this backdrop, Farrell and her colleagues (2017) decided to examine links between early parenting quality, adult attachment security, and a measure of cardiometabolic risk during adulthood within the MLSRA. They hypothesized that higher-quality early parenting would longitudinally forecast lower cardiometabolic risk in middle adulthood, and that adult attachment security (i.e., memories and interpretations of how one was treated by parents during childhood) would mediate this link.

Measures and Methods

To assess the quality of early care, mother-child interactions were videotaped during semi-structured tasks and then coded for maternal sensitivity when MLSRA participants were 3, 6, 24, and 42 months old. At 3 months, each mother and child were observed in the home during a routine feeding situation. When infants were 6 months old, two feeding situations and one play interaction were observed in the home on two different days. For these early assessments, maternal sensitivity was operationalized using Ainsworth's sensitivity scale (Ainsworth et al., 1978), which assesses each mother's ability to perceive and accurately interpret her infant's signals and respond appropriately and promptly. When participants were 24 and 42 months old, they and their mothers were observed in a laboratory setting while attempting to solve several problem-solving and teaching tasks. At each age, the tasks gradually increased in complexity, eventually becoming too difficult for the child to complete on his or her own. Mothers were instructed to initially allow their child to try to solve each task independently, and then to give their child any help they thought was needed. Maternal sensitivity at 24 and 42 months was evaluated with a rating of each mother's supportive presence, which assessed the extent to which each mother provided a secure base for her child (i.e., helped the child feel comfortable with the task) as well as each mother's positive involvement during the interaction. A single composite measure of early maternal sensitivity (i.e., quality of maternal caregiving) was then created by standardizing and averaging all four maternal sensitivity ratings.

Adult attachment security was assessed by secure base script knowledge coded from Adult Attachment Interviews (AAIs), which were conducted twice when participants were 19 and 26 years old. The AAI is a semi-structured audiotaped interview that assesses adults' state of mind with respect to their attachment relationships with their primary caregivers (Main, Goldwyn, & Hesse, 2003). It contains questions that elicit recollections of experiences with caregivers early in life, typically between ages 5 to 12. Each participant's secure base script knowledge was rated from his or her interview on a scale that assessed the extent to which each narrative followed or implied knowledge of the secure base script (Waters et al., 2013, 2016). Raters focused on: (a) explicit or implied expectations consistent with the secure base script (e.g., caregivers were available, responsive, and/or provided comfort effectively), and (b) recall of specific autobiographical memories that follow the secure base script. Narratives receiving high scores contained several events that followed the secure base script structure. Those receiving a low score had several events that directly violated secure base script structure (e.g., the caregiver was rejecting or did not offer help when the participant reported being hurt, ill, or afraid in childhood) or reflected other relationship expectations (e.g., recurring abuse).

At age 37, four biomarkers of cardiometabolic risk were assessed. During a laboratory assessment, participants' blood pressure was measured at the start and end of the assessment. Participants' body mass index (BMI) was also calculated from their height and weight measurements. Their waist-to-hip ratio (WHR) was assessed by dividing the measurement of each participant's waist at the narrowest point from the measurement of his or her hips at the widest point. Their level of C-reactive protein (CRP), a marker of inflammation in the blood, was assayed from blood samples. A composite measure of cardiometabolic risk was then created by standardizing and averaging these four biomarker measures.

We also measured variables that could be confounds. They included participants' gender, race, and the life stress experienced by the mother during the early life of her child.

Findings

In line with our expectations, individuals who received higher-quality care early in life from their mothers (rated by observers) had greater attachment security in early adulthood (based on secure base script knowledge coded from the AAIs) and lower levels of cardiometabolic risk at age 37. Moreover, being securely attached in adulthood proved to be a significant mediator of this connection (see Figure 15.2). These effects also held when the potential confounds of sex, race, and mother's stress were controlled. These mediation findings are noteworthy because they identify one of the psychological variables that may carry the impact of early parenting forward to eventually impact adult health. However, attachment did not fully mediate the link between maternal sensitivity and adult cardiometabolic risk (i.e., a significant direct path between maternal sensitivity and cardiometabolic risk remained, despite the significant mediational path). This suggests that other psychological or biological variables may also serve as important mechanisms that need to be identified.

Study 3: Life Stress, Early Caregiving, and Adult Health

According to Miller and Chen (2013), being socially or economically disadvantaged early in life should render people more susceptible to early onset health problems

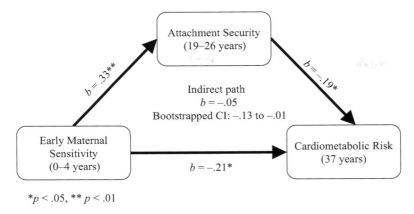

FIGURE 15.2 A Mediation Model Showing That the Effect of Higher-Quality Maternal Care Early in Life on Health Outcomes in Middle Adulthood Is Mediated by Secure Base Representations of Childhood in Early Adulthood; Standardized Betas Are Reported

later in life (see also Huppert, this volume). A great deal of cross-sectional research has focused on one major consequence of being disadvantaged—experiencing high levels of stress (e.g., Cohen et al., 2007). As we discuss below, some more recent evidence suggests that *when* stress is encountered during life might also uniquely impact later health outcomes (e.g., Lupien et al., 2009; Miller, Chen, & Parker, 2011). Moreover, there are compelling reasons to believe that certain experiences, such as receiving better maternal care early in childhood, may protect (buffer) individuals from the adverse effects of life stress. Little longitudinal research, however, has examined the impact of stress at different life stages, and very few studies have explored protective factors.

Being aware of these gaps in our knowledge, Farrell, Simpson, Englund, Carlson, and Sung (2017) sought answers to two questions: (1) When during life does stress more strongly predict later adult health problems? and (2) Does receiving better maternal care early in life reduce the negative effects that stress typically has on adult health outcomes? Some prior research indicates that there could be sensitive periods during development when stress has a somewhat stronger impact on later adult health (e.g., Fagundes & Way, 2014; Miller, Chen, & Parker, 2011). Miller and colleagues (2011), for example, propose that early life stress affects adult health by programming the immune system to be hyperactive to potential threats, which produces chronic inflammation and associated health problems later in life (e.g., high blood pressure, poor immune functioning). Consistent with this idea, exposure to higher levels of stress early in life prospectively forecasts a myriad of deleterious health outcomes, including coronary heart disease (Dong et al., 2004) and premature death (Galobardes et al., 2006).

Life stages other than early childhood, however, might also impact long-term health. Experiencing greater life stress during adolescence, for example, is associated with higher levels of inflammation (Ehrlich et al., 2016) and more chronic health problems (Gustafsson et al., 2012). In addition, experiencing greater current life stress is also associated with poorer health outcomes (DeLongis et al., 1988; Uchino, Cacioppo, Malarkey, & Glaser, 1995). Complementing these ideas, animal studies have shown that early life and adolescence are two critical periods for the development of chronic health issues (e.g., Meaney & Szyf, 2005; McCormick, Mathews, Thomas, & Waters, 2010). The long-term effects of stress beyond early childhood on health in humans, however, remain largely unknown.

To our knowledge, two prospective studies have investigated the impact of early life stress on later physical health. Essex and colleagues (2011) followed children from infancy to adolescence and found that greater stress in infancy and preschool (operationalized as having depressed parents and being exposed to anger in the family) resulted in atypical diurnal cortisol patterns in middle childhood and adolescence, which usually are associated with health problems. Raposa and colleagues (2014) investigated how young adult health outcomes were affected by early adversity (measured by mother's psychopathy, parental discord, harsh discipline, family income, and parental criminal behavior during the first five years of life). Children who experienced greater adversity early in life had higher levels of inflammation, BMI, and smoking at age 20. These two studies, however, examined the effects of stress only from early childhood.

Although the stress-to-health link is robust, one protective factor may be the quality of early maternal care (see also Crano & Donaldson, this volume). It is well established that social support promotes better health, partly because it buffers the deleterious effects of stress (Cohen & Syme, 1985; Uchino, Cacioppo, & Kiecolt-Glaser, 1996). In a similar manner, higher-quality parenting serves as a protective factor for many non–health-relevant outcomes linked with child adversity because it reduces children's stress responses. Thus, higher-quality parenting ought to have a buffering effect on the relation between early stress and adult health outcomes (Cicchetti & Blender, 2006; Gunnar & Quevedo, 2007). Consistent with this view, greater self-reported maternal warmth and nurturance early in life buffers the impact of low SES on inflammation and metabolic syndrome in adulthood (Chen et al., 2011; Miller, Chen, & Parker, 2011). Moreover, parenting interventions tend to be effective in improving child health (Miller, Brody, Yu, & Chen, 2014).

Similar to research on stress, however, virtually all prior research on parenting as a protective factor has relied on retrospective accounts, typically by asking adults to report on their mother's warmth and nurturance when they were young (e.g., Chen et al., 2011; Miller, Lachman, et al., 2011). As with retrospective reports of stress, there may be disparities between what actually happened during childhood and adult perceptions of those experiences (Roisman et al., 2002). To complicate matters, past studies have conflated parenting quality and life stress by including parenting or parenting-relevant issues (e.g., maternal depression; Essex et al., 2011) in life stress measures.

Working with the MLSRA, Farrell and her colleagues (2017) hypothesized that exposure to greater stress at three life stages—early in life, during adolescence, and currently—should have somewhat stronger prospective effects on adult health. They also explored whether experiencing greater stress at two or more of these life stages revealed a "dual-risk" pattern, with higher stress at two or more stages resulting in worse health outcomes than the main effects of each stage alone. Most importantly, they also anticipated that higher-quality maternal care would have a buffering effect on adult health, with higher-quality parenting reducing or perhaps eliminating the negative effects of earlier life stress on adult health.

Measures and Methods

Three health measures were collected on MLSRA participants when they were 32 years old: (1) a self-rating of their overall physical health (on a scale from *Excellent* to *Poor*); (2) their body mass index (BMI), calculated from their height and weight; and (3) self-reports as to whether they had any one of several chronic illnesses within the past year, assessed by the Adult Health Survey (coded 1 if they reported one or more illnesses, and 0 if they had none).

Life stress was assessed at 16 time-points when participants were between 12 months and 32 years old. At each time-point, life stress was measured by an interview (the Life Events Schedule [LES]; Egeland, Breitenbucher, & Rosenberg, 1980), which assessed whether and the extent to which several potentially stressful life events had occurred during the prior year (e.g., financial issues, conflict with romantic partners, being a victim of crime, losing a job). The audio-recorded answers were then rated by coders for how disruptive each potential stressor was on a scale ranging from 0 (*no disruption*; e.g., minor changes in job responsibilities) to 3 (*extreme disruption*; e.g., having a parent commit suicide). Each mother completed the LES until her child (the participant) was 17.5 years old, after which each participant completed the LES. Stress ratings for each potential stressor were summed within each assessment period to create a total stress score for each participant. Assessments were then grouped into four life stages: early childhood (ages 0–5), middle childhood (ages 6–12), adolescence (ages 13–19), and young adulthood (ages 20–31). Total life stress scores were standardized at each assessment and were then averaged within each life stage to create a total stress composite for that stage. Life stress at age 32 was also standardized to measure current life stress.

As described earlier, ratings of the quality of maternal caregiving earlier in life were based on several observational assessments of mother-child interactions that were conducted in the home and in the lab.

The control measures included the sex and race/ethnicity of each participant (white = 1; non-white = 0) and his or her self-reported level of neuroticism, which was assessed at age 32 by the Berkeley Personality Profile (John & Srivastava, 1999). Neuroticism was controlled because it correlates with self-reported health problems (Watson & Pennebaker, 1989).

Findings

When the three health outcomes at age 32 were examined, nearly all of the significant stress → adult health correlations were found for the three hypothesized life stages: early childhood (ages 0–5), adolescence (ages 13–19), and currently (age 32). Further analyses revealed that experiencing higher levels of stress during certain stages yielded interaction effects. For example, early childhood and adolescent stress significantly interacted to predict participants' BMI (see Figure 15.3, panel B), such that individuals who encountered greater stress at both of these life stages had the highest BMI at age 32. A marginally significant interaction was also found involving early childhood and adolescent stress predicting overall self-rated physical health (see Figure 15.3, panel A). Specifically, individuals who experienced higher stress at both life stages rated their physical health as somewhat worse than those who experienced higher stress at only one or neither life stage.

Tests of the buffering effects of maternal sensitivity on life stress-adult health connections revealed a significant three-way interaction predicting BMI (see Figure 15.4, panels B_1 and B_2) and a marginal three-way interaction predicting chronic illness counts (see Figure 15.4, panels A_1 and A_2). In both cases, experiencing higher stress at both life stages as well as lower maternal sensitivity predicted poorer adult health outcomes, whereas experiencing lower life stress at both life stages along with higher maternal sensitivity predicted lower BMI and fewer illnesses. As hypothesized, however, individuals who experienced higher life stress during both early childhood and adolescence but also experienced higher maternal sensitivity had *equally good* health outcomes as those with no risk factors (i.e., lower life stress at both life stages and higher maternal sensitivity). The majority of these effects held when we controlled for participants' sex, ethnicity, and self-reported neuroticism (see Farrell et al., 2017).

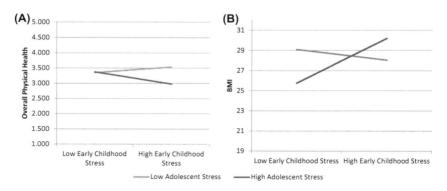

FIGURE 15.3   Interaction Effects of Early Childhood and Adolescent Life Stress on Subjective Ratings of Overall Physical Health (A) and BMI (B)

Source: From Farrell et al., 2017

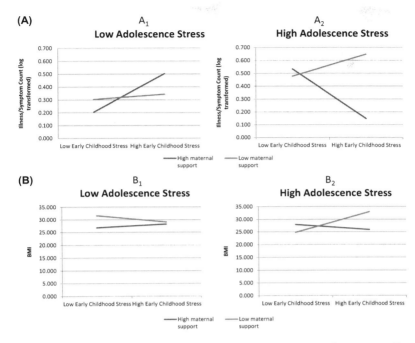

FIGURE 15.4 Buffering Effects of Maternal Supportive Care on Life Stress on Illness/
Symptom Counts (A) and BMI (B)

Source: From Farrell et al., 2017

Conclusions and Future Directions

As we noted at the beginning of the chapter, one critical component of a good
life is the quality of one's physical health. Although a lot is known about how
current life events, such as the amount of current life stress, social support, and
access to resources, are correlated with physical health outcomes, only a few prospective studies have examined whether and how early life events—particularly
interpersonal ones—prospectively predict physical health outcomes in adulthood.
Following the lives of individuals involved in a 40-year longitudinal project (the
Minnesota Longitudinal Study of Risk and Adaptation; MLSRA), we are beginning to identify some of the specific early life events that prospectively forecast
better versus worse physical health outcomes in middle adulthood, controlling
for the confounding effects of current life events that also systematically correlate
with health outcomes.

Viewed together, the MLSRA findings summarized in this chapter provide
some of the best and most direct evidence to date that certain early life experiences leave long-term, enduring effects on physical health. Consistent with
biological programming ideas (e.g., Boyce, 1985; Miller & Chen, 2013), our studies using the MLSRA document that being securely attached to one's mother

very early in life, receiving higher-quality maternal care during childhood, and encountering less life stress all predict better health outcomes in middle adulthood. Moreover, the association between receiving better maternal care during childhood and having better health in middle adulthood is mediated (i.e., carried forward) by having more secure attachment representations of childhood in early adulthood. Corroborating animal models and research (e.g., Meaney & Szyf, 2005), we have also found that stress encountered at certain life stages—especially early in life (ages 0–5), during adolescence (ages 13–19), and concurrently (at the time of the health assessment in adulthood)—has interactive effects on adult health outcomes. Importantly, however, receiving higher-quality maternal care appears to protect (buffer) individuals who experienced higher levels of stress early in life from experiencing health problems in middle adulthood.

Future research should head in several different directions. Returning to Miller and Chen's (2013) biological programming model (see Figure 15.1), we need to learn more about how accentuating effects (e.g., threat vigilance, social difficulties, poor self-regulation) affect adult health and whether certain accentuating effects statistically interact with certain programming effects (e.g., family instability, low nurturance, exposure to conflict) to impact health outcomes years later. If, for example, individuals grow up in low nurturance homes and become highly vigilant to threats later in life, does the combination of low nurturance and threat vigilance result in especially poor adult health outcomes? Alternatively, instead of operating in parallel, the programming effects of social experiences stemming from early adversity may be the cause of accentuating behavioral proclivities, making the path to a pro-inflammatory phenotype more linear. Testing causal mechanisms between each construct in this model can clarify the pathways linking early adversity to adult health problems.

We also need to learn more about whether and how genetic liabilities in combination with other harmful (or protective) environmental factors influence adult health outcomes via specific programming or accentuating effects. If, for instance, children are born with genetically compromised immune systems and are raised in environments containing more pathogens, how does this interface with their nutritional status or health-related lifestyle to affect their health status in adulthood? Finally, we need to better understand how different early life variables "get under the skin" to affect or perhaps reprogram biological systems known to regulate health outcomes (see, for example, Farrell & Simpson, 2017). Our recent findings from the MLSRA open the door to addressing each of these important future issues in order to help people live healthier and more fulfilling lives.

Bibliography

Ainsworth, M. D. S., Blehar, M., Waters, E., & Wall, S. (1978). *Patterns of attachment: A psychological study of the strange situation.* Hillside, NJ: Lawrence Erlbaum.

Anderson, S. A., & Whitaker, R. C. (2011). Attachment security and obesity in U.S. preschool-aged children. *Archives of Pediatric and Adolescent Medicine, 165,* 235–242.

Barker, D. J. P., Gluckman, P. D., Godfry, K. M., Harding, J. F., Owens, J. A., & Robinson, J. S. (1993). Fetal nutrition and cardiovascular disease in adult life. *The Lancet, 341,* 938–941.

Bell, B. G., & Belsky, J. (2008). Parents, parenting, and children's sleep problems: Exploring reciprocal effects. *British Journal of Developmental Psychology, 26,* 579–593.

Blum, R. W., Resnick, M. D., & Bergeisen, L. G. (1989). *The state of adolescent health in Minnesota.* Minneapolis, MN: University of Minnesota Adolescent Health Program.

Bowlby, J. (1969). *Attachment Vol. 1: Attachment and loss.* New York: Basic Books.

Bowlby, J. (1973). *Attachment Vol. 2: Separation and loss.* New York: Basic Books.

Boyce, W. T. (1985). Social support, family relations, and children. In S. Cohen & S. S. Leonard (Eds.), *Social support and health* (pp. 151–173). San Diego, CA: Academic Press.

Brody, G. H., Yu, T., Beach, S. R. H., Kogan, S. M., Windle, M., & Philibert, R. A. (2014). Harsh parenting and adolescent health: A longitudinal analysis with genetic moderation. *Health Psychology, 33,* 401–409.

Carroll, J. E., Gruenewald, T. L., Taylor, S. E., Janicki-Deverts, D., Matthews, K. A., & Seeman, T. E. (2013). Childhood abuse, parental warmth, and adult multisystem biological risk in the Coronary Artery Risk Development in Young Adults study. *Proceedings of the National Academy of Sciences, 110,* 17149–17153.

Ceichanowski, P. S., Walker, E. A., Katon, W. J., & Russo, J. E. (2002). Attachment theory: A model for healthcare utilization and somatization. *Psychosomatic Medicine, 64,* 660–667.

Chen, E., Miller, G. E., Kobor, M. S., & Cole, S. W. (2011). Maternal warmth buffers the effects of low early-life socioeconomic status on pro-inflammatory signaling in adulthood. *Molecular Psychiatry, 16,* 729–737.

Christakis, N. A., & Fowler, J. H. (2007). The spread of obesity in a large social network over 32 years. *New England Journal of Medicine, 357,* 370–379.

Cicchetti, D., & Blender, J. A. (2006). A multiple-levels-of-analysis perspective on resilience. *Annals of the New York Academy of Sciences, 1094,* 248–258.

Coan, J. A., Schaefer, H. A., & Davidson, R. J. (2006). Lending a hand: Social regulation of the neural response to threat. *Psychological Science, 17,* 1032–1039.

Cohen, S., Janicki-Deverts, D., & Miller, G. E. (2007). Psychological stress and disease. *Journal of the American Medical Associate, 298,* 1685–1687.

Cohen, S. E., & Syme, S. (1985). *Social support and health.* San Francisco: Academic Press.

Danese, A., Pariante, C. M., Caspi, A., Taylor, A., & Poulton, R. (2007). Childhood maltreatment predicts adult inflammation in a life-course study. *Proceedings of the National Academy of Sciences, 104*(4), 1319–1324.

DeLongis, A., Folkman, S., & Lazarus, R. S. (1988). The impact of daily stress on health and mood: Psychological and social resources as mediators. *Journal of Personality and Social Psychology, 54,* 486–495.

Dong, M., Giles, W. H., Felitti, V. J., Dube, S. R., Williams, J. E., Chapman, D. P., & Anda, R. F. (2004). Insights into causal pathways for ischemic heart disease adverse childhood experiences study. *Circulation, 110,* 1761–1766.

Egeland, B., Breitenbucher, M., & Rosenberg, D. (1980). Prospective study of the significance of life stress in the etiology of child abuse. *Journal of Consulting and Clinical Psychology, 48,* 195–205.

Ehrlich, K. B., Miller, G. E., Rohleder, N., & Adam, E. K. (2016). Trajectories of relationship stress and inflammatory processes in adolescence. *Development and Psychopathology, 28,* 27–138.

Essex, M. J., Shirtcliff, E. A., Burk, L. R., Ruttle, P. L., Klein, M. H., Slattery, M. J., & Armstrong, J. M. (2011). Influence of early life stress on later hypothalamic—pituitary—adrenal axis functioning and its covariation with mental health symptoms: A study of the allostatic process from childhood into adolescence. *Development and Psychopathology, 23,* 1039–1058.

Fagundes, C. P., Bennett, J. M., Derry, H. M., & Kiecolt-Glaser, J. K. (2011). Relationships and inflammation across the lifespan: Social developmental pathways to disease. *Social and Personality Psychology Compass, 5,* 891–903.

Fagundes, C. P., & Way, B. (2014). Early-life stress and adult inflammation. *Current Directions in Psychological Science, 23,* 277–283.

Farrell, A. K., & Simpson, J. A. (2017). Effects of relationship functioning on the biological experience of stress and physical health. *Current Opinion in Psychology, 13,* 49–53.

Farrell, A. K., Simpson, J. A., Englund, M. M., Carlson, E. A., & Sung, S. (2017). The impact of stress at different life stages on physical health and the buffering effects of maternal sensitivity. *Health Psychology, 36,* 35–44.

Farrell, A. K., Young, E., Simpson, J. A., Rosiman, G., Englund, M., & Carlson, E. (2017). *The quality of early caregiving, adult attachment representations, and health in adulthood: A longitudinal investigation.* Unpublished manuscript, University of Minnesota, Minneapolis, MN.

Fearon, R. M. P., & Belsky, J. (2016). Precursors of attachment security. In J. Cassidy & P. R. Shaver (Eds.), *Handbook of attachment: Theory, research, and clinical applications* (pp. 291–313). New York, NY: Guilford Press.

Felitti, V. J., Anda, R. F., Nordenberg, D., Williamson, D. F., Spitz, A. M., Edwards, V., & Marks, J. S. (1998). Relationship of childhood abuse and household dysfunction to many of the leading causes of death in adults: The adverse childhood experiences (ACE) study. *American Journal of Preventative Medicine, 14,* 245–258.

Fraley, R. C., & Brumbaugh, C. C. (2004). A dynamical systems approach to conceptualizing and studying stability and change in attachment security. In S. W. Rholes & J. A. Simpson (Eds.), *Adult attachment: Theory, research, and clinical implications* (pp. 86–132). New York, NY: Guilford Press.

Galobardes, B., Smith, G. D., & Lynch, J. W. (2006). Systematic review of the influence of childhood socioeconomic circumstances on risk for cardiovascular disease in adulthood. *Annals of Epidemiology, 16,* 91–104.

Gouin, J. P., Glaser, R., Loving, T. J., Malarkay, W. B., Stowell, J., Houts, C., & Kiecolt-Glaser, J. K. (2008). Attachment avoidance predicts inflammatory responses to marital conflict. *Brain, Behavior, and Immunity, 22,* 699–708.

Gunnar, M. R., & Quevedo, K. (2007). The neurobiology of stress and development. *Annual Review of Psychology, 58,* 151–173.

Gustafsson, P. E., Janlert, U., Theorell, T., Westerlund, H., & Hammarstrom, A. (2012). Do peer relations in adolescence influence health in adulthood? Peer problems in the school setting and the metabolic syndrome in middle age. *Plos One, 7,* 39385.

House, J. S., Landis, K. R., & Umberson, D. (1988). Social relationships and health. *Science, 241,* 540–545.

John, O. P., & Srivastava, S. (1999). The Big Five trait taxonomy: History, measurement, and theoretical perspectives. In L. A. Pervin & O. P. John (Eds.), *Handbook of personality: Theory and research* (2nd ed., pp. 102–138). New York, NY: Guilford Press.

Kidd, T., Poole, L., Leigh, E., Ronaldson, A., Jahangiri, M., & Steptoe, A. (2014). Attachment anxiety predicts IL-6 and length of hospital stay in coronary artery bypass graft surgery (CABG) patients. *Journal of Psychosomatic Research, 77,* 155–157.

Kiecolt-Glaser, J. K., Glaser, R., Cacioppo, J. T., & Malarkay, W. B. (1998). Marital stress: Immunologic, neuroendocrine, and autonomic correlates. *Annals of the New York Academy of Sciences, 840,* 656–663.

Lehman, B. J., Taylor, S. E., Kiefe, C. I., & Seeman, T. E. (2009). Relationship of early life stress and psychological functioning to blood pressure in the CARDIA study. *Health Psychology, 28*, 338–346.

Lupien, S. J., McEwan, B. S., Gunnar, M. R., & Heim, C. (2009). Effects of stress throughout the lifespan on the brain, behavior, and cognition. *Nature Reviews Neuroscience, 10*, 434–445.

Main, M., Goldwyn, R., & Hesse, E. (2003). *Adult attachment scoring and classification systems.* Unpublished manuscript, Department of Psychology, University of California, Berkeley.

McCormick, C. M., Mathews, I. Z., Thomas, C., & Waters, P. (2010). Investigations of HPA function and the enduring consequences of stressors in adolescence in animal models. *Brain and Cognition, 72*, 73–85.

McWilliams, L. A., & Bailey, S. J. (2010). Associations between adult attachment ratings and health conditions: Evidence from the national comorbidity survey replication. *Health Psychology, 29*, 446–453.

Meaney, M. J., & Szyf, M. (2005). Environmental programming of stress responses through DNA methylation: Life at the interface between a dynamic environment and a fixed genome. *Dialogues in Clinical Neuroscience, 7*, 103–123.

Miller, G. E., Brody, G. H., Yu, T., & Chen, E. (2014). A family-oriented psychosocial intervention reduces inflammation in low-SES African American youth. *Proceedings of the National Academy of Sciences, 111*, 11287–11292.

Miller, G. E., & Chen, E. (2013). The biological residue of childhood poverty. *Child Development Perspectives, 7*, 67–73.

Miller, G. E., Chen, E., & Parker, K. J. (2011). Psychological stress in childhood and susceptibility to the chronic diseases of aging: Moving toward a model of behavioral and biological mechanisms. *Psychological Bulletin, 137*, 959–997.

Miller, G. E., Lachman, M. E., Chen, E., Gruenwald, T. L., Karlamangla, A. S., & Seeman, T. E. (2011). Pathways to resilience: Maternal nurturance as a buffer against the effects of childhood poverty on metabolic syndrome at midlife. *Psychological Science, 22*, 1591–1599.

Okun, M. A., & George, L. K. (1984). Physician-and self-ratings of health, neuroticism and subjective well-being among men and women. *Personality and Individual Differences, 5*(5), 533–539.

Okun, M. A., & Stock, W. A. (1987). Correlates and components of subjective well-being among the elderly. *Journal of Applied Gerontology, 6*, 95–112.

Pietromonaco, P. R., Uchino, B., & Dunkel Schetter, C. (2013). Close relationship processes and health: Implications of attachment theory for health and disease. *Health Psychology, 32*(5), 499.

Puig, J., Englund, M. M., Simpson, J. A., & Collins, W. A. (2013). Predicting adult physical illness from infant attachment: A prospective longitudinal study. *Health Psychology, 32*, 409–417.

Raposa, E. B., Bower, J. E., Hammen, C. L., Najman, J. M., & Brennan, P. A. (2014). A developmental pathway from early life stress to inflammation: The role of negative health behaviors. *Psychological Science, 25*, 1268–1274.

Reis, H. T., Collins, W. A., & Berscheid, E. (2000). The relationship context of human behavior and development. *Psychological Bulletin, 126*, 844.

Repetti, R. L., Taylor, S. E., & Seeman, T. E. (2002). Risky families: Family social environments and the mental and physical health of offspring. *Psychological Bulletin, 128*, 330.

Roisman, G. I., Padrón, E., Sroufe, L. A., & Egeland, B. (2002). Earned-secure attachment status in retrospect and prospect. *Child Development, 73*, 1204–1219.

Rubin, D. C., Rahhal, T. A., & Poon, L. W. (1998). Things learned in early adulthood are remembered best. *Memory and Cognition, 26*, 3–19.

Russek, L. G., & Schwartz, G. E. (1997). Feeling of parental caring predict health status in midlife: A 35-year follow-up of the Harvard Mastery of Stress Study. *Journal of Behavioral Medicine*, *20*, 1–13.

Scharfe, E., & Eldredge, D. (2001). Associations between attachment representations and health behaviors in late adolescence. *Journal of Health Psychology*, *6*, 295–307.

Simpson, J. A., Collins, W. A., Tran, S., & Haydon, K. C. (2007). Attachment and the experience and expression of emotions in romantic relationships: A developmental perspective. *Journal of Personality and Social Psychology*, *92*(2). 355–367.

Simpson, J. A., & Rholes, W. S. (2012). Adult attachment orientations, stress, and romantic relationships. In P. Devine & A. Plant (Eds.), *Advances in experimental social psychology* (Vol. 45, pp. 279–328). New York, NY: Elsevier.

Slopen, N., Loucks, E. B., Appleton, A. A., Kawachi, I., Kubzansky, L. D., Non, A. L., & Gilman, S. E. (2015). Early origins of inflammation: An examination of prenatal and childhood social adversity in a prospective cohort study. *Psychoneuroendocrinology*, *51*, 403–413.

Sroufe, L. A., Egeland, B., Carlson, E. A., & Collins, W. A. (2005). *The development of the person*. New York, NY: Guilford Press.

Tobin, E. T., Kane, H. S., Saleh, D. J., Wildman, D. E., Breen, E. C., Secord, E., & Slatcher, R. B. (2015). Asthma-related immune responses in youth with asthma: Associations with maternal responsiveness and expressions of positive and negative affect in daily life. *Psychosomatic Medicine*, *77*(8), 892–902.

Uchino, B. N., Cacioppo, J. T., & Kiecolt-Glaser, J. K. (1996). The relationship between social support and physiological processes: A review with emphasis on underlying mechanisms and implications for health. *Psychological Bulletin*, *119*, 488–531.

Uchino, B. N., Cacioppo, J. T., Malarkey, W., & Glaser, R. (1995). Individual differences in cardiac sympathetic control predict endocrine and immune responses to acute psychological stress. *Journal of Personality and Social Psychology*, *69*, 736–743.

van IJzendoorn, M. (1995). Adult attachment representations, parental responsiveness, and infant attachment: A meta-analysis on the predictive validity of the Adult Attachment Interview. *Psychological Bulletin*, *117*, 387–403.

Waters, E., Merrick, S., Treboux, D., Crowell, J., & Albersheim, L. (2000). Attachment security in infancy and early adulthood: A twenty-year longitudinal study. *Child Development*, *71*, 684–689.

Waters, T. E. A., Brockmeyer, S., & Crowell, J. A. (2013). AAI coherence predicts caregiving and care seeking behavior in couple problem solving interactions: Secure base script knowledge helps explain why. *Attachment and Human Development*, *15*, 316–331.

Waters, T. E. A., Ruiz, S. K., & Roisman, G. I. (2016). Origins of secure base script knowledge and the developmental construction of attachment representations. *Child Development*, *88*, 198–209.

Watson, D., & Pennebaker, J. W. (1989). Health complaints, stress, and distress: Exploring the central role of negative affectivity. *Psychological Review*, *96*, 234.

Zayas, V., Mischel, W., Shoda, Y., & Aber, J. L. (2011). Roots of adult attachment maternal caregiving at 18 months predicts adult peer and partner attachment. *Social Psychological and Personality Science*, *2*, 289–297.

16

POSITIVE PARENTING, ADOLESCENT SUBSTANCE USE PREVENTION, AND THE GOOD LIFE

William D. Crano and Candice D. Donaldson

Although the effects of traumatic parent-child interactions can be overcome, optimal family relationships are widely viewed as powerful foundational forces for productivity, rewarding social relations, and long-term contentment. Dysfunctional relations, conversely, often are viewed as an open doorway to hell. Positive parenting practices and constructive family relationships are significant predictors of appropriate youth adjustment (Leidy, Guerra, & Toro, 2012; Zhou et al., 2002) and offer protection against evolving delinquent behaviors (Donaldson, Nakawaki, & Crano, 2015; Hemovich & Crano, 2009; Hemovich, Lac, & Crano, 2011). The effects of positive parenting are long lasting (Donaldson et al., 2016) and crucial for youth well-being (DeVore & Ginsburg, 2005; Schwarz et al., 2011), and so it is imperative to understand ways in which parents' actions motivate and facilitate their own, and by extension, their children's, attainment of the "good life," a central concept in the discipline of positive psychology and the study of optimal human functioning (Seligman & Csikszentmihalyi, 2000; see also Simpson et al., this volume).

Social psychology can contribute to our understanding and attainment of the good life in many ways. It can highlight new approaches for understanding health promotion and psychological resilience (Jané-Llopis, Barry, Hosman, & Patel, 2005; Kobau et al., 2011; Moore & Charvat, 2007; see also Frederickson, this volume), and indicate areas where social researchers might shift their focus toward understanding and preventing illness and self-destructive behaviors, rather than rehabilitation and recovery from engagement in those behaviors (see also Shah, this volume). Few scientific disciplines are as well positioned as social psychology to advance the goal of the good life. We contend that the application of principles of persuasion to prevent (self-)destructive behaviors, or in promoting positive actions, can and should be a fundamental concern of social psychology.

Our particular focus as social psychologists involves study of the formation and change of attitudes related to the use of illicit and illegal substances, which is damaging to youth development and decreases their and their families' overall quality of life (Hemovich et al., 2011; Topolski et al., 2001; Zullig, Valois, Huebner, Oeltmann, & Drane, 2001). For social psychologists, the prevention of destructive behaviors should play a prominent role in defining what it means to live the "good life." The current chapter centers specifically on adolescent substance use prevention and the importance of positive parenting practices in promoting the goal of abstinence from use of harmful substances, which we view as a fundamental necessity to reaching the goal of achieving happiness, the good life. We first outline our views on the role of parents as facilitators of youth development and subjective well-being, and then consider recent developments in adolescent substance use prevention. Finally, we will draw implications for future prevention efforts aimed at preventing adolescent substance use initiation.

Subjective Well-Being and Positive Youth Development

The meaning of "the good life" is fundamental to the study of positive psychology, which centers on understanding factors that help individuals live fulfilling and satisfying lives, rather than directing efforts toward treating mental illness and other negative mental states (see also Baumeister; and Dunn & Dwyer, this volume; Seligman, 2003; Seligman & Csikszentmihalyi, 2000). A central focus of positive psychology is the concept of subjective well-being (SWB) as a fundamental component of the good life (Diener, 1984; see also Sheldon, this volume). SWB refers to people's evaluations of their quality of life, and involves both cognitive and emotional factors (Diener, 1994). It is characterized by high levels of positive affect, low levels of negative affect, and judgments of one's overall quality of life (Diener, 1984). A facet of SWB that has received increased attention is youth life satisfaction, and recent research has focused on the correlates and possible consequences of this construct. Considerable research, for example, has shown that deficits in life satisfaction place teens at an increased risk for psychological and social problems (Huebner & Alderman, 1993; Lewinsohn, Redner, & Seeley, 1991; Suldo & Huebner, 2004a). Conversely, high levels of adolescent life satisfaction have been associated positively with enhanced well-being (Huebner, Suldo, Smith, & McKnight, 2004) and negatively connected to health-damaging behaviors such as substance use (Bogart, Collins, Ellickson, & Klein, 2007; Zullig et al., 2001).

Positive psychologists have argued that psychology has focused too much on negative affect and mental illness (Seligman & Csikszentmihalyi, 2000). However, some have held that the study of optimal human functioning should not ignore issues related to the avoidance of negative states (e.g., Lazarus, 2003; see also Fiedler and Arslan; and Forgas, this volume). In support of this argument, the good life is seen to involve using one's strengths to produce happiness and gratification, which cannot be accomplished without preventing or avoiding unhealthy behaviors while promoting positive ones. Thus, study of substance use prevention and resultant positive mental health should be incorporated into the social psychological analysis of human thriving, as study of prevention is arguably central to promoting individual strengths, virtues, abilities, and overall happiness—in short, the good life.

The Role of Positive Parental Influence in Children's Substance Use

Social relationships affect quality of life (Diener, Suh, Lucas, & Smith, 1999; see also Gable, this volume). Children's relations among family members have been shown to influence life satisfaction throughout adolescence (Rask, Åstedt Kurki, Paavilainen, & Laippala, 2003; Schwarz et al., 2011; Suldo & Huebner, 2004b; see also Simpson et al., this volume). During adolescence, interactions between parents and their children evolve. This evolution often is accompanied by the emergence and escalation of conflict (Allison, 2000). Parents must learn to balance the promotion of adolescent independence effectively, while simultaneously counteracting development of problem behaviors.

Warmth and Limits

Positive parenting behaviors are among the most important influences on healthy youth development (Castro-Schilo et al., 2013; McKee et al., 2007; Skinner, Johnson, & Snyder, 2005). These behaviors are characterized by warmth, acceptance, support, positive reinforcement, affection, involvement, and setting reasonable limits (Donaldson et al., 2015, 2016; Morrill, Hawrilenko, & Córdova, 2016; Sanders, 2003). This parenting style fosters cooperation and mutual enjoyment of parent-child interactions (Kochanska, Aksan, Prisco, & Adams, 2008), higher levels of youth well-being and life satisfaction (DeVore & Ginsburg, 2005; Schwarz et al., 2011), and is associated with a decreased risk of delinquency (Menting, Van Lier, Koot, Pardini, & Loeber, 2016).

Parents play an important role in attenuating adolescents' initiation of illicit or illegal substances (e.g., marijuana, alcohol, tobacco, etc.). Our research has shown parental *warmth* and *monitoring* operate in tandem as important moderators of youth deviance (Donaldson et al., 2015, 2016; Handren, Donaldson, & Crano, 2016; Hemovich et al., 2011; Lac & Crano, 2009; Lac, Alvaro, Crano, & Siegel, 2009; Siegel et al., 2014). *Parental warmth* concerns the extent to which adolescents perceive their parents as loving, caring, and responsive to their individual needs (Lowe & Dotterer, 2013). Teens who experience high levels of parental warmth are more likely to comply with parental attempts to set behavioral rules and guidelines (Grusec, Goodnow, & Kuczynski, 2000). In addition, parental warmth is associated with enhanced perception of well-being (Chang, McBride-Chang,

Stewart, & Au, 2003; Fredrickson, this volume), better psychosocial development, and lower levels of stress (Lippold, Davis, McHale, Buxton, & Almeida, 2016).

Monitoring/Surveillance

As a complementary factor, Dishion and McMahon (1998) described *parental monitoring* as a set of parenting behaviors focused on the child's whereabouts and activities. Youth who experience inadequate monitoring may be more susceptible to associating with deviant peers and adopting deviant behavior (Donaldson et al., 2015; Hemovich & Crano, 2009; Hemovich et al., 2011). In addition, poorly monitored youth are more likely to engage in risky activity, have higher rates of illicit substance use (Lac et al., 2009), and associate with peer groups that approve of substance use (Chassin, Pillow, Curran, Molina, & Barrera, 1993; Donaldson et al., 2015).

Although the link between monitoring and antisocial outcomes has been consistently acknowledged (DeVore & Ginsburg, 2005; Donaldson et al., 2015; Hemovich et al., 2011; Lac & Crano, 2009), the impact and efficacy of various monitoring tactics is less clear, as parents can make use of a variety of strategies to monitor their children. For example, parents can use surveillance, where they closely and consistently track their child's whereabouts and activities (Dishion & McMahon, 1998; Kerr & Stattin, 2000; Kerr, Stattin, & Özdemir, 2012; Stattin & Kerr, 2000), or they can rely on the child's voluntary disclosures (Lac et al., 2009; Ramirez et al., 2004).

The relative importance of monitoring and warmth variations is the focus of considerable discussion and debate (DeVore & Ginsburg, 2005). For example, Stattin and Kerr's (2000) results contradicted the long-held belief that surveillance and direct control of children's behavior promoted healthy development, and showed instead that voluntary disclosure was more important in promoting healthy outcomes. Parenting that facilitated positive parent-child communication was highly protective against deviant behavior. Fletcher, Steinberg, and Williams-Wheeler (2004) supported this view when they argued that parental control surveillance deterred teen substance use when combined with warmth.

Over-Monitoring

Following conflicting evidence on the effectiveness of different monitoring techniques (e.g., Fletcher et al., 2004; Kerr et al., 2012; Stattin & Kerr, 2000), researchers have begun to assess the potentially harmful effects of parental control, or "over-monitoring," which involves their exerting extreme control over their children's behavior (Donaldson et al., 2015; Gere, Villabø, Torgersen, & Kendall, 2012; Roche, Ghazarian, Little, & Leventhal, 2011). By this definition, parental control involves parents' invasive attempts to control, invalidate, and manipulate children so they think and behave in parentally approved ways (Barber, 1996; Barber & Harmon, 2002; Barber, Olsen, & Shagle, 1994). Parents who over-monitor tend to employ tactics that involve withdrawal of warmth and support while inducing guilt, shame, and anxiety, limiting verbal expression, invalidating a child's feelings, using personal attacks, inducing feelings of guilt and anxiety, and withdrawing love (Barber, 1996; Barber & Harmon, 2002; Barber et al., 1994; Smetana & Daddis, 2002). This type of maladaptive parenting is detrimental to adolescent development and is related to several emotional and behavioral problems, including anxiety (Duchesne & Ratelle, 2010), depression (Barber, 1996), and juvenile delinquency (Pettit, Laird, Dodge, Bates, & Criss, 2001).

In research on the detrimental effects of parental control, Donaldson and associates (2016) showed how high levels of monitoring combined with low relative levels of parental warmth negatively impacted on youth development. This research was designed to assess parental correlates of teen prescription stimulant (e.g., Adderall) and opioid (e.g., Vicodin) misuse. It used a nationally representative survey of adolescent respondents. Results showed that high levels of strict monitoring combined with low parental warmth were related to young adolescents' (ages 12 to 14) heightened misuse of prescription stimulants. Among younger teens, high levels of monitoring had a positive influence on social relationships and drug-related attitudes, but a negative impact on usage behavior when combined with low warmth. Parents who monitored their children closely without providing support and warmth appeared to have driven their children into prescription stimulant misuse to meet the parents' overly ambitious academic standards. This is not a recipe for the good life, of either parents or their offspring.

Consistent with these findings, Donaldson and colleagues (2016) used a nationally representative longitudinal panel survey of parents and their children to show that parental over-monitoring had lasting and negative effects on the development of their children. Responses were collected across four irregularly spaced measurement periods. At the first measurement period (Wave 1), respondents were between the ages of 10 and 20 ($M = 14.89, SD = 1.64$). At Wave 2, one year later, respondents' ages ranged from 11 to 21 ($M = 15.89, SD = 1.64$). In Wave 3, seven years later, respondents were between the ages of 18 and 27 ($M = 21.81, SD = 1.84$), and at Wave 4, seven years later, the original respondents were between the ages of 25 to 34 years ($M = 28.54, SD = 1.82$). Analysis revealed that parents' behaviors (measured at Wave 1) were related to binge drinking both one year later (at Wave 2) and six to seven years after the initial assessment (at Wave 3). Parental expectations that their child was an alcohol user, along with parent consumption of alcohol, were predictive of their child's binge drinking during adolescence (Wave 2) and young adulthood (Wave 3). Adolescent (Wave 2) and adult (Wave 3) binge drinking was most common for respondents whose parents practiced low levels of monitoring and warmth, highlighting the importance of parental communication style and proper monitoring on later teen outcomes. Finally, and perhaps most surprisingly, analysis showed that binge drinking during both adolescence and young adulthood was associated with increased odds of incarceration in Wave 4, eight to 14 years after the first survey was administered.

Parents' Expectations

Research by Lamb and Crano (2014) on self-fulfilling prophecy effects in adolescent substance use showed that the expectancy cues transmitted by parents in their interactions with children did not need to be excessive or pronounced. In their research, transference of apparently subtle parental cues and expectancies predicted subsequent adolescent substance use. Discrepancies between parents' expectations of their children's marijuana use and children's reported usage had lasting behavioral consequences. Abstinent adolescents in the first year (T1) of a U.S. nationally representative survey were significantly *more* likely to initiate marijuana use over the next year (T2) if their parents reported the belief at T1 that their child *had* used the substance. Conversely, self-reported adolescent marijuana users at T1 were significantly *less* likely to continue usage at T2 if their parents reported the belief at T1 that their child had *never* used drugs. Odds that abstinent children whose parents believed they used marijuana would initiate use at T2 were 4.4 times greater than those of abstinent respondents whose parents judged them abstinent. Odds of self-reported users quitting by T2 were 2.7 times greater if parents reported a belief at T1 that their children had never used drugs. These results were found despite data indicating that the majority of the adolescent respondents, users and nonusers alike, did not think their parents would be aware of their usage. The relation between youths' marijuana usage and their estimates of their parents' likelihood of knowing that they had used the drug was practically nonexistent ($r = .005$). These results support Stattin and Kerr's (2000) contention by demonstrating that close parental surveillance and inconsistencies between parents' expectations and their children's actions can exacerbate the risk of youth substance use initiation or reduce the likelihood of a child's continuance of substance use. The source of such inconsistencies is difficult to pinpoint precisely, but surely one of the contributing factors concerns the lack of clear parental attention and communication. If a child is using an illicit substance, and parents know it but the child believes they do not, then the parents have exhibited a failure of communication, concern, or capacity to face a difficult and potentially unpleasant interaction. Similarly, if the child is drug-abstinent and the parent believes he or she is not, their failure to confront the issue, for surely it is the parents' duty to do so, reveals an astonishing failure of parental responsibility, and a loss of an opportunity to establish a stronger connection with the child. These problems are remedial, but the remedies used in substance use prevention are not immediately obvious to many parents, and that is the fault of the society for not providing such information in their publicly funded prevention communications, which almost inevitably target youth, telling them what to do but not how to do it. This information, while often ignored by the primary target audience (youth), could be immeasurably valuable to parents whose good intentions are stifled by ignorance of the proper preventive approach and a reluctance to display it.

Self-Determination

These results, and those of Donaldson and associates (2015, 2016) are consistent with self-determination theory (SDT), a model of social development that argues that adolescents have innate psychological needs to experience autonomy and freedom (Ryan & Deci, 2000, 2002). Youth seek voluntarily to engage in interesting and novel activities (i.e., in intrinsically motivated actions), in addition to integrating their sense of self into their values and behaviors (i.e., internalization). Youth can either accept different values as their own, integrating them into their sense of self (integration), or they can behave in accord with a value without accepting it as their own (introjection; Deci, Eghrari, Patrick, & Leone, 1994). Parents can play a positive role in helping their children adopt the appropriate motivational framework informing behavior relevant to substance use.

SDT research distinguishes intrinsic from extrinsic motivation and suggests the ways they are differentially associated with underage alcohol consumption (Chawla, Neighbors, Logan, Lewis, & Fossos, 2009; Wormington, Anderson, & Corpus, 2011). *Intrinsic motivation* concerns behaviors that are freely chosen and pleasurable or interesting in their own right. This type of motivation is associated with an autonomy orientation and is related to positive outcomes, such as less alcohol consumption. In contrast, *extrinsic motivation* is associated with behavior that is influenced by external sources and regulatory processes, and is related to a control orientation. Extrinsic motivation is associated with negative outcomes, as it leads individuals to feel forced to take a given course of action.

Research indicates that extrinsic motivation is associated with drinking and alcohol-related consequences and leads to external forms of regulation (Chawla et al., 2009; Wormington et al., 2011). Youth who attribute their behavior to external circumstances are more likely to succumb to peer pressures (Knee & Neighbors, 2002). Thus, it has been postulated that the link between SDT and alcohol use is mediated by perceived peer approval (Chawla et al., 2009). Teens might use substances to establish their own sense of autonomy or to diminish stress from outside sources. SDT reinforces the idea that parents who coldly enforce rules and restrict personal freedom to make decisions suppress their children's innate need for autonomy and independence. In turn, these restrictions are likely to render teens more susceptible to negative peer pressures, which is likely to result in negative outcomes such as using substances to regain control and cope with problems.

Positive Parenting

The importance of monitoring and warmth was anticipated by Baumrind (1978, 1991, 2013), who distinguished authoritative from authoritarian parenting and their resulting outcomes. *Authoritative* parents inspire children to be independent, while simultaneously placing reasonable limits on their behaviors. This style is characterized by extensive communication, warmth, and nurturance, and is related to positive developmental outcomes (Baumrind, 1978; Dornbusch, Ritter, Leiderman, Roberts, & Fraleigh, 1987), including increased life satisfaction (Stevenson, Maton, & Teti, 1999). *Authoritarian* parenting, conversely, is characterized by restrictive and punitive parenting, where parents pressure children to follow their commands and harshly enforced rules. Research indicates that adolescents with authoritarian parents are more likely to develop resistance to authority (Trinkner, Cohn, Rebellon, & Van Gundy, 2012) and are more susceptible to substance use than children with authoritative parents (Adalbjarnardottir & Hafsteinsson, 2001; Kenney, Lac, Hummer, Grimaldi, & LaBrie, 2015).

Overall, monitoring and supervision have been shown consistently to play a crucial role in facilitating healthy childhood development (Hemovich et al., 2011); however, the literature reviewed here suggests that harsh discipline combined with strict observation are not efficient factors in preventing adolescents' substance use initiation. Rather, positive parent-child interactions are crucial in facilitating positive relationships and youth well-being (Donaldson et al., 2015; Kaminski, Valle, Filene, & Boyle, 2008; Lac & Crano, 2009; Lac et al., 2009). These interactions are characterized by warmth, understanding, and respect. They promote reciprocal and cooperative relationships between parents and their children, enhancing mutual enjoyment of their interactions (see also Huppert, this volume; Kochanska et al., 2008). Positive parenting, involving warmth *and* setting reasonable boundaries on acceptable behavior, results in more effective implementations of discipline, owing to the quality of the parent-child relationship (McNeil & Hembree-Kigin, 2010). These findings indicate that positive parenting should be an important feature in future efforts designed to prevent youth substance use initiation.

Substance Use Prevention: The Role of Media Campaigns

In addition to parenting, the media play a crucial role in prevention of substance use, as parents may prove a key factor in transmitting positive evaluations of preventive media to their children. Applied health research shows the importance of prevention campaigns, targeting individuals who have not engaged in illicit substance use, as users have more positive perceptions of illicit substances than nonusers (Crano, Siegel, Alvaro, Lac, & Hemovich, 2008; Lac & Donaldson, 2016), and usually are less receptive to persuasive communications (Crano, Siegel, Alvaro, & Patel, 2007). In line with this research, many large-scale mass media interventions have been designed to prevent substance use initiation in adolescents whose history of past use is almost necessarily less involved than those found in older populations. However, adolescents often are characterized by high levels of reactivity, exhibiting heightened sensitivity to threats to personal freedom, which render them difficult targets for mass media substance use prevention appeals (Miller & Quick, 2010).

Parent-Child Communication and the Two-Step Flow Model

To circumvent reactance or resistance, we have suggested that parents may prove a more expedient target for campaigns designed to prevent adolescent substance use, thereby enhancing overall life satisfaction. In line with this suggestion, parent-child communication has been applied as a central component of some studies designed to attenuate adolescent substance use (Beatty, Cross, & Shaw, 2008; Donaldson et al., 2016; Huansuriya, Siegel, & Crano, 2014) and has been a significant feature of some antidrug campaign efforts as well (Stephenson, 2002). Many small-scale, person-to-person interventions maintain that targeting parent-child communication can enhance the success of efforts designed to reduce the likelihood of adolescent substance use (Koutakis, Stattin, & Kerr, 2008; O'Donnell, Myint-U, Duran, & Stueve, 2010; Strandberg & Bodin, 2011); however, evaluations of large-scale national campaigns demonstrate that multimedia messages promoting the importance of parent-child drug communication are not always successful (Hornik, MacLean, & Cadell, 2003).

Since research consistently highlights the important role of parents in attenuating the risks of adolescent substance initiation and continuance (Donaldson et al., 2015, 2016; Hemovich et al., 2009, 2011), application of more comprehensive frameworks modeling the flow of interpersonal communication from parents to their children might be useful in evaluating large-scale prevention efforts. In particular, integrating the two-step flow model of communication (Katz & Lazarsfeld, 1955; Lazarsfeld, Berelson, & Gaudet, 1944), which is a model of media influence, with a person-to-person approach of attitude change known as the theory of planned behavior (Ajzen, 1985, 1991), might be useful in developing a more precise understanding of media influence and the vital role of parents in substance prevention.

The two-step flow of communication model (Katz & Lazarsfeld, 1955; Lazarsfeld et al., 1944) postulates that mass media campaigns convey information to intended audience members via two distinct stages. Opinion leaders (e.g., parents) first attend to and react to persuasive messages. These opinion leaders, in turn, relay and interpret the message content to their opinion followers (e.g., their children), thereby influencing followers' responses to the message. According to this model, opinion leaders are individuals perceived as authoritative and knowledgeable about the message topic. In the context of substance use, teens tend to characterize their parents as credible sources of information about drugs (Kelly, Comello, & Hunn, 2002). Thus, in applying the two-step flow framework, we conceptualize parents as opinion leaders about drug use information; their children are opinion followers that may be influenced by the information conveyed by parents, as shown clearly in research by Huansuriya and colleagues (2014). This model indicates that parents can be powerful opinion leaders for their children in transmitting important information; in turn, this observation suggests that targeting parents in our preventive campaigns may be a highly effective tactic in reducing the substance use of their offspring. Indeed, even the parenting behaviors of a teen's friends' parents can affect substance use. As Cleveland, Feinberg, Osgood, and Moody (2012) showed, higher parental knowledge of one's friendship-group's parents was associated with decreased alcohol, tobacco, and marijuana use. Targeting parents in efforts to attenuate adolescent substance use, in other words, might have positive indirect influences on teens' peer groups (see also Myers, this volume).

Two-Step Flow and TPB

The theory of planned behavior (TPB: Ajzen, 1985, 1991) can be integrated with the two-step flow of communication model, thereby suggesting the pathways through which communications might influence parents' (as opinion leaders) attitudes, opinions, and behaviors toward substance use. The TPB holds that intentions directly influence behavior, and that intention to participate in a behavior is influenced by attitudes, subjective norms, and perceived behavioral control (PBC). Attitudes represent positive or negative evaluations. Subjective norms involve perceptions of what important others think about an actor's behavior. PBC is concerned with the extent to which a person feels capable to perform a given behavior.

Combining the two-step flow model with the TPB results in a conceptual model in which the theories synergistically interact to create a useful model of the ways parents might be incorporated as communicators into adolescent substance use prevention campaigns. The two-step flow model describes the ways in which mass media influence people, whereas the TPB is informative with respect to the variables that should be the targeted. Combining the theoretical frameworks suggests that parents' (i.e., opinion leaders) exposure to a substance use prevention message may encourage them to converse with their children (opinion followers) about substance use and its dangers. Doing so, parents can influence their children's attitudes, subjective norms, percieved behavioral control, and subsequent intentions to engage in substance use. This is important, as meta-analyses have consistently shown a strong and positive association between intentions and subsequent behavior (Ajzen & Fishbein, 2005; Webb & Sheeran, 2006).

Research supporting incorporating both theories into future prevention efforts was performed by Huansuriya and associates (2014), who combined the two theories in their research on the outcomes of a national adolescent substance use prevention campaign. Their results revealed that parents' exposure to the campaign was indirectly linked via parental communication, which influenced their children's attitudes, and which in turn affected children's intentions to use marijuana one year later. The authors reported that extent of campaign exposure resulted in positive changes in parents' attitudes about communicating with their children about drug use, in addition to facilitating changes in parent's subjective norms (i.e., perceptions that significant others would approve of their substance-centered conversations with their children), which increased parents' intentions to initiate a substance-related conversation with their children. This intention to communicate was confirmed by their children's self-reports one year later. In turn, parent-child conversation had a positive influence on adolescents' attitudes about marijuana, which had a strong influence on their marijuana usage intentions.

An intriguing feature of this research is that parents' self-perceived capability to communicate with their children (perceived behavioral control: PBC) was not affected by exposure to the campaign, nor was their children's. The authors attributed this apparent null campaign effect on PBC to its failure to provide information about *how* to resist the offer of illicit substances, a critical antecedent to adolescent substance use (Benjet et al., 2007; Siegel, Tan, Navarro, Alvaro, & Crano, 2015; Voelkl & Frone, 2000; Wagner & Anthony, 2002). The role of parents in fostering adolescents' resisting offers of illicit substances has been explicated in research, which indicated that children who perceived high levels of parental knowledge received fewer offers of illicit substances than those who perceived their parents as being less knowledgeable (Siegel et al., 2015).

Huansuriya and colleagues' (2014) research provides further evidence that parenting behaviors can play a crucial role in preventing adolescent substance use. It indicates that targeting parents may be an effective way to reduce adolescent substance use. Their findings fit well with research on positive parenting and the importance of parental warmth and understanding in guiding the content of thoughtful, evidence-based prevention campaigns designed to educate parents about effective ways of influencing their children when dealing with issues of substance use. Such campaigns should stress the importance of parental responsiveness and respect, and the utility of using reason in rule setting (Donaldson et al., 2016). An experimental intervention conducted by Glatz and Koning (2015) revealed that providing parents with specific and concrete instructions about how to deal with their children's potential substance use enhanced their overall self-efficacy and confidence in implementing prevention strategies. This does not mean that parents should abrogate their responsibilities in guiding their children, but rather that arbitrary and capricious rules must be avoided, whereas reasonable rules of conduct should be honored. In light of this research, it stands to reason that future prevention efforts should contain three critical elements, which often are lacking in adolescent substance use prevention campaigns.

The first requisite for success is that the campaign must provide useful and relevant content (information) about substance use and its potential dangers. Many parents are not confident that they know enough about the multitude of illicit substances available today to discuss substance use with their children knowledgeably and persuasively. This perception may be true, but it need not be so if proper evidence-based, media-based prevention campaigns were mounted (Crano, 2010; Crano, Alvaro, & Siegel, 2015). A second element is that the importance of effective parent-child communication is stressed when disseminating substance use preventive information. Finally, and consistent with the second element, specific strategies for implementing clear guidelines that maintain mutual respect while communicating clear expectations regarding substance use should be a part of every parent-centered prevention campaign (Donaldson et al., 2015).

The application of both the two-step flow model and the TPB when disseminating persuasive information aimed at parents has an added benefit of being less likely to be resisted by adolescents. Crano and associates' (2007) research examined in a factorial experiment the effects of source (doctor or peer), suggested harm (social or physical), and target (direct or indirect) on adolescents' evaluations of several anti-inhalant messages. Their analysis showed that indirect messages (i.e., those apparently targeted at parents rather than the adolescents themselves) more effectively influenced youth to avoid inhalant use. The authors suggested that persuasive messages targeted at parents might be less likely to be resisted by adolescent respondents, thereby attenuating reactance and counter-argumentation. Thus, adopting a parent-targeted approach to prevention might have important direct implications for parents and indirect effects on adolescents as well, by attenuating their tendency to counter-argue, thereby maximizing campaign effects.

The upshot of this argument is clear—parents are valuable but largely untapped resources in adolescent substance use prevention. In part, this is the result of prevention campaigns that have largely ignored this important resource. To succeed, campaigns should leverage the inherent authoritative positions of parents as persuasive communication sources for their children. First, the prevention community must provide parents with the necessary information; to the extent necessary, parents must be motivated to learn this information, and keep current with the changing topography of substance use; they must be motivated to monitor their children's behavior; and they must disseminate the information they have absorbed to their children in a reasoned and reasonable manner.

To succeed, proper dissemination requires knowledge and effort. Firm but reasonable rule setting, a warm and open environment to encourage conversation and discussion, and mutual respect will have a measurable impact on adolescents' substance-related behaviors. The theories and empirical research that bolster this claim are readily available, and have been since the time of Lasswell and Hovland. It is time we took them more seriously in combatting one of society's most vexing issues, the misuse of dangerous psychotropic substances by youth.

Limitations and Future Directions

Despite the importance of positive parenting, effective strategies can be difficult for parents to enact, and in addition may arouse parental resistance and fade over time (McNeil & Hembree-Kigin, 2010). People are predisposed to focus on others' negative thoughts and actions (Baumeister, Bratslavsky, Finkenauer, & Vohs, 2001), and even the best-behaved children do not always comply with parental ideals. Noncompliance can be frustrating for parents, and in consequence, about 90% of parents in the United States have resorted to acts of psychological aggression (e.g., shouting or cursing) in response to their children's misbehavior. This reaction is associated with increased susceptibility of youth to delinquent actions and mental health problems (McKee et al., 2007; Straus & Field, 2003). Thus, future investigations might focus on sustained parental educational strategies that help prevent psychological aggression and reinforce positive parenting. Clearly, one-shot interventions are not likely to succeed (see Fiedler & Arslan, this volume).

Another difficulty requiring consideration is that most parents avoid participating in parent education programs, and economically disadvantaged parents are least likely to do so (Sanders et al., 1999). This is a challenging problem, because substance use is more common among low-income and single-parent families (Hemovich et al., 2011). Thus, a multi-level, population-based approach to prevention might be required to enhance parental competence to implement positive parent behaviors. Sanders (2003) argued that an approach targeting multiple prevention contexts including the media, schools, and community institutions would be more effective than single-mode diffusion models in disseminating persuasive substance use prevention information.

Individual differences in youth personality (Smack, Kushner, & Tackett, 2015) and temperament (Slagt, Dubas, Deković, & van Aken, 2016) also might be an important consideration for future interventions. Child personality traits that reflect a predisposition to experience negative emotions (e.g., neuroticism) and poor self-regulation (e.g., low conscientiousness) might respond differently to harsh versus positive parenting practices, as these traits have been shown to moderate relationships between parent actions and externalizing behaviors (De Clercq, Van Leeuwen, De Fruyt, Van Hiel, & Mervielde, 2008; Prinzie et al., 2003; Smack et al., 2015). Similarly, a meta-analysis of parenting and child temperament revealed that children with more difficult temperaments were more vulnerable to negative parenting, but also benefited more from positive parenting (see Forgas, and Fritz & Lyubomirsky, this volume; Slagt et al., 2016).

Research has identified youth at the highest risk for substance use initiation by recategorizing nonusers into two groups based on systematic differences in their reported certainty of continued abstinence (Crano et al., 2007; Crano, Gilbert, Alvaro, & Siegel, 2008; Siegel, Alvaro, & Burgoon, 2003; Siegel et al., 2014). In this research, substance-abstinent youth who reported absolute certainty that they would never initiate substance use were categorized as *resolute nonusers*. In contrast, teens who were uncertain that they would remain abstinent were termed *vulnerable nonusers*. Compared to resolute nonusers, vulnerable nonusers experienced less parental monitoring, lower academic performance, and were more approving of substance use, putting them at a greater risk of engaging in drug use in adolescence (Siegel et al., 2014).

Collectively, the literature suggests that different characteristics of adolescents might influence the effectiveness of certain parenting practices on developmental outcomes. Neurotic teens might be particularly sensitive to a stern parenting style devoid of adequate warmth, whereas vulnerable nonusers might benefit from stricter parenting. Thus, the cited literature implies that tailored health messages might be more effective than a generic one-size-fits-all approach (Hirsh, Kang, & Bodenhausen, 2012; Simpson et al., this volume). In implementing such an approach, researchers could assess characteristics of adolescents prior to educating parents about strategies appropriate for facilitating healthy development, or inform parents in the prevention campaign about variations in approach that might fit best with their child's psychological characteristics.

Conclusions

The social psychological study of the "good life" is concerned with learning how to enhance well-being and life satisfaction (see also Baumeister; Sheldon; Huppert, this volume). We have argued that social psychological approaches to prevention are fundamental to this concern. If the family is a major determinant of life satisfaction, then family dysfunction will have a major impact on perceived life satisfaction—and there are few things that are more destructive of family life than an addicted child. Thus, programs to limit substance use and subsequent addiction in youth can have appreciable effects on the experience of "the good life." Given its foundational concern with attitudes and attitude change (Allport, 1935), social psychology can make a substantial positive contribution to life satisfaction by bringing an evidence-based focus to substance use prevention in youth. Because youth typically have their first encounters with illicit substances in early or middle adolescence (Patrick & Schulenberg, 2010), prevention is critical to facilitating their optimal development. Considerable research indicates that parents are a trusted source of information about drugs (Kelly et al., 2002) and thus can function as important opinion leaders for communicating antidrug persuasive information to their adolescent children. For this reason, we have argued that campaigns that affect parents' communicative behaviors about substance use might prove effective in affecting adolescents' substance-related behaviors. A well-designed prevention campaign might focus on more than the diffusion of substance use information for parents. It also should involve instructing parents about the importance of positive parent-child communication, warmth, and setting democratic and fair guidelines and boundaries. This requires parents to learn communication strategies conveying warmth and understanding to guide adolescent children without threatening their autonomy. These goals can be met with effective, persuasive prevention communications. The necessary knowledge has been available for years (Fiedler & Arslan, this book); questions regarding the will to enact such programs remain to be answered.

Bibliography

Adalbjarnardottir, S., & Hafsteinsson, L. G. (2001). Adolescents' perceived parenting styles and their substance use: Concurrent and longitudinal analyses. *Journal of Research on Adolescence, 11*, 401–423. doi:10.1111/1532-7795.00018

Ajzen, I. (1985). From intentions to actions: A theory of planned behavior. In J. Kuhland & J. Backman (Eds.), *Action-control: From cognitions to behavior* (pp. 11–39): Heidelberg: Springer.

Ajzen, I. (1991). The theory of planned behavior. *Organizational Behavior and Human Decision Processes, 50,* 179–211.

Ajzen, I., & Fishbein, M. (2005). The influence of attitudes on behavior. In D. Albarracin, B. T. Johnson, & M. P. Zanna (Eds.), *The handbook of attitudes.* New York, NY: Psychology Press.

Allison, B. N. (2000). Parent-adolescent conflict in early adolescence: Precursor to adolescent adjustment and behavior problems. *Journal of Family and Consumer Sciences, 92,* 53–56.

Allport, G. W. (1935). Attitudes. In C. Murchison (Ed.), *Handbook of social psychology* (pp. 798–884). Worcester, MA: Clark University Press.

Barber, B. K. (1996). Parental psychological control: Revisiting a neglected construct. *Child Development, 67,* 3296–3319. doi:10.2307/1131780

Barber, B. K., & Harmon, E. L. (2002). Violating the self: Parental psychological control of children and adolescents. In B. K. Barber & B. K. Barber (Eds.), *Intrusive parenting: How psychological control affects children and adolescents* (pp. 15–52). Washington, DC: American Psychological Association.

Barber, B. K., Olsen, J. E., & Shagle, S. C. (1994). Associations between parental psychological and behavioral control and youth internalized and externalized behaviors. *Child Development, 65,* 1120–1136. doi:10.2307/1131309

Baumeister, R. F., Bratslavsky, E., Finkenauer, C., & Vohs, K. D. (2001). Bad is stronger than good. *Review of General Psychology, 5,* 323–370.

Baumrind, D. (1978). Parental disciplinary patterns and social competence in children. *Youth and Society, 9,* 239–276.

Baumrind, D. (1991). The influence of parenting style on adolescent competence and substance use. *The Journal of Early Adolescence, 11,* 56–95. doi:10.1177/0272431691111004

Baumrind, D. (2013). Authoritative parenting revisited: History and current status. In R. E. Larzelere, A. S. Morris, & A. W. Harrist (Eds.), *Authoritative parenting: Synthesizing nurturance and discipline for optimal child development* (pp. 11–34). Washington, DC: American Psychological Association.

Beatty, S. E., Cross, D. S., & Shaw, T. M. (2008). The impact of a parent-directed intervention on parent-child communication about tobacco and alcohol. *Drug and Alcohol Review, 27,* 591–601. doi:10.1080/09595230801935698

Benjet, C., Borges, G., Medina-Mora, M. E., Blanco, J., Zambrano, J., Orozco, R., Feliz, C., Rojas, E. (2007). Drug use opportunities and the transition to drug use among adolescents from the Mexico City Metropolitan Area. *Drug and Alcohol Dependence, 90,* 128–134.

Bogart, L. M., Collins, R. L., Ellickson, P. L., & Klein, D. J. (2007). Are adolescent substance users less satisfied with life as young adults and if so, why? *Social Indicators Research, 81,* 149–169. doi: 10.1007/s11205-006-0019-6

Castro-Schilo, L., Taylor, Z. E., Ferrer, E., Robins, R. W., Conger, R. D., & Widaman, K. F. (2013). Parents' optimism, positive parenting, and child peer competence in mexican-origin families. *Parenting: Science and Practice, 13,* 95–112. doi:10.1080/15295192.2012.709151

Chang, L., McBride-Chang, C., Stewart, S. M., & Au, E. (2003). Life satisfaction, self-concept, and family relations in chinese adolescents and children. *International Journal of Behavioral Development, 27,* 182–189. doi: 10.1080/01650250244000182

Chassin, L., Pillow, D. R., Curran, P. J., Molina, B. S., & Barrera, M. (1993). Relation of parental alcoholism to early adolescent substance use: A test of three mediating mechanisms. *Journal of Abnormal Psychology, 102,* 3–19.

Chawla, N., Neighbors, C., Logan, D., Lewis, M. A., & Fossos, N. (2009). Perceived approval of friends and parents as mediators of the relationship between self-determination and drinking. *Journal of Studies on Alcohol and Drugs, 70,* 92–100.

Cleveland, M. J., Feinberg, M. E., Osgood, D. W., & Moody, J. (2012). Do peers' parents matter? A new link between positive parenting and adolescent substance use. *Journal of Studies on Alcohol and Drugs, 73,* 423–433.

Crano, W. D. (2010). Applying established theories of persuasion to problems that matter: On becoming susceptible to our own knowledge. In J. P. Forgas, J. Cooper, & W. D. Crano (Eds.), *The psychology of attitudes and attitude change.* New York, NY: Psychology Press.

Crano, W. D., Alvaro, E. M., & Siegel, J. T. (2015). The media campaign as a focal prevention strategy: A guide to design, implementation, and evaluation. In L. M. Scheier (Ed.), *Handbook of drug prevention* (pp. 397–414). Washington, DC: American Psychological Association.

Crano, W. D., Gilbert, C., Alvaro, E. M., & Siegel, J. T. (2008). Enhancing prediction of inhalant abuse risk in samples of early adolescents: A secondary analysis. *Addictive Behaviors, 33,* 895–905.

Crano, W. D., Siegel, J. T., Alvaro, E. M., Lac, A., & Hemovich, V. (2008). The at-risk adolescent marijuana nonuser: Expanding the standard distinction. *Prevention Science, 9,* 129–137.

Crano, W. D., Siegel, J. T., Alvaro, E. M., & Patel, N. M. (2007). Overcoming adolescents' resistance to anti-inhalant appeals. *Psychology of Addictive Behaviors, 21,* 516–524.

De Clercq, B., Van Leeuwen, K., De Fruyt, F., Van Hiel, A., & Mervielde, I. (2008). Maladaptive personality traits and psychopathology in childhood and adolescence: The moderating effect of parenting. *Journal of Personality, 76,* 357–383. doi:10.1111/j.1467-6494.2007.00489.x

Deci, E. L., Eghrari, H., Patrick, B. C., & Leone, D. R. (1994). Facilitating internalization: The self-determination theory perspective. *Journal of Personality, 62,* 119–142. doi:10.1111/j.1467-6494.1994.tb00797.x

DeVore, E. R., & Ginsburg, K. R. (2005). The protective effects of good parenting on adolescents. *Current Opinion in Pediatrics, 17,* 460–465.

Diener, E. (1984). Subjective well-being. *Psychological Bulletin, 95,* 542–575. doi:10.1037/0033-2909.95.3.542

Diener, E. (1994). Assessing subjective well-being: Progress and opportunities. *Social Indicators Research, 31,* 103–157. doi:10.1007/BF01207052

Diener, E., Suh, E. M., Lucas, R. E., & Smith, H. L. (1999). Subjective well-being: Three decades of progress. *Psychological Bulletin, 125,* 276–302.

Dishion, T. J., & McMahon, R. J. (1998). Parental monitoring and the prevention of child and adolescent problem behavior: A conceptual and empirical formulation. *Clinical Child and Family Psychology Review, 1,* 61–75. doi:10.1023/A:1021800432380

Donaldson, C. D., Handren, L. M., & Crano, W. D. (2016). The enduring impact of parents' monitoring, warmth, expectancies, and alcohol use on their children's future binge drinking and arrests: A longitudinal analysis. *Prevention Science, 17,* 606–614. doi:10.1007/s11121-016-0656-1

Donaldson, C. D., Nakawaki, B., & Crano, W. D. (2015). Variations in parental monitoring and prediction of adolescent prescription opioid and stimulant misuse. *Addictive Behaviors, 45,* 14–21. doi:10.1016/j.addbeh.2015.01.022

Dornbusch, S. M., Ritter, P. L., Leiderman, P. H., Roberts, D. F., & Fraleigh, M. J. (1987). The relation of parenting style to adolescent school performance. *Child Development*, 1244–1257.

Duchesne, S., & Ratelle, C. (2010). Parental behaviors and adolescents' achievement goals at the beginning of middle school: Emotional problems as potential mediators. *Journal of Educational Psychology*, *102*, 497–507.

Fletcher, A. C., Steinberg, L., & Williams-Wheeler, M. (2004). Parental influences on adolescent problem behavior: Revisiting stattin and kerr. *Child Development*, *75*, 781–796.

Fredrickson, B. L. (2001). The role of positive emotions in positive psychology: The broaden-and-build theory of positive emotions. *American Psychologist*, *56*, 218–226. doi:10.1037/0003-066X.56.3.218

Gere, M. K., Villabø, M. A., Torgersen, S., & Kendall, P. C. (2012). Overprotective parenting and child anxiety: The role of co-occurring child behavior problems. *Journal of Anxiety Disorders*, *26*, 642–649. doi:10.1016/j.janxdis.2012.04.003

Glatz, T., & Koning, I. M. (2015). The outcomes of an alcohol prevention program on parents' rule setting and self-efficacy: A bidirectional model. *Prevention Science*, *13*, 377–385. doi: 10.1007/s11121-015-0625-0

Grusec, J. E., Goodnow, J. J., & Kuczynski, L. (2000). New directions in analyses of parenting contributions to children's acquisition of values. *Child Development*, *71*, 205–211.

Handren, L. M., Donaldson, C. D., & Crano, W. D. (2016). Adolescent alcohol use: Protective and predictive parent, peer, and self-related factors. *Prevention Science*, *17*, 862–871. doi:10.1007/s11121-016-0695-7

Hemovich, V., & Crano, W. D. (2009). Family structure and adolescent drug use: An exploration of single-parent families. *Substance Use & Misuse*, *44*, 2099–2113. doi:10.3109/1082 6080902858375

Hemovich, V., Lac, A., & Crano, W. D. (2011). Understanding early-onset drug and alcohol outcomes among youth: The role of family structure, social factors, and interpersonal perceptions of use. *Psychology, Health, and Medicine*, *16*, 249–267. doi:10.1080/ 13548506.2010.532560

Hirsh, J. B., Kang, S. K., & Bodenhausen, G. V. (2012). Personalized persuasion tailoring persuasive appeals to recipients' personality traits. *Psychological Science*, *23*, 578–581. doi:10.1177/0956797611436349

Hornik, R., MacLean, D., & Cadell, D. (2003). *Evaluation of the national youth anti-drug media campaign: 2003 report of findings: Executive summary*. Washington, DC: Westat.

Huansuriya, T., Siegel, J. T., & Crano, W. D. (2014). Parent—child drug communication: Pathway from parents' ad exposure to youth's marijuana use intention. *Journal of Health Communication*, *19*, 244–259. doi:10.1080/10810730.2013.811326

Huebner, E. S., & Alderman, G. L. (1993). Convergent and discriminant validation of a children's life satisfaction scale: Its relationship to self-and teacher-reported psychological problems and school functioning. *Social Indicators Research*, *30*, 71–82.

Huebner, E. S., Suldo, S. M., Smith, L. C., & McKnight, C. G. (2004). Life satisfaction in children and youth: Empirical foundations and implications for school psychologists. *Psychology in the Schools*, *41*, 81–93. doi:10.1002/pits.10140

Jané-Llopis, E., Barry, M., Hosman, C., & Patel, V. (2005). Mental health promotion works: A review. *Global Health Promotion*, 9–25.

Kaminski, J. W., Valle, L. A., Filene, J. H., & Boyle, C. L. (2008). A meta-analytic review of components associated with parent training program effectiveness. *Journal of Abnormal Child Psychology*, *36*, 567–589. doi:10.1007/s10802-007-9201-9

Katz, E., & Lazarsfeld, P. F. (1955). *Personal influence: The part played by people in the flow of mass communications*. New York, NY: Free Press.

Kelly, K. J., Comello, M. L. G., & Hunn, L. C. (2002). Parent-child communication, perceived sanctions against drugs use, and youth drug involvement. *Adolescence, 37*, 775–787.

Kenney, S. R., Lac, A., Hummer, J. F., Grimaldi, E. M., & LaBrie, J. W. (2015). Pathways of parenting style on adolescents' college adjustment, academic achievement, and alcohol risk. *Journal of College Student Retention: Research, Theory & Practice, 17*, 186–203.

Kerr, M., & Stattin, H. (2000). What parents know, how they know it, and several forms of adolescent adjustment: Further support for a reinterpretation of monitoring. *Developmental Psychology, 36*, 366–380. doi:10.1037/0012–1649.36.3.366

Kerr, M., Stattin, H., & Özdemir, M. (2012). Perceived parenting style and adolescent adjustment: Revisiting directions of effects and the role of parental knowledge. *Developmental Psychology, 48*, 1540–1553. doi:10.1037/a0027720

Knee, C. R., & Neighbors, C. (2002). Self-determination, perception of peer pressure, and drinking among college students. *Journal Of Applied Social Psychology, 32*, 522–543. doi:10.1111/j.1559–1816.2002.tb00228.x

Kobau, R., Seligman, M. E., Peterson, C., Diener, E., Zack, M. M., Chapman, D., & Thompson, W. (2011). Mental health promotion in public health: Perspectives and strategies from positive psychology. *American Journal of Public Health, 101*, e1–e9.

Kochanska, G., Aksan, N., Prisco, T. R., & Adams, E. E. (2008). Mother-child and father-child mutually responsive orientation in the first 2 years and children's outcomes at preschool age: Mechanisms of influence. *Child Development, 79*, 30–44. doi:10.1111/j.1467-8624.2007.01109.x

Koutakis, N., Stattin, H., & Kerr, M. (2008). Reducing youth alcohol drinking through a parent-targeted intervention: The örebro prevention program. *Addiction, 103*, 1629–1637. doi:10.1111/j.1360–0443.2008.02326.x

Lac, A., Alvaro, E. M., Crano, W. D., & Siegel, J. T. (2009). Pathways from parental knowledge and warmth to adolescent marijuana use: An extension to the theory of planned behavior. *Prevention Science, 10*, 22–32. doi:10.1007/s11121-008-0111-z

Lac, A., & Crano, W. D. (2009). Monitoring matters: Meta-analytic review reveals the reliable linkage of parental monitoring with adolescent marijuana use. *Perspectives on Psychological Science, 4*, 578–586. doi:10.1111/j.1745–6924.2009.01166.x

Lac, A., & Donaldson, C. D. (2016). Alcohol attitudes, motives, norms, and personality traits longitudinally classify nondrinkers, moderate drinkers, and binge drinkers using discriminant function analysis. *Addictive Behaviors, 61*, 91–98.

Lamb, C. S., & Crano, W. D. (2014). Parents' beliefs and children's marijuana use: Evidence for a self-fulfilling prophecy effect. *Addictive Behaviors, 39*, 127–132. doi: 10.1016/j.addbeh.2013.09.009

Lazarsfeld, P. F., Berelson, B., & Gaudet, H. (1944). *The people's choice: How the voter makes up his mind in a presidential campaign.* Oxford, UK: Duell, Sloan & Pearce.

Lazarus, R. S. (2003). Does the positive psychology movement have legs? *Psychological inquiry, 14*, 93–109.

Leidy, M. S., Guerra, N. G., & Toro, R. I. (2012). Positive parenting, family cohesion, and child social competence among immigrant latino families. *Journal of Latina/o Psychology, 1*, 3–13. doi: 10.1037/2168–1678.1.S.3

Lewinsohn, P. M., Redner, J., & Seeley, J. R. (1991). The relationship between life satisfaction and psychosocial variables: New perspectives. In F. Strack, M. Argyle, & N. Schwarz (Eds.), *Subjective well-being: An interdisciplinary perspective* (pp. 141–172). Oxford: Pergamon.

Lippold, M. A., Davis, K. D., McHale, S. M., Buxton, O. M., & Almeida, D. M. (2016). Daily stressor reactivity during adolescence: The buffering role of parental warmth. *Health Psychology, 9*, 1027–1035. doi: 10.1037/hea0000352

Lowe, K., & Dotterer, A. M. (2013). Parental monitoring, parental warmth, and minority youths' academic outcomes: Exploring the integrative model of parenting. *Journal of Youth and Adolescence, 42*, 1413–1425. doi: 10.1007/s10964-013-9934-4

McKee, L., Roland, E., Coffelt, N., Olson, A. L., Forehand, R., Massari, C., . . . Zens, M. S. (2007). Harsh discipline and child problem behaviors: The roles of positive parenting and gender. *Journal of Family Violence, 22*, 187–196. doi: 10.1007/s10896-007-9070-6

McNeil, C., & Hembree-Kigin, T. L. (2010). *Parent-child interaction therapy.* New York, NY: Springer.

Menting, B., Van Lier, P. A. C., Koot, H. M., Pardini, D., & Loeber, R. (2016). Cognitive impulsivity and the development of delinquency from late childhood to early adulthood: Moderating effects of parenting behavior and peer relationships. *Development and Psychopathology, 28*, 167–183. doi:10.1017/S095457941500036X

Miller, C. H., & Quick, B. L. (2010). Sensation seeking and psychological reactance as health risk predictors for an emerging adult population. *Health Communication, 25*, 266–275.

Moore, S. M., & Charvat, J. (2007). Promoting health behavior change using appreciative inquiry: Moving from deficit models to affirmation models of care. *Family and Community Health, 30*, S64–S74.

Morrill, M. I., Hawrilenko, M., & Córdova, J. V. (2016). A longitudinal examination of positive parenting following an acceptance-based couple intervention. *Journal of Family Psychology, 30*, 104–113.

O'Donnell, L., Myint-U, A., Duran, R., & Stueve, A. (2010). Especially for daughters: Parent education to address alcohol and sex-related risk taking among urban young adolescent girls. *Health Promotion Practice, 11*, 70S–78S. doi:10.1177/1524839909355517

Patrick, M. E., & Schulenberg, J. E. (2010). Alcohol use and heavy episodic drinking prevalence and predictors among national samples of american eighth- and tenth-grade students. *Journal of Studies on Alcohol and Drugs, 71*, 41–45.

Pettit, G. S., Laird, R. D., Dodge, K. A., Bates, J. E., & Criss, M. M. (2001). Antecedents and behavior-problem outcomes of parental monitoring and psychological control in early adolescence. *Child Development, 72*, 583–598.

Prinzie, P., Onghena, P., Hellinckx, W., Grietens, H., Ghesquiére, P., & Colpin, H. (2003). The addictive and interactive effects of parenting and children's personality on externalizing behavior. *European Journal of Personality, 17*, 95–117. doi: 10.1002/per.467

Ramirez, J. R., Crano, W. D., Quist, R., Burgoon, M., Alvaro, E. M., & Grandpre, J. (2004). Acculturation, familism, parental monitoring, and knowledge as predictors of marijuana and inhalant use in adolescents. *Psychology of Addictive Behaviors, 18*, 3–11. doi: 10.1037/0893–164X.18.1.3

Rask, K., Åstedt Kurki, P., Paavilainen, E., & Laippala, P. (2003). Adolescent subjective well-being and family dynamics. *Scandinavian Journal of Caring Sciences, 17*, 129–138.

Roche, K. M., Ghazarian, S. R., Little, T. D., & Leventhal, T. (2011). Understanding links between punitive parenting and adolescent adjustment: The relevance of context and reciprocal associations. *Journal of Research on Adolescence, 21*, 448–460. doi: 10.1111/j.1532–7795.2010.00681.x

Ryan, R. M., & Deci, E. L. (2000). Self-determination theory and the facilitation of intrinsic motivation, social development, and well-being. *American Psychologist, 55*, 68–78. doi: 10.1037/0003–066X.55.1.68

Ryan, R. M., & Deci, E. L. (2002). Overview of self-determination theory: An organismic-dialectical perspective. In E. L. Deci, R. M. Ryan, E. L. Deci, & R. M. Ryan (Eds.), *Handbook of self-determination research* (pp. 3–33). Rochester, NY: University of Rochester Press.

Sanders, M., Tully, L., Baade, P., Lynch, M., Heywood, A., Pollard, G., & Youlden, D. (1999). A survey of parenting practices in queensland: Implications for mental health promotion. *Health Promotion Journal of Australia, 9*, 105–114.

Sanders, M. R. (2003). Triple P—Positive Parenting Program: A population approach to promoting competent parenting. *Australian e-Journal for the Advancement of Mental Health, 2*, 1–17. doi:10.5172/jamh.2.3.127

Schwarz, B., Mayer, B., Trommsdorff, G., Ben-Arieh, A., Friedlmeier, M., Lubiewska, K., . . . Peltzer, K. (2011). Does the importance of parent and peer relationships for adolescents' life satisfaction vary across cultures? *The Journal of Early Adolescence, 32*, 55–80.

Seligman, M. E. P. (2003). Positive psychology: Fundamental assumptions. *The Psychologist, 16*, 126–127.

Seligman, M. E. P., & Csikszentmihalyi, M. (2000). Positive psychology: An introduction. *American Psychologist, 55*, 5–14. doi:10.1037/0003-066X.55.1.5

Siegel, J. T., Alvaro, E. M., & Burgoon, M. (2003). Perceptions of the at-risk nonsmoker: Are potential intervention topics being overlooked? *Journal of Adolescent Health, 33*, 458–461.

Siegel, J. T., Crano, W. D., Alvaro, E. M., Lac, A., Hackett, J. D., & Hohman, Z. P. (2014). Differentiating common predictors and outcomes of marijuana initiation: A retrospective longitudinal analysis. *Substance Use and Misuse, 49*, 30–40. doi:org/10.3109/10826084.2013.817427

Siegel, J. T., Tan, C. N., Navarro, M. A., Alvaro, E. M., & Crano, W. D. (2015). The power of the proposition: Frequency of marijuana offers, parental knowledge, and adolescent marijuana use. *Drug and Alcohol Dependence, 148*, 34–39. doi:10.1016/j.drugalcdep.2014.11.035

Skinner, E., Johnson, S., & Snyder, T. (2005). Six dimensions of parenting: A motivational model. *Parenting: Science and Practice, 5*, 175–235. doi:10.1207/s15327922par0502_3

Slagt, M., Dubas, J. S., Deković, M., & van Aken, M. A. G. (2016). Differences in sensitivity to parenting depending on child temperament: A meta-analysis. *Psychological Bulletin, 142*, 1068–1110.

Smack, A. J., Kushner, S. C., & Tackett, J. L. (2015). Child personality moderates associations between parenting and relational and physical aggression. *Journal of Aggression, Maltreatment & Trauma, 24*, 845–862. doi:10.1080/10926771.2015.1062450

Smetana, J. G., & Daddis, C. (2002). Domain-specific antecedents of parental psychological control and monitoring: The role of parenting beliefs and practices. *Child Development, 73*, 563–580.

Stattin, H., & Kerr, M. (2000). Parental monitoring: A reinterpretation. *Child Development, 71*, 1072–1085. doi:10.1111/1467-8624.00210

Stephenson, M. T. (2002). Anti-drug public service announcements targeting parents: An analysis and evaluation. *Southern Journal of Communication, 67*, 335–350.

Stevenson, W., Maton, K. I., & Teti, D. M. (1999). Social support, relationship quality, and well-being among pregnant adolescents. *Journal of Adolescence, 22*, 109–121. doi:10.1006/jado.1998.0204

Strandberg, A. K., & Bodin, M. C. (2011). Alcohol-specific parenting within a cluster-randomized effectiveness trial of a swedish primary prevention program. *Health Education, 111*, 92–102. doi:10.1108/09654281111108526

Straus, M. A., & Field, C. J. (2003). Psychological aggression by american parents: National data on prevalence, chronicity, and severity. *Journal of Marriage and Family, 65*, 795–808.

Suldo, S. M., & Huebner, E. S. (2004a). Does life satisfaction moderate the effects of stressful life events on psychopathological behavior during adolescence? *School Psychology Quarterly, 19*, 93–105.

Suldo, S. M., & Huebner, E. S. (2004b). The role of life satisfaction in the relationship between authoritative parenting dimensions and adolescent problem behavior. *Social Indicators Research*, *66*, 165–195. doi:10.1023/B:SOCI.0000007498.62080.1e

Topolski, T. D., Patrick, D. L., Edwards, T. C., Huebner, C. E., Connell, F. A., & Mount, K. K. (2001). Quality of life and health-risk behaviors among adolescents. *Journal of Adolescent Health*, *29*, 426–435.

Trinkner, R., Cohn, E. S., Rebellon, C. J., & Van Gundy, K. (2012). Don't trust anyone over 30: Parental legitimacy as a mediator between parenting style and changes in delinquent behavior over time. *Journal of Adolescence*, *35*, 119–132.

Voelkl, K. E., & Frone, M. R. (2000). Predictors of substance use at school among high school students. *Journal of Educational Psychology*, *92*, 583–592. doi.org/10.1037/0022–0663.92.3.583

Wagner, F. A., & Anthony, J. C. (2002). Into the world of illegal drug use: Exposure opportunity and other mechanisms linking the use of alcohol, tobacco, marijuana, and cocaine. *American Journal of Epidemiology*, *155*, 918–925. doi: 10.1093/aje/155.10.918

Webb, T. L., & Sheeran, P. (2006). Does changing behavioral intentions engender behavior change? A meta-analysis of the experimental evidence. *Psychological Bulletin*, *132*, 249–268. doi:10.1037/0033–2909.132.2.249

Wormington, S. V., Anderson, K. G., & Corpus, J. H. (2011). The role of academic motivation in high school students' current and lifetime alcohol consumption: Adopting a self-determination theory perspective. *Journal of Studies on Alcohol and Drugs*, *72*, 965–974.

Zhou, Q., Eisenberg, N., Losoya, S. H., Fabes, R. A., Reiser, M., Guthrie, I. K., . . . Shepard, S. A. (2002). The relations of parental warmth and positive expressiveness to children's empathy-related responding and social functioning: A longitudinal study. *Child Development*, *73*, 893–915. doi:10.1111/1467-8624.00446

Zullig, K. J., Valois, R. F., Huebner, E. S., Oeltmann, J. E., & Drane, J. W. (2001). Relationship between perceived life satisfaction and adolescents' substance abuse. *Journal of Adolescent Health*, *29*, 279–288.

17

INTERNET AND WELL-BEING

Yair Amichai-Hamburger and Shir Etgar

You are sitting at the office, reading emails, listening to songs from YouTube. Now you've left work and you are using a navigation application to avoid traffic, and back at home you watch a new Netflix series while participating in a heated discussion via WhatsApp. Wherever you look, the Internet plays a crucial part in our lives and has a major influence on us: It affects our work environment, our leisure time and the way we communicate with others. As such, we will claim in this chapter that it also impacts on our psychological processes. The chapter will open by examining the seven unique psychological components of the Internet environment. Then, we will move on to describe the way these factors impact on our well-being. This influence will be assessed in four different domains: personality, intimate relationships, e-therapy and online intergroup contact.

The Unique Components of the Internet Environment

There is no dispute that the online world is different from the offline world (Amichai-Hamburger, 2005, 2008, 2012; Hamburger & Ben-Artzi, 2000; Amichai-Hamburger & Hayat, 2013; McKenna, Green & Gleason, 2002). These differences can be summarized into seven factors, each of which has a psychological effect that distinguishes it from the offline world:

Anonymity

Our offline life is full of visual cues that can easily lead to social labels and stereotypes. Offline, people cannot hide, for example, their race, their gender or their accent—nor even their social status, as there are numerous social cues, from one's car key to dress code, that can supply a myriad of pieces of social information. In the online world, these visual and social cues can easily disappear. In a lot of online environments, such as blogs, chats, talkbacks or online gaming, people can decide how much they choose to disclose. Much of this type of anonymous interaction occurs by text (Riordan & Kreuz, 2010), which reduces to a minimum the social and the visual cues. Surprising as it might sound, anonymity in the online world can be beneficial for well-being. First, anonymity helps people to feel protected and confident. Thus, they tend to feel a greater freedom to express themselves and disclose more personal information (Amichai-Hamburger, 2005; Joinson, 2001; Turkle, 1995). Second, this secure feeling may well encourage people to allow themselves to take part in activities or learning environments that they would find much harder to join in the offline world. Thus, anonymity can lead individuals to explore aspects of their identity they would not dare or feel capable of exploring offline. Moreover, they can also validate these newly revealed aspects of themselves in the online world (Turkle, 1995). Third, this exploration of their identity might be especially important to people from a group or community that has a negative stigma. In this case, anonymity is critical as it allows participants safely to investigate their identity, without any social stigma. Such investigation may result in increasing self-esteem (Amichai-Hamburger & Hayat, 2013).

We are identified in many of our online activities. For example, many people use Facebook, Instagram, Twitter or LinkedIn accounts in their own names, in which they disclose information about themselves. People frequently use email addresses that identify them fully, writing blogs with their full signature, and so on. It should be taken into account, however, that these forms of identification may be partially or wholly false, as in fact are many profiles found on social network sites. This is achieved either by inventing a totally false identity, or by giving wrong or inaccurate information about oneself (Bumgarner, 2007; Grimmelmann, 2009). As we will discuss below, even when our given identity is genuine, the online world enables us to have a greater amount of control over the way it will appear.

Control Over Physical Appearance

In the offline world, people are being constantly appraised according to their physical appearance. People are judged differently due to their skin color, weight, visible disabilities or degree of attractiveness. For example, the more attractive an individual is perceived, the greater his or her chances of being liked, receiving help and even of being regarded as possessing superior personality traits (Horai, Naccari, Fatoullah, 1974; Nisbett & Wilson, 1977; Wilson, 1978). People who do not measure up to perceived beauty standards may well internalize these judgments and tend to suffer from a negative body image (Annis, Cash, Hrabosky, 2004; Schwartz & Brownell, 2004; Taleporos & McCabe, 2002), which, in turn, is related to lower self-esteem (McCaulay, Mintz, & Glenn, 1988) and to eating disorders (Cash & Deagle, 1997). The online world is very different, since on the Internet, people are free to expose as much of their physical appearance as they want. Even on social network sites, when a photo is required, participants can choose to represent themselves in any way they choose. Some choose to show themselves as a baby, a pet or another figure, such as a superhero. Even in a case when people choose to display a photograph of themselves, it is still very different from the offline reality. This is due to the ability to maintain and control their impression management. In fact, people work very hard to create and sustain their online impression through their online photos, even when this impression is actually directed at people whom they already know and may frequently meet offline (Amichai-Hamburger & Vinitzky, 2010; McAndrew & Jeong, 2012). In terms of physical appearance, people often work to ensure they produce and upload only their most flattering photos; thus, overweight people will choose to display pictures that make them look thinner (Amichai-Hamburger & Hayat, 2013). Another method is to upload only carefully chosen photos, in which the subjects are happy, good-looking, and taking part in hugely enjoyable activities (Amichai-Hamburger & Hayat, 2013). In fact, this type of behavior has become the norm, so much so that a study of kids between the ages 11 to 16, carried out in the UK, Italy and Spain, showed that across all three countries the youth believed that they must look "perfect" in photos uploaded to social network sites (Mascheroni, Vincent & Jimenez, 2015).

One interesting phenomenon that has emerged from the need to have control over one's physical impression is the selfie. A selfie is a photograph of oneself, taken by oneself, usually using a cell phone or webcam, and usually with the intention of uploading it to a social network site (Weiser, 2015). One of the motivations to take a selfie, instead of a regular photo, is due to the ease with which one can control all the photo's environment (Mehdizadeh, 2010; Qiu, Lu, Yang, Qu & Zhu, 2015). In a survey of youth from the USA, UK and China, it was found that between 96% and 100% of the participants take and upload selfies to social network sites. However, all of the participants reported that due to concerns as to their appearance, they take far more selfies than the number they actually upload to such sites (Katz & Crocker, 2015). It seems that one of the great advantages of the selfie is that it grants the protagonist the ability to perform as many attempts as he or she believes is necessary, under his or her total control, until the "perfect" photo is achieved.

Greater Control Over Interaction

The online world also grants people a high degree of control over their social interactions, far greater than that that exists offline. Offline, during any social interaction, we are obliged to keep focused and to give an immediate response to the other side, whereas online the social norms are very different. Online, we are not committed immediately to respond to a communication, and should a chat reach an uncomfortable topic, it is possible to simply to leave. The feeling that an online interaction can be stopped whenever one chooses was found to enhance feelings of security (McKenna, Green & Gleason, 2002). Since online many inter-actions are asynchronous, this allows for time to think, rewrite and revise our comments. This delayed communication gives us greater sense of control over the interaction (Riva, 2002). Another aspect of control flows from the location in which the interaction takes place. Online, this is wherever we choose; and being able to interact from a secure place can, even of itself, increase the participant's sense of security (Amichai-Hamburger, 2005).

This improved feeling of security provides great benefits, as was suggested by a study by Ben Ze'ev (2005). Ben Ze'ev examined participants in online versus offline dating situations. His results showed that participants felt less anxious, and were more open to disclosure, when the interaction was online rather than offline. This was because online, participants felt more secure, since they had the ability to finish the interaction whenever they chose.

Finding Similar Others

Two basic needs in Maslow's (1971) pyramid are the need to belong and esteem needs. Tajfel and Turner (1979) suggested that being part of a group that shares an individual's own interests can have positive influence on his or her self-esteem. It is highly important for people to feel validated, and sharing interests and goals with others is a way to achieve such a confirmation. Gable (this volume) suggested that social relationships are one of the main generators of well-being, as they help to regulate emotions, arouse positive feelings, and supply meaning. However, the offline world is very limited; we know and interact with a finite number of people who may well not share our points of view or our interests, particularly if they are unusual. Conversely, the online world contains infinite numbers of people, with an inestimable number of interests and hobbies. Moreover, it is easy to find those who have similar pursuits, simply by "googling" or searching on social network sites. It is unsurprising that "belonging" was cited as a leading motivator for using Facebook (Seidman, 2013) and Instagram (Oh, Lee, Kim, Park & Suh, 2016; Sheldon & Bryant, 2016).

The validation found due to finding similar others on the net has many benefits. One of them is that people from stigmatized groups can find similar others, and thus be strengthened. For example, in research by Cserni and Talmud (2015) about LGBT (lesbian, gay, bisexual and transgender) youths, it was found that locating an online group for LGBT youth helped them to cope more easily with the challenges of validating their sexual identity. The research found that higher participation in LGBT online groups was related to greater social capital. This was found to be true, even when the participation was passive, suggesting that sometimes just knowing that there are similar others can be a powerful enough reinforcement. In another study, McKenna and Bargh (1998) compared people from a stereotyped group and from a non-stereotyped group. They found that those from the stereotyped group were more likely to belong to an online group that was related to their main offline group identity, and that those who actively participated considered their belonging to the online group as much more important to their identity as compared with those who actively participated from a non-stereotyped group. All of this would suggest that the Internet can be an intensifying tool for individuals from stigmatized groups. It is important to note that such benefits are not just limited to stigmatized groups. Another interesting advantage of the ease of finding similar others is that by being able to find similar others for most of the components of our identities, it is much more easy for us to explore the many domains of our identity. In this way, the Internet may serve as a tool to enrich people's identities (Amichai-Hamburger & Hayat, 2013). And moreover, even connecting with familiar others on social network sites was found to result in similar advantages, as it increases social capital, since connecting online makes connections more powerful (Liu, Ainsworth & Baumeister, 2016). This may be because connecting people online is done on the basis of their similarities, which in some cases could not be exposed offline.

High Accessibility

We can surf the Internet from anywhere, at any time. Those times in which we had to reach the computer are a distant memory, thanks to the appearance of smartphones (Adler & Benbunan-Fich, 2012; Amichai-Hamburger, 2009; Ames, 2013). With smartphones, we feel as if we really have got the whole world in our hands, as we can stay connected anytime from anywhere. In fact, in 2013, college students reported that they use smartphones for almost every purpose: learning, working, entertaining and socializing (Ames, 2013). And younger people already perceive their smartphones as "everything" in their own lives, and use them constantly (Turner, 2015). We are so highly connected that we are used to engaging with our smartphone even when we are taking part in other activities (David, Kim, Brickman, Ran & Curtis, 2014). In contrast, offline, we are not always connected, we don't have constant access to all information, and our friends are not omnipresent. Online, we do have unlimited access to information, as well as to social support. The unlimited amount of information found there leads to more opportunities for learning, exposure to new ideas, and a greater ability to gain knowledge. These result in higher construal learning, which widens mental abilities (see also Kalkstein, Hubbard & Trope, this volume). The social support results in people feeling strong and capable, as they feel that they are no longer alone and that their social group is ubiquitously accessible. Therefore, no wonder that higher amount of smartphone use was found to be related to increased feelings of social support, which lead to higher self-esteem and to a decrease in feelings of loneliness and depression (Park & Lee, 2012). Similarly, smartphone apps that are specifically used for communication with others were found to help build and enhance social capital, which in turn leads to a reduction in the feelings of social isolation (Cho, 2015). All of this may be even more important to people belonging to stereotyped groups. As mentioned earlier, stereotyped groups receive a lot of social capital from finding similar others on the web (Cserni & Talmud, 2015; McKenna & Bargh, 1998). Now, these similar others and the feelings of empowerment they promote are their constant companions, with them, in their pocket (see also Dunn & Dwyer, this volume, on the impact of smartphones on well-being).

Fun

The Internet is exciting, interactive, colorful and enjoyable, and so naturally people want more of it (Wiggins, 2007). The enjoyment we receive from the Internet is in no small part due to the effort and thought on the part of web designers to create a net in which our needs will be fulfilled and we will continuously like to remain on their websites (Ehmke & Wilson, 2007). The Internet environment provides a leisure time that involves entertainment, play and sociability (Nimrod, 2010), and engaging in fun leisure activities has a positive connection to subjective well-being (Kuykendall, Tay & Ng, 2015; Newman, Tay & Diener, 2014).

Equality

The Internet is deeply rooted in the value of equality, and this value comes from the numerous people who helped to create it, mostly on a voluntary basis (Amichai-Hamburger, 2008). As the previous six components testify, the Internet is an environment that decreases status symbols, is open to anyone, and is accessible from most places. This promotes feelings of equality and makes people feel that they are significant and that their opinions count. This emphasis on equality is strongly expressed in the marketing world. Nowadays, it is common to use ordinary people or community experiences shared in social network sites to create positive attitudes, customer engagement and higher incomes for a product (Le Roux & Maree, 2016; Mir, 2014). And it is not just marketing: In today's online world, anyone can upload their own unique content that they have created, and it is all valid. From uploading an entry to Wikipedia to playing in a fantasy web game, on the Internet, anyone can find a way to express themselves (Amichai-Hamburger & Hayat, 2013). Sometimes this expression can even upgrade your social status, as happened with the young singer Justin Bieber, who first found fame by uploading his own material to YouTube (Khrabrov & Cybenko, 2010). This kind of success story induces feelings of equality in many people, suggesting to them that the Internet has the ability to make anyone a star.

A Brief Summation

As mentioned earlier, the Internet provides a readily available, protected environment, full of like-minded people world, which meets people's needs and allows them to explore many aspects of their identity (Turkle, 1995), all of this while they experience excitement and fun. So it is really not surprising that many people seem to prefer the online world over the offline (Amichai-Hamburger & Hayat, 2013).

The Dark Side of the Seven Factors: When the Online Environment Can Hurt

From the description of the seven components, one can get the impression that the Internet is a perfect world that can only empower individuals and make them happier. Unfortunately, not all of the ways in which the Internet impacts on our well-being are positive. Below we briefly contrast some of these disadvantages with the positive aspects of the Internet described earlier.

First, the anonymity: Anonymity certainly decreases inhibitions (Suler, 2004). This lowering of reticence can easily lead to non-normative behavior, and online anonymity has been clearly shown to be linked to Internet harassment and cyber-bullying (for example, Ševčíková & Šmahel, 2009; Tsikerdekis, 2012). Moreover, in one study, participants were asked to use a sexual harassment hashtag on Twitter, either anonymously or with identifiable details. Afterwards, participants were asked to evaluate resumes from men and women; concurrently, the degree to which they displayed hostile sexism was measured. Results showed that in this assignment, those who had shared the anonymous tweet, and those who wrote sexist tweets, showed higher levels of hostile sexism than those who had shared an identified tweet or wrote a non-sexist tweet (Fox, Cruz & Lee, 2015). This research indicates that the impact of online anonymity can be harsher than expected and extend beyond the online world.

Another disadvantage flows from the high degree of control over physical appearance. One of the major risks attached to this component is an obsessive preoccupation about personal appearance online. One major example is that use of social network sites is related to higher social comparison in terms of appearance (Chae, 2017). This comes to fruition in the gap, which we mentioned earlier, between the amount of selfie taking and actual posting, suggesting that people take many more selfies than they are uploading (Katz & Crocker, 2015). It can also be seen in a new phenomenon of selfie-editing, which is a "virtual makeover" for online self-presentation (Chae, 2017).

Control over the interaction may also have some negative outcomes. The ability to control the interaction makes it be perceived as slower, harder and less convincing as compared to face-to-face interactions. While evidence suggests that online communication is much more effective for easy and simple tasks, it may not be that valuable when it comes to more complicated assignments, such as difficult learning tasks (An & Frick, 2006) or tasks that require long and collaborative dialogues (Groenke, 2007).

As for finding similar others, while of great benefit when it comes to positive similar others, it is also empowering groups such as terror operatives or neo-Nazi cells, which can easily locate and meet up with similar others online. ISIS is an example of a terror organization that has become more familiar and more powerful by using online media to distribute its beliefs (Farewell, 2014).

Accessibility is another benefit of the online world that can easily backfire, and many people pay a heavy price for their permanent online status. A major part of this is a pressure to multitask, which stems from the need to be available all the time (Ames, 2013; Oulasvirta, Rattenbury, Ma & Raita, 2012). Evidence suggested that multitasking, and especially multitasking with multimedia, such as with a computer or a smartphone, damages attention span and decreases performance (David et al., 2014; Oulasvirta, Tamminen, Roto & Kuorelahti, 2005; Rosen, Lim, Carrier & Cheever, 2011). Another psychological price is the fear of missing out, often labelled according to its acronym, FOMO. This has been defined as a "pervasive apprehension that others might be having rewarding experiences from which one is absent. FOMO is characterized by the desire to stay continually connected with what others are doing" (Przybylski, Murayama, DeHaan & Gladwell, 2013, p. 1841). This phenomenon, the intense feeling that one is simply missing out on things, relates to the need to be highly connected, and is positively correlated to engagement in social media activities (Alt, 2015). It can be destructive for the individual, as it is known to lower mood and lessen life satisfaction (Przybylski et al., 2013), and to hurt mindfulness abilities, which alone are important to well-being (see also Huppert, this volume). Multitasking and fear of missing out both demonstrate that permanent online connectivity can have a negative side.

And what about the fun factor? Can there be any "dark sides" when it comes to fun? It seems that there might be. The fun factor of the Internet is also one of the reasons that people become addicted to it (Turel & Serenko, 2012; Young, 1998). Another point is what happens when the accessibility comes at the expense of time spent in the offline world. A meta-analysis of social network sites showed that greater use of social network sites is related to greater feelings of loneliness (Liu & Baumeister, 2016). This suggests that while social network sites might be used instead of offline friendship and activities, their use does not decrease feelings of loneliness.

The seeming equality found on the Internet can raise serious issues, since, in order to be equal with the other—for example, to experience similar levels of life satisfaction and sadness or difficulty—people feel obligated to produce inordinate amounts of content in order to be "unique" and to receive attention. This frequently leads to inappropriately high levels of disclosure online. In fact, these levels need to increase constantly in order to have an effect, since the bar of what is stimulating is continuously being raised. Such self-disclosure online, together with the high use of social network sites, has been shown to be linked to higher stress levels and to decreased well-being (Bevan, Gomez & Sparks, 2014; Chen & Lee, 2013).

The Unique Impact of the Internet Environment

The first part of this chapter was devoted to demonstrating the qualities that together make the Internet into a unique psychological environment. In the second part, we will move on to discuss the way this unique environment may influence a number of domains in our lives: personality, romantic relationships, group contact, and e-therapy.

Personality

Does personality, the basic building block of psychology, relate to our behavior on the Internet? Hamburger and Ben-Artzi (2000) demonstrated that the personality of the online user is relevant to their online behavior. A later study showed that people with introverted personalities are more likely to use the net for socializing than extroverts (Amichai-Hamburger Wainapel & Fox, 2002). It seems that the protection people feel provides a compensative environment that allows such people, who frequently find socializing in a face-to-face setting challenging, to do so online. These findings were later confirmed in many online environments, such as the Wikipedia community, chat, and online fantasy games (for a review, see Amichai-Hamburger & Hayat, 2013). It is, however, important to point out that the Internet milieu has undergone major changes since these initial studies. The Internet, which started as a mainly anonymous environment, has changed dramatically with the advent of social networks, which are becoming increasing dominant on the net. Amichai-Hamburger, Kaplan and Dorpatcheon (2008) showed that social network use gives an advantage to extroverts. Extroverts who used social networks were frequently more active socially on the net than introverts using the social networks. This appears to stem from the fact that extroverts simply moved their offline social network onto the online and so gained a significant numerical advantage. In addition, they replicated the psychological dominance they enjoyed offline to the online. In line with these studies, Amichai-Hamburger and Vinitzky (2010) found that extroverts have more social ties and more social interaction on Facebook than do introverts. However, interestingly, it was found that introverts invest more time in the construction of their profile page than extroverts do. The introverted users tend to supply quantities of information relating to various personal spheres, such as activities, interests and favorites in music, television and literature. It seems that for introverts working on the profile is a sheltered activity, with little of the tension related to real-time interactions. Thus, although the social networks do tend to strengthen those with an extroverted personality, introverts have found opportunities for compensation.

It is important to stress that although the social networks seem to have become more dominant than the anonymous online environments, the anonymous environments are still powerful and play a significant role in the online lives of many people. People who are shy are still more likely to utilize the anonymous online environments. However, there are also some extroverts who feel that they cannot express themselves freely on an identified website, and so do so on anonymous websites. The Internet and especially the anonymous environment seem to serve introverts well. However, whether this ability to remain anonymous serves introverts well in the long term still remains an open question, and longitudinal studies in this area are required to provide answers. Presently, it appears that while the online, especially the anonymous parts, might serve as a compensative environment that allows introverts to express themselves, and may even help this population to develop their social skills and encourage them to socialize offline, there may be a danger that their online success might preoccupy introverts and may even be responsible for a weakening in their offline social activities.

The extroversion-introversion personality theory is an important demonstration of the relevance of personality to the Internet. This theory received a lot of interest from researchers, who saw it as being particularly relevant to online behavior. Amichai-Hamburger (2002) suggested that a number of personality theories are also relevant when considering the reasons for online behavior. (For a review, see Amichai-Hamburger, 2017.)

The Internet and Romantic Relationships

A romantic relationship is based on romantic intimacy, which is defined as positive affect and feelings of commitment towards a person, accompanied by tendencies for self-disclosure from both partners (Laurenceau, Barrett & Pietromonaco, 1998; Moss & Schwebel, 1993; Prager, 1989; Reis & Shaver, 1988). Romantic intimacy has been shown to be very beneficial for humans. It leads to an increase in well-being (see also chapter by Gable, this volume; and Gable & Reis, 2010), a decrease in negative feelings (Otto, Laurenceau, Siegel & Belcher, 2015), and helps one to cope with difficult life events (Manne & Badr, 2008). The influence of the Internet in our lives has changed our patterns of romantic intimacy. In one study, which examined the way that the form of interaction influences relationship satisfaction, it was found that within the immediate family, only face-to-face interaction, and not any other type of communication (email, text messages, social network sites, video calls, etc.), is positively related to relationship satisfaction (Goodman-Deane, Mieczakowski, Johnson, Goldhaber & Clarkson, 2016). A more direct examination of the influence of the Internet on romantic intimacy followed 190 newly married couples during the first year of their marriage, and subsequently one year and two years afterwards. The researchers reported that if one partner was found to be a heavy Internet user during the first data collection, this led to lower intimacy and less passionate feeling and to greater conflicts between the partners, as reported in the second and third data collections (Kerkhof, Finkenauer & Muusses, 2011). Other studies that were focused specifically on social networks showed that the time spent on social networks has a negative effect on romantic relationships (Hand, Thomas, Buboltz, Deemer & Buyanjar-gal, 2013). More specifically, Facebook use is negatively related to relationship satisfaction and positively related to jealousy (Elphinston & Noller, 2011), and higher amount of Facebook use is even related to breakups and divorce (Clayton, Nagurney & Smith, 2013). And it is not just about Facebook: Greater amounts of Twitter and Instagram use also leads to increased romantic conflict, which leads to breakups and divorce (Clayton, 2014; Ridgway & Clayton, 2016).

Today's pervasive smartphone use has also led to diminished intimacy levels. In this case, when partners were together, each reported that it was the partner's, rather than their own, smartphone use that was negatively connected to intimacy. However, when smartphones are used for shared reasons, smartphone use was not connected to intimacy levels. These findings demonstrate that it is not the smart-phone multitasking itself that harms intimacy; rather, it is the use of the smart-phone to connect with others at a time that was supposed to be dedicated to the partner (Amichai-Hamburger & Etgar, 2016). We suspect that such smartphone multitasking influence is not limited only to romantic intimacy; it may influence other types of relationship, such as that between family members. It may well impact on well-being in the short and in the long term (see Crano & Donaldson; Simpson, Farrell, Huelsnitz & Eller, this volume).

We would speculate that Internet use arouses all these negative feelings due to the unique qualities of the online environment. When using the Internet each partner now has his or her own individual fun place that is not necessarily shared with the other partner. Moreover, the Internet can easily fulfill the need for self-disclosure, as each partner can disclose in front of other people, and so lessens the intimacy that comes from self-disclosure to a partner. They can also find similarities with other people, and those people can provide immediate feelings of comfort and belonging. Moreover, unlike partners, such Internet contacts are less likely to say the wrong thing, and differently from any other relationship, this comfort, support and belonging is always accessible, from anywhere, at any time, a demand that any specific individual, however loving, would not be able to accomplish.

Practically, it means that most of what is defined as romantic intimacy can be fulfilled, or at least give a sense that it is fulfilled, in the online world, and all of this without the partner's involvement. Thus, we suggest that it is not the Internet use by itself that impacts on romantic intimacy, but the needs that can be accomplished by the Internet instead of by a romantic partner. Therefore, it is of little wonder that intimacy levels are hurt when the Internet is not used for shared purposes (Amichai-Hamburger & Etgar, 2016).

Online Group Contact

This is a harnessing of the unique components of the Internet environment to promote an improvement in intergroup relations. The original group contact theory (Allport, 1954) suggests that in order to decrease prejudice and discrimination, a real positive acquaintance between the two oppositional groups must be formed. Allport stipulated a number of conditions that must be in place in order to make such a meeting effective: First, both groups should feel they have equal status during the contact. Second, they have to agree on a common goal. Third, this goal can be achieved only through the cooperation of the two groups. Fourth, both sides should be supported by their own authority or institution.

These conditions are challenging to fulfill. First, it is difficult, as well as costly, to organize several meetings between two conflicted groups that may well have issues in even agreeing where to hold the meetings (Amichai-Hamburger, Hasler & Shani-Sherman, 2015). Second, face-to-face meetings tend to provoke a lot of anxiety on the part of participants, and such anxiety may well hinder their ability to be patient and cognitively available to the contact (Islam & Hewstone, 1993; Wilder, 1993). As a solution for these challenges, Amichai-Hamburger and Mc-Kenna (2006) recommended using the online as a location in which to hold the contact meetings. Online intergroup contact uses the unique online environment as an advantage to maintain a contact that meets with all of Allport's conditions. First, it is practical, as the Internet is accessible, free to use, and does not demand any physical place in order for participants to take part in group meetings. Therefore, online meetings are much easier to arrange as compared with face-to-face meetings (Amichai-Hamburger, 2013). Moreover, contrary to face-to-face encounters, this ease of producing the meetings supports the continuity of the contact, as most of the practical barriers that prevented face-to-face meetings are diminished in the online world. Second, as seen earlier, status differences are also reduced in the online world (Amichai-Hamburger & McKenna, 2006; Spears, Postmes, Lea & Wolbert, 2002). It means that naturally a more equal-status contact will take place via the web, where physical and social cues can be straightforwardly controlled. The need to cooperate towards a superordinate goal can also be fulfilled online by performing a joint online task that is important to both groups (Amichai-Hamburger 2008). Online contact can also raise feelings of control and belonging, which will decrease anxiety from both groups. As shown earlier, this can be achieved through a number of components: First, in online meetings, each participant attends the meeting from their own secure place. In this way, there is both a physical distance between the group members, and the sense of security is much higher compared to face-to-face interactions (Amichai-Hamburger, 2005). Second, the greater degree of control that participants feel during the session may well serve to reduce anxiety, and this promotes a secure online contact (Amichai-Hamburger et al., 2015).

In addition to these benefits, which meet Allport's conditions, there are other advantages to the online as a contact environment. The anonymity it provides, for example, can encourage people to participate in a group, without experiencing shame or embarrassment before and during the process. Anonymity is especially important when the rival groups come from an area of violent conflict and group members are afraid to reveal any personal information (Amichai–Hamburger et al., 2015). The ease of finding similar others can also be a benefit. Finding similarities with other group members, regardless of their group identity, will probably happened spontaneously. And this will encourage them to sustain the dialogue, both before and after the formal contact is over (Amichai–Hamburger et al., 2015). The fact that the online contact takes part on the web will for some people serve as a factor in making it more fun and exciting. Moreover, meeting the outgroup online may also help the intergroup contact indirectly, as it decreases negative feelings, which form the basis of any discrimination (Neuberg & Cottrell, 2002).

Implementation of the Online Contact Theory

It is important to note that the online contact theory is not just a theoretical framework; it has in fact been implemented successfully in several leading intergroup projects. Below we briefly describe two of them: "Dissolving Boundaries" is a project that aims to use the online group contact as a basis to bridge the gap between pupils from the Republic of Ireland and Northern Ireland. In this project, small groups of children from Catholic and Protestant schools, each in their own schools, collaborated using online interaction in order to work together on a long-term mutual project (Amichai–Hamburger et al., 2015; Austin, Abbott, Mulkeen & Metcalfe, 2003). The results showed that children from both groups experienced higher levels of similarity with the other group and that each group's understanding of the other group's identity increased (Austin, 2006).

Another project is the "Good Neighbors" project (McKenna, Samuel-Azran & Sutton-Balaban, 2009). Good Neighbors was a blog in which bloggers from all around the Middle East wrote about their experiences living in this area. Visitors to the blog were encouraged to comment and discuss the articles. In order to preserve the feelings of equality and anonymity, the actual identities of the project-writers and respondents remained hidden, but in order to maintain feelings of closeness, writers were encouraged to introduce themselves and share some personal attitudes. This platform ran for about three years and received about 100 responses per day. Overall, the researchers found that either writing or responding decreased participants' negative attitudes toward the outgroups. Sadly, during the third year war broke out, and participants' opinions hardened and sometimes seemed to revert to their initial positions, suggesting that these attitude changes are not as robust as we would like to believe (Hasler & Amichai–Hamburger, 2013).

E-therapy

One of the most amazing psychological developments on the net is online therapy. This refers to "a licensed mental health care professional providing mental health services via email, video conferencing, virtual reality technology, chat technology, or any combination of these" (Manhal-Baugus, 2001, p. 551). Online therapy has major advantages: In the offline world, the stigma surrounding mental health issues causes many people to feel anxious about starting a course of therapy. In the online world, there is no such fear; there is no danger of bumping into someone you know on your way in or out of your therapy session. Moreover, for many people the Internet is perceived as a safer, more secure environment than the offline world (Amichai-Hamburger & Hayat, 2013; Hamburger & Ben-Artzi, 2000). The Internet also solves the logistical issues involved in reaching the therapist. This is frequently a concern for people who live in outlying areas or who have issues with mobility; in such cases, the possibility of receiving therapy in their own home can be a pivotal factor in their ability to obtain therapy (Rochlen, Zack & Speyer, 2004). There is also the cost. Therapy itself may well be expensive on- and offline, but for some, the cost of traveling may make it prohibitively expensive. As well, online therapy may also reduce waiting times and solve the problem of relocation (Wright et al., 2005).

Online therapy has proved successful in treating a variety of problems, ranging from eating disorders, depression and addictions (e.g., nicotine, alcohol, gambling) to various forms of anxiety that harm a person's functioning by generating tension and unease (Amichai-Hamburger et al., 2014). E-therapy is constantly evolving. Initially, it was a text-only concept, but now many e-therapists are using Skype and similar technologies that allow both parties to see and hear one another. Amichai-Hamburger et al. (2014) suggested some technological directions that in the future could assist therapists in providing a more comprehensive service. First was sophisticated software that will analyze the therapy session more fully and come up with some directions for the therapist to explore. For example, such software might detect a repetition of metaphors and words used, or of specific body movements made in association with specific words. This might lead in turn to directions that the therapist would be able to explore and examine with the patient. A second suggestion was that, in the future, therapists will be able to utilize applications that will help them to follow and assess the behavior of their patients outside of the therapy sessions, and so help to build a more comprehensive diagnosis of the patient and a greater understanding his or her state. In addition, the therapist will be able to utilize technology to provide the patients with tools that can help them cope with their own specific challenges. For example, the utilization of a combination smart watch with pulse measurements and GPS abilities and a smartphone will be able to record the context in which the patient becomes anxious and nervous. Such a device may well enable the therapist to work with the patient to assess when certain reactions occur, and this knowledge could be employed in the sessions to further help the patient in finding more healthy reactions to certain stimuli. This ability to continue therapeutic work outside of the confines of session may well lead to much more successful outcomes.

Virtual reality (VR) environments may serve as another tool for the modern therapist to put together a better therapeutic process. VR refers to a "computer-generated, three-dimensional landscape in which we would experience an expansion of our physical and sensory powers" (Ryan, 2000, p. 1). VR CBT refers to cognitive behavioral therapy that uses virtual reality technology to help people with a variety of psychological disorders. Amichai-Hamburger et al. (2014) suggested that, using VR components, patients may be able to revisit and repeat different cognitive and/or behavioral skills learned in different virtual situations. In addition, VR may be used to practice adaptive interpersonal skills. As a component of e-therapy, VR may increase motivation by allowing patients to witness changes in their behavior, emotion and cognition. Moreover, patients may well experience feelings of empowerment as they observe changes in their behavior and reach their conclusions based on their experiences. For example, patients who suffer from difficulties or anxieties in interpersonal communication may well benefit from an opportunity to enhance their skills through virtual exposure to a social environment, such as a dinner party. Such settings have been studied using VR (e.g., Pan, Gillies, Barker, Clark & Slater, 2012). In these VR studies, subjects interacted with virtual characters who were controlled either autonomously or semi-autonomously by confederates. Recent studies have established that participants can be virtually embodied in forms that are radically different from their own, including a strong sense of gender swapping (Slater, Spanlang, Sanchez-Vives & Blanke, 2010). Virtual embodiment was suggested as a tool for reducing erroneous body perception and for the treatment of obesity and eating disorders (Riva, 2011), and it has indeed been shown that virtual embodiment can affect individuals' assessment of the size of their belly (Normand, Giannopoulos, Spanlang & Slater, 2011). All these tools can now be integrated into a much more comprehensive therapeutic intervention.

Last Word

In its first stages, the psychological impact of the Internet was unclear. We now know that the Internet creates a unique psychological environment that provides many of its users with a feeling of protection and empowerment. The impact on us is very complex, with extremes of both positive and negative, and it is especially interesting to study the generation that was born into a world replete with the Internet and that developed its most basic concepts in the Internet era. Research of the Internet is challenging since the Internet is perpetually changing in all kinds of different directions. One of these amazing changes happening currently is the integration of virtual reality into the Internet—the additional abilities to smell and touch will clearly increase the psychological impact of the Internet and will behoove scholars to carry out in-depth research.

Bibliography

Adler, R. F., & Benbunan-Fich, R. (2012). Juggling on a high wire: Multitasking effects on performance. *International Journal of Human-Computer Studies, 70*, 156–168.

Allport, G. W. (1954). *The nature of prejudice*. Cambridge, MA: Addison-Wesley.

Alt, D. (2015). College students' academic motivation, media engagement and fear of missing out. *Computers in Human Behavior*, *49*, 111–119.

Ames, M. G. (2013, February). Managing mobile multitasking: The culture of iPhones on Stanford campus. In *Proceedings of the 2013 conference on Computer supported cooperative work* (pp. 1487–1498). New York, NY: ACM.

Amichai-Hamburger, Y. (2002). Internet and personality. *Computers in Human Behavior*, *18*, 1–10.

Amichai-Hamburger, Y. (2005). Personality and the Internet. In Y. Amichai-Hamburger (Ed.), *The social Net: Human behavior in cyberspace* (pp. 27–55). New York: Oxford University Press.

Amichai-Hamburger, Y. (2008). The contact hypothesis reconsidered: Interacting via Internet: Theoretical and practical aspects. In A. Barak (Ed.), *Psychological aspects of cyberspace: Theory, research, applications* (pp. 209–227). Cambridge: Cambridge University Press.

Amichai-Hamburger, Y. (2009). Technology and well-being: Designing the future. In Y. Amichai-Hamburger (Ed.), *Technology and well-being* (pp. 260–278). New York, NY: Cambridge University Press.

Amichai-Hamburger, Y. (2012). Reducing intergroup conflict and promoting intergroup harmony in the digital age. In H. Giles (Ed.), *The handbook of intergroup communication* (pp. 181–193). New York, NY: Routledge.

Amichai-Hamburger, Y. (2013). Reducing intergroup conflict and promoting intergroup harmony in the digital age. In H. Giles (Ed.), *The handbook of intergroup communication* (pp. 181–193) New York, NY: Routledge.

Amichai-Hamburger, Y. (2017). *Internet psychology*. New York: Routledge.

Amichai-Hamburger, Y., & Etgar, S. (2016). Intimacy and Smartphone Multitasking—a new oxymoron?. *Psychological Reports*, *119*, 826–838.

Amichai-Hamburger, Y., Hasler, B. S., & Shani-Sherman, T. (2015). Structured and unstructured intergroup contact in the digital age. *Computers in Human Behavior*, *52*, 515–522.

Amichai-Hamburger, Y., & Hayat, Z. (2013). Internet and personality. In Y. Amichai-Hamburger (Ed.), *The social Net: Understanding our online behavior* (2nd ed., pp. 1–20). New York: Oxford University Press.

Amichai-Hamburger, Y., Kaplan, H., & Dorpatcheon, N. (2008). Click to the past: The impact of extroversion by users of nostalgic website on the use of Internet social services. *Computers in Human Behavior*, *24*, 1907–1912.

Amichai-Hamburger, Y., Klomek, A. B., Friedman, D., Zuckerman, O., & Shani-Sherman, T. (2014). The future of online therapy. *Computers in Human Behavior*, *41*, 288–294.

Amichai-Hamburger, Y., & McKenna, K. Y. A. (2006). The contact hypothesis reconsidered: Interacting via the Internet. *Journal of Computer-Mediated Communication*, *11*, article 7. Retrieved from http://jcmc.indiana.edu/vol11/issue3/amichai-hamburger.html

Amichai-Hamburger, Y., & Vinitzky, G. (2010). Social network use and personality. *Computers in Human Behavior*, *26*, 1289–1295.

Amichai-Hamburger, Y., Wainapel, G., & Fox, S. (2002). "On the internet no one knows I'm an introvert": Extroversion, neuroticism, and internet interaction. *Cyberpsychology and Behavior*, *2*, 125–128.

An, Y. J., & Frick, T. (2006). Student perceptions of asynchronous computer-mediated communication in face-to-face courses. *Journal of Computer-Mediated Communication*, *11*, 485–499.

Annis, N. M., Cash, T. F., & Hrabosky, J. I. (2004). Body image and psychosocial differences among stable average weight, currently overweight, and formerly overweight women: The role of stigmatizing experiences. *Body Image*, *1*, 155–167.

Austin, R. (2006). The role of ICT in bridge-building and social inclusion: Theory, policy and practice issues. *European Journal of Teacher Education, 29*, 145–161.

Austin, R., Abbott, L., Mulkeen, A., & Metcalfe, N. (2003). Dissolving boundaries: Cross-national co-operation through technology in education. *Curriculum Journal, 14*, 55–84.

Ben-Ze'ev, A. (2005). "Detattachment": The unique nature of online romantic relationships. In Y. Amichai-Hamburger (Ed.), *The social net: Understanding human behavior in cyberspace* (pp. 115–138). New York, NY: Oxford University Press.

Bevan, J. L., Gomez, R., & Sparks, L. (2014). Disclosures about important life events on Facebook: Relationships with stress and quality of life. *Computers in Human Behavior, 39*, 246–253.

Bumgarner, B. A. (2007). You have been poked: Exploring the uses and gratifications of Facebook among emerging adults. *First Monday*, 12, Number 11–5. Retrieved December 12, 2011, http://firstmonday.org/htbin/cgiwrap/bin/ojs/index.php/fm/article/view/2026/1897

Cash, T. F., & Deagle, E. A. (1997). The nature and extent of body-image disturbances in anorexia nervosa and bulimia nervosa: A meta-analysis. *International Journal of Eating Disorders, 22*, 107–126.

Chae, J. (2017). Virtual makeover: Selfie-taking and social media use increase selfie-editing frequency through social comparison. *Computers in Human Behavior, 66*, 370–376.

Chen, W., & Lee, K. H. (2013). Sharing, liking, commenting, and distressed? The pathway between Facebook interaction and psychological distress. *Cyberpsychology, Behavior, and Social Networking, 16*(10), 728–773.

Cho, J. (2015). Roles of Smartphone app use in improving social capital and reducing social isolation. *Cyberpsychology, Behavior, and Social Networking, 18*, 350–355.

Clayton, R. B. (2014). The third wheel: The impact of Twitter use on relationship infidelity and divorce. *Cyberpsychology, Behavior, and Social Networking, 17*, 425–430.

Clayton, R. B., Nagurney, A., & Smith, J. R. (2013). Cheating, breakup, and divorce: Is Facebook use to blame? *Cyberpsychology, Behavior, and Social Networking, 16*, 717–720.

Crano, W. D., & Donaldson, C. D. (2017). Positive parenting, adolescent substance use prevention, and the good life. In J. Forgas & R. Baumeister (Eds.), *The social psychology of the good life*. New York: Psychology Press.

Cserni, R. T., & Talmud, I. (2015). To know that you are not alone: The effect of internet usage on LGBT youth's social capital. *Communication and Information Technologies Annual (Studies in Media and Communications), 9*, 161–182.

David, P., Kim, J. H., Brickman, J. S., Ran, W., & Curtis, C. M. (2014). Mobile phone distraction while studying. *New Media & Society*, 1461444814531692.

Ehmke, C., & Wilson, S. (2007, September). Identifying web usability problems from eye-tracking data. In *Proceedings of the 21st British HCI Group Annual Conference on People and Computers: HCI . . . but not as we know it* (Vol. 1, pp. 119–128). London: British Computer Society.

Elphinston, R. A., & Noller, P. (2011). Time to face it! Facebook intrusion and the implications for romantic jealousy and relationship satisfaction. *Cyberpsychology, Behavior, and Social Networking, 14*, 631–635.

Farwell, J. P. (2014). The media strategy of ISIS. *Survival, 56*(6), 49–55.

Fox, J., Cruz, C., & Lee, J. Y. (2015). Perpetuating online sexism offline: Anonymity, interactivity, and the effects of sexist hashtags on social media. *Computers in Human Behavior, 52*, 436–442.

Gable, S. L. (2017). Satisfying and meaningful close relationships. In J. Forgas & R. Baumeister (Eds.), *The social psychology of the good life*. New York: Psychology Press.

Gable, S. L., & Reis, H. T. (2010). Good news! Capitalizing on positive events in an inter-personal context. *Advances in experimental social psychology, 42,* 195–257.

Goodman-Deane, J., Mieczakowski, A., Johnson, D., Goldhaber, T., & Clarkson, P. J. (2016). The impact of communication technologies on life and relationship satisfaction. *Computers in Human Behavior, 57,* 219–229.

Grimmelmann, J. (2009). Saving Facebook. *Iowa Law Review, 94,* 1137–1206.

Guadagno, R. E., Okdie, B. M., & Eno, C. A. (2008). Who blogs? Personality predictors of blogging. *Computers in Human Behavior, 24,* 1993–2004.

Groenke, S. L. (2007). Collaborative dialogue in a synchronous CMC environment? A look at one beginning English teacher's strategies. *Journal of Computing in Teacher Education, 24,* 41–46.

Hamburger, Y. A., & Ben-Artzi, E. (2000). The relationship between extraversion and neuroticism and the different uses of the Internet. *Computers in Human Behavior, 16,* 441–449.

Hand, M. M., Thomas, D., Buboltz, W. C., Deemer, E. D., & Buyanjargal, M. (2013). Facebook and romantic relationships: Intimacy and couple satisfaction associated with online social network use. *Cyberpsychology, Behavior, and Social Networking, 16,* 8–13.

Hasler, B. S., & Amichai- Hamburger, Y. (2013). Online intergroup contact. In Y. Amichai-Hamburger (Ed.), *The social net. Human behavior in cyberspace* (2nd ed.). New York, NY: Oxford University Press.

Hewstone, M., & Brown, R. J. (1986). Contact is not enough: An intergroup perspective on the contact hypothesis. In M. Hewstone & R. J. Brown (Eds.), *Contact and conflict in intergroup encounters* (pp. 1–44). Oxford: Blackwell.

Horai, J., Naccari, N., & Fatoullah, E. (1974). The effects of expertise and physical attractiveness upon opinion agreement and liking. *Sociometry,* 601–606.

Huppert, F. (2017). Living life well: The role of mindfulness and compassion. In J. Forgas & R. Baumeister (Eds.), *The social psychology of the good life.* New York, NY: Psychology Press.

Islam, M. R., & Hewstone, M. (1993). Dimensions of contact as predictors of inter-group anxiety, perceived out-group variability, and out-group attitude: An integrative model. *Personality and Social Psychology Bulletin, 19,* 700–710.

Joinson, A. (2001). Self-disclosure in computer-mediated communication: The role of self-awareness and visual anonymity. *European Journal Social Psychology, 31,* 177–192.

Katz, J. E., & Crocker, E. T. (2015). Selfies and photo messaging as visual conversation: Reports from the United States, United Kingdom and China. *International Journal of Communication, 9,* 1861–1872.

Kerkhof, P., Finkenauer, C., & Muusses, L. D. (2011). Relational consequences of compulsive Internet use: A longitudinal study among newlyweds. *Human Communication Research, 37,* 147–173.

Khrabrov, A., & Cybenko, G. (2010, August). Discovering influence in communication networks using dynamic graph analysis. In *Social Computing (SocialCom), 2010 IEEE Second International Conference on Social Computing*(pp. 288–294). Washington, DC: IEEE.

Kuykendall, L., Tay, L., & Ng, V. (2015). Leisure engagement and subjective well-being: A meta-analysis. *Psychological Bulletin, 141,* 364–403.

Laurenceau, J. P., Barrett, L. F., & Pietromonaco, P. R. (1998). Intimacy as an interpersonal process: The importance of self-disclosure, partner disclosure, and perceived partner responsiveness in interpersonal exchanges. *Journal of Personality and Social Psychology, 74,* 1238–1251.

Le Roux, I., & Maree, T. (2016). Motivation, engagement, attitudes and buying intent of female Facebook users. *Acta Commercii, 16*, a340. http://dx.doi.org/10.4102/ ac.v16i1.340

Liu, D., Ainsworth, S. E., & Baumeister, R. F. (2016). A meta-analysis of social networking online and social capital. *Review of General Psychology, 20*, 369–391.

Liu, D., & Baumeister, R. F. (2016). Social networking online and personality of self-worth: A meta-analysis. *Journal of Research in Personality, 64*, 79–89.

Manhal-Baugus, M. (2001). E-therapy: Practical, ethical and legal issues. *Cyberpsychology and Behavior, 4*(5), 551–563.

Manne, S., & Badr, H. (2008). Intimacy and relationship processes in couples' psychosocial adaptation to cancer. *Cancer, 112*, 2541–2555.

Mascheroni, G., Vincent, J., & Jimenez, E. (2015). "Girls are addicted to likes so they post semi-naked selfies": Peer mediation, normativity and the construction of identity online. *Cyberpsychology: Journal of Psychosocial Research on Cyberspace, 9*, article 5, doi:10.5817/CP2015-1-5

Maslow, A. (1971). *Farther reaches of human nature.* New York, NY: Viking.

McAndrew, F. T., & Jeong, H. S. (2012). Who does what on Facebook? Age, sex, and relationship status as predictors of Facebook use. *Computers in Human Behavior, 28*, 2359–2365.

McCaulay, M., Mintz, L., & Glenn, A. A. (1988). Body image, self-esteem, and depression-proneness: Closing the gender gap. *Sex Roles, 18*, 381–391.

McKenna, K. Y., & Bargh, J. A. (1998). Coming out in the age of the Internet: Identity "Demarginalization" through virtual group participation. *Journal of Personality and Social Psychology, 75*, 681–694.

McKenna, K. Y. A., Green, A. S., & Gleason, M. J. (2002). Relationship formation on the Internet: What's the big attraction? *Journal of Social Issues, 58*, 9–32.

McKenna, K. Y. A., Samuel-Azran, T., & Sutton-Balaban, N. (2009). Virtual meetings in the Middle East: Implementing the contact hypothesis on the Internet. *The Israeli Journal of Conflict Resolution, 1*, 63–86.

Mehdizadeh, S. (2010). Self-presentation 2.0: Narcissism and self-esteem on Facebook. *Cyberpsychology, Behavior, and Social Networking, 13*, 357–364.

Mir, A. A. (2014). Effects of pre-purchase search motivation on user attitudes toward online social network advertising: A case of university students. *Journal of Competitiveness, 6*, 42–55.

Moss, B. F., & Schwebel, A. I. (1993). Defining intimacy in romantic relationships. *Family Relations, 42*, 31–37.

Newman, D. B., Tay, L., & Diener, E. (2014). Leisure and subjective well-being: A model of psychological mechanisms as mediating factors. *Journal of Happiness Studies, 15*, 555–578.

Neuberg, S. L., & Cottrell, C. A. (2002). Intergroup emotions: A biocultural approach. In D. M. Mackie & E. R. Smith (Eds.), *From prejudice to intergroup relations: Differentiated reactions to social groups* (pp. 265–283). New York, NY: Psychology Press.

Nimrod, G. (2010). The fun culture in seniors' online communities. *The Gerontologist, 51*, 226–237.

Nisbett, R. E., & Wilson, T. D. (1977). The halo effect: Evidence for unconscious alteration of judgments. *Journal of Personality and Social Psychology, 35*, 231–259.

Normand, J. M., Giannopoulos, E., Spanlang, B., & Slater, M. (2011). Multisensory stimulation can induce an illusion of larger belly size in immersive virtual reality. *PLoS One, 6*, e16128.

Oh, C., Lee, T., Kim, Y., Park, S., & Suh, B. (2016, May). Understanding participatory hashtag practices on Instagram: A case study of weekend hashtag project. In *Proceedings* of the 2016 CHI Conference Extended Abstracts on Human Factors in Computing Systems (pp. 1280–1287). New York: ACM.

Otto, A. K., Laurenceau, J. P., Siegel, S. D., & Belcher, A. J. (2015). Capitalizing on everyday positive events uniquely predicts daily intimacy and well-being in couples coping with breast cancer. *Journal of Family Psychology, 29*, 69–79.

Oulasvirta, A., Rattenbury, T., Ma, L., & Raita, E. (2012). Habits make smartphone use more pervasive. *Personal and Ubiquitous Computing, 16*, 105–114.

Oulasvirta, A., Tamminen, S., Roto, V., & Kuorelahti, J. (2005). Interaction in 4-second bursts: The fragmented nature of attentional resources in mobile HCI. In *Proceedings of the SIGCHI conference on Human factors in computing systems* (pp. 919–928). New York, NY: ACM.

Pan, X., Gillies, M., Barker, C., Clark, D. M., & Slater, M. (2012). Socially anxious and confident men interact with a forward virtual woman: An experimental study. *PloS One, 7*(4), e32931.

Park, N., & Lee, H. (2012). Social implications of smartphone use: Korean college students' smartphone use and psychological well-being. *Cyberpsychology, Behavior, and Social Networking, 15*, 491–497.

Prager, K. J. (1989). Intimacy status and couple communication. *Journal of Social and Personal Relationships, 6*, 435–449.

Postmes, T., Spears, R., Sakhel, K., & De Groot, D. (2001). Social influence in computer-mediated communication: The effects of anonymity on group behavior. *Personality and Social Psychology Bulletin, 27*, 1243–1254.

Przybylski, A. K., Murayama, K., DeHaan, C. R., & Gladwell, V. (2013). Motivational, emotional, and behavioral correlates of fear of missing out. *Computers in Human Behavior, 29*, 1841–1848.

Qiu, L., Lu, J., Yang, S., Qu, W., & Zhu, T. (2015). What does your selfie say about you?. *Computers in Human Behavior, 52*, 443–449.

Reis, H. T., & Shaver, P. (1988). Intimacy as an interpersonal process. In S. W. Duck (Ed.), *Handbook of personal relationships* (pp. 367–89). Oxford, UK: Wiley.

Ridgway, J. L., & Clayton, R. B. (2016). Instagram unfiltered: Exploring associations of body image satisfaction, Instagram# selfie posting, and negative romantic relationship outcomes. *Cyberpsychology, Behavior, and Social Networking, 19*, 2–7.

Riordan, M. A., & Kreuz, R. J. (2010). Emotion encoding and interpretation in computer-mediated communication: Reasons for use. *Computers in Human Behavior, 26*, 1667–1673.

Riva, G. (2002). The sociocognitive psychology of computer-mediated communication: The present and future of technology-based interactions. *Cyberpsychology & Behavior, 5*, 581–598.

Riva, G. (2011). The key to unlocking the virtual body: Virtual reality in the treatment of obesity and eating disorders. *Journal of Diabetes Science and Technology, 5*, 283–292.

Rochlen, A. B., Zack, J. S., & Speyer, C. (2004). Online therapy: Review of relevant definitions, debates, and current empirical support. *Journal of Clinical Psychology, 60*(3), 269–283.

Rosen, L. D., Lim, A. F., Carrier, L. M., & Cheever, N. A. (2011). An empirical examination of the educational impact of text message-induced task switching in the classroom: Educational implications and strategies to enhance learning. *Psicologia Educativa, 17*, 163–177.

Ryan, M. (2000). *Narrative as virtual reality*. Baltimore, MD: Johns Hopkins University Press.

Schwartz, M. B., & Brownell, K. D. (2004). Body image and obesity. *Body Image, 1*, 43–56.

Seidman, G. (2013). Self-presentation and belonging on Facebook: How personality influences social media use and motivations. *Personality and Individual Differences, 54*, 402–407.

Ševčíková, A., & Šmahel, D. (2009). Online harassment and cyberbullying in the Czech Republic: Comparison across age groups. *Journal of Psychology, 217*, 227–229.

Sheldon, P., & Bryant, K. (2016). Instagram: Motives for its use and relationship to narcissism and contextual age. *Computers in Human Behavior, 58*, 89–97.

Simpson, J. A., Farrell, A. K., Huelsnitz, C., & Eller, J. (2017). Early social experiences and living well: A longitudinal view of adult physical health. In J. Forgas & R. Baumeister (Eds.), *The social psychology of the good life*. New York, NY: Psychology Press.

Slater, M., Spanlang, B., Sanchez-Vives, M. V., & Blanke, O. (2010). First person experience of body transfer in virtual reality. *PLoS One, 5*, e10564.

Spears, R., Postmes, T., Lea, M., & Wolbert, A. (2002). When are net effects gross products? Communication. *Journal of Social Issues, 58*, 91–107.

Suler, J. (2004). The online disinhibition effect. *Cyberpsychology & Behavior, 7*, 321–326.

Tajfel, H., & Turner, J. (1979). An integrative theory of intergroup conflict. In W. Austin & S. Worchel (Eds.), *The social psychology of intergroup relations* (pp. 33–47). Monterey, CA: Brooks/Cole.

Taleporos, G., & McCabe, M. P. (2002). Body image and physical disability—personal perspectives. *Social Science & Medicine, 54*, 971–980.

Thompson, L., & Nadler, J. (2002). Negotiating via information technology: Theory and application. *Journal of Social Issues, 58*, 109–124.

Trope, Y., Kalkstein, D., & Hubbard, A. (2017). Expansive and contractive learning experiences: Mental construal and living well. In J. Forgas & R. Baumeister (Eds.), *The social psychology of the good life*. New York: Psychology Press.

Tsikerdekis, M. (2012). The choice of complete anonymity versus pseudonymity for aggression online. *eMinds International Journal on Human-Computer Interaction, 2*, 35–57.

Turel, O., & Serenko, A. (2012). The benefits and dangers of enjoyment with social networking websites. *European Journal of Information Systems, 21*, 512–528.

Turkle, S. (1995). *Life on the screen: Identity in the age of the Internet*. New York, NY: Simon & Schuster.

Turner, A. (2015). Generation Z: Technology and social interest. *The Journal of Individual Psychology, 71*, 103–113.

Weiser, E. B. (2015). # Me: Narcissism and its facets as predictors of selfie-posting frequency. *Personality and Individual Differences, 86*, 477–481.

Wiggins, A. (2007). Information architecture: Data-driven design: Using web analytics to validate heuristics system. *Bulletin of the American Society for Information Science and Technology, 33*, 20–24.

Wilder, D. A. (1993). The role of anxiety in facilitating stereotypic judgments of outgroup behavior. In D.M. Mackie & D.L. Hamilton (Eds.), *Affect, cognition, and stereotyping: Interactive processes in group perception* (pp. 87–109). San Diego, CA: Academic Press.

Wilson, W. J. (1978). The declining significance of race. *Society, 15*, 56–62.

Wright, J., Stepney, S., Clark, J. A., & Jacob, J. L. (2005). Formalizing anonymity: A review. University of York Technical Report YCS 389.

Young, K. S. (1998). Internet addiction: The emergence of a new clinical disorder. *CyberPsychology & Behavior, 1*, 237–244.

18

TECHNOLOGY AND THE FUTURE OF HAPPINESS

Elizabeth W. Dunn and Ryan J. Dwyer

In 1965, Intel cofounder Gordon Moore made a bold prophecy. He predicted that the speed and power of microchips would double every year for at least a decade. Although he later revised this prediction slightly (noting that the doubling would occur every two years), the exponential growth he envisioned has now held up for five decades—and has been enshrined as "Moore's Law." Because it's difficult to comprehend the overwhelming rate of change that exponential growth creates, engineers at Intel recently calculated what a 1971 Volkswagen Beetle would look like today if it had evolved at the same rate as microchips: You could drive the Beetle 300,000 miles per hour, you would only need to buy one tank of gas in your life, and the car would cost you a grand total of four cents (Friedman, 2016). By its very nature, exponential growth means that the faster something gets, the faster it gets faster. All of this growth hit a tipping point between 2006 and 2007, when a series of breakthroughs enabled the advent of the iPhone, Facebook, Twitter, and other platforms that now permeate our everyday lives. But have all of these advances increased our chances of living the Good Life?

Around the world, advances in computing technology have provided people with access to the entire store of human knowledge at little or no cost. A young woman growing up in Nairobi can now sign up for a free online computer science course offered by Harvard, and people can lift themselves out of poverty with the help of micro-loans delivered via their smartphones. Friends who are oceans apart can connect with each other anytime for free on Skype, and children who are running late getting home can reassure their worried parents with a simple text message. As Amichai-Hamburger and Etgar (this volume) describe, the Internet makes it easier for people to seek others who are like them, which may be particularly important for members of marginalized groups (e.g., LGBT youths). While appreciating the myriad ways in which rapid advances in technology are increasing access to the Good Life, it is important to recognize that enhancing well-being is not the driving force shaping these advances.

The spread of new technologies can be thought of in much the same way as the spread of "selfish genes." As Hamilton (1963, p. 355) put it, "the ultimate criterion which determines whether [a gene] G will spread is not whether the behavior is to the benefit of the behaver, but whether it is to the benefit of the gene." Likewise, new technologies can spread if they are effectively designed to propagate themselves, even if they do not enhance the lives of their users. For example, apps that push notifications to the front of their users' screens may be more likely to capture attention, even though users may not benefit from having their limited attentional resources captured. This idea is taken to its logical extreme with "clickbait," sensational—and often false—online news stories created entirely to attract clicks and shares; these questionable news stories are unlikely to provide real informational value, and some commentators suggest that such misleading stories may have played a key role in enabling the election of Donald Trump (e.g., Parkinson, 2016).

Given the unprecedented current pace of technological innovation, we propose that well-being researchers have a critical role to play in ensuring that these advances are harnessed to promote, rather than undermine, the pursuit of the Good Life. In this chapter, we begin with the rapidly evolving present, highlighting how today's most ubiquitous microchips—smartphones—can both support and subvert well-being. We then look forward to the near future, in which this advancing technology could be used to more effectively promote the Good Life. Finally, we take a long view, considering how deploying well-being research now can help us prepare for a not-so-distant future, in which robots render much of human work unnecessary. Taken together, this chapter sheds light on the future of the Good Life.

Back to the Present

One of the clearest conclusions from happiness research is that positive social interactions and relationships are of paramount importance in the pursuit of the Good Life (e.g., Baumeister & Leary, 1995; Diener & Seligman, 2002; Gable, this volume; Sandstrom & Dunn, 2014). It should therefore come as no surprise that people around the world have harnessed the power of microchips for social purposes. Although mobile apps offer a vast array of tools, the five most popular apps in the world—WhatsApp, Messenger, Facebook, Snapchat, and Instagram—primarily offer the opportunity to connect with others (Richter, 2016).

But a growing body of research suggests that these virtual interactions may be less likely to promote happiness compared to actual face-to-face interactions (e.g., Kross et al., 2013; Holtzmann et al., 2017; Sacco & Ismail, 2014; but see Sheldon, Abad, & Hinsch, 2011 for important nuances). For example, after completing a stressful speech, young women were randomly assigned to receive social support from a close friend either in-person or via text messaging (Holtzmann et al., 2017). Although they rated the two types of support as equally satisfactory, they felt significantly happier after receiving support in-person. In fact, receiving support via text messaging provided negligible benefits compared to not receiving support at all. Turning to social media, in a longitudinal study of Facebook users, Kross et al. (2013) found that increases in Facebook use were linked to decreases in mood over time; meanwhile, increases in actual (e.g., face-to-face) social interactions were linked to improvements in mood. Using Facebook to actively engage with others (e.g., by commenting on posts) can produce positive effects for mood, but people spend more time using Facebook passively (e.g., scrolling through posts), which appears detrimental for mood (Verduyn et al., 2015). Taken together, this research suggests that spending time on our screens may not be a good substitute for spending time with other people.

The Role of Distraction

The siren song of our screens may impair our ability to connect with people in our immediate social environment. Being barraged with notifications from our attention-seeking apps may make it difficult to remain focused and present. In a sample of over 200 undergraduates, Kushlev, Proulx, and Dunn (2016) found that individuals who reported getting interrupted more often by their phones scored higher on measures of inattention and hyperactivity. Half of the students were then randomly assigned to disable all notifications on their phones for one week and to keep their phones out of sight; the following week, these students were assigned to turn notifications on and keep their phones within reach. The other half of students were assigned to follow the same instructions in the reverse order. Participants scored higher on both inattention and hyperactivity when their smartphones were configured to enable notifications. And the more inattentive people felt, the lower they scored on a wide range of variables related to well-being, including environmental mastery, meaning in life, and social connectedness.

From our theoretical perspective, inattention should reduce the ability to derive well-being benefits from valued daily activities, including social interactions (Brown & Ryan, 2003; Huppert, this volume; Quoidbach et al., 2010). To test this idea, Kushlev and Dunn (2017) recruited parents who were visiting a science museum with their children and randomly assigned them to maximize or minimize their smartphone use during the visit. By the time they left the museum, parents in the high-use (vs. low-use) group felt more distracted and less socially connected, and even reported feeling less meaning and purpose. Interestingly, these negative effects on social connectedness emerged even when people were using their phones to engage in social activities, such as texting or using social media. In fact, phone use only enhanced feelings of social connectedness when parents utilized their phones to access content relevant to their child's experience at the science museum (e.g., supplementary information about exhibits). These findings suggest that any phone use that directs attention away from the immediate social environment may make it more difficult to derive benefits from spending time with close others.

Of course, life has always been filled with potential distractions. But by offering access to an unlimited array of information and entertainment—in a portable device that can be taken anywhere—phones are uniquely poised to permeate important social interactions. Indeed, in a nationally representative survey of over 3,000 cell phone owners in the United States, almost 90% of respondents said that they had used their phones during their most recent social gathering (Pew Research Center, 2015a). And in a qualitative, observational study of parents eating out with their children at Boston-area fast-food restaurants, researchers observed that many parents exhibited a high degree of absorption in their phones (Radesky, Kistin, Augustyn, & Silverstein, 2014).

Because sharing a meal with family and friends represents a central form of daily social interaction across cultures, we manipulated phone use in this context (Dwyer, Kushlev, & Dunn 2017). We invited over 300 people, including students and community members from Vancouver, Canada, to have dinner at a local café with their family or friends. In the phone condition, participants were told that they would be asked to answer a question via text partway through the meal, and that they should keep their phones on the table with ringer or vibration on to ensure they received the question; this approach enabled us to ensure that phones were present without revealing that their presence was the focus of the study. Meanwhile, groups assigned to the phoneless condition were also told that they would be handed a survey (on paper) partway through the meal, and they were instructed to turn their phones on silent and place them in a container on the table; this request was embedded within other instructions about the study to avoid making it salient. At the end of the meal, all participants were asked to complete a survey about their experience. Despite the subtlety of our manipulation, participants in the phone condition reported feeling more distracted during the meal and reported enjoying it significantly less.

Moving beyond this specific context, we conducted an experience sampling study with over 100 students in the southern United States (Dwyer et al., 2017). Over the course of a week, participants received five text messages per day asking them what they had been doing and feeling in the preceding 15 minutes. When participants had been engaging in face-to-face interactions, they felt more distracted and reported lower interest and enjoyment, as well as lower social connectedness, if they had also been using smartphones than if they had not. In an observational study conducted at coffee shops, Misra, Cheng, Genevie, and Yuan (2014) studied the behavior of pairs of people sitting together, and then asked them to complete surveys about their feelings. They found that participants reported lower levels of social connectedness in dyads where either member accessed a mobile device (e.g., smartphone, laptop). Although distraction was not measured and the correlational nature of the study precludes causal conclusions,

Misra et al. (2014) theorize that the presence of phones may divide attention, undermining feelings of social connection. There is even some evidence that the mere presence of phones in the visual field may undermine feelings of closeness during face-to-face interactions (Przybylski & Weinstein, 2012), possibly by priming people to think of their broader social networks and thereby dividing attention. Taken together, this growing body of research points to the conclusion that phones may undercut the benefits of face-to-face interactions by distracting people from their immediate social environment.

Negative Social Signals

In addition to these intrapsychic costs, using phones during social interactions may produce interpersonal costs by acting as a negative social signal. In 2016, the *Oxford English Dictionary* added the word "phubbing" to describe the act of snubbing others by devoting attention to one's phone. Not surprisingly, individuals who say they are frequently phubbed by their romantic partners report lower relationship satisfaction, which in turn predicts lower life satisfaction (Roberts & David, 2016). To test the causal role of phone use in social perception, researchers brought pairs of unacquainted students into the lab, and asked one member of each pair to serve as a confederate (Vanden Abeele, Antheunis, & Schouten, 2016). When confederates were randomly assigned to reach for a smartphone several times during a ten-minute social interaction, they were rated as being significantly less attentive and polite than when smartphones were absent. These negative effects were magnified when participants proactively accessed phones, rather than responding to an obvious notification. This finding suggests that phone use may be particularly detrimental when it conveys an internal lack of interest in the conversation rather than a response to external demands.

Of course, in some cases, phone use may provide an accurate social signal of disinterest; in a recent Pew survey, almost half of young people (ages 18–29) reported using their smartphones to avoid others around them over the course of a week (Pew Research Center, 2015b). But phone use may be a noisy signal. A key property of smartphones—their capacity to serve so many different functions— makes it difficult to infer whether people are using their phones for an essential purpose, such as responding to an urgent text message, or simply seeking casual entertainment by surfing social media. This property should create a high degree of attributional ambiguity, which may make people reluctant to strike up a conversation with phone users—even when phones are used merely to pass the time in a manner that is less satisfying than engaging in face-to-face social interaction.

An Easy Substitute for Social Interactions

Given these important social costs, why have smartphones been adopted more rapidly than any other technology in history? According to the Principle of Least Effort, organisms will seek out the easiest, most convenient route to achieving a goal (Ferrero, 1894). Because smartphones enable us to accomplish a vast array of goals quickly and easily, we may turn to them for information and entertainment, even if doing so comes at the potential cost of social connection. To explore this idea, Kushlev, Proulx, and Dunn (2017a) asked university students to find an unfamiliar building on campus, either with or without using their smartphones. Stripped of their smartphones, the typical participant talked to about two to three other people in the course of trying to find the building. In contrast, those who were allowed to rely on their smartphones typically talked to no one. Although eliminating these social interactions might seem trivial (or even beneficial), participants who were able to rely on their smartphones arrived at the building feeling significantly less socially connected, compared to people who had to find the building without using smartphones.

At the same time, of course, smartphones made the task of finding the building much easier; armed with their smartphones, participants got to the building several minutes earlier and rated the task as being less difficult, compared to phoneless participants. And the easier participants found the task, the happier they felt afterward, as we would expect based on the Principle of Least Effort. Although this was a large effect, participants who were carrying powerful computers in their pockets ended up only slightly happier than participants whose phones had been taken away. Why? The massive benefit that phones provided in terms of convenience was significantly undercut by the cost they created in terms of foregone human connections. That is, by relying on technology rather than other people, phone users were able to accomplish the task more easily and efficiently, but in doing so, they missed an opportunity for casual interpersonal encounters when asking for directions.

When other participants simply imagined trying to find the building with and without their phones, they accurately forecasted that they would (a) find the task easier and (b) end up feeling less socially connected if they used their phones (Kushlev, Proulx, & Dunn, 2017). They also recognized that the convenience provided by phones would make them happier. But they failed to recognize that the loss of social connectedness would have a countervailing, negative effect on their happiness. These findings point to the conclusion that new technologies that reduce effort may be readily adopted, even if people recognize that this efficiency might come at the cost of social connection. For example, people may recognize that scrolling through Facebook or texting a friend will provide less social connection than having a real face-to-face interaction, but the minimal effort required for social media and texting may drive people to opt for these less rewarding activities.

Integrative Summary

Taken together, the research reviewed above highlights three key mechanisms—distraction, negative social signals, and substitution—through which powerful microchips that keep us constantly connected may actually undermine feelings of social connection and happiness. First, by providing a pervasive source of distraction, phones may make it more difficult to derive emotional benefits from potentially rewarding social activities, such as spending time with friends and family. Second, by sending negative social signals, phone use may exert interpersonal costs, impeding the development and maintenance of relationships. Third, by enabling people to access information and entertainment with minimal effort, smartphones may act as a substitute for actual interactions with people in the immediate social environment.

Toward a Happier Horizon

By identifying these three mechanisms, it is possible to envision how the negative effects of today's smartphones and tomorrow's microchips could be minimized or even reversed. Although individual apps benefit from clamoring for attention, the negative effects of distraction point to the potential value of "meta-apps" that keep the resulting cacophony under control. A company called Ringly recently introduced rings that vibrate or light up in response to certain notifications, selected by the user, making it possible to keep smartphones out of sight. For example, during a night out with friends, a single mother could put her phone away, entrusting the ring to light up only if the babysitter called. As sensors become more advanced, it may be possible for smartphones and other mobile devices to automatically detect what we are doing and who we are with, enabling them to minimize distractions when we are engaging in valuable activities, such as spending time with loved ones.

By recognizing that screens can send negative—and noisy—social signals, it may also be possible to re-engineer new and existing technologies. For example, the light already built into the back of smartphones could produce a faint colored glow that would provide a more informative social signal, turning red to indicate phone use that should not be interrupted and otherwise glowing green to invite social interactions. Already, dating apps such as Tinder, Grindr, and Happn make it easy to meet up with potential romantic or sexual partners who happen to be nearby, but this existing technology could be repurposed to promote nonsexual interactions by enabling precise and frictionless social signaling. As one example, imagine that you installed an app indicating where and when you were open to talking to strangers. If you were knowledgeable about your hometown and liked to share this knowledge, you could indicate this openness; visiting tourists who had the app and happened to be riding the same public bus would know to approach you for a mutually rewarding chat about this topic. And if you were finding your way around an unfamiliar city, you could use the app to identify people in the immediate vicinity who would be happy to help you. In this way, technology could be harnessed to send clearer social signals, such that screens could facilitate, rather than supplant, face-to-face interactions.

Extremely successful technology developers have recently voiced concerns that their rapidly adopted products may be undermining human well-being; as Twitter cofounder Evan Williams put it in 2017, "The internet is broken." This growing recognition can potentially provide an opening for well-being researchers and technologists to work together in beginning to reverse this trend.

Promoting Well-Being Directly

Indeed, the ubiquity of current smartphones and future microchips may be harnessed to promote well-being directly. In conjunction with the rapidly evolving mHealth movement—whereby mobile technology is utilized to improve health—developers have created a number of smartphone apps that offer to enhance happiness. Unfortunately, there is a dearth of rigorous research to evaluate the efficacy of these apps (see Konrath, 2015, for a review). There is, however, some intriguing preliminary evidence that well-designed smartphone apps may promote behaviors linked to well-being, such as helping others (Konrath, 2015) and expressing gratitude (Ghandeharioun, Azaria, Taylor, & Picard, 2016; see also Huppert, this volume). As Konrath (2015) argues, interventions that harness mobile technology offer a number of important advantages. Thanks to the widespread adoption of this technology, interventions can potentially reach large and diverse populations around the world. As a result, mobile technology is poised to help researchers address two fundamental problems in social psychology: the use of small samples and the reliance on samples that are Western, Educated, Industrialized, Rich, and Democratic (Henrich, Heine, & Norenzayan, 2010).

In addition, mobile technology makes it possible to deliver interventions in everyday contexts, increasing their capacity to affect behavior in daily life. This is important because simply asking people to alter their behavior may be insufficient to change deeply ingrained habits (Konrath, 2015). For example, our lab has found that people feel happier and report a greater sense of belonging on days when they take the time to interact with strangers and acquaintances—but we also found that simply instructing people to increase these interactions had no effect on their behavior (Sandstrom & Dunn, 2014). Smartphones could be harnessed to deliver this intervention more effectively by utilizing location-detection capacities to provide people with reminders to change their behavior when they entered relevant contexts. As sensors improve, it may be possible for smartphones (and their technological descendants) to detect a wide range of information about the social setting, making it possible to tailor interventions even more precisely.

Monitoring Happiness

Sensors may also make it possible to detect current happiness levels automatically, enabling the deployment of interventions at key time points—as well as the evaluation of their efficacy. There is some preliminary evidence that state-like changes in mood can be detected using current smartphone technology. In a small pilot study, researchers collected data from six patients with bipolar disorder over a period of months (Karam et al., 2014). Using an app installed on their smartphones, all outgoing speech was recorded during their phone calls (thereby capturing the voices of the patients, but not their conversation partners). By harnessing machine learning, the researchers were able to use the acoustical properties of participants' voices during these calls to infer their mood states, as rated by trained clinicians on the same days as the phone calls. Building on this work, our lab is currently investigating whether we can use smartphones to assess momentary happiness unobtrusively in nonclinical populations. Eventually, this approach could enable us to examine the efficacy of novel interventions designed to promote happiness, while minimizing the demand characteristics that often plague this area of research. We believe this goal is especially important to pursue now, given that advances in technology may soon provoke dramatic changes in the fabric of everyday life, a topic we turn to in the next section.

A Fundamentally Different Future

In 1930, John Maynard Keynes famously predicted that the increasing efficiency of machines would reduce the workweek to 15 hours by 2030 (Keynes, 1930). While the 40-hour week is still the norm, recent advances in technology are paving the way for a world in which robots do much of the work for us. Some of our most dreaded tasks may soon be automated—such as flipping burgers, manual labor, and customer service (Kim, 2016). But the potential of machines is now stretching far beyond simple and repetitive tasks. For example, a driverless semi-truck named "Otto" recently completed the world's first automated commercial truck delivery (Bloomberg, 2016). This may be just the beginning of a much bigger trend; Oxford researchers claim that machine learning and other advances in information processing could automate as many as half of all jobs by 2050, including many white-collar and creative jobs (Frey & Osborne, 2013).

The potential changes spurred on by technological advances have raised serious questions about how to prepare for a future where human labor is no longer needed. How would people make a living if they did not work? Universal basic income—a guaranteed livable income for all citizens without regard to work status—has generated a lot of interest as a potential solution. The idea of a basic income has been around in various forms for centuries (Vanderborght & Van Parijs, 2005), and despite its radical nature, both liberal and conservative thinkers have supported it (De Rugy, 2014).

If people could rely on a basic income, would the trend toward a workless world usher in an era of happiness? On the one hand, working hours are among the most unpleasant in many people's days (e.g., Kahneman, Krueger, Schkade, Schwarz, & Stone, 2004; Krueger et al., 2009), and nearly 70% of employees are not engaged at their job (Gallup, 2016). If society's most dull and menial jobs were replaced by automation, the "daily grind" could be replaced by relaxation and leisure. On the other hand, research shows that people who are unemployed are less satisfied with their lives than their employed counterparts, even after controlling for relevant factors like income (Knabe, Rätzel, Schöb, & Weimann, 2010). In addition, unemployment can have severe and long-lasting negative psychological effects (Knabe & Rätzel, 2011) that remain even after reemployment (Anusic, Yap, & Lucas, 2014; Clark, Georgellis, & Sanfey, 2001). And across seven Western countries, almost half of respondents reported that work provided an important source of meaning in life (Delle Fave, Brdar, Wissing, & Vella-Brodrick, 2013; see also Baumeister, this volume).

While there has been much speculation about the potential impact of basic income and a workless world, there has been little data directly examining these issues, until recently. A number of government projects are now underway in countries like Canada, the Netherlands, and Finland (Henley, 2017). Even Silicon Valley has taken interest, in the hope of better understanding how the benefits of technological progress might be spread throughout society. A renowned startup incubator, Y Combinator, is currently investing millions of dollars to study the impact of implementing a guaranteed basic income in the United States (Altman, 2016). The company put out a request for research in January of 2016, and they are now working with researchers on a pilot project that will pay 100 Oakland residents \$2,000 a month for a year—no matter what they do. The goal is to see how basic income influences people's financial and psychological health, and to see how they spend their time. If the methods work, they hope to expand the basic income study to more people over a longer time period.

Studies of this sort will provide unprecedented insight into the psychology of the Good Life, by allowing us to see what people do when working is unnecessary. But they also highlight the need to consider impending societal changes that will result from rapid technological advances. Well-being researchers are in a unique position to advocate for progress that promotes— rather than undermines—the Good Life. Of course, recommendations about *how* to enhance the Good Life should be grounded in psychological theory and backed by evidence.

Decades of research in positive psychology have found that humans are more likely to be happy if they meet: (a) basic physical and health needs (Angner, Ghandhi, Williams Purvis, Amante, & Allison, 2013; Deaton, 2008; Veenhoven, 1991), and (b) psychological needs for autonomy, competence, and relatedness (see Gagné & Lydon, 2004, for cross-cultural evidence; Ryan & Deci, 2000; Baumeister, this volume). We argue that a universal basic income—setting aside all economic and political hurdles—would certainly help citizens live *better* lives by ensuring their basic physical needs are met. However, in order to promote *the Good Life*, basic income must further enhance autonomy, competence, and relatedness. In the remaining sections of this chapter, we use self-determination theory (Ryan & Deci, 2000) as a framework for understanding the conditions under which people could be most likely to find happiness in a world where basic needs are met and work is no longer a necessity.

Autonomy. People want to choose what they do in life (Ryan & Deci, 2000), but they must sacrifice their time by working in order to make ends meet each month. In a world where machines have replaced human labor, a basic income could provide people with more freedom to choose how to spend their time without worrying about paying rent. This could allow people to invest their time into achieving self-directed goals, such as gaining higher education or creating art. In fact, people are motivated to stay busy and to be productive (Hsee, Yang, & Wang, 2010), especially on tasks that are intrinsically rewarding (Ryan & Deci, 2000). According to the General Social Survey, nearly three-quarters of Americans say they wouldn't quit their jobs even if a financial windfall enabled them to live in luxury for the rest of their lives (Brooks, 2013). In sum, people want to spend time on tasks they care about, so a basic income will likely only promote the Good Life if it helps people pursue intrinsically motivated goals. Thus, jobs that are dull and disliked, such as repetitive or low-skilled labor and service industry jobs, should be targeted for automation, while jobs that are intrinsically satisfying might be better left to humans. In the transition to an automated workforce, a basic income could help displaced workers retrain for jobs that are not easily automated or allow them pursue their interests beyond work.

Competence. While basic income could provide people with autonomy over how they spend their time, people also need to feel that they are competent and efficacious in order to be happy (Ryan & Deci, 2000). For example, research shows that people are more likely to be happy when they are in flow—exercising expertise in a task with full engagement (Csikszentmihalyi, 1990). Many people experience competence at work, so some have suggested that automatization could deprive people of satisfying this need and lead to meaninglessness and depression (Thompson, 2015). Unemployment can also negatively affect self-perceptions of competence due in part to failing to meet the cultural expectation to work (Schöb, 2013). For example, a study using a German sample found that life satisfaction increased when retirement-age job seekers changed their status from "unemployed" to "retired," suggesting that the expectation to work affects the psychological impact of unemployment (Hetschko, Knabe, & Schöb, 2014). To the extent that mass automation reduces the cultural expectation to work, people who are unemployed may be less likely to be perceived—by themselves and others—as incompetent, potentially reducing the detrimental effects of unemployment on well-being (Stutzer & Lalive, 2004).

A basic income could promote competence by enabling people to devote their time to engaging hobbies instead of dull work, but research suggests people may need assistance in dealing with the extra time. Time use surveys, for example, reveal that unemployed people spend much of their extra free time sleeping and watching TV (Aguiar, Hurst, & Karabarbounis, 2011), and retired seniors watch nearly five hours of television a day (Bureau of Labor Statistics, 2015), likely to the detriment of their own well-being (Frey, Benesch, & Stutzer, 2005). Thus, in moving toward a workless world, it may be important to provide people with "leisure training," helping them build the skills necessary to engage deeply with challenging hobbies that satisfy the need for competence.

Relatedness. People have a need to feel connected to others (Ryan & Deci, 2000), and social relationships are one of the best predictors of happiness (Lyubomirsky, King, & Diener, 2005; see also Gable, 2017; Lyubomirsky & Fritz, 2017), but working necessitates spending time away from loved ones. In fact, one of the most common complaints of working adults is lack of work-life balance (Ernst & Young, 2015), and at the end of life, people often regret working so much and not having spent more time with loved ones (Ware, 2012). A world without work could enhance well-being by allowing people to spend more time with close friends and family. Research on the time use of retired Dutch seniors shows that they become more engaged in civic activities and provide more instrumental support to their family after they retire compared to seniors who continue to work (Van Den Bogaard, Henkens, & Kalmijn, 2014). Data from the American Time Use Survey also shows that the unemployed spend about 50% more time socializing compared to employed individuals (Katz, 2015). At the same time, working forces us to interact with others, and the workplace can also be socially rewarding in its own right (Mottaz, 1985). To prepare for a future in which the workplace no longer provides a central source of social interaction, communities should strive to create more public spaces that encourage social interactions (Montgomery, 2013). In fact, Putnam (2000) has argued that civic engagement has been declining for decades in the United States. By providing people with more free time, a world without work—aided by thoughtful urban design—has the potential to reverse this trend, thereby helping to fulfill our need to connect.

Conclusion

One of the most puzzling findings in happiness research is known as the Easterlin Paradox. Over the past five decades, many countries have witnessed substantial economic growth, but this progress has not been consistently accompanied by sustained increases in happiness (e.g., Easterlin et al., 2010). Looking ahead to the next five decades, this finding provides a cautionary tale: Progress does not inevitably lead to increased well-being. Indeed, recent research on smartphones suggests that the powerful microchips designed to connect us can sometimes leave us feeling more disconnected. As a result, even though smartphones make life easier, this major technological advance may fail to substantially increase happiness. By shaping the way new technologies are developed and utilized, however, well-being researchers may be able to increase the odds that rapid growth in technology will be accompanied by growth in human happiness. Researchers have already begun to use modern microchips to measure and enhance happiness, although this work is in its infancy and demands much more attention. As the fabric of daily life is resewn and work becomes increasingly unnecessary, well-being researchers should play a vital role in ensuring that these fundamental changes nourish—rather than neglect—fundamental human needs. Although these changes lie in the future, the time to prepare for them is now.

Bibliography

Aguiar, M. A., Hurst, E., & Karabarbounis, L. (2011). Time use during recessions. *NBER Working Paper Series*. https://doi.org/10.1007/s13398-014-0173-7.2

Altman, S. (2016). *Moving forward on basic income*. Retrieved December 30, 2016, from https://blog.ycombinator.com/moving-forward-on-basic-income/

Amichai-Hamburger, Y., & Etgar, S. (2017). Internet and wellbeing. In J. P. Forgas & R. F. Baumeister (Eds.), *Sydney symposium of social psychology*. New York, NY: Psychology Press.

Angner, E., Ghandhi, J., Williams Purvis, K., Amante, D., & Allison, J. (2013). Daily functioning, health status, and happiness in older adults. *Journal of Happiness Studies, 14*(5), 1563–1574. https://doi.org/10.1007/s10902-012-9395-6

Anusic, I., Yap, S. C. Y., & Lucas, R. E. (2014). Testing set-point theory in a swiss national sample: Reaction and adaptation to major life events. *Social Indicators Research*, 1–24. https://doi.org/10.1007/s11205-013-0541-2

Baumeister, R. F. (2017). Happiness and meaningfulness as two different and not entirely compatible versions of the good life. In J. P. Forgas & R. F. Baumeister (Eds.), *Sydney symposium of social psychology*. New York, NY: Psychology Press.

Baumeister, R. F., & Leary, M. R. (1995). The need to belong: Desire for interpersonal attachments as a fundamental human motivation. *Psychological Bulletin, 117*(3), 497–529. http://doi.org/10.1037/0033-2909.117.3.497

Bloomberg (2016, October 25). Uber Self-Driving Truck Packed With Budweiser Makes First Delivery in Colorado. Retrieved from https://www.bloomberg.com/news/articles/2016-10-25/uber-self-driving-truck-packed-with-budweiser-makes-first-delivery-in-colorado

Brooks, A. C. (2013, December 14). A formula for happiness. *The New York Times*.

Brown, K. W., & Ryan, R. M. (2003). The benefits of being present: Mindfulness and its role in psychological well-being. *Journal of Personality and Social Psychology, 84*(4), 822–848. https://doi.org/10.1037/0022-3514.84.4.822

Bureau of Labor Statistics. (2015). *American time use survey*. Washington, DC: Bureau of Labor Statistics.

Clark, A. E., Georgellis, Y., & Sanfey, P. (2001). Scarring: The psychological impact of past unemployment. *Economica, 68*(270), 221–241. https://doi.org/10.1111/1468-0335.00243

Csikszentmihalyi, M. (1990). *Flow: The psychology of optimal experience*. New York, NY: Harper and Row.

De Rugy, V. (2014). *What's the welfare initiative uniting liberals and conservatives?* Retrieved December 30, 2016, from www.pbs.org/newshour/making-sense/whats-welfare-initiative-uniting-liberals-conservatives/

Deaton, A. (2008, Spring). Income, health, and well-being around the world: Evidence from the gallup world poll. *Journal of Economic Perspectives, 22*(2), 53–72. https://doi.org/10.1257/jep.22.2.53

Delle Fave, A., Brdar, I., Wissing, M. P., & Vella-Brodrick, D. A. (2013). Sources and motives for personal meaning in adulthood. *The Journal of Positive Psychology*, 8(6), 517–529. https://doi.org/10.1080/17439760.2013.830761

Diener, E., & Seligman, M. E. P. (2002). Very happy people. *Psychological Science*, 13(1), 81–84. https://doi.org/10.1111/1467-9280.00415

Dwyer, R., Kushlev, K., & Dunn, E. (2017). Smartphone use undermines enjoyment of face-to-face social interactions. *Journal of Experimental Social Psychology*. Advance online publication. https://doi.org/10.1016/j.jesp.2017.10.007

Easterlin, R. A., McVey, L. A., Switek, M., Sawangfa, O., & Zweig, J. S. (2010). The happiness-income paradox revisited. *Proceedings of the National Academy of Sciences*, 107(52), 22463–22468. https://doi.org/10.1073/pnas.1015962107

Ernst & Young (2015). Global generations: A global study on work-life challenges across generations. Retrieved from http://www.ey.com/Publication/vwLUAssets/EY-global-generations-a-global-study-on-work-life-challenges-across-generations/%24FILE/EY-global-generations-a-global-study-on-work-life-challenges-across-generations.pdf

Ferrero, G. Mental inertia and the law of least effort. Revue Philosophique, 1894 (In French).

Frey, B. S., Benesch, C., & Stutzer, A. (2005). Does watching tv make us happy?

Frey, C. B., & Osborne, M. A. (2013). The future of employment: How susceptible are jobs to computerisation? *Technological Forecasting and Social Change*, 114, 254–280. https://doi.org/10.1016/j.techfore.2016.08.019

Friedman, T. (2016). *Thank you for being late: An optimist's guide to thriving in the age of accelerations*. New York, NY: Farrar, Straus & Giroux.

Gable, S. L. (2017). Satisfying and meaningful close relationships. In J. P. Forgas & R. F. Baumeister (Eds.), *Sydney symposium of social psychology*. New York, NY: Psychology Press.

Gagné, F. M., & Lydon, J. E. (2004). Bias and accuracy in close relationships: An integrative review. *Personality and Social Psychology Review: An Official Journal of the Society for Personality and Social Psychology, Inc*, 8(4), 322–338. https://doi.org/10.1207/s15327957pspr0804_1

Gallup. (2016). *Employee engagement in U.S. stagnant in 2015*. Retrieved December 30, 2016, from www.gallup.com/poll/188144/employee-engagement-stagnant-2015.aspx

Ghandeharioun, A., Azaria, A., Taylor, S., & Picard, R. W. (2016). "Kind and Grateful": a context-sensitive smartphone app utilizing inspirational content to promote gratitude. *Psychology of well-being*, 6(1), 1–21.

Global generations: A global study on work-life challenges across generations. (2015). London: Ernst and Young.

Hamilton, W. D. (1963). The evolution of altruistic behavior. *The American Naturalist*, 97(896), 354–356. https://doi.org/10.1086/497114

Henley, J. (2017). Finland trials basic income for unemployed. *The Guardian*.

Henrich, J., Heine, S. J., & Norenzayan, A. (2010). The weirdest people in the world? *The Behavioral and Brain Sciences*, 33(2–3), 61–83–135. https://doi.org/10.1017/S0140525X0999152X

Hetschko, C., Knabe, A., & Schöb, R. (2014). Changing identity: Retiring from unemployment. *Economic Journal*, 124(575), 149–166. https://doi.org/10.1111/ecoj.12046

Holtzmann, S., DeClerck, D., Turcotte, K., Lisi, D., & Woodworth, M. (2017). Social support during times of stress: Can text messaging compete with in-person communication? *Computers in Human Behavior*, 71, 130–139.

Hsee, C. K., Yang, A. X., & Wang, L. (2010). Idleness aversion and the need for justifiable busyness. *Psychological Science*, 21(7), 926–930. https://doi.org/10.1177/0956797610374738

Huppert, F. A. (2017). Living life well: The role of mindfulness and compassion what is mindfulness and how does it promote living well ? In J. P. Forgas & R. F. Baumeister (Eds.), *Sydney symposium of social psychology*. New York, NY: Psychology Press.

Kahneman, D., Krueger, A. B., Schkade, D., Schwarz, N., & Stone, A. A. (2004). A survey method for characterizing daily life experience: The day reconstruction method. *Science (New York, N.Y.)*, *306*(5702), 1776–1780. https://doi.org/10.1126/science.1103572

Karam, Z. N., Provost, E. M., Singh, S., Montgomery, J., Archer, C., Harrington, G., & McInnis, M. G. (2014, May). Ecologically valid long-term mood monitoring of individuals with bipolar disorder using speech. In *Acoustics, Speech and Signal Processing (ICASSP), 2014 IEEE International Conference*, pp. 4858–4862. New York: IEEE.

Katz, J. (2015). How nonemployed americans spend their weekdays: Men vs. women. *The New York Times*.

Keynes, J. M. (1930, June). Economic possibilities for our grandchildren. *Essays in Persuasion*, 358–373. https://doi.org/10.1007/978-1-349-59072-8_25

Kim, Q. (2016). *As our jobs are automated, some say we'll need a guaranteed basic income*. Retrieved December 30, 2016, from www.npr.org/2016/09/24/495186758/as-our-jobs-are-automated-some-say-well-need-a-guaranteed-basic-income

Knabe, A., & Rätzel, S. (2011). Quantifying the psychological costs of unemployment: The role of permanent income. *Applied Economics*, *43*(21), 2751–2763. https://doi.org/10.1080/00036840903373295

Knabe, A., Rätzel, S., Schöb, R., & Weimann, J. (2010). Dissatisfied with life but having a good day: Time-use and well-being of the unemployed. *Economic Journal*, *120*(547), 867–889. https://doi.org/10.1111/j.1468-0297.2009.02347.x

Konrath, S. (2015). Positive technology: Using mobile phones for psychosocial interventions. In *Encyclopedia of mobile phone behavior* (pp. 871–897). IGI Global. https://doi.org/10.4018/978-1-4666-8239-9.ch072

Kross, E., Verduyn, P., Demiralp, E., Park, J., Lee, D. S., Lin, N., . . . Ybarra, O. (2013). Facebook use predicts declines in subjective well-being in young adults. *PLoS One*, *8*(8), 1–6. https://doi.org/10.1371/journal.pone.0069841

Krueger, A. B., Kahneman, D., Fischler, C., Schkade, D., Schwarz, N., & Stone, A. A. (2009). Time use and subjective well-being in France and the U.S. *Social Indicators Research*, *93*(1), 7–18. http://doi.org/10.1007/s11205-008-9415-4

Kushlev, K., & Dunn, E. W. (2017). Smartphone use distracts parents from cultivating feelings of connection when spending time with their children. Manuscript submitted for publication.

Kushlev, K., Proulx, J., & Dunn, E. W. (2016). "Silence Your Phones": Smartphone notifications increase inattention and hyperactivity symptoms. *Proceedings of the 2016 CHI Conference on Human Factors in Computing Systems*, 1011–1020. http://doi.org/10.1145/2858036.2858359

Kushlev, K., Proulx, J. D. E., & Dunn, E. W. (2017). Digitally connected, socially disconnected: The effects of relying on technology rather than other people. *Computers in Human Behavior*, *76*, 68–74. http://doi.org/10.1016/j.chb.2017.07.001

Lyubomirsky, S., & Fritz, M. M. (2017). Wither happiness? When, how, and why might positive activities undermine well-being. In J. P. Forgas & R. F. Baumeister (Eds.), *Sydney symposium of social psychology*. New York, NY: Psychology Press.

Lyubomirsky, S., King, L., & Diener, E. (2005). The benefits of frequent positive affect: Does happiness lead to success? *Psychological Bulletin*, *131*(6), 803–855. https://doi.org/10.1037/0033-2909.131.6.803

Misra, S., Cheng, L., Genevie, J., & Yuan, M. (2014). The iphone effect: The quality of in-person social interactions in the presence of mobile devices. *Environment and Behavior*, 1–24. https://doi.org/10.1177/0013916514539755

Montgomery, C. (2013). *Happy city: Transforming our lives through urban design*. London: Palgrave Macmillan.

Mottaz, C. J. (1985). The relative important of intrinsic and extrinsic rewards as determinants of work satisfaction. *The Sociological Quarterly*, *26*(3), 365–385. https://doi.org/10.1111/j.1533-8525.1985.tb00233.x

Parkinson, H. J. (2016). *Click and elect: How fake news helped donald trump win a real election*. Retrieved December 30, 2016, from www.theguardian.com/commentisfree/2016/nov/14/fake-news-donald-trump-election-alt-right-social-media-tech-companies

Pew Research Center (2015a). Americans' views on mobile etiquette. Retrieved from http://www.pewinternet.org/2015/08/26/americans-views-on-mobile-etiquette/

Pew Research Center (2015b). U.S. Smartphone Use in 2015. Retrieved from http://www.pewinternet.org/2015/04/01/us-smartphone-use-in-2015/

Przybylski, A. K., & Weinstein, N. (2012). Can you connect with me now? How the presence of mobile communication technology influences face-to-face conversation quality. *Journal of Social and Personal Relationships*, *30*(3), 237–246. https://doi.org/10.1177/0265407512453827

Putnam, R. D. (2000). *Bowling alone*. New York, NY: Simon & Schuster.

Quoidbach, J., Dunn, E. W., Petrides, K. V., & Mikolajczak, M. (2010). Money giveth, money taketh away: The dual effect of wealth on happiness. *Psychological Science*, *21*(6), 759–763. https://doi.org/10.1177/0956797610371963

Radesky, J. S., Kistin, C. J., Augustyn, M., & Silverstein, M. (2014). Patterns of mobile device use by caregivers and children during meals in fast food restaurants. *Pediatrics*, *133*(4), e843–e849. https://doi.org/10.1542/peds.2013-3703

Richter, F. (2016). *The most popular apps in the world*. Retrieved December 30, 2016, from www.statista.com/chart/5055/top-10-apps-in-the-world/

Roberts, J. A., & David, M. E. (2016). My life has become a major distraction from my cell phone: Partner phubbing and relationship satisfaction among romantic partners. *Computers in Human Behavior*, *54*, 134–141. https://doi.org/10.1016/j.chb.2015.07.058

Ryan, R. M., & Deci, E. L. (2000). Self-determination theory and the facilitation of intrinsic motivation. *American Psychologist*, *55*(1), 68–78. https://doi.org/10.1037/0003-066X.55.1.68

Sacco, D. F., & Ismail, M. M. (2014). Social belongingness satisfaction as a function of interaction medium: Face-to-face interactions facilitate greater social belonging and interaction enjoyment compared to instant messaging. *Computers in Human Behavior*, *36*, 359–364. https://doi.org/10.1016/j.chb.2014.04.004

Sandstrom, G. M., & Dunn, E. W. (2014). Social interactions and well-being: The surprising power of weak ties. *Personality & Social Psychology Bulletin*, *40*(7), 910–922. https://doi.org/10.1177/0146167214529799

Schöb, R. (2013). Unemployment and identity. *CESifo Economic Studies*, *59*(1), 149–180. https://doi.org/10.1093/cesifo/ifs040

Sheldon, K. M., Abad, N., & Hinsch, C. (2011). A two-process view of facebook use and relatedness need-satisfaction: Disconnection drives use, and connection rewards it. *Psychology of Popular Media Culture*, *1*(S), 2–15. https://doi.org/10.1037/2160-4134.1.S.2

Stutzer, A., & Lalive, R. (2004, June). The role of social work norms in job searching ans subjective well-being. *Journal of the European Economic Association*, *2*, 696–719. https://doi.org/10.1162/1542476041423331

Thompson, D. (2015, July/August). A world without work. *The Atlantic.*

Van Den Bogaard, L., Henkens, K., & Kalmijn, M. (2014). So now what? Effects of retirement on civic engagement. *Ageing and Society, 34*(7), 1170–1192. https://doi.org/10.1017/S0144686X13000019

Vanden Abeele, M. M. P., Antheunis, M. L., & Schouten, A. P. (2016). The effect of mobile messaging during a conversation on impression formation and interaction quality. *Computers in Human Behavior, 62,* 562–569. https://doi.org/10.1016/j.chb.2016.04.005

Vanderborght, Y., & Van Parijs, P. (2005). *L'allocation universelle.* Paris: La découverte.

Veenhoven, R. (1991). Is happiness relative? *Social Indicators Research, 24*(1), 1–34. https://doi.org/10.1007/BF00292648

Verduyn, P., Lee, D. S., Park, J., Shablack, H., Orvell, A., Bayer, J., . . . Kross, E. (2015). Passive facebook usage undermines affective well-being: Experimental and longitudinal evidence. *Journal of Experimental Psychology: General, 144*(2), 480–488. https://doi.org/10.1037/xge0000057

Ware, B. (2012). *The top five regrets of the dying: A life transformed by the dearly departing.* Carlsbad, CA: Hay House, Inc.

INDEX

Note: Page numbers in italics indicate figures and those in bold indicate tables.

Aaker, J. L. 22
Abeyta, A. A. 183–184, 185, 186, 190
abstraction: construal levels of 226–227; as evolutionary adaptation 227–229; expansive/contractive learning and 226–229; role of, in social learning 229–234
accessibility, Internet and 302–303, 305
accommodative, bottom-up processing style 205
activity, eudaimonia as 120
adult physical health, living well and 257–272; biological programming model *258*, 258–259; child attachment insecurity study 260–263; early maternal care and adult attachment insecurity study 263–266; future research for 271–272; life stress and early caregiving study 266–270, *267*, *270–271*; Minnesota Longitudinal Study of Risk and Adaptation 259–270, *271*; overview of 257–258
advertising, identity/connectedness and 6–7
affect, study of 203; *see also* negative affect
affect-as-information (AAI) model 204–205
affect priming 204
Ainsworth, M. D. S. 265
Algoe, S. B. 247, 248

allostatic load 263
Allport, G. W. 309
ambiguous communication, negative affect influence on 213–214, *214*
Amichai-Hamburger, Y. 306, 307, 309, 311, 312
anonymity, Internet and 298–299, 304
approach orientation: contamination and 183; nostalgia and 182–184; redemption and 182–183
arguing 27
Aristotle 66, 75, 116, 120, 257
Aron, A. 250
Arslan, P. 59
Asbeck, J. 206
Aspinwall, L. G. 194
assimilative, top-down processing style 205
attentional control, mindfulness and 67
Aurelius, M. 4
Australopithecines 40
authoritarian parenting 284
authoritative parents 283–284
autonomy, basic income and 329
Awakening Compassion at Work: The Quiet Power That Elevates People and Organizations (Worline & Dutton) 76
awareness, mindfulness and 67

Baldwin, M. 184
Bargh, J. A. 301–302

basic income, happiness and 327–330
Bauer, J. J. 117–118
Baumeister, R. F. 22, 26, 27, 29, 30, 240
belonging, social media use and 301–302
Belsky, J. 165
Ben-Artzi, E. 306
Bentham, J. 3, 202
Ben Ze'ev, A. 301
biological programming model, childhood
    socioeconomic disadvantage *258*,
    258–259
Biswas-Diener, R. 130
Bless, H. 205
Bolger, N. 245
Bowlby, J. 248, 261
Boyce, W. T. 261
broaden-and-build theory 164–165
Brody, G. H. 263
Brunhart, S. M. 194
Buddhism 4, 66

Cacioppo, J. T. 241
calm and connect autonomic response
    168
Campbell, D. 143
capitalization, social relationships and
    246–247
cardiac vagal tone: loving-kindness
    meditation and 169–170; positive
    emotions and purpose and 168–170;
    and social interactions 171–172
Carlson, E. A. 267
Chaplin, S. 183
charitable giving, religious people and 143,
    144, 145
Chen, E. 258–259, 264, 266–267, 272
Cheng, L. 322–323
Cheung, W. Y. 187
child attachment insecurity and adult
    health study 260–263
Cicero 4
Cleveland, M. J. 286
Clore, G. L. 204
cognition, informational effects and
    204–205
cognitive dissonance theory 53
Colantuoni, A. 189–190
Cole, S. 165–167, 241
compassion 73–77; living well and 73–74;
    mindfulness and 76–77; self-compassion
    74; towards others 74–75; well-being
    benefits of 75–76
competence, basic income and 329–330

conserved transcriptional response to
    adversity 166
constant *vs.* variable evolutionary environments,
    selection pressures in 224–225
construal level theory (CLT), social
    learning and 229
consumption, well-being and 6–7
contamination 183
cooperation, social coordination and
    40–41
Cox, C. R. 186, 194
Crano, W. D. 282, 288
crear 60
creativity, nostalgia and 191–193
crescere 60
crime, religious engagement and 147–148,
    152, 153
Critelli, J. W. 23
Cserni, R. T. 301
cyber-bullying 304
Cyrenaics 2

Danese, A. 264
dating apps 325
Davis, F. 182, 183, 186
Dawkins, R. 137
Deaton, A. 149
deception, negative affect and detection of
    210, 210–211
Deci, E. L. 85, 86–87, 129
decision affect theory 51
De Graaf, N. D. 143
Democritus 2, 202
deprivation, satisfaction and 52–54
development, personality and 43–44
Dickerson, S. S. 241
Diener, E. 149, 155
Dishion, T. J. 280
"Dissolving Boundaries" (intergroup
    project) 310
distraction, app notifications as 321–323
diverse contexts, navigating 226
Donaldson, C. D. 281, 283
Donner Party 240
Dorpatcheon, N. 306
Dunedin Multidisciplinary Health and
    Development Study 264
Durkheim, E. 240
dysphoria: behavioural/motivational
    benefits of 211–217, *212, 213, 214, 215,
    216*; cognitive benefits of, on memory/
    judgements 205–211, *206, 207, 208,
    209, 210*; negative affect and 201

early maternal care, adult attachment insecurity, and adult health study 263–266
Easterlin Paradox 330
Economist, The 137
Ee, J. S. 23
Elliot, A. J. 87, 188–189
emotional well-being religious engagement and 146–147, *147*, *148*
emotion regulation, social relationships and 248–249
empathy 74
enacted support 244–245
end of life planning, regulatory focus and 93–96, *94*, *95*
Englund, M. M. 267
enjoyment of Internet 303, 305
environmental constraints, navigating 226
Epic of Gilgamesh (Siduri) 2, 202
Epictetus 2, 4
Epicurus 2, 202
equality of Internet 303, 305–306
Essex, M. J. 268
e-therapy 310–312
eudaimonia: concept of 116; critique of 116–117; defining, as type of conative activity 120–122; growth of 116
Eudaimonic Activity Model (EAM) 117, 126–130, *129*; full version of 128–130, *129*; for problem solving in EWB literature 130; psychosocial content and 127–128; simple version of 126; subjective well-being and 126–127
eudaimonic well-being (EWB) 116–131; concept of, problems with 117–119, *118*; defining eudaimonia and 120–122, *121*; defining well-being and 119–120; elements of 118; empirical meaning of 117–118; Eudaimonic Activity Model and 126–130, *129*; evaluating, using subjective well-being 122–125; expanding conceptions of well-being and 125–126; meaning of 117; overview of 116–117; *see also* subjective well-being (SWB)
evaluative conditioning, relativity in 51–52
Event Reflection Task (ERT) 182
evolutionary imperatives, good life and 34–45; competition and 40–41; cooperation and 40–41; development, personality and 43–44; learning and 41–43; modern world pitfalls 44–45; overview of 34–35; reproduction and 35–39; survival and 39–40
EWB *see* eudaimonic well-being (EWB)

expansive and contractive learning 223–235; abstraction and 226–234; in constant *vs.* variable evolutionary environments 224–225; construal level theory, social learning and 229; diverse contexts, navigating 226; evolutionary perspective of 224–229; higher-level "why?" questions and 232–234; overview of 223–224; psychological distance and 229–231; social learning across constant and variable contexts 225–226; socially acquired *vs.* direct experience evidence 231–232
extrinsic motivation 283
extroversion-introversion personality theory 306–307
eyewitness memories, mood effects on *206*, 206–208, *207*

Facebook 299, 301, 306, 308, 319, 320, 321, 324
faith-happiness correlation 138–140, *139*
false consciousness 9, 10
Farrell, A. K. 265, 267, 269
fear of missing out (FOMO) 305
Feinberg, M. E. 286
Festinger, L. 53
Fiedler, K. 52, 58, 59, 60, 205, 206
fight or flight autonomic response 168
Fincham, F. D. 111
Fisher, R. R. 30
Fletcher, A. C. 280
focus of good life 88–89
FOMO (fear of missing out) 305
Forgas, J. P. 60
Foxen-Craft, E. 189–190
Franklin, B. 11
Fredrickson, B. L. 75, 76, 86, 104–105
French Revolution, human well-being and 5
Freud, S. 31
fundamental attribution error (FAE) 209
Future of an Illusion, The (Freud) 137
future planning, mindfulness and 69–70

Gable, S. L. 245
Gabriel, M. T. 23
Gabriel, S. 29–30
Galen, L. 143
Gallup Organization 138
Garbinsky, E. N. 22
Gardner, W. L. 250
General Social Surveys 138
Genevie, J. 322–323

Germer, C. K. 68

Gilbert, D. T. 86

Gilkey, L. 137

Glatz, T. 287

goal pursuit, nostalgia and 189–191

God Is Not Great, How Religion Poisons Everything (Hitchens) 137

good life: achieving 1, 2–3; adaptive functions of 48–61; aggregation errors symptom of 49; basic income and 328–329; desires and requirements for 89–93, **91**, **92**, *92*, 93, **93**; end of life planning and 93–96, *94*, *95*; evolutionary imperatives and (*see* evolutionary imperatives, good life and); focus of 88–89; happiness and (*see* happiness); health and 11; meaning and (*see* meaningfulness); negative affect and (*see* negative affect); neglected-theory symptoms of 48–49; pleasure and purpose of 85–88; with purpose 96; reification symptom of 48–49; reverse inference symptom of 49; technology and 7, 319–320, 328–329; virtue/achievement and 10–11; *see also* eudaimonic well-being (EWB); happiness *vs.* meaning in good life

good life, adaptive functions of 48–61; deprivation and 52–54; evaluative conditioning and 51–52; introduction to 48–49; mood states and 57–60; positive/negative valence and 49–50; relativity and 49–52; self-generated reinforcement and 54–56; well-being, pleasant experiences and 50–51

Good Neighbors project (intergroup project) 310

Google 70

Google sex searches, religious engagement and 151

Goyal, M. 72

gratitude, social relationships and 247–248

gratitude interventions 105–106

Grayson, D. 240

Grindr 325

Gross, J. J. 249

Gschneidinger, E. 56

gullibility, negative affect and 210–211

Haidt, J. D. 247

halo effects, negative mood and *208*, 208–209, *209*

Hamilton, W. D. 35, 320

Handbook of Eudaimonic Well-Being (Vitterso) 118

Hansen, J. 232

Hansen, K. B. 118

happiness: arguing and 27; basic income and 327–330; boredom and 24; caring for children and 27; defined 101, 119; feelings and 23–24; future of (*see* technology); and good life 21; present time perspective of 24, 25–26; religion and 138–140, *139*; self-control and 30–31; self-esteem and 22–23; self-reward and 30; social relationships and 26–27; society involvement effects on 27–28; survey questions to learn about 22; technology to monitor levels of 326–327; *see also* well-being

happiness *vs.* meaning in good life 21–32; overview of 21; past, present and future thoughts and 24–26; satisfying needs and wants 23–24; self-expression and 29–30; self-reward/self-control and 30–31; social relationships and 26–27; societal involvement and 27–28; studies pertaining to 22–23

Happn 325

Harlow, H. 239, 248

health: good life and 11; religion and 140–142, *142*

Health Enhancement Program (HEP) 72

hedonic well-being (HWB) 118–119, 126; *see also* subjective well-being (SWB)

hedonism 2; defined 202; negative affect and 202–203

helping, prosociality and 193–194

helping behaviors, religious engagement and 142–145, *144*

Hertel, G. 60

Hertwig, R. 54

Hitchens, C. 137, 142–143

Hofmann, W. 30, 31

Holt-Lunstad, J. 240

House, J. S. 240

Houser-Marko, L. 86–87

Huansuriya, T. 285–286, 287

Huismans, S. 143

humanistic psychology movement 8

human labor, technology and 327–328

Huta, V. 85, 87, 129, 130

Ianakieva, I. 189–190

imagination, mindfulness and 69–70

impulse control, religious engagement and 140

Inagaki, T. K. 109
income and life satisfaction 37–38, *38*
informational effects, cognition and 204–205
information processing styles, affect and 205
inspiration, nostalgia and 187–189
Instagram 299, 301, 308, 320
intergroup relations, Internet and 308–310
Internet, psychological components of 298–312; accessibility 302–303, 305; anonymity 298–299, 304; disadvantages of 304–306; enjoyment 303, 305; equality 303, 305–306; e-therapy and 310–312; impact of 306–312; online group contact and 308–310; overview of 298; personality and 306–307; physical appearance 299–300, 304; romantic relationships and 307–308; similar others, finding 301–302, 305; social interactions, control over 300–301, 304
intrinsic motivation 283
invisible support 245
iPhone 319
Isgett, S. 168–169, 171–172

Joplin, J. 239
Jost, J. T. 9–10
Juhl, J. 186, 190

Kabat-Zinn, J. 66
Kalkstein, D. A. 233
Kaplan, H. 306
Kark, J. 141
Kashdan, T. B. 130
Kasser, T. 87
Keltner, D. 128
Kemeny, M. E. 241
Kerr, M. 280, 282
Kersten, M. 186, 194
Keynes, J. M. 327
Kiaei, Y. A. 118
Kibbutz communities, religious engagement and 141
Kiecolt-Glaser, J. K. 241
kindness interventions 102–103
King, L. A. 125, 130
King, M. L., Jr. 140
Koestner, R. 189–190
Kok, B. 169
Koning, I. M. 287
Konrath, S. 326

Krause, N. 244
Kross, E. 321
Kushner, H. 140

Lamb, C. S. 282
Landau, M. J. 184
Landis, K. R. 240
language processing, negative affect influence on 212–213, *213, 214*
Lawrence, D. H. 53
learning, evolution and 41–43
Leary, M. R. 240
leukocyte gene expression, positive emotions/purpose and 165–168
Levontin, I. B. 123
liberal countries, religious engagement and 151
life expectancy, religious engagement and 147, *149, 150*
life satisfaction: income and 37–38, *38*; religiosity and, by country *146*
Lincoln, A. 10
LinkedIn 299
living well, religious engagement and *see* religious engagement, living well and
living well, social psychology of: consumption and 6–7; evolutionary considerations of 4–6; hedonism and 2; overview of 11–16; philosophical orientations of 1–4; psychology's contribution to 7–11; Stoicism and 3–4; technology and 7; utilitarianism and 2–3; wealth and 4–5
loneliness 5–6
longevity, religious engagement and 141, *142*
love, social relationships and 248
loving-kindness meditation (LKM) 74–75, 169–170, 172
Luhmann, M. 30
Lyubomirsky, S. 86

MacCoon, D. G. 72
Maimonides 140
Maisel, N. C. 245
marketing, identity/connectedness and 6–7
Marx, K. 9, 10
Maslow, A. 301
McAdams, D. P. 117–118
McCullough, M. 140
McKenna, K. Y. 301–302, 309
McMahan, E. A. 118

McMahon, R. J. 280
McNulty, J. K. 111
meaningfulness: arguing and 27; boredom and 24; caring for children and 27; and good life 21; nostalgia and 190–191; past/future thinking and 24–26; religious engagement and 140, 151; self-esteem and 22–23; self-reward and 30; social relationships and 26–27, 249; society involvement effects on 27–28; survey questions to learn about 22; time span and 24
meditation, mindfulness and 69
Meditations (Aurelius) 4
Medline 141
men's/women's longevity, religious engagement and 141, *142*
Messenger 320
meta-apps 325
Michelangelo Phenomenon 250
Mill, J. S. 3
Miller, G. E. 258–259, 263, 266–267, 272
Milyavskaya, M. 189–190
mindfulness 24, 65–73; compassion and 76–77; defined 66–67; development/ strengthening of skills through 68; future planning and 69–70; how to practice 68; imagination and 69–70; introduction to 65–66; living well and 66–68; meditation and 69; well-being benefits of 70–73
Mindfulness-Based Cognitive Therapy (MBCT) 66, 69, 71
Mindfulness-Based Stress Reduction (MBSR) 66, 69, 72–73
Mindfulness-Based Stress Reduction Clinic 66
mindfulness training (MT) 71–72
Mindful Self-Compassion (MSC) 74
Minnesota Longitudinal Study of Risk and Adaptation (MLSRA) 259–270; child attachment insecurity and adult health, study 1 260–263; early maternal care, adult attachment insecurity and adult health, study 2 263–266; life stress, early caregiving, and adult health, study 3 266–270, *267, 270–271*
Misra, S. 322–323
modern world pitfalls, good life and 44–45
monetary donations to charity, prosociality and 193
moods, defined 203–204
mood states, impact on behavior of 57–60

Moody, J. 286
Moore, G. 319
Moore's Law 319
motivation: for goal pursuit, nostalgia and 189–191; positive/negative affect on 216
Murray, H. 239

National Longitudinal Study of Adolescent Health 148
National Survey on Youth and Religion 148
needs and wants, satisfying 23–24
negative affect 200–218; acceptance of 200–201; behavioural/motivational benefits of 211–217, *212, 213, 214, 215, 216*; cognition and 203–204; cognitive benefits on memory/judgements 205–211, *206, 207, 208, 209, 210*; described 200–201; dysphoria and 201; hedonism and 202–203; history of 200–202; informational effects and 204–205; introduction to 200–204; processing effects and 205
negative social signals, cell phones and 323
Nickel, S. 206
nostalgia 181–194; approach orientation and 182–184; conceptualization of 181; creativity and 191–193; defined 181; future well-being and 182–189; inspiration and 187–189; motivation for goal pursuit and 189–191; openness to experience and 192–193; optimism and 184–187; overt behavior and 193–194; physical activity and 194; potentiates future well-being 189–194; properties of 181; prosociality and 193–194; self-esteem and 186–187, 188–189; social connectedness and 187, 189
Nostalgia (periodical) 183
nurturance, as human motive 36

Okun, M. 138
online contact theory 310
openness to experience, nostalgia and 192–193
optimism: health-related 185–186; nostalgia and 184–187; scent-induced nostalgia and 185; self-esteem and 186–187
Orehek, E. 109
Orth, U. 9
Osgood, D. W. 286

overt behavior, nostalgia and 193–194
oxytocin: described 170–171; physical
health and 171; positive emotions
and purpose and 170–173; and social
interactions 171–172; spirituality and
172–173

Papies, E. K. 68
Parducci, A. 50
parental control 280–281
parental monitoring 280
parental over-monitoring 280–281
parental warmth 279–280
parenthood paradox 27
PEP Lab (Positive Emotions and
Psychophysiological Laboratory) 164
PERMA model 124
personality: development and 43–44;
Internet behavior and 306–307
personality system, subjective well-being as
indicator of 122
persuasive arguments, negative affect and
quality/effectiveness of 211–212, *212*
phenotypic indulgences 35
phubbing 323
physical activity, nostalgia and 194
physical appearance, Internet and control
over 299–300, 304
physical health, social relationships and
240–242
physical proximity, prosociality and 193
Plato 66, 203
pleasure and purpose of good life 85–88
pleasures, subjective levels of 3
Pleskac, T. J. 54
Pluess, M. 165
politics, religious engagement and 149
Popper, K. 123
Porges, S. W. 169
positive activities, well-being and 101–112;
activity overdose and 105–106;
examples of 102; interventions
of 102–103; kindness-recipient/
kindness-giver relationship and
108–110; mediators for 104–105;
motivation extremes and 106–107;
overview of 101–102; person-activity
fit, role of *103*, 104; person-activity
misfit and 107–108; person-level
features *103*, 103–104; positive activity
model 102–105, *103*; social costs of
110–111; study findings 111–112
positive activity interventions 102–103
positive activity model 102–105, *103*
positive affect, consequences of 203

positive constructive daydreaming 69
positive emotions: defined 164; and
purpose 164; relationships and 245–248;
see also positive emotions and purpose
Positive Emotions and Psychophysiological
Laboratory (PEP Lab) 164
positive emotions and purpose 163–175;
biological underpinnings of 164;
broaden-and-build theory of 164–165;
cardiac vagal tone and 168–170;
correlation between 163; defined 164;
evidence-based overarching model *173*,
173–175; leukocyte gene expression and
165–168; natural selection and 163–164;
oxytocin and 170–173; self-reports of
165; vantage resources and 165
positive/negative life events by church
attendance *139*
positive parenting 277–290; behaviors
279–280; children's substance use
and 279–284; elements of 283–284;
limitations and future directions
for 288–290; media campaigns and
284–288; overview of 277–278;
subjective well-being and 278–279; *see
also* substance use, positive parenting and
children's
positive psychology movement 8
Potts, R. 228
Pressman, S. D. 108
prevention focus of good life 90
primary effects 208
Principle of Least Effort 323–324
processing effects, negative affect and 205
promotion focus of good life 90
prosociality, nostalgia and 193–194
PsychInfo 116
psychological distance: defined 229; social
learning and 229–231
Psychological Well-Being (PWB) model
124–125, 127
psychosocial content: defined 123;
subjective well-being and 123–124
Puig, J. 262
Puritan hypothesis 30
purpose: defined 164; religious
engagement and 140; social relationships
and 249
Putnam, R. 143, 330

Questionnaire for Eudaimonic Well-Being
(QEWB) 118

Raposa, E. B. 268
received support 244, 245

redemption 182–183
regulatory focus, end of life planning and 93–96, *94, 95*
regulatory focus theory 88–89
Reio, T. J. 118
relatedness, basic income and 330
relationships: positive emotions and 245–248; reduced negative affect and 243–245; satisfying and meaningful 239–240; social support and 244–245; *see also* social relationships
relativity 49–52; in evaluative conditioning 51–52; of pleasant experiences and well-being 50–51; of positive and negative valence 49–50
"Religion in America" (Gallup survey) 138
religious engagement, living well and 137–156; crime and 147–148, *152, 153*; emotional well-being and 146–147, *147, 148*; happiness and 138–140, *139*; health and 140–142, *142*; helping behaviors and 142–145, *144*; income and 152–155; life expectancy and 147, *149, 150*; by nations and states 145–148, *146–147*; overview of 137–138; paradoxical results of 148, 149, 151, 152–156; smoking and 147, *150–151*; teen pregnancy/birth rates and 148, *153–155, 156*
reproduction, evolution and 35–39
requesting, negative affect and 213–214, *215*
resolute nonusers 289
responsiveness to the self 247
Ringly 325
Rini, C. 245
risky family environments 263
Robinson, W. S. 151
Rogers, C. 8
romantic relationships, Internet and 307–308
Routledge, C. 183–184, 185, 186, 190
Ruiter, S. 143
Rusbult, C. E. 250
Ryan, R. M. 85, 86–87, 129–130
Ryff, C. 124–125, 127

sadness, negative affect and 203
Sanders, M. R. 289
Satisfaction with Life Scale (SWLS) 90, 94, *95*, 124
Schwarz, N. 56, 204
Schwartz, S. 143

"Search Inside Yourself" (Google mindfulness course) 70
self-acceptance, religious engagement and 140
self-compassion 74
self-concordance model 86–87
self-control 10–11, 30–31
self-determination theory (SDT) 128, 283
self-esteem: inspiration and 188–189; nostalgia and 186–187; social connectedness and 187
self-esteem movement 8–10
self-expansion theory 250
self-expression, happiness/meaning and 29–30
self-generated reinforcement, well-being and 54–56
self-growth, social relationships and 250
self-handicapping, mood effects on 217
selfie 300
selfie-editing 304
selfish genes, spread of 320
selfishness *versus* fairness to others, mood and 215–216, *216*
self-regulation, mindfulness and 67
self-reward 30–31
Seligman, M. E. P. 8, 124
Seneca 4
sexual desire, as human motive 35–36
Shah, J. Y. 90, 91, 93–94
Sheldon, K. M. 87, 106
Siduri 2
similar others, Internet and finding 301–302, 305
Simpson, J. A. 267
Singer, P. 77
Slotter, E. B. 250
smartphones 325; as distraction 321–322; to monitor happiness levels 327; to promote well-being directly 326; as substitute for social interactions 302, 308, 323–324
smoking, religious engagement and 147, *150–151*
Snapchat 320
social connectedness, nostalgia and 187, 189
social costs of positive activities 110–111
social interactions: Internet and control over 300–301, 304; smartphones as substitute for 323–324
social learning: abstraction role in 229–234; across constant and variable contexts, challenges of 225–226;

construal level theory and 229; psychological distance and 229–232

social relationships: capitalization and 246–247; emotion regulation and 248–249; engagement and 26–27; gratitude and 247–248; love and 248; meaning and purpose in life and 249; physical health and 240–242; positive emotions and 245–248; psychologists/ scientific view of 239–240; reduced negative affect and 243–245; self-growth and 250; social support and 244–245; well-being and 242–243

social support: relationships and 244–245; religious engagement and 139–140, 142

society involvement, effects of, on happiness and meaning 27–28

Socrates 2, 66, 120

spirituality: defined 172; oxytocin and 172–173

Stattin, H. 280, 282

Steinberg, L. 280

Stock, W. 138

Stoicism 3–4, 202–203

Stone, A. 149

storytelling 42, 44

Strack, F. 56

stress 28

stress protection, religious engagement and 142

subjective well-being (SWB): for comparing/winnowing eudaimonic theories 124–125; components of 118; defining 119–120; distinguishing eudaimonic factors from *121*, 121–122; Eudaimonic Activity Model and 126–127; eudaimonic well-being and 122–125; as free of psychosocial content 123–124; as indicator of personality system 122; positive youth development and 278–279; as unitary and economical 122–123; valuing/living and 124

substance use, positive parenting and children's 279–284; authoritarian parenting and 284; authoritative parents and 283–284; media campaigns and 284–288; monitoring/surveillance and 280; over-monitoring 280–281; parents' expectations and 282; self-determination theory and 283; warmth and limits of 279–280

substance use prevention, media campaigns and 284–288; theory of planned behavior and 286–288; two-step flow of communication model and 285–286

suicide risk, religious engagement and 141

Sung, S. 267

survival goals 39–40

system justification 9–10

Tajfel, H. 301

Talmud, I. 301

Tay, L. 155

technology: autonomy and 329; basic income and 327–330; competence and 329–330; as distraction 321–323; efficient use of 327; future of happiness and 325–330; good life and 7, 319–320, 328–329; human labor and 327–328; to monitor happiness levels 326–327; as negative social signal 323; overview of 319–320; to promote well-being 326; relatedness and 330; as social interaction substitute 323–324; virtual *vs.* face-to-face interactions and 320–321

teen pregnancy/birth rates, religious engagement and 148, *153–155*, *156*

terror management, religious engagement and 140

theory of cognitive dissonance 53

theory of planned behavior (TPB) 286–288

Thrash, T. M. 188–189

Tillich, P. 140

Tinder 325

Trivers, R. 35

Trump, D. 320

Turner, J. 301

Twitter 299, 304, 308, 319, 326

two-step flow of communication model 285–286; theory of planned behavior and 286–288

Tyszkowski, K. A. 93

Uchino, B. N. 241

Umberson, D. 240

Unkelbach, C. 52

utilitarian ethics 3

utilitarianism 2–3, 202

Valenti, J. 29–30

Van Cappellen, P. 172–173

VanderWeele, T. 141, 142

Van Enkevort, E. A. 186, 194

vantage resources 165

Vinitzky, G. 306
virtual reality (VR) 311–312
Vitterso, J. 125
Vohs, K. D. 22, 30
volunteerism, religious people and 143, *144*
vulnerable nonusers 289

Waterman, A. S. 116
Ways of Living scale (Morris) 90
wealth, well-being and 4–5
well-being: compassion and 75–76; conception of, expanding 125–126; consumption and 6–7; defined 119; French Revolution and 5; Internet and (*see* Internet, psychological components of); measurement and 11; mindfulness and 70–73; pleasant experiences and, relativity of 50–51; psychology's contribution to 7–11; religious engagement and 142; self-control and 10–11; self-esteem movement 8–10; self-generated reinforcement and 54–56; social relationships and 242–243; technology for promoting 326; wealth and 4–5
WhatsApp 320
Williams, E. 326
Williams-Wheeler, M. 280
Willoughby, B. 140
Wilson, D. S. 143
Wilson, E. O. 143
Wilson, T. D. 86
Winthrop, J. 139–140
women's longevity, religious engagement and 141, *142*
World 2 123
World Values Survey 41
worry, defined 28

Y Combinator 328
Young, A. F. 29–30
Yuan, M. 322–323

Zalizniak, A. A. 123
Zeno 2, 3, 202